RESISTANCE AND CARIBBEAN LITERATURE

RESISTANCE AND CARIBBEAN LITERATURE

SELWYN R. CUDJOE

OHIO UNIVERSITY PRESS

Chicago   Athens, Ohio   London

Copyright © 1980 by Selwyn R. Cudjoe
All rights reserved
Printed in the United States of America
by the Oberlin Printing Company

Library of Congress Cataloging in Publication Data

Cudjoe, Selwyn Reginald.
    Resistance and Caribbean Literature

    Bibliography: p. 301
    Includes index.
    1. Caribbean fiction—History and criticism.
2. Government, Resistance to, in literature.
3. Caribbean area—Social conditions. I. Title.
PN849.C3C8   809.3'03   76-25616
ISBN 0-8214-0353-2 (clothbound)
ISBN 0-8214-0573-X (paperbound)

CONTENTS

CONTENTS

Acknowledgments

A first work is never the exclusive property of the author but reflects a lifetime of influences. The people most responsible for my development have been my teachers, and to them my thanks must go. Those from Trinidad include the late Vernon Scott, Walter Clarke, Cecil Ifill, Utris Thomas and Grace Griffith.

In the United States, I want to thank Mr. Frank Jay, Dr. William Hines and Dan Sullivan at Fordham University. I wish to thank my committee at Cornell University—Dr. Saunders Redding, who acted as my chairman and surrogate father; Dr. Robert Elias, who niggled at times but always demanded the highest quality of scholarship; Dr. Cushing Strout, the gentleman-scholar who was always fun to talk to; and Dr. Roberto Gonzalez Echevarría, who later chaired my committee and whose suggestions and insights proved invaluable. A very special word of thanks goes to Michael J. Colacurcio, who was a reservoir of consolation and strength when things were bad.

I must also thank the master, Robert Rhodes, assistant professor of Afro-American Studies at Ohio University, whose influence becomes manifest in the transposition from a dissertation into a book. My thanks also go to Mrs. Herman, who gave her valuable time to help translate *Au seuil d'un nouveau cri*; to Mrs. Slater who was very patient in typing my dissertation; and to Susan Barnhart, whose editorial changes made a better manuscript. To my two student research assistants at Harvard University: Roberto Lewis (who assisted in some translations) and Constance Russell who tracked down innumerable works at Widener Library, my fondest thanks.

To my foster parents, Ray and Mabel, who made it possible for me to start school in this country and who sustained me for those important first years, a special thank you and God Bless; to Brother John Terrence Reilly and his lovely wife, April, thanks for all the encouragement; to Brother James Turner, thanks for all the kindness; to my beautiful wife, Gwen, who continues to be my chief source of strength, inspiration and pride, a special thank you. Finally, to my moms, my first great teacher and the one who set it all in motion, thanks that can never be adequately expressed. To my brother Winston and sisters, Mags and Yvonne, thanks for all the assistance; to the many others who assisted, a final thank you.

List of Abbreviations

The following abbreviations are used for citing references within the text. For example, (EC, p. 44) refers the reader to page 44 of Alejo Carpentier's *Explosion in a Cathedral.*

APO   Price-Mars, Jean. *Ainsi parla l'oncle.* Haiti: Compeigne, 1928. (My own translation.)

ARS   Montejo, Esteban. *Autobiography of a Runaway Slave.* New York: Pantheon Books, 1968.

ASNC   Juminer, Bertène. *Au seuil d'un nouveau cri.* Paris: Presence Africaine, 1963.

BJ   McKay, Claude. *Banjo: A Story Without a Plot.* New York: Harcourt, Brace, Jovanovich, 1929.

BM   Mais, Roger. "Brother Man" in *The Three Novels of Roger Mais.* London: Jonathan Cape, 1970.

BR   Juminer, Bertène. *Bozambo's Revenge.* Washington, D.C.: Three Continents Press, 1976.

BT   Maran, René. *Batouala: A True Black Novel.* Greenwich, Conn.: Fawcett Publications, 1972.

CS   Galván, Manuel de Jesús. *The Cross and the Sword* (trans. Robert Graves). Bloomington: Indiana University Press, 1954.

CV   Villaverde, Cirilo. *Cecilia Valdés* (trans. Sydney G. Gest). New York: Vantage Press, 1962.

EC   Carpentier, Alejo. *Explosion in a Cathedral.* London: Victor Gollanez, 1973.

ELNP   Manzano, Juan Francisco. *Early Life of the Negro Poet.* London: Thomas Ward and Co., 1840.

G   Naipaul, V.S. *Guerrillas.* New York: Ballantine Books, 1976.

HWJT   Mais, Roger. "The Hills Were Joyful Together" in *The Three Novels of Roger Mais.* London: Jonathan Cape, 1970.

I   Vega, Garcilaso de la. *The Incas.* New York: Avon Books, 1964.

KW Carpentier, Alejo. *Kingdom of this World*. New York: Collier Books, 1957.

MD Roumain, Jacques. *Masters of the Dew*. New York: Collier Books, 1971.

ND Reid, V.S. *New Day*. London: Heinemann Educational Books, 1949.

OAI Lamming, George. *Of Age and Innocence*. London: Michael Joseph, 1958.

R Glissant, Édouard. *The Ripening*. New York: George Braziller, Inc., 1959.

RNL Césaire, Aimé. *Return to My Native Land*. Middlesex: Penguin Books, 1970.

TI Casas, Bartolomé de las. *The Tears of the Indians*. New York: Oriole Chapbooks, 1972.

WA Harris, Wilson. *The Whole Armour*. London: Faber and Faber, 1973.

WWB Lamming, George. *Water With Berries*. New York: Holt, Rinehart, and Winston, 1971.

Introduction

Analysis, literary or otherwise, not only involves the quantification of data and description of events but also seeks to discover what Engles described as "the inner causal connection in the course of a development"[1] of these events. The search should be for the essence that yields a more critical study and helps predict further development of the phenomenon. Thus, when we examine Caribbean literature, we look for a continuous thread giving this literature its particular resonance, tonality and, most important of all, content.

I have dispensed with a strict chronology of the works because the uneven economic development of the Caribbean islands has created varying social development. For example, Barbados in the seventeenth century was more developed than, say, Jamaica, and the consciousness of writers reflected this. In Cuba today, the social consciousness of writers is more advanced than that of writers in Haiti. In dispensing with chronology, I have correlated similar socio-political experiences with their concomitant artistic forms. Thus *Autobiography of a Runaway Slave* (1963) is treated as arising necessarily and logically out of *Slave Narrative of Juan Manzano* (1840); *Kingdom of This World* (1949) is dealt with in the same context as *The Whole Armour* (1962).

This is valid because it reflects a given level of social consciousness even though different countries achieved that level at different times. This is not merely the aesthetic imposition of judgment but the real reflection of social development and illustrates the belief that the "imaginative content of a work of art should correspond to the objective image of reality."[2]

My major concern is to reflect a literary theory which emanates from the "objective reality" rather than vice versa and to present a cohesive and gnostical view of the literature which, developing out of the Caribbean experience, has been fashioned by resistance at various levels. The approach, which is holistic and organic, proceeds from the premise that "every serious work of literature is a live human document reflecting the epoch's actual historical processes and phenomena."[3]

To yield a richer understanding of literary works, criticism should show an understanding of the "historical processes and phenomena" out of which a literature grows and should examine artistic form as a vehicle for carrying forward ideological content. For this reason I examine the artistic forms used to carry the ideological content of Caribbean literature forward: This work is meant to consolidate what we now know, to open possibilities for further study and to see literary scholarship in a "holistic" manner.

Cambridge, Mass. 1980

PART I

I

CARIBBEAN RESISTANCE:
AN HISTORICAL BACKGROUND

I

In overthrowing me, you have cut down in San Domingo only the trunk of the tree of liberty. It will spring up again by the roots for they are numerous and deep.[1]

To write at all was and is for the West Indian a revolutionary act. Any criticism that does not start from this very real recognition is invalid.[2]

CARIBBEAN history, beginning with the European incursion, can best be understood against its international background. Feudal social forces in Europe had been disintegrating for three hundred years before Columbus discovered Hispaniola in 1492. Markets came into closer contact with each other, and "world trade" grew steadily. As Julio Le Riverend puts it:

> While commerce flourished in the Near East—that is, in the regions to the east of the Mediterranean Sea—there emerged since the thirteenth century an active trade in the western Mediterranean. Barcelona and Marseilles, Pisa and Genoa had established contact among themselves and with the Barbary and other points located in the north of Africa and in the south of Spain. Navigation on the Atlantic was destined to favor the development of the new colonial-commercial powers. The Portuguese and the Spaniards, among whom expansive commercial capitalism emerged, we might say prematurely, launched out into the ocean and re-discovered and conquered the Madeira, Canary, and Cape Verde Islands, colonizing them; the Portuguese, on the other hand, pounced upon Africa and sailed along its coasts since the middle of the fifteenth century.[3]

By the end of the fifteenth century, other events (such as the growth of iron mining, better mining techniques, the invention of water machines and water wheels, and increased use of the compass) accelerated production and awakened interest in the rich raw materials of East Asia. As a result, the search for new sea routes became important.

3

The dissolution of feudalism and the emergence of nascent capitalism brought about the primitive accumulation of capital, and this process had devastating consequences for the metropolitan (home) countries as well as for their overseas colonies. At home, thousands of serfs were separated from their lands without recompense, thus creating a landless, propertyless class which would become the proletariat. An unbelievable amount of cruelty accompanied this transition. Karl Marx puts it this way:

> . . . the historical movement which changes the producers into wage-workers, appears, on the one hand, as the emancipation from serfdom and from the fetters of the guilds, and this side alone exists for our bourgeois historians. But, on the other hand, these new freedmen became sellers of themselves only after they had been robbed of all their own means of production, and all the guarantees of existence afforded by the old feudal arrangements. *And the history of this, their expropriation, is written in the annals of mankind in letters of blood and fire.* [Italics mine][4]

But this cruelty towards the expropriated European serfs was only a prelude to what was to come in Africa, Asia, and the Americas. The European thirst for new wealth led to an alliance between an emerging bourgeois class and the centralized monarchy, which supported the bourgeoise in order to consolidate its power against the nobility. One or two individuals could not assume the cost of further exploration; thus, the pooling of state and private resources was a necessary prerequisite to further exploitation of new territories in the East. With scholars and sailors knowledgeable about the earth's roundness and aware of lands beyond the sea, the development of trade and the desire for new trade routes led to European overseas expansion. This expansion was further necessitated by

> . . . the existence of a large impoverished nobility, which after the completion of the expulsion of the Moors (1492) was unable to find suitable occupation and feverishly sought means of acquiring wealth, dreaming of discovering the fabulous "golden land" of Eldorado.[5]

Displaced criminal elements and this large impoverished nobility set out for the new lands.

Eldorado, a land of a thousand myths, drew these people to explore its fabled gold. By the late fifteenth and early sixteenth centuries the brutality once used towards serfs in the metropolitan countries was inflicted with even greater intensity upon people in the colonized lands. Marx says:

> The discovery of gold and silver in America, the extirpation, enslavement and entombment in mines of the aboriginal population, the beginning of the

conquest and looting of the East Indies, the turning of Africa into a warren for the commercial hunting of blackskins, signalised the rosy dawn of the era of capitalist production. These idyllic proceedings are the chief momenta of primitive accumulation.[6]

Portugal and Spain, the major feudalist countries at the time, led in the extirpation of aboriginal populations as a means of private accumulation.

The original populations had already achieved cultural advances. The oldest civilization, the Mayan, which developed along the northwestern part of Central America and later shifted to the Yucatan peninsula, had created a culture in which agriculture, architecture, sculpture, and painting flourished. The Toltec culture of Central Mexico had devised a calendar and made impressive advances in writing. The Aztecs, located in Central America, had constructed buildings, dams, and canals.

In South America, the Quechua and the Amymara had achieved a high level of culture. The Incas, who had subdued a number of tribes and formed a large and progressive state, "were fairly advanced in agriculture, stock breeding, crafts (metal-working, pottery, weaving, etc.), and architecture. They achieved notable successes in mathematics, astronomy, medicine and other sciences, and used a hieroglyphic script. Road building and trade were also advanced."[7] All these civilizations had reached an advanced stage of culture before the arrival of Europeans.

The influx of Europeans halted the development of these societies. Hernando Cortés destroyed the Indians of Central America in three years (1519–1522) while Francisco Pizarro and Diego de Almagro wiped out the splendid Inca civilization (1532–1537). The decimation of the Indian population in Central and South America must not be seen as a unique or novel phenomenon, for European expansion meant the same kind of harrowing cruelty toward, and the destruction of, indigenous Indian populations in North, Central, and South America.

Our particular concern remains the Caribbean, which, as part of the Americas, played a decisive role in the development of capitalism, a point Eric Williams makes in his work *Capitalism and Slavery*. The Caribs that inhabited the Caribbean at the time of Columbus' arrival had recently emigrated from the Amazon basin and the Orinoco valley—which opens toward Trinidad, the southernmost island of the Caribbean—and were, in the process, subduing the less advanced cultures of the Taínos, Arawaks and Ciboneyes. Although, as Felipe Moya contends, "no West Indian cultural group knew the architectural use of stones, nor how to work metals, and therefore monumental constructions and the technique and richness of gold and silver work were skills alien to all of them."[8] A group such as the Taínos had a strong economy based on tobacco and cocoa.

Colonization in the Caribbean involved social and economical organization. At the beginning of the seventeenth century, we find the Spanish colonies in the Americas organized as follows:

> Within the Spanish colonies two groups stood out especially: colonies based on mining and ranches; colonies founded on the planting of tropical crops. In a general way, the former included high areas, mountains or plateaus (Mexico, Colombia, Peru), where, besides, Indian population was abundant; the others were insular or coastal areas, of a climate that was hard on the Europeans— especially at a time of no great hygienic progress—and of scarce or very backward native population: examples of this are the Antilles and the area around the Caribbean. The former made up the great viceroyships; the latter had governments of lesser institutional development.[9]

The native depopulation that occurred in the Caribbean took place from Columbus' arrival in 1492 to the middle of the sixteenth century. Spanish gold mining, begun in 1520, brought disastrous consequences for the Indians. It is believed that small numbers of African slaves came on Columbus' second voyage in 1494 but with the destruction of the Indians, the demand for African slaves increased so that by 1530, large "loads" of African slaves were imported to work in the mines since they could produce twice as much as the Indians. In the latter part of the sixteenth century, the attempt to "establish the sugar industry coincided with the emphatic petition for importing Africans"[10] by the European powers. As sugar production increased, the demand for more and more slaves accelerated. The successful use of African slaves allowed the development of large-scale plantation economy, monoculture, and many other ills of Caribbean society.

Since slavery existed in feudal Europe, Caribbean slavery was not racial in origin. Julio Le Riverend says:

> . . . African slavery in America is a historical *continuity*. Christian slavery in Europe and the slave trade established with the Arabs is a proof of this *continuity*—a continuity which acquired a faster and deeper rhythm even before the discovery of America, that is, at the end of the fourteenth and all during the fifteenth centuries, due to the fact that the Europeans came out into the Atlantic, especially the Portuguese.[11]

Slavery was the continuation of political systems that had their origins in the exploitation of one man for the benefit of another; it was the logical culmination of a process that was accelerated by the dissolution of feudalism and the emergence of capitalism. Professor Eric Williams notes:

Slavery in the Caribbean has been too narrowly identified with the Negro. A racial twist has thereby been given to what is basically an economic phenomenon. Slavery was not born of racism: rather, racism was the consequence of slavery. Unfree labor in the New World was brown, white, black, and yellow; Catholic, Protestant and pagan.[12]

We must perceive the rise of the Caribbean in this historical context. It must be pointed out again that the European thrust into the Caribbean was the culmination of certain political, economic, and social forces that peaked at the end of the fifteenth century. That thrust was as much a result of greed and the need for profit as of the objective laws of social development demanded by the contradictions of European society. The corresponding resistance on the part of the Indians and the Africans in the New World was the necessary corrective to that expansion and dehumanization, one action bringing an equal and opposite reaction in order to retain equilibrium. Resistance, then, was the reaction needed to maintain the equilibrium, to preserve human dignity, and to ennoble the human spirit.

II

Since Christopher Columbus set foot on San Salvador, the history of the Caribbean has been one of social, economic and physical violence. As Professor Williams reminds us, it has been said of the Spanish conquistadores that, "first they fell on their knees, and then they fell on the aborigines."[13] Observing the timid and unwarlike nature of the Indians, Columbus "shipped six hundred Indians back to Spain" in 1498, thus creating the curious phenomenon: "the slave trade in the Caribbean thus began as outward and not inward cargoes."[14]

At that time the Spaniards were murdering the Indians in a brutal manner. The injustices were first inflicted upon the indigenous peoples, the Caribs and the Arawaks, the Taínos and the Ciboneyes, and then upon the Africans. One reason the Spanish were able to enslave the Indians was the fact that the Indians believed the Spaniards to be gods. However, resistance began when the brutality of the Spaniards became clear to the Indians. Juan Angel Silén reports that in Puerto Rico:

In 1511, the Indians drowned a Spaniard named Diego Salcedo to prove that Spaniards were mortal, not gods. With his death armed rebellion broke out. It was bloody and treacherous, and major battles were fought against the Spaniards by Arawaks and Caribs. The battle of Rio Coayuco (between the Aguada and Culebrinas Rivers), of the Culebrinas Valley, and in the province of Yagueca (now Mayaguez and Añasco) live in our history. The immortal heroes of our first fight for liberty are the Arawak chiefs of *caciques* Agüeybaná and Guarionex, who have passed into our literature and history deformed by Hispanists scornful of our true roots.[15]

The Indians were overcome, but not before they joined the Africans. As early as 1503, for example, people called for a direct prohibition of slave trade to Cuba because of combined Indian and African rebellions. As Julio Le Riverend puts it:

> . . . in 1501, the entrance of Moorish slaves [Santa Domingo-Haiti] was forbidden, while that of African slaves born in Catholic countries was permitted. And, undoubtedly because of the number existing in 1503, Ovando asked for the complete prohibition of the trade, for, in previous years, the Negroes had shown an open tendency towards rebellion and conspiracy with the Indians.[16]

Bartolomé de las Casas, seeing the brutality and responding as one of the enlightened thinkers of his time, made the following proposal to King Ferdinand in 1511: ". . . as the labour of one Negro was more valuable than that of four Indians, every effort should be made to bring to Hispaniola many Negroes from Guinea."[17] Resistance began from the time blacks were captured in the interior of Africa and continued after their arrival through their disposal in the New World. We can begin to see the rise of political resistance in the Caribbean, typified by the Cuban rebellion in 1503, as we observe the first known organized slave revolt in 1522 in Hispaniola. This first phase of resistance I have characterized as non-ideological. The Negroes in the Caribbean fought long and strenuously for their freedom. Dr. Williams records revolts in Puerto Rico in 1527, Honduras in 1548, and New Spain in 1612.[18] The revolts, however, did not end there. Sidney King points out:

> The Caribbean tradition is, taken as a whole, a revolutionary tradition. It is the stage on which acted Cudjoe, and Cuffe, Accabreh and Accra, Toussaint, Quamina and Damon, Adoe and Araby [all leaders of the slave revolts]. Blows delivered against the European system in 1750 or in 1850 served to shake that system, sometimes to its foundations, and to cause it to make democratic concessions as a price of recovery. It was never the same again; and although financial exploitation became more intense and complicated, a constitutional superstructure was raised for dealing with human anger and for sidetracking revolution into peaceful awe-inspiring chambers.[19]

By 1509 the Spaniards settled in Jamaica and in 1517 brought Africans to Jamaica as body servants. When the English under Captain Venables and Admiral Penn captured the island for the British in 1655, some African slaves took to the hills and joined other Africans who had been hunters and herdsmen and who knew the mountainous territory. These were the first Maroons, a group which refused to accept slave status and which, by constant and effective guerrilla warfare, eventually forced the English to negotiate treaties.[20]

The Maroons learned guerrilla warfare when they joined the Spanish effort against the English. General Sedgewick, writing to Secretary Thurloe about the effectiveness of the Maroons, gave the following account: "They gave no quarter to his men, but destroyed them at every opportunity and, he reported that, as his own soldiers grew more confident and careless, the Africans became more enterprising and bloody-minded."[21]

In fact, the decisive moment in the battle between the English and the Spanish forces came in February of 1660 when the Maroon leader Juan de Bolas deserted the Spanish and went over to the English forces. By May 9, 1660, Yassi, the Spanish leader, had fled the island, and Jamaica was in British hands.

The English granted Juan de Bolas and his followers lands and privileges. Despite inducements, including twenty acres of land, freedom from slavery and pardon for those who had fought with the Spanish, many Maroons preferred to live apart from the English. In an effort to wipe out the Maroons who had refused their offer, the British engaged the services of Juan de Bolas, which proved disastrous. Bolas was killed, and his forces were scattered and destroyed by former comrades who resented his attempt to take away their freedom.

By 1668 the British were importing large numbers of West African slaves to cultivate sugarcane. The ethnic origins of these slaves included Eboes from the Bight of Benin, Mandingoes from Sierra Leone, Coromantees (or Karomantees) from present-day Ghana, Papawas from Whiddah, and others from the Congo and Angola. The Coromantees led the majority of the nineteenth century slave revolts; great leaders such as Cudjoe of Jamaica, Kofi of Guyana, and Marcus Garvey were of Coromantee origin.

Although a number of slave revolts known as the "Akan revolts" took place between 1680 and 1686, the largest and most dangerous Jamaican slave insurrection took place in 1690 on the Sutton estates in the parish of Clarendon. Seizing arms and ammunition, slaves escaped into the Clarendon hills and set up a base under the leadership of Captain Kwadwo, popularly known as Captain Cudjoe.

From 1690 until 1740 the Maroons harassed the English with guerrilla tactics and were so disruptive that the Jamaica "Assembly was to pass 44 acts and spend £240,000 in its attempts at suppression."[22] By 1733 the assembly offered a bounty of £10 a head for each captured Maroon. Unable to contend with the Maroons, the English introduced Mosquito Indians from Honduras with their hunting dogs in 1737 and recruited slave military police companies called Blackstones. These efforts proved ineffective against the Maroons, who retreated into the rugged terrain of the inaccessible Cockpit country.*

After open warfare for more than forty years, the English resorted to pacification. On 1 March 1739, Cudjoe, Captain Guthrie, and Captain Sadler signed a treaty calling for an end to hostilities between the Maroons and the English. Three months later the Windward Maroons under Captain Quao signed a similar treaty and hostilities came to a temporary halt.

The peace settlement with the British cost a tremendous price since the treaty was replete with falsehoods. Of the 1,500 acres the Maroons had received under the treaty, only 100 acres were arable. The treaty forbade the admission of new runaway slaves into the Maroon community and required that the Maroons "use their best endeavors to take, kill, suppress or destroy"[23] any other rebel slaves in the country. As Carey Robinson points out, "These were the articles which were to change the entire character of the Maroons and reverse their way of life."[24]

Hostilities temporarily ceased in Jamaica, but the Coromantees were to be found in other Caribbean islands. Robinson points out that "Almost every slave revolt [in Jamaica] was inspired or led by Coromantees and the planters were divided between admiration of their superior strength and activity, and apprehension of their fierceness."[25] Their effectiveness was not limited to Jamaica alone. Monica Schuler notes that:

> The records of slave rebellions from the Virgin Islands to Surinam, from the seventeenth through the nineteenth century, show that the rebel slaves *par excellence* were the Akan and Ga/Adangme speaking peoples who originated in the area of modern Ghana. These are the "Koromantine" or "Coromantees," "Delminas" or "Eliminas" of the slave traders' and planters' description.[26]

These fierce Coromantees with their Obeah, a belief similar to Voodoo, made life a violent affair for Caribbean colonists. They were so terrifying that "the Barbados Assembly later passed a law banning the importation of Akan slaves."[27]

Although the Maroon revolts led by the Coromantees were dying down

---

* The Cockpits are deep depressions or glens which are found in the mountains of Jamaica. They are separated from one another by precipitious towers of rock which are covered with dense bushes. The Cockpits are found mostly in the parishes of St. James, St. Elizabeth and Trelawny. (C. Robinson, *The Fighting Maroons of Jamaica*, p. 43)

in Jamaica, the Caribbean people kept up their fight for liberation. The Bush Negro Movement in Surinam (i.e., the Djuka) attacked the Dutch so intensely that it caused the Dutch to beg for peace, and so a treaty was concluded between the African leader, Adoe, and the Dutch governor, Mauricus, in 1749. In Berbice, Guyana in South America, there were a number of slave uprisings from 1733 to 1763, when the most serious rebellion took place.

On 23 February 1763, a rebellion broke out at the Plantation Magdalenenburg on the Canje River and by March had spread to other plantations. Kofi, a Coromantee who was elected the new revolutionary governor of Guyana, took up residency at the Governor's house and lived in the same style as the previous European Governor.

At first Kofi ordered the Dutch Governor, van Hoogenheim, and the white inhabitants to leave the country, but then he compromised with the Governor by allowing the Dutch to retain half the land. With victory over the colonists (the Dutch Governor had escaped to Surinam), the economy became the first priority. Kofi assigned "some of the rebels to harvest the sugarcane and make the rum. This led to complaints that life under the new regime was no different from life under the old."[28] Many of the rebels disliked Kofi's style and ignored his wishes, and by July dissension and disunity began to occur among Kofi's men. Meanwhile, another Coromantee, Atta, set himself up as a rival governor to Kofi.

As was to be expected, hostilities broke out between the two leaders. Most of Kofi's forces were defeated, and eventually Kofi blew himself up with ammunition the insurgent colony needed for its fight against the Dutch rather than let the ammunition fall into the hands of his rival. In the end, "Coffy [Kofi] was defeated, not by the Dutch, but by another leader, Atta."[29] Schuler reports that, "Kofi's death seems to indicate the point at which disunity took over among the rebels."[30] This internal rivalry weakened the young colony and assured its defeat when reinforcements arrived by the English ship *Betsy* six months after the February outbreak. Nonetheless, two things seemed clear after this rebellion. The Africans were determined, as Kofi had said, that they would "never be slaves again,"[31] and as King puts it, this rebellion "was part and parcel of the Caribbean Movement, begun by the Caribs against the European penetration and domination."[32]

The Africans' failure to rout the Europeans in the New World was caused by squabbling, the inability to understand the necessity of sacrificing for independence, and the scarcity of decisive leaders in times of relative stability. In Jamaica, for example, a feud began between the Trelawny Maroons and the Accompong Maroons over who should keep the original treaty signed by Captain Cudjoe. The Accompongs (named after Cudjoe's brother) claimed the right to the treaty since they had kept it from the time of its signing, while the Trelawnys felt they should keep it because Trelawny Town had been Cudjoe's headquarters. Indeed, the Trelawny Maroons, who were fighting the colonists, found that the Accompongs were assisting the English and had even agreed that their young people would be baptized.

At this time, the Maroons, who had always been free, began to look upon slaves as inferior. This view included Creoles (those slaves born in the islands) and new arrivals, known derisively as "freshwater Negroes." Tension also occurred between the Creole slaves and the Africans, the former accusing the latter of tempting them to rebel. Given these divisions, it became impossible for Africans to maintain the sense of cohesiveness necessary to overthrow the Europeans and develop their own national state.

The trouble between the Maroons and the colonists was not yet over. Disturbances broke out once more in 1773, and sporadic outbreaks of fighting occurred until 1795 when the Maroons, influenced by the San Domingo revolution, became more turbulent. Fighting broke out once more between the Trelawny Maroons and the British. The British, who used trained dogs imported from Cuba, achieved a surrender on January 1, 1796. Some Maroons were transported to Sierra Leone while others remained in Jamaica. They had struggled long and hard to gain their freedom, yet had used their freedom and effective guerrilla tactics to prevent the slaves from achieving theirs. As Robinson points out:

> Their love of freedom was outstanding, and their inability to live in harmony with the Jamaican slave society resulted in their banishment, which was the only thing that they feared.[33]

While other revolts led by Akans took place in Antigua and St. Croix, the next insurrection of importance took place in San Domingo where Toussaint L'Ouverture (Pierre Domingo) was aware that the Maroons under Cudjoe had extracted a treaty from the British. Toussaint knew he had an advantage over the Maroons of Jamaica because he could call upon another colonial power, Britain, to aid his war against the French. He decided he would govern San Domingo, and in a heart-to-heart talk with his general, Moise, declared:

> General H'edouville does not know that at Jamaica there are in the mountains blacks who have forced the English to make treaties with them? Well, I am black like them, I know how to make war, and besides I have advantages that they didn't have; for I can count on assistance and protection.[34]

What were these advantages? How did this black man who had been nothing but a slave until the age of forty-five learn to make war? How could he speak so confidently? The story of his resistance is one of the greatest epics in history.

As in the other Caribbean islands, the cruelty of slavery was unspeakable. C. L. R. James documents it:

> . . . there was no ingenuity that fear or a depraved imagination could devise which was not employed to break their spirit and satisty the lusts and resentment of their owners and guardians—irons on the hands and feet, blocks of wood that the slaves had to drag behind them wherever they went, the tin-plate mask designed to prevent the slaves from eating the sugarcane, the iron collar. Whipping was interrupted in order to pass a piece of hot wood on the buttocks of the victim; salt, pepper, citron, cinders, aloes, and hot ashes were poured on the bleeding wounds. Mutilations were common, limbs, ears and sometimes the private parts, to deprive them of the pleasures which they could indulge in without expense. Their masters poured burning wax on their arms and hands and shoulders, emptied the boiling cane sugar over their heads, burned them alive, roasted them on slow fires, filled them with gunpowder and blew them up with a match; buried them up to the neck and smeared their heads with sugar that the flies might devour them; fastened them to nests of ants or wasps; made them eat their excrement; drink their urine, and lick the saliva of other slaves. One colonist was known in moments of anger to throw himself on his slaves and stick his teeth into their flesh.
>
> Were these tortures, so well authenticated, habitual or were they merely isolated incidents, the extravagances of a few half-crazed colonists? Impossible as it is to substantiate hundreds of cases, yet all the evidence shows that these bestial practices were normal features of slave life. The torture of the whip, for instance, had 'a thousand refinements', but there were regular varieties that had special names, so common were they. When the hands and arms were tied to four posts on the ground, the slave was said to undergo 'the four post.' If the slave was tied to a ladder it was 'the torture of the ladder'; if he was suspended by four limbs, it was 'the hammock,' etc. The pregnant woman was not spared her 'four post.' A hole was dug in the earth to accommodate the unborn child. The torture of the collar was specially reserved for women who were suspected of abortion, and the collar never left their necks until they produced a child. The blowing up of a slave had its own name—'to burn a little powder in the arse of a nigger': obviously this was no freak but a recognized practice.[35]

Such were the inhuman conditions under which blacks lived in San Domingo, otherwise a glittering and prosperous colony. Even the biased and racist analysis of Lothrod Stoddard acknowledges:

> In 1789, San Domingo had attained a height or prosperity not surpassed in the history of European colonies . . . And the degree of this prosperity was increasing by leaps and bounds. Since 1786, the planters had doubled their

products, and a large amount of French capital had poured into the island for investments—a hundred million from Bordeaux alone. The returns were already splendid and still greater were expected . . . Such a colony was patently the most precious overseas possession of France. The imports from her American colonies for the year 1789 totaled two-hundred and eighteen million livres, fully three-fourths of which came from San Domingo . . . Lastly, to all these profits there must be added the rich returns from the slave trade, and San Domingo's predominant share in maintaining the fleet of one-thousand ships and fifteen-thousand sailors trading with the colonists.[36]

This great wealth was procured through great inhumanity to the slaves on whose labor it depended. The cruelty was such that by 1787 the "annual excess of deaths (over births) was fully two and one-half percent—over 11,000 persons,"[37] and San Domingo was importing more than 40,000 slaves a year. It is, therefore, no surprise that at the time of the revolution, approximately two-thirds of the slaves were African born—no doubt an important factor.

As elsewhere, the Maroons of San Domingo were the first to raise the banner for freedom. Under Mackandal, the greatest of their leaders, they planned to poison the whites and drive them out of the island. Mackandal organized the blacks for six years, but he was betrayed and executed when he got drunk at one of the neighboring plantations. This was 1751, but the slaves had already vowed at their Voodoo ceremonies: "We swear to destroy the whites and all that they possess; let us die rather than fail to keep this vow."[38]

In 1791, Boukman, a high priest, used arson followed by slave uprisings as his plan for rebellion. Boukman's plot was much better organized than Mackandal's. After three weeks the slaves had destroyed Cap Haitien, known locally as Le Cap, and settled down to reorganize themselves. It was at this point that the famous Toussaint joined them.

The story of Toussaint's victory in San Domingo is well known. Not only did he defeat the French but the English and Spanish as well. Toussaint was determined to stop the slave trade at its source and secreted millions of francs from the United States banks for this purpose. The success of the San Domingo revolution culminated in the establishment of Haiti as the first black republic of the New World,[39] and marked the first phase in Caribbean liberation. France had been defeated in Haiti as had Britain in Jamaica, and in 1816 Bolívar would leave Haiti, taking with him a detachment of men and arms to free Latin America from the Spanish. By the end of 1825, Spain, no longer a world power, only held on to Cuba and Puerto Rico in the Caribbean. She would lose those islands to the United States, which would become the next colonial power.

III

Although development of the Hispanic Caribbean was different from and slower than that of the French and British Caribbean, all areas followed the same cycle and became "plantation colonies."

The differences between the Hispanic and the French and British Caribbean were numerous. First, there was greater centralization in the Hispanic islands. Second, where "the English [colonial] practice was designed to enrich the individual, the Spanish was designed to promote their colonization of the Indies,"[40] an attitude which made the islands part of the Spanish Empire and resulted in fewer absentee landlords.

Third, in the middle of the eighteenth century, the slave population of Cuba and the other Hispanic islands numbered about fifty percent of the population while the slave population of the French and British islands constituted from eighty-five to ninety percent. The higher proportion of slaves in the French and British islands created a situation ripe for violence with the white-settler class living in constant fear of revolt.

Fourth, Spain neglected Cuba since there was no gold to be found there. As a consequence, there were few markets for Hispanic goods because Spain had a low demand for sugar and prevented Cuba from trading with other industrial countries. Further, Cuban planters were unable to import the slaves they needed since Spain had no trading establishments on the African coast.

Fifth, up to the eighteenth century, the development of Hispanic slave rights proceeded along a less barbarous route than that of the slaves in the British and French Caribbean because Hispanic law recognized slaves not as property but as persons with the right to marry and own property.

Sixth, the system of the *coartación* (the legal right by which slaves paid their masters money that guaranteed that they could not be sold and allowed them eventually to buy their freedom at a fixed price) created greater stability. Further, the ratio of free blacks and mulattoes to the slave population (twenty thousand free blacks and mulattoes in a slave population of only thirty-two thousand) contrasted to the insignificant number of free blacks and mulattoes found in the French and British Caribbean.

Thus, up to the eighteenth century, the overall condition in the Hispanic Caribbean was one of greater normalcy and less development than in the French and British Caribbean. This is not to suggest that the treatment of slaves was less cruel than that practiced in the other islands but to point out the kinds of circumstances that mitigated against the rapid growth of the plantation in the Hispanic Caribbean in general and in Cuba in particular.[41]

Cuba's development up to the eighteenth century was slow. Cuba eventually followed the other Caribbean territories, where one found "the conveyance of the land to the wealthiest sugar planters (for the most part absentee); the disappearance of small and medium-sized properties; the emigration of the white farmer; and the wholesale importation of slaves."[42] Poverty was inevitable, given the presence of a monoculture and the resulting underutilization of labor and resources.

In *Sugar and Society in the Caribbean*, the Cuban historian and economist Ramiro Guerra y Sánchez demonstrates the violence personified by the latifundium on the one hand and the peasants' reaction on the other. Speaking of the latifundium, he says:

> It did not seek to promote the welfare or the material and moral advancement of the people of a cane-growing country, but was entirely dedicated to obtaining a high profit on invested capital. By supplying sugar at a very low price to the consumer, the producer country becomes an economic fief of a distant metropolis and its working class lives in poverty so that the country that dominates and exploits it can live better and more cheaply.[43]

Because latifundium monopolizes the land in its concern for profit, it challenges peasants who work to maintain small holding that insure their survival and dignity. A constant struggle ensues as in the Caribbean experience.

The demise of the Haitian economy after its war of independence propelled Cuba out of a "state of isolation and thrust it into the turmoil of the outside world"[44] when French exiles fled to Cuba, taking with them capital and sugar-production techniques. Capital also came from other parts of the Caribbean, Latin America, and even from Louisiana in the United States. Ramiro Guerra y Sánchez says:

> The sugar latifundium created so precarious a social structure in Haiti and inflicted such grievous suffering upon the slave population that as soon as the mother country, convulsed with internal revolutionary struggles, momentarily relaxed its coercive grip, the slaves rose in revolt. A catastrophe ensued which in a few months ruined the economy of this wealthy colony, principal supplier of Europe's sugar and coffee. The prices of both articles shot up, initiating in 1790 a period of prosperity, perhaps the most famous in Cuban history, which lasted almost a decade.[45]

The newly independent United States added new markets for Cuban sugar. As John Adams pointed out, "West Indian molasses was an essential ingredient in American independence," and as another writer has shown, "a fundamental cause of the British North American colonies in the 1770s was their desire to trade with Cuba and the French West Indies." This impetus to the economy created a need for labor so that from 1823 to 1865, four hundred thousand African slaves arrived in Cuba. Cuban merchants, indebted to English and United States capitalists, engaged in slave trade that brought millions of dollars into Cuba itself. At this point, the United States had entered into Caribbean life.

But this newly enjoyed prosperity in Cuba would insure the suffering of millions of inhabitants and guarantee violence. As Guerra suggests:

When all this toil of centuries seemed to be almost completed and the fruits could at last be enjoyed by the children, the sugar latifundium, which had ruined the West Indies with its two formidable instruments, foreign capital and imported cheap labor, invaded the island. Its appearance marked the beginning of the wholesale destruction of our small and medium-sized properties and the reduction of our rural land owners and independent farmers, backbone of our nation, to the lowly condition of a proletariat being stifled by that economic asphyxiation which afflicts the country today from one end to the other.[46]

The chief beneficiary of this toil and destruction was the United States of America, whose merchants were selling food and clothing in return for slaves.

It must be understood that violence was not only used in a physical sense to subjugate the people of the Caribbean but was implicit in the economic arrangements of the islands. By far the most oppressive and violent element was that same latifundium system, which

. . . consolidates thousands of small farms into immense agrarian units; it uproots the farmer from his land; it destroys the rural landowning and independent farming class, backbone of the nation; and finally, it puts an end to national economic independence by converting the society into a mere dependency, a satellite, a workshop, at the service of some foreign power.[47]

It is no wonder that Barbados, where the latifundium system reached its perfection, is the setting for one of the most important Caribbean novels, *In the Castle of My Skin*. The novel deals with the violent removal of a peasant who, defenseless against the latifundium, clings to his plot of land. In Vic Reid's novel, *New Day*, a Jamaican peasant struggles against the very same socioeconomic forces. In fact, the latifundium was so destructive that Guerra warns:

The rising tide of the latifundium irresistibly destroys, as demonstrated by the history of twenty prosperous Antillean islands—everything that stands in the way of its final goal: to produce at minimum cost a basic commodity or luxury article for a distant market at a profit, even though that policy will in the long run ruin the producing country economically, socially and politically.[48]

Cuba found herself in precisely this position at the end of the nineteenth century.

II

CARIBBEAN RESISTANCE:
AN HISTORICAL ANALYSIS

I

A Note on Resistance

THE history of the Caribbean can be divided into three periods: 1500–1800; 1800–1960; 1960 to the present—all characterized by violence perpetrated against Caribbean peoples and their political resistance. Political resistance has usually been defined as active or passive, with active resistance involving open revolts and rebellions and with passive resistance including suicide, voluntary abortion, poisoning masters and sabotaging crops.

In his work, *African Civilizations in the New World*, Roger Bastide distinguishes between "spontaneous revolts," which were "ideological" and "expressed the Negro's opposition to the whole concept of servile labor," and "cultural resistance," which was "organized" and represented "a symptom of Negro protest against compulsory Christianization, the imposition of European customs and values."[1] For the purposes of this study, I shall define resistance as any act or complex of acts designed to rid a people of its oppressors, be they slave masters or multinational corporations. I will further categorize resistance as follows:

Cultural resistance: the motive of resistance emanates from the beliefs, mores, or indigenous ways of life and is expressed in religion or the arts.

Socioeconomic resistance: resistance is expressed by suicide, abortion, work sabotage, withholding labor, poisoning masters, etc.

Political resistance: the motive of resistance emanates from an ideological framework in which the goal of the enslaved people is to control their destiny—be it full independence or some other form of government—and may be expressed in revolts, rebellions or revolutions.

These categories are by no means static. They can occur simultaneously, and one may precede the other. However, one generally predominates at crucial moments in history. The goals are always the same: "to oppose the concept of servile labor," and to reject "compulsory Christianization [and] the imposition of European customs and values."[2] The following examples illustrate these three types of resistance.

The predominance of the slave mode of production and the physical violence against Caribbean peoples, which culminated in the San Domingo revolution, characterized the first period of Caribbean history. C. L. R. James says that "West Indians first became aware of themselves as a people in the Haitian revolution, [and that] whatever its ultimate fate, the Cuban revolution marks the ultimate stage of a Caribbean quest for national identity."[3]

In the second phase of Caribbean history one sees the development of a well defined dimension of political, socioeconomic and cultural resistance. While physical violence was just as intense in this phase, the colonizers also tried to control the intellectual and mental faculties of the slaves by presenting the outer veneer of freedom, yet regulating the people through institutional means. This period saw the rise of wage workers as slaves were transformed into a growing and more aggressive proletariat, thereby creating the basis for a capitalist society. This second period culminated with the Cuban Revolution of 1959 and formal independence for most other Caribbean countries after 1960.

With the demise of slavery and the slave trade, European colonization became the order of the day. Speaking of colonization in the Caribbean territories, Bill Riviere contends:

The advent of colonialism introduced a new dimension. The colonial relationship is based, on the one hand, on the power and domination of the coloniser and, on the other, on the impotence and submissiveness of the colonised. Colonies and the colonised exist to generate wealth for the coloniser in a compact that is cemented with the guns of the coloniser and the blood of the colonised; the colonisers are in the small minority and the colonised in the vast majority. *Thus, physical violence is a necessary condition of colonial domination. But it has consistently proven not nearly sufficient, and has had to be complemented by institutionalized violence. The principle agency in the business of institutionalized violence has been education.*[4] [Italics mine.]

The Europeans introduced religious and secular education into the Caribbean to inculcate the new values a budding capitalist society would require. Both Dr. Walter Rodney and Julius Nyerere, speaking about the same colonial experience in different geographical regions, discuss this problem. Rodney comments: ". . . colonial schooling was education for subordination, exploitation, the creation of mental confusion and the development of underdevelopment."[5] Dr. Nyerere puts it this way: "The education provided by the colonial government . . . was not designed to prepare young people for the service of their own country; instead it was motivated by a desire to inculcate the values of the colonial society and to train individuals for the service to the colonial state."[6] This was the case in Africa, and it has relevance for the Caribbean as well. Speaking more particularly about Puerto Rico, Juan Angel Silén notes:

> The school exists to shape the student to a social order, to give him continuity in an order based on exploitation. As a ruling-class instrument it penalizes students and teachers to make them conform to an authoritarian structure. It aims to brutalize them by psychological manipulation. Thus the school stresses the "smallness" of the Puerto Ricans, develops a whole theory of our "limitations" and "defencelessness." It plays down our culture in relation to the "great" and "powerful" one of the United States.[7]

Thus, the purpose of colonial education was to prepare obedient boys and girls to participate in a new capitalist enterprise.

Brutality and oppression took a different emphasis in the post-slavery epoch. As the Brazilian writer Paulo Freire recognizes, education carried forward "institutional violence"

> . . . which begins with the egoistic interests of the oppressors (an egoism cloaked in the false generosity of paternalism) and makes of the oppressed the objects of its humanitarianism, itself maintains and embodies oppression. It is an instrument of dehumanization. This is why, as we affirmed earlier, the pedagogy of the oppressed cannot be developed or practised by the oppressor. It would be a contradiction in terms if the oppressor not only defended but actually implemented a liberating education.[8]

This is one reason the British granted £30,000 per annum for the education of former slaves in the British colonies. The grant was neither "humanitarian" nor "humanistic"; rather, it was designed to serve colonial interests of the transitional period by ensuring that obedient and submissive slaves became obliging and willing wage earners. It is in this sense that Freire carefully differentiates in his work between "humanistic generosity" and "humanitarian generosity." (Paulo Freire differentiates between "the pedagogy of the oppressed, animated by authentic, humanistic (not humanitarian) generosity, [which] presents itself as a pedagogy of man.")[9]

In this period, education was brought under the auspices of the church, which sought to maintain control through religious and secular education. This was particularly true in the Spanish empire where one of the main pretexts for colonization was the conversion of "infidel" Indians. But in many cases throughout the New World, religious leaders organized and led the political resistance. For example, Riviere points out that in Jamaica "Preaching and teaching by religious denominations like the Baptist . . . had produced in the minds of the slaves a belief that they could serve both a spiritual and a temporal master; thereby occasioning them to resist the lawful authority of their temporal, under the delusion of rendering themselves more acceptable, to a spiritual leader."[10]

But the planter class continued the violence against the peasantry at other levels as well. They imported laborers from China, India and some European countries to keep wages low and the peasantry in a state of perpetual poverty. As Guerra shows, this was the pattern followed throughout the Caribbean. For instance, during the sugar boom in Cuba, black labor was imported from Haiti, Jamaica, Puerto Rico and Panama. Although the colonizers passed laws which prevented the peasantry from owning property, these measures did not contain the resistance. Revolts and rebellions would continue with renewed intensity into the twentieth century.

Meanwhile, colonial theorists tried to justify slavery in hopes of resurrecting it. By 1833, when slavery had ended in the British territories, all major decisions were still made through the "colonial office." The people did not yet control their own affairs and were only a little better off than slaves.

II

The second period of Caribbean history begins in 1800. Between 1801 and 1807, Jamaica had its heaviest period of slave imports, with more than sixty-three thousand slaves brought to the island. By 1830 a high percentage of blacks were still African-born, with the largest being the Coromantees. Both the formal church and African cults grew between 1809 and 1823. As a result, legislation was passed to ban unlicensed preaching, and planters prevented their slaves from holding religious meetings for fear the meetings would inflame the slaves with visions of equality.

The period from 1831 to 1865 brought intensified growth of both the formal church and authentic African cults, with the latter

> . . . offering a reinterpretation of Christianity closer to the religious belief of the community . . . that was able to reflect or represent the national life in a way that was more closely analogous to the belief that the people had known, i.e., its own African ways. Far from disappearing after emancipation, there's every evidence that the growth of the cults parallels the growth of missionary churches and this movement was not confined to the hills.[11]

While European religious leaders tried to exterminate the whole panoply of

African life, African church members emphasized and retained their religious ways because they knew the indispensible role their church played in emancipating Caribbean peoples. In this sense, African religion was the spearhead of cultural resistance.

Bill Riviere makes the distinction between "disseminating missionaries" and the "established clergyman"—the former, who did not consciously teach subversion but by "their methodology, greatly assisted the slaves in shaping religious doctrine to the needs of liberation," and the latter, "who shared [and I might add, perpetuated] the class interest of the plantocracy."[12] This lends support to Brathwaite's theory that Caribbean culture is essentially one in which religion fashions the sensibilities of the people and becomes the *modus operandi* for most of their actions.[13] It is no wonder, then, that the central force (i.e., the Baptist Church) in the 1831 revolution was a cadre of religious organizations just as Voodoo and Obeah were the mainsprings of previous revolutionary struggles.

The sheer barbarity of the slavery system led to the 1831 revolution in Jamaica. As in Haiti, arson was the foremost weapon. On December 28, 1831, Kensington Estates burst into flames, and the burning of buildings in the western part of the island followed. Samuel Sharpe, a "house slave" and Native Baptist Church minister known as the "ruler" or "daddy" among his followers, led the rebellion. Sharpe was an eloquent and passionate preacher, and when he spoke, the slaves were "wrought up almost to a state of madness."[14] Sharpe believed that the church's demand of "obedience" from its followers was inconsistent with the teachings of the Bible and that slaves were entitled to their freedom. He used the contacts he had made while preaching to organize the slaves and to work with the Black Regiment, which launched attacks against the British. One account explains:

The rebel's military core was the Black Regiment, about one hundred and fifty strong with fifty guns among them. The Black Regiment under the command of Colonel Johnson of Retrieve Estate, fought a successful action on the 28th of December 1831 against the Western Interior militia, which had retreated from its barracks in the interior to Old Montpelier Estate, near Montego Bay and put the country between Montego Bay, Lucea and Savannah-la-Mar in rebel hands. The Black Regiment then carried rebellion into the hills, invading estates and inviting recruits, burning properties on the border of St. James and setting off a trail of fires through the Great River Valley in Westmoreland and St. Elizabeth. Its commanders, "Colonels" Dove and Gardner, set up headquarters at Greenwich, Gardner's estate on the border of Hanover and Westmoreland, and from there a sketchy organization held sway over the surrounding estates. The slaves were organized into companies, each responsible for guarding its estate boundaries and holding allegiance to

Gardner and Dove at Greenwich. This sort of activity was carried on by a number of rebel leaders, also Baptist members, notably Captain Dehany operating in the Salters Hill area, and Captain Tharp in the interior. Their work was supplemented by the activity of self-appointed leaders, who took the opportunity to roam the country collecting recruits, looting and destroying and intimidating other slaves; enjoying a little brief authority.[15]

The slaves held out for three days. When the attack ended in defeat, white retaliation was brutal, with 323 slaves executed. However, black resistance was not in vain, for "the rebellion contributed indirectly to the abolition of slavery" and speeded up the ultimate liberation of the Caribbean peoples.

The first act of the planters after the Baptist War was to form the Colonial Church Union, which destroyed all the chapels on the island. The revolt had shown both Jamaican planters and the British Crown that the black man was to be enslaved no longer. It also gave the British government the arguments necessary to abolish slavery. But abolition did not end the servile condition under which blacks lived; inhumane practices continued long after slavery since political control resided within a small band of ruling-class whites and some colored Jamaicans who together controlled the Jamaican assembly.[17]

With the abolition of slavery in 1834,

> Jamaica had not yet lost her supremacy as the wealthiest of West Indian colonies or as the most prized of all British overseas possessions. She was still one of the 'richest jewels of the British crown.' The prestige of the governship of Jamaica was second only to that of India and Canada, and it would remain so for twenty years more.[18]

Around the end of the 1840s there were signs that all was not well on the island. Economic decline began when Jamaica found she could not sell coffee and sugar below the price offered by the world market. The price of sugar dropped, and the British removed special rates given to Jamaican sugar. Cuba, which still employed slave labor, was in better shape since new techniques had lowered the cost of sugar production.

A parallel movement of the "little man" or the peasant took place. After emancipation, ex-slaves left the sugar and coffee estates and went into the hills, where they worked their own "little plots" and became their own "massas." By 1865 there were more than fifty thousand small landholders producing and trading for and among themselves and creating the necessary conditions for independence. While the sugar industry was declining, these small peasant farmers began to enjoy relative prosperity. But there was hardly enough land, and the condition of the peasantry as a whole continued to deteriorate.

Against this background, Edward John Eyre became the lieutenant governor of Jamaica on 26 March 1862. From the beginning of his tenure, Eyre was in conflict with the people. Even by standards of his day, Eyre was incapable of running a country. He had left school at the age of sixteen and gone to New Zealand, where he made his fortune by selling sheep. By intellect, temperament, character, and education he was unsuited to govern. He was a disciple of Thomas Carlyle and accepted in an unquestioned manner the ideas of Carlyle which he put forward in his pamphlet, *Occasional Discourse on the Negro Question* (1849) which was later amended to read *Occasional Discourse on the Nigger Question* (1853). In this pamphlet Carlyle not only described West Indian blacks as being inferior to whites but also saw them as forever condemned to be servants unto whites. As he argued:

> You are not "slaves" now; nor do I wish, if it can be avoided, to see you slaves again: but decidedly you will have to be servants to those that are born *wiser* than you,—servants to the whites, if they are (as what mortal can doubt they are?) born wiser than you. That, you may depend on it, my obscure Black friends, is and was always the Law of the World, for you and for all men: To *be* servants, the more foolish of us to the more wise; and only sorrow, futility and disappointment will betide both, till both in some approximate degree get to conform to the same.[19]

Most of the ideas in the infamous "Queen's Advice," sent to the people in 1865, were Carlyle's and was a carbon copy of recommendations made by Eyre to the Queen regarding the situation in Jamaica. They were instrumental in causing the Morant Bay Rebellion in 1865.

Although slavery was abolished in Jamaica in 1834, by the time of the Morant Bay Rebellion, the condition of the poor had not changed materially, and they still did not participate in the governmental processes of the island. Writing in 1850, one observer comments on Jamaica as follows: "The poor are utterly excluded from all participation in its privileges or responsibility [i.e., of government in the island]. All the energies of legislation are exerted to promote the growth and sale of sugar and rum. . . ."[20]

Although white absentee owners controlled most of the large estates, they abandoned a large number of plantations because of heavy mortgages and decreasing profits. As a result, unemployment became more severe, and peasants secured more "little plots" in order to offset approaching starvation. The authorities, however, believed that their salvation lay in sugar estates and tried to prevent the peasantry from acquiring their plots by drawing up class legislation to discourage them. The ex-slaves were forced to work for wages, hut taxes were imposed, and high rents were charged for lands on which blacks lived. But the peasantry would not give up their freedom for what was in effect another system of forced labor. In fact, their reaction proved another form of socioeconomic resistance to European enslavement and plantation economy.[21]

There were other problems, including lack of sanitation, a decline in the number of medical doctors by one-quarter since emancipation, and a cholera epidemic which took thirty thousand lives in 1850–1851. In the face of these crises, the authorities should have been an assembly representing mostly the peasants' interest. But conflict was inevitable, given a Crown Colony form of government (where there was an executive council selected by the Crown), an assembly representing mostly the planters' interest, and the gradual encroachment by those representing the interest of the coloreds.

One of the first incidents that fostered public discontent was the Tramway affair. A resolution by the House of Assembly calling for Eyre's impeachment followed, and House members subsequently refused to conduct any further public business with him. Even the normally pro-Eyre newspaper, *Morning Journal*, concluded that "the feebleness of his understanding makes him unfit to represent the Majesty of the Crown and to conduct the grave business of State."[22]

At this point Eyre had alienated most of the people from him. The educated ones might have articulated the problems among themselves and might have been concerned in their own way, but the masses instinctively perceived that Eyre was not acting in their best interests. George William Gordon and Paul Bogle's approaches illustrate these different attempts to deal with Eyre. Gordon, a colored Native Baptist and champion of people's rights, pursued independence through legislative means, whereas Bogle, a black man, and his followers used violent political resistance.* Both found it difficult to assist their people since they were persecuted constantly. In May, 1855 Gordon complained to the London Antislavery Society that "I have to contend with hatred and persecution of no ordinary kind at present. You will, by a paper sent you herewith, see that the Governor, the Judge (of the Circuit Court), the Attorney General and a special jury, are all conspiring against me here: and I believe that if some of them found the opportunity, they would unscrupulously dispatch me."[23] Gordon continued his efforts at home and, rebuffed by authorities in Jamaica, decided to take the people's petition to the Queen.

Paul Bogle on the other hand, who believed that he was an instrument of

---

* The coloreds in Jamaica (like the mulattoes in Haiti) form a well-defined and distinctive group in Jamaican society. George William Gordon was a product of a white father and a black mother and therefore was a colored rather than a black. Paul Bogle was a black.

God, built the Nature Baptist Church at Stoney Gut, educated the dispossessed and landless peasantry, and organized the people. Thus while a deputation of Jamaican citizens was to be sent to the Queen, Paul Bogle was selected to head another delegation to see Governor Eyre to present the grievances of his people. When Eyre refused to receive his delegation, Bogle called secret meetings and organized his people to resist the authorities.

On 7 October 1865 Bogle and his men marched to Morant Bay court house to protest the injustices which were being committed against their people. Mavis Campbell describes what took place on that fateful day:

> The first protest occurred 7 October 1865 during a court of petty session where an accused, on a charge of assault, was found guilty and ordered to *pay a fine of 4/. plus 12/6 costs.* The court was then interrupted by one of Bogles's men who advised the accused to pay only the fine but not the costs. The dual charge was quite a feature of the magistrates and it was felt that the greater part of these costs went secretly to the clerk of the court who, in this case, was the *son of Rector Cooke, Gordon's enemy.*
>
> The second protest arose from a protracted dispute over the ownership of land on a certain estate near Morant Bay. This case was representative of many. As estates were abandoned, the practice of squatting by ex-slaves increased considerably since the 1840s; partly from lack of purchase money, partly because many planters were unwilling to sell lands to "Negroes," and partly because in many cases "owners" themselves had no longer a clear title to the lands. Often owners of doubtful legality "sold" lands to the land-thirsty peasantry, as happened in this case. When their ownership was disputed they held on doggedly until finally one of their numbers was prosecuted for trespassing. The case was heard on the 9th, and as would be expected the accused was found guilty and ordered to pay a fine with costs. Once more there was an interruption, this time advising the man to appeal. The next day warrants were issued for the arrest of Paul Bogle, the "ringleader," and others for the interruptions on both occasions.[24]

On 11 October 1865 Bogle and his men again marched to Morant Bay court house to present their grievances. The Custos, who knew that they were coming, mustered the militia at the court house and ordered Bogle and his men not to enter the square at the front of the court house. When Bogle and his men disobeyed the Custos's order he read the riot act. While the act was being read some persons from the crowd which had gathered threw some stones at the militia and then the Custos ordered the militia to fire into the crowd.

In the ensuing confrontation several people were killed and injured. On 13 October Eyre moved against Bogle and on 23 October 1865 captured and executed him. Whereas fifteen people were killed and thirty-one wounded during the rebellion, Eyre's men executed thirty blacks for each white man killed and flogged the same proportion for each wounded. More than a thousand black homes were burned to the ground. Gordon, who had not taken part in the revolt, was arrested on 17 October in Kingston, shipped to Morant Bay, where martial law had been proclaimed, and executed. Eyre was recalled to England and indicted for murder but acquitted. The rebellion had come to an end.

As in San Domingo, the Morant Bay Rebellion was not one against color; it just happened that the ruling class was white. As Mr. Henry Clare wrote after the rebellion, "It was a great mistake to leave a country of free blacks in the hands of a pro-slavery government."[25] Bogle and his men had declared that "if the land was given up to them they did not want anything from the white people; they would try to make their own living themselves."[26] It was the same self-reliance Garvey would preach fifty years later, the same "do for self" the Nation of Islam would call for some years following, and the same self-reliance Nyerere advocates in Tanzania. "Colour for colour! Buckra country for us!" would be the rallying cry which the Morant Bay Rebellion started.

Marcus Garvey said that Bogle and Gordon

> . . . sounded the call of un-molested liberty, but owing to the suppression of telegraphic communication, they were handicapped and suppressed, otherwise Jamaica would be as free today as Haiti, which threw off the French yoke under the leadership of the famous Negro General, Toussaint L'Ouverture.[27]

It is difficult to accept this assessment of the Morant Bay Rebellion since Bogle had neither Toussaint's organization nor decisiveness and Gordon advised handling the problem through legitimate channels. As Gordon admitted, "all I ever did was to recommend the people who complained to seek redress in a legitimate way."[28] But the Morant Bay Rebellion does illustrate the continued use of political resistance as the Caribbean people challenged a constituted power in their quest for national liberation.

CARIBBEAN RESISTANCE: TOWARDS VICTORY

I

THE Jamaican peasants had lost the battle, but they continued the war. The Assembly handed power back to Britain, even though a year after the Morant Bay Rebellion, revolutionary activity increased in Cuba and Puerto Rico where slavery still existed. Both countries exploded three years after the Morant Bay Rebellion.

In Puerto Rico, where the first revolt took place in 1527, *repartimiento* and *encomienda** had gone hand in hand with suppression of indigenous people and Africans. Although there were other rebellions in the sixteenth, seventeenth and eighteenth centuries, as Manuel Maldonado-Denis contends, Puerto Rico was at "the stages during which preparations served for the future of our nation were made."[1] The nineteenth century was replete with revolutionary figures: Ramón Emeterio Betances, Ruiz Belvis, the brothers Andrés and Juan Vizcarrondo, Buenaventura Quiñones, Eugenio María de Hostos and others. But the one who personified the revolutionary spirit more than anyone else was Betances, acknowledged as a "revolutionary by conviction."[2]

---

* *Encomienda:* The Spaniards who emigrated at the beginning of the Spanish conquest of the Americas took Indian women to serve as concubines. The men were enslaved and made to work in the agricultural fields and the mines to supply the Spaniards with food and gold respectively. The creation of a legal institution to regularize this relationship became known as *encomienda* and was inaugurated by Nicolás de Ovando, the first royal governor of Hispaniola, when he arrived in 1502.

While the system of *encomienda* gave the Spaniards the right to exploit the labor of the Indians and to receive tribute from them, the *encomendors* had the corresponding obligation to provide the Indians with religious instructions and to defend the land against any invasion. This system was known as *repartimientos* even though the term later came to be mean a *grant* or *distribution* of Indian forced labor. (See Lewis Hanke, *The Spanish Struggle for Justice in the Conquest of America*, p. 19)

During the nineteenth century, organized plots began to surface in Puerto Rico as early as 1812, which helped bring about the imposition of the infamous Negro Code which brought even more cruelty upon blacks. In 1867 Betances proclaimed his "Ten Commandments of Liberty" in St. Thomas with the first commandment calling for the abolition of slavery. A second proclamation later in the year called for an end to Spanish domination. Betances was consistent in his position, for when the 1865 Morant Bay Rebellion was in full swing, he acknowledged that

> . . . only by the force of arms can we wrest from the government and the Spanish nation the right to manage our own affairs, enjoy our liberty, insure and defend our interests, and occupy the position that is due us among the nations of the earth.[3]

It is therefore not coincidental that, beginning with his exile from Puerto Rico in July 1867 to the fateful War of Lares in September 1868, Betances raised funds, purchased arms and advocated liberation, becoming, as Maldonado-Denis reminds us, the "chief organizer and the intellectual and tangible inspiration of the Cry of Lares."[4]

When the authorities discovered the plot, the revolution, planned for 29 September 1868, was advanced to 23 September 1868. Betances and his expeditionary force of three thousand men were prevented from leaving St. Thomas to join the revolution. Left in the command of the Venezuelan Manuel Rojas, the revolutionary fighters marched from Rojas' estate to the town of Lares carrying a white flag with the inscription, *Muerte o Libertad; Viva Puerto Rico Libre, Año 1868*, by which they proclaimed Puerto Rico a republic. However, on the same day, the Spanish routed the revolutionaries when they moved from Lares to Sebastian del Pepino. But, as Silén puts it, "Grito de Lares marked the birth of our Puerto Rican nationality"[5] and led to the abolition of slavery in 1873. Indeed, a war was lost, but a nation was born. At the same time, the Cuban War of Yara, which would give continuity to the Caribbean struggle for justice and freedom, began.[6]

Unlike Puerto Rico, Cuba had risen to economic ascendency after the demise of Haiti and was the focus of attention in the Caribbean during the nineteenth century. Cuba had raised tobacco and cattle from the time of discovery until 1763. But when the English occupied Havana for ten months in 1763, the commercial importance of the island increased and precipitated changes that resulted in a full-blown plantation economy by 1838. Franklin Knight in his work, *Slave Society in Cuba*, catalogs the major events responsible for the transformation of Cuba into a plantation economy. He says:

Among these powerful agents of change in the history of Cuban society at this time must be included the shifts in international market demands, the English occupation of Havana in 1763–64, the far-reaching economic and administrative reforms of Charles III (1759–88), the sudden destruction of the French colony of St. Dominique, and the disruptive wars of the Latin American independence movement.[7]

The desire for African slaves increased once this commercial and agricultural transformation was made. From 1512 to 1761, sixty thousand slaves were imported, while from 1762 to 1838 more than four hundred thousand slaves were imported.[8] In 1789 a royal cedula removed all restriction on the slave trade, and free trade with American sources rose considerably.

The United States began to immerse herself more fully in the economic life of the Caribbean during Cuba's ascendency to a plantation economy. Emerging as the new colonial power under President Jefferson, the United States began to toy with purchasing Cuba, and the American consul in Cuba held secret negotiations of which nothing ever came.

At this time, revolutionary activity increased in Latin America and Cuba with the 1820 conspiracy of José Antonio Aponte being of particular importance because of its failure led to further repression. José Francisco Lemus discussed plans for revolution with the Latin American liberator, Simon Bolívar, but the conspiracy was revealed through bribery and treachery, and Lemus and his chief lieutenants were imprisoned. Conspiracies were uncovered frequently in 1826 and 1827 and their leaders hung. Cuba became an armed camp, and the Spanish authorities prohibited persons born in Cuba from serving in the Spanish army in Cuba.

The United States did not remain neutral but warned that Cuba must not follow Haiti's example. Of course, the effect another revolution might have on slaves in the southern part of the United States influenced the Americans. Henry Clay warned:

> Would not the freed slaves of Cuba be tempted by the very fact of that independence to employ all the means which vicinity, similarity of origin and sympathy could supply, to foment and stimulate insurrection, in order to join ultimate strength to their cause (to stir up insurrection, that is, among the slaves in the southern states of the U.S.). *The U.S. has too much at stake in the fortunes of Cuba to allow them to see . . . a war of invasion.*[9] [Italics mine.]

This threat of a United States slave insurrection fed by Caribbean events caused apprehension in the United States. Alarmed by the rumor that Toussaint was about to invade soon after his successful revolution in Haiti, the United States consul to Haiti sought assurances, and on 13 July 1799, Toussaint signed a secret treaty in which he promised that he would not attack the United States. The fear was real, given the fact that Toussaint had defeated both the British and the French and had commanded more men than George Washington. Toussaint, however, was more concerned with the liberation of his own people and had no plans for invading the United States.[10] The United States was not prepared to risk another Haiti in Cuba; and the large contingent of Spanish forces, combined with controls over slave movement, contained serious revolts until 1868.

In 1860 Cuba reached the height of her prosperity. Sugar exports had grown from $160,000 in 1760 to $8 million in 1825 and to $20 million in 1860. Unlike the other Caribbean plantation owners during the height of their prosperity, most Cuban sugar planters lived in Cuba, and by 1830 the largest slave merchants were "Europeans who had settled in . . . Cuba."[11] The United States had actively entered into this trade, with nine-tenths of the ships employed in Cuban slave trade built in the United States and captained by United States citizens. As Hugh Thomas reminds us, ". . . about half the slave trade to Cuba was, during the 1850s at least, in U.S. hands, an adjunct of the still grandiose slave trade to Texas and the U.S. south (perhaps 300,000 slaves were brought into the U.S. south between 1808 and 1860)."[12]

This alliance of the Cuban planter class with the United States was important since United States acquisition of Cuba would help guarantee the continuance of United States slavery. The purchase of Cuba and maintenance of slavery played a large role in the American Civil War since the South hoped to annex Cuba and continue the profitable slave trade after seceding from the Union.[13] The Confederates had to abandon the idea of annexing Cuba when they needed the support of Europe.

The Ten Years' War that erupted in 1868 continued the liberation process instigated by the Cuban Maroons ("the guardians of the flag of liberation," as José L. Franco calls them), who "joined en masse the ranks of the Cuban Liberation Army"[14] when the war began. The war started when Carlos Manuel de Céspedes, commander of the Bayone area, freed his thirty slaves and placed them in his army of 147 men. By the end of October the uprising was so popular that he had more than twelve thousand men and had captured both Bayone and Holguin. In 1868, Céspedes and the Oriente rebels formed their own rebel government while Agramonte and his followers, mostly free Negroes, established themselves in Puerto Príncipe. In 1869 a revolutionary assembly, criticizing Céspedes' position on gradual emancipation, abolished slavery in areas it commanded. Guerrilla warfare continued in 1869 and the rebels, like the Maroons in Jamaica, used the terrain to their advantage. Out of this movement emerged Antonio Maceo, a mulatto, one of the great heroes of Cuban independence, and Máximo Gómez, who came from Santo Domingo where he had learned guerrilla warfare while fighting against the Haitians.

It is important to take exception to the statement that

> Nothing could be more misleading than to think that slavery was an important factor contributing to the outbreak of the civil war in Cuba that lasted from 1868 to 1878. Instead, as Rafael María de Labra correctly pointed out to the Spanish Cortes, the causes were basically political and economic.[15]

We know this is manifestly absurd since slavery was the backbone of Cuban "political and economic" life. Second, the very nature of revolutionary activity explains the fact that the *criollos* (Cuban born Spanish) took the initial impetus in the Ten Years' War. A. N. Yakovlev suggests:

> . . . general economic prerequisites alone cannot bring about a revolutionary explosion; the presence of a *revolutionary situation* is also essential.
> A revolution matures only when society becomes entangled in economic contradictions and the situation of the masses drastically deteriorates. . . . In principle, however, a revolutionary situation does not necessarily develop as a result of war. It can be engendered by the exacerbation of society's internal contradictions.[16]

We know that Cuba was always on the brink of revolution. We also know that the Cuban *criollos* needed Spanish protection in the event of serious slave insurrections, which meant greater Spanish control of their internal affairs. On the other hand, the excessive taxation the Cuban planters were forced to pay (". . . the Spanish government, without consulting the colonies, imposed a new tax ranging from 6–12 per cent on real estate, incomes, and all types of business") became doubly burdensome during a depression when sugar prices fell to the lowest level in thirteen years.[17] Coming on the eve of the Ten Years' War, the taxes provided the necessary spark for a revolutionary situation. The internal and external condition of war (the September revolution of Serrano and others, which drove the Spanish Queen Isabel II into exile, created a weakened monarchy abroad), plus the internal contradictions in Cuban economic conditions (i.e., the need for greater hegemony in trade and thus greater profits for the *criollos*) presented the revolutionary situation necessary for the oppressed masses to rise.

The war, started by white planters and perceived as between the *criollos* and the *peninsulares*, turned into a war of liberation centering on the question of slavery. It mattered not that Céspedes' "early plans in general, seemed to be merely to bring an end to Spanish rule and taxation, substituting creole domination of the same political structure and bureaucracy,"[18] since once the war began, Céspedes had to address himself to slavery, the major contradiction within the society. Franklin W. Knight is forced to admit that while slavery was not among the issues considered at first by the rebels, once the war broke out it assumed greater importance. Indeed, it became of major importance. The attempt to separate "slavery" from the "political and economic" causes of the Ten Years' War is potentially misleading.

Destruction of sugar estates by fire during the next phase of the struggle encouraged the slaves to rise. Like the French in Haiti, the Spanish executed reprisals against the Cubans, and as in Guyana (formerly British Guiana), rebel disorder and violence negated their victories. As a result, Gómez was removed from his command in 1872, and Céspedes was killed in an ambush in 1874.

Gómez was in charge of the rebels again by 1874, with Maceo acting as his second in command. Fearing that the brilliant Maceo might create a black republic, Gómez replaced him with the less prominent black, Cecilio González. Gómez continued the war by burning eighty-three plantations in Sancti Spiritus and freeing the slaves there. Nonetheless, Maceo's prestige continued to grow; again, conservative elements attacked him, leading him to complain:

> . . . a small circle exists which has indicated that it did not wish to serve under my orders because I belong to the colored race. . . . Since I form a not inappreciable part of this democratic republic, which has for its basis the fundamental principles of liberty, equality and fraternity, I must protest energetically with all my strength that neither now nor at any time am I to be regarded as an advocate of a Negro Republic or anything of that sort. . . .[19]

Again, the problem of race presented itself in what was essentially a nationalist struggle, and that struggle continued. In 1876 the new rebel president, Estrada Palma, was captured, and many rebels deserted. Maceo and Martínez Campos, who represented the Spanish, discussed peace terms which provided for neither the abolition of slavery nor Cuban independence. Maceo held that the two were inseparable for the liberation of the Cuban people. Campos was unrelenting in his demands, and Maceo was unshakeable in his resolve. After an eight-day truce, hostilities resumed. Capitulation was inevitable, given the desertion by Maceo's men and his weakened position. The Pact of Zanjón, signed on 10 February 1878, ended the war.

The Ten Years' War had yet another result, for apart from keeping "military revolt alive in Cuba for a decade . . . it awoke the immediate attention of the United States."[20] The United States moved to fill the economic vacuum during the sugar crisis of 1880, and by 1895 became one of the largest investors in Cuba with close to $30 million. Defeated, Gómez and Maceo formed their base of operations in New York where they were in exile with José Martí.

By 1891 Martí reorganized his party into the Cuban Revolutionary Party and encouraged New York Cubans to contribute one-tenth of their annual earnings towards liberating Cuba. Later in the same year he extended revolutionary instruction to include the tobacco workers in Tampa while maintaining the support of Cubans in New York, Florida and New Orleans. Martí brought Máximo Gómez, who was then in Santo Domingo, and Maceo, then in Costa Rica, together. Although often sick, Martí determined that no uprising would take place unless backed by strong support. With evidence that four out of six Cuban provinces were ready for revolutionary activity, he labored hard for the revolution.

It seemed that all was ready by the end of 1894. Unrest was so great in Cuba that planters' homes were virtual fortresses.[21] Plans for the invasion had begun in New York. Martí shipped six hundred thousand rounds of ammunition and eight hundred rifles to Florida; three fast steamers were chartered, and arrangements were made to pick up Gómez, Maceo and other generals of the Ten Years' War. On 14 January 1895, the whole group of revolutionaries was caught as it prepared to sail to Cuba. Nonetheless, secret orders had been sent, and the revolution began on the night of 4 February 1895.

Arriving in Cuba a few months later, Martí and his comrades took up the struggle with renewed intensity. In April of that year Martí was killed while riding conspicuously into battle on a white horse. Only hours before he had written to a friend, the Mexican Manuel Mercado, saying, "Everything I have done to this day, and everything I shall do is to that end . . . to prevent in time the expansion of the U.S. into the Antilles and to prevent her from falling with even greater force, upon our American lands."[22] Martí was dead, but the war continued under the leadership of Máximo Gómez, Antonio Maceo and his brother José. Up to October, the war had taken place on the east side of the island, but on 29 October, Gómez slipped over the military "trocha" that divided Camagüey from Santa Clara province and began to ravage the western provinces, raising the people to arms and leaving fire and destruction in his path. By 6 January of the following year, Gómez was near Havana; Arsenio Martínez de Campos, leader of the Spanish forces, sensed defeat and submitted his resignation.

By 22 January Maceo had reached Matua. Both he and Gómez were brilliant in victory. They were not in an advantageous position, but the

Cuban people displayed the same bravery in the face of insurmountable odds as the Haitians had one hundred years before. Armed only with machetes, they fought stoutly. General Miró Argentes, Maceo's chief of state, describes their valor:

> Untrained men under the command of Pedro Delgado, most of them equipped only with machetes, were virtually annihilated as they threw themselves on the solid ranks of the Spaniards. It is not an exaggeration to assert that of every fifty men, 25 were killed. Some even attacked the Spaniards with bare fists, without pistols, without machetes; without even knives. Searching through the reeds by the Hondo River, fifteen more dead of the Cuban party were found and it was not immediately evident to what group they belonged. They did not appear to have shouldered arms, their clothes were intact and only tin drinking cups hung from their waists; a few steps ahead lay a dead Spanish horse, all its equipment intact. We reconstructed the climax of the tragedy. These men, following their daring chief, Lieutenant Colonel Pedro Delgado, had earned hero's laurels; they had thrown themselves against bayonets with bare hands; the clash of metal which was heard around them was the sound of their drinking cups banging against the saddlehorn.[23]

Fidel Castro also comments about this spectacle:

> Maceo was deeply moved. This man so accustomed to seeing death in all its forms, murmured this praise: "I had never seen this—untrained and unarmed men, attacking the Spaniards with only a drinking cup for a weapon. And I called it an *impedimenta!*" This is how the people fight when they want to win their liberty; they throw stones at airplanes and overturn tanks![24]

It is doubtful whether the Cubans used the American press to publicize their struggle, though it has been claimed that the Cubans in New York assisted the campaign so successfully that Millis commented, "the Cuban patriots seem to have been the first of modern peoples fully to grasp the military value of propaganda."[25] By 1898, victory was almost in Cuban hands.

At this point the Spanish unleashed a reign of terror equalling what took place in Haiti one hundred years before and in Jamaica after the 1865 Morant Bay Rebellion. Like Toussaint, Maceo was lured by a truce and assassinated. It was evident that the Spanish were losing, which posed an immediate threat to United States commercial interests on the island. Fearing Cuban victory, the United States sent the battleship *Maine* to the island in January, 1898. The *Maine* exploded in Havana harbor. With 260 lives lost, the United States demanded restitution, which Spain refused to give. After three months of diplomatic maneuvering and fighting, "Spain sued for peace, preferring annexation of Cuba by the United States in order to guarantee Spanish life and property and Cuba's external debts to Spain."[26] But the United States refused. Under pressure from the United States, the Treaty of Paris, signed on 10 December 1898, ended Spanish sovereignty over Cuba; Puerto Rico was annexed, and a United States military government was established in Cuba. The *Platt Amendment* of 1901 gave the United States complete control of all Cuban affairs. A struggle was lost, but once more the people of the Caribbean were being forged into even stauncher revolutionaries.

II

The U.S. was in an expansionist mood by the end of the Spanish-American War. The twentieth century marked the triumph of "manifest destiny" and U.S. dollar diplomacy in the Caribbean, culminating in "the emergence of the United States as world imperialist power"[27] occupying Cuba (1895–1902 and 1906–1909), Haiti (1915–1934) and the Dominican Republic (1916–1924), purchasing the Virgin Islands in 1917 and building the Panama Canal after provoking a war between Panama and Columbia. During World War II, the United States continued penetration by establishing military bases in most of the British Caribbean.

United States exploitation of these countries was no less abominable than that of her predecessors. Major-General Smedley D. Butler, one of the most decorated marines in the U.S. armed forces, commented in 1935:

> I spent 33 years and 4 months in active service as a member of our country's most agile military force—the Marine Corps. I served in all commissioned ranks from a second lieutenant to major-general. And during that period I spent most of my time being a high-class muscle man for Big Business, for Wall Street, and for the bankers. In short, I was a racketeer for capitalism. . . Thus, I helped make Mexico and especially Tampico safe for American oil interest in 1914. I helped make Haiti and Cuba a decent place for the National City Bank boys to collect revenues in . . . I helped purify Nicaragua for the international banking house of Brown Brothers in 1909–1912. I brought light to the Dominican Republic for American sugar interests in 1916. I helped make Honduras "right" for American fruit companies in 1903. . . . During those years, I had, as the boys in the back room would say, a swell racket. I was rewarded with honors, medals, promotion. Looking back on it, I feel I might have given Al Capone a few hints. The best *he* could do was to operate his racket in three city districts. We Marines operated on three *continents*.[28]

After winning independence in 1804, Haiti was virtually cut off from intercourse with the world for the next sixty years. In 1806, the United States Congress passed an act prohibiting trade with Haiti; during the War of 1812 the British Navy again prevented the United States from trading with Haiti; and the "double indemnity" loan of 150 million francs in 1825 added a heavy drain on Haiti's resources. In fact, Haiti had retrogressed from exports amounting to 11 million pounds in 1793 to only 2.5 million pounds in 1863.

It was a long time before Haiti was officially recognized by other nations. France was first to recognize Haiti in 1825, but the United States, fearing recognition might have an adverse effect on her slaves, did not recognize Haiti until 1862. Even the Latin American liberator, Bolívar, who was aided by Haitian President Pétion on at least two occasions that enabled him "to renew the struggle that won independence for Venezuela, Columbia, Peru, Ecuador and Bolivia, not only refused to recognize the independence of Haiti; he also did not invite it [Haiti] to the Congress of Panama which met in 1826."[29]

From 1870, when Bismarck demanded an indemnity of 3,000 pounds, up until World War I, "Haiti was dominated by the play of strong rivalries among the imperialist powers, above all France, Germany, and the United States."[30] In order to protect their interest these countries openly intervened in the domestic affairs of Haiti, encouraged rivalries among different local groups and thereby consciously obstructed the economic growth and political stabilization of the country. Because of the inability to stabilize the country and to plan for its social and economic development, the growth of this country was stymied. In the process, Haiti became a country of poverty, overpopulation, and illiteracy. Added to all these problems was the inability of political leaders to handle the island's problems. Political chaos plagued the country, and by 1904, "the last vestiges of a more or less stable government in Haiti disappeared."[31] The island's independence began under difficult conditions, for

> . . . the great plantations and sugar cane industry were ruined. Likewise destroyed was the underlying technology, together with great infrastructural accomplishments imposed by French colonialism that had made possible the high production of the erstwhile "*Pearl of the Antilles*," San Domingue.[32]

One of Haiti's most important innovations was a massive agrarian reform begun by President Pétion and described by Rayford Logan as "the first large scale distribution of land in the western hemisphere."[33] It is incorrect to suggest, as Logan does, that "this noble experiment, which was continued by Boyer and a few other presidents, actually contributed in the long run to the worsening of Haiti's agrarian problems."[34] Haiti's agrarian problems increased first, because of the former freed men's opposition to the agrarian program, and second, because under "the Agrarian Code of Jean Boyer, modeled on the *Code Napoléon* . . . A majority of the peasantry labored as serfs on the great plantations."[35] Haiti's basic problem was not caused by the peasantry or agrarian reform but primarily by the landholding classes' constant struggle for power and by the predominance of *caudillismo*, in which "popular sovereignty, suffrage, and constitutions represented unreal affirmations in those societies [which were] characterized by the predominance of direct, personal bonds between the oligarchy and the mass of the people."[36] This led to a unique situation in which local chieftains and military chiefs dominated certain regions, commanding loyalty from the local populace and constituting resistance to the national government. When one local group felt dissatisfied with the national government, it marched into the capital and, if strong enough, took over the government. If unable to do this, it still created enough conflict to keep the government politically unstable. Obviously this would create a climate rife with violence.

United States penetration of the island began against this background. "From 1847 onward, the United States had shown great interest in Haiti's strategic position, and with the construction of the Panama Canal, strong pressure was exerted on Haiti to obtain the transfer of môle Saint Nicolas as a coaling and naval station."[37] By the turn of the century, the United States controlled Haitian fiscal activities through the National City Bank of New York. Fearing the avowed intention of the United States to do in Haiti what they had done in Santo Domingo, the Haitian government in 1916 "asked for assistance by the United States in obtaining a loan to consolidate Haiti's debt and to reform the monetary system; the appointment of an arbitral commission to settle the differences between Haiti and the United States; [and] the good offices of the United States in securing a modification of the contract between Haiti and the bank."[38] But the United States, determined to secure Haiti by any means, landed on the island, disarmed the peasants, seized $500,000 in gold reserves and sent them back to New York. The sentiments of the Haitian people were neither considered nor accepted.

Because of the imperialist penetration of Haiti there were two important results: "the establishment of plantation economy and the subjugation of the political apparatus to the sole and exclusive benefit of American monopolies, particularly the First National City Bank."[39]

As we have seen earlier, in the British colonies and later in Cuba, the latifundia was always established at the expense and to the detriment of the peasantry. In the other Caribbean territories, the expansion of a plantation economy led to increased brutality and violence against the peasantry, and Haiti was no exception. As Suzy Castor reminds us: " . . . efforts to impose a plantation economy were carried out with excessive violence in both countries to the detriment of the small peasant holders."[40] In Haiti,

American companies were granted more than 100,000 hectares of land, while more than 50,000 peasants were driven from the land. Given this dispossession and accompanying violence, the peasantry took to armed resistance against military conquest, resulting in the emergence of the *coco* revolts, where the peasants fought with all their might to remove the forces of oppression which had come to dominate their lives and the resultant plantation economy which ensued.*

The entrance of the United States into Haitian affairs intensified the economic and political fragmentation of the society. As Naomi M. Garret, an American critic who supported the intervention of the United States was forced to conclude:

> If the Americans had made inexcusable mistakes in the political, financial, and educational administration of Haiti, greater blunders were yet to come. One of these was the restoration of the corvée which, though reasonable and acceptable in its conception, was so gravely mismanaged that its operation was fraught with abuses and was followed by dire results. That most of the atrocities were committed by Haitian gendarmes instead of their American officers did not lessen the wave of anti-American sentiment created among the peasantry. Members of the elite who were bitter in their resentment against the Americans wasted no time in using all propaganda at hand to fan to a white heat the feeling of race hatred among the masses. This, added to the forced recruitment and the ill treatment of the workers, caused a surge of uprisings of the cocos. The gendarmerie doubted its ability to cope with the situation and appealed to the Marines to help subdue the ill-equipped but determined peasants whose subsequent casualties were many.[41]

In 1922 the cocos' revolt was put down with the assistance of the United States Army but the cultural resistance of the people continued.

Perhaps one of the most salutary effects of all the ostracism imposed upon Haiti during the nineteenth century was the fact that African culture remained intact and became the base of Haitian culture. Edward Brathwaite has described the hostility imposed upon Haiti, not only as sanctions that had to be raised against these slave upstarts but as a device against the cultural subversion of the hemisphere.[42] This ostracism, nonetheless, led to the continued use of cultural resistance on the part of the

---

* During the period 1900-1915 there was tremendous internal unrest in Haiti. For example, there were a number of insurrections and four presidents were killed. Because of this unrest many peasants were impressed into the army. These conscripted peasants were called "cocos" and most of them came from the hills. During the U.S. occupation of the island, these cocos turned their guns against the U.S. army. Also, see James G. Leyburn, *The Haitian People* (New Haven: Yale University Press, 1941) Chapter 6, for an account of this period.

Haitian people and gave the impetus for the further cultural awakening of Caribbean peoples. It had its implications for the Harlem Renaissance, Negritude, and the ultimate explosion of a whole new dimension of cultural resistance of negroid peoples in the New World.

The Caribbean region, therefore, entered the twentieth century as a society in great poverty, stubbornly resisting enslavement and striving towards liberation. Given the ever-growing sophistication of weaponry against them, and the growing concentration of economic power in the heads of the colonizing powers, at an individual or collective level, the peasantry added another weapon to their repertoire of resistance, this time at the economic level. There is, therefore, among the masses, a great sense of class consciousness, a greater intensification and understanding of the vertical demarcation of the oppressed and the oppressors, and a coming together of these classes under the ambit of some sort of ideological framework. At first it is a rather unsophisticated consciousness, merely to respond to an impulse, as it were, but gaining greater clarity as it goes along and culminating in Fidel Castro's Marxist-Leninist state.

III

Against this background one can begin to understand the spate of strikes-turned-riots found through the Caribbean in the twentieth century. These began in Guyana in 1905; Cuba, 1912; and Trinidad, 1919; and continued with greater intensification throughout the Caribbean until 1940. Gordon Lewis comments about these strikes-turned-riots:

> . . . the underlying causes lay in the nature of the colonial economy itself; . . . the disturbances represented no longer a mere blind protest against a worsening of conditions, but a positive demand for the creation of new conditions that would render possible a better life; and, further, as the 1937 Commission that reported more particularly on the Trinidadian explosion noted, the demand had been made possible, in part, by the recent formation of a Trinidadian working-class opinion increasingly affected by the Great War experience of West Indian soldiers, industrial unrest in the United States and the spread of elementary education in the colony.[43]

Lewis was speaking of the British Caribbean case, but his analysis holds for the entire Caribbean.

In Jamaica, a process which began with Cudjoe continued with the Baptist War and the Morant Bay Rebellion, gave way to Garveyism in the twentieth century and culminated in the 1938 riots, which marked the "formal lowering of an already well established way for the masses of the population."[44]

Twentieth century Caribbean working-class consciousness and the use of strikes had their origins in slavery. Slaves struck during the 1831 Jamaican rebellion to support other slaves who were already striking for their freedom. The result of their action was to reinforce the rights of the liberated blacks to remain free. Mary Reckford reports:

> Strike action was effectively organized in some areas. In Trelawny, for example, the slaves on Carlton estate "sat down" firmly after Christmas. The Presbyterian missionary, Reverend Waddell, went to the estate to persuade them they were not yet free, but they accused him of being paid by the magistrates to deceive them.[45]

The strike failed because it wasn't organized on a widespread basis, and the government used murder to intimidate the slaves. For example,

> On a Georgia estate, Trelawny, where the slaves put up a determined and well-disciplined opposition, the negro village was subjected to a daybreak attack by the militia using a field-piece; when they still refused to move, they were dragged out, one-by-one, and one man was shot as an example.[46]

The earliest twentieth century strikes took place in Guyana in 1905. Bill Riviere describes the confrontation:

> The turning point in what, in the initial stages of the strike, was officially regarded as a "not disorderly" affair was an unprovoked shooting by white police officers of four labourers, one of whom died from his wounds on Rulmvelt estate on the outskirts of Georgetown. The victims were placed in a cart and pushed through the city enroute to the hospital. The sight of innocently shed blood sent three-quarters of Georgetown it has been estimated, "stark raving mad." The masses, frequently shouting slogans such as "Blood for blood" and "A life for a life," looted business premises, assaulted "respected citizens," damaged a telephone exchange, raided residential places, stoned the Government Buildings in search of the Inspector-General of Police and battled in the streets for an entire afternoon with his subordinates. The scale of the disturbance necessitated the declaration of a state of emergency in Georgetown and adjacent areas extending high up on the East and West banks of the Demerara River, and the reading of the Riot Act on a number of occasions. The toll read 58 policemen injured of whom one died and four were hospitalized; 1 lieutenant in the Salvation Army fatally killed by a bullet lodged in the head; on the other side, by 3 p.m. on the 2nd of November, 8 had been killed and 20 seriously injured. Subsequently, more than 35 civilians were brought to trial on charges involving disorderly conduct, throwing stones, assaulting police and carrying dangerous weapons. Interestingly enough, *the militia unlike their police counterparts continued a tradition that was in evidence as early as the 1860's by remaining loyal to the people. Not only did*

large numbers of them reject a call to go into action against the people, they even joined the rioteers, jeered at their colleagues who expressed reluctance to follow their lead, and were "even bold enough to propose to the police that they should put down their rifles and throw in their lot with rioters." Forty-six were committed to trial.[47] [Italics mine.]

This confrontation, known as the Sandback-Parker confrontation, represents one of the first acts in which the workers had a conscious awareness of their power. However, although now aware of the power of withholding their labor, the workers' inability to organize completely and to develop wage-bargaining machinery proved detrimental. In fact, the workers were represented by a company "spokesman" rather than by their own representative at the initial stages of negotiations.

The masses understood the strike as another tactic of resistance, and their growing class consciousness had important ramifications for other strikes-turned-riots that followed in Guyana in 1924. The 1924 confrontation demonstrated more effective leadership and greater cohesion among the workers, who were determined to demonstrate their "greater consciousness as a class sharing interests in direct conflict with the plantation and mercantile capitalists" and the strength of their interracial solidarity.[48]

The 1905 and 1924 confrontations in Guyana, the 1919 confrontation in Trinidad, the demonstration and strikes that culminated in the Negro revolt in Cuba in 1912, and the triumph of the Puerto Rican Socialist Workers Party in Arecibo municipality in 1914 ("the first time in all of America that a workers' and peasants' party had won control of an administration"[49]) all showed the growing class consciousness and solidarity of Caribbean workers and led to greater socioeconomic resistance during the 1930s.

The thirties were a tumultuous time for the Caribbean. The 1929 economic crisis in the United States had a devastating effect on the Caribbean economy because it was tied to that of the United States. Because of the nature of capitalist economies to export their contradictions from the center to the periphery, the people of the Caribbean generally felt the effects of the Great Depression with harsher severity than the people who lived in the United States.

These economic contradictions were manifested primarily in the increased prices of the commodities which were exported to the Caribbean and the decreased prices which were paid for the imports from the Caribbean, resulting in a drastic decline in the living standards for workers and peasants of the area. As a consequence, this was a period in which the sharpest attacks were made against foreign imperialism and colonialism and can be called truly the beginning of the anti-imperialist struggle in the Caribbean. In speaking about the Jamaican situation, Dr. Walter Rodney made an observation that could have been extended to the entire Caribbean region:

> In 1938, exactly one hundred years after the supposed Emancipation of the Black Man in Jamaica, the masses once again were driven into action to achieve some form of genuine liberation under the new conditions of oppression. The beneficiaries of that struggle were a narrow, middle-class sector whose composition was primarily brown, augmented by significant elements of white and other groups, such as Syrians, Jews and Chinese. Of late, that local ruling elite has incorporated a number of blacks in positions of prominence. However, irrespective of its racial or colour composition, this power-group is merely acting as representatives of metropolitan-imperialist interests. Historically white and racist-oriented, these interests continue to stop attempts at creative social expression on the part of the black oppressed masses.[50]

The impetus for this transformation, which was taken first by Puerto Rico and Cuba, spread over the Caribbean. Nineteen-thirty saw the rise of Albizu Campos, who, "placing himself in the Betances tradition of revolutionary independence," gave the Puerto Rican Nationalist Party a new sense of radical direction.[51] The party took the position that:

> Under the harsh yoke of North American colonialism, from a nation of proprietors we have changed into a mass of peons, a rich economic mine for exploitation by the capitalist invader.[52]

Declaring himself anti-imperialist and anti-colonialist, Campos waged the struggle for Puerto Rican independence until he and his colleagues were suppressed in the 1935 Massacre of Río Piedras where four nationalists and one policeman were killed and forty people injured. Charged with conspiracy to overthrow the government of the United States by force and violence (a charge designed to suppress the nationalist movement and remove its leadership), Campos was found guilty by a jury of ten North Americans and two Puerto Ricans after a trial by Puerto Rican peers ended in a hung jury. Sentenced to fifteen years in an Atlanta, Georgia prison, Campos still managed, in the words of Maldonado-Denis

> . . . to personify the spirit of resistance to colonialism, the fight against cultural assimilation, the termination of our handing-over of our national patrimony, the respect for our traditional values, the revolutionary tradition of Betances and Martí, the spirit of sacrifice reflected so perfectly in his sentence, "The fatherland is courage and sacrifice."[53]

The Communist Party, small in Puerto Rico, had a larger following in Cuba where, as early as 1925, a commission of inquiry sent by the Foreign Policy Association of the United States found that "these Cubans have welcomed communism as a redemptive force capable of freeing them from the misery and poverty which Cuba now suffers."[54] Up to the mid-1930s, the Communist Party played a constructive and revolutionary roll in Cuban politics, only to be betrayed by its secretary-general, Blas Roco, who collaborated with Batista in 1938.

Cuba felt the Great Depression more severely than any other island, with the sugar slump of the 1930s leading to unemployment and famine. The 19 March 1830 general strike paralyzed the country; later, in September, one person was killed when university students marched to the house of the famed philosopher, Enrique José Varona, to protest President Gerardo Machado, referred to as "the Butcher." The presence of United States Ambassador Sumner Welles in Havana precipitated another strike three years later. According to K. S. Karol,

> On August 2, 1933, a bus depot in the capital went on strike; two days later the entire transport system of Havana was paralyzed. On August 6, the strike spread to the whole country. On August 7, the rumor went around that the dictator had resigned, whereupon the overjoyed population came out into the streets and marched on the capitol. They were met and fired upon by the police; dozens lay dead, and hundreds were wounded.[55]

This brutality led to the ultimate removal of Machado, who fled the country a few days later. It took eighteen months of Batista's "unprecedented brutality" to crush the workers' organized resistance.[56]

The British Caribbean also felt the Great Depression. In 1935 there were sugar strikes in St. Kitts and Guyana, a coal strike in St. Lucia, and a strike protesting customs duties in St. Vincent; in 1936 there was a general strike of waterfront workers in Guyana; in 1937 a general strike tied up the entire island of Trinidad, with Barbados workers striking in sympathy, and there were sugar strikes again in Guyana and St. Lucia, spreading this time to Jamaica; in 1938 there was further unrest in Jamaica and Guyana.

Of the 1935–1939 strikes-turned-riots, workers in the 1937 Trinidad strike took the lead in confronting the social order.[57] Led by Uriah "Buzz" Butler, dubbed the "chief servant of the people," Trinidad oil field workers struck for higher wages. One policeman was killed when the government tried to arrest Butler while he was addressing a meeting. Later, workers fired upon the police and killed another subinspector. The strike spread over the island. Whereas during the 1919 riots, armed British troops had landed on the island, in 1937, the British cruisers could only remain outside in the harbor while negotiations proceeded.

Workers used their new found striking power and interracial solidarity to raise the level of resistance. Concomitant with these two qualities was the further politicization of the society. Ideology, incompletely understood in some cases, was injected into the resistance movement and gradually the struggle was analysed within the context of class. C. L. R. James noted that:

> . . . trade unions are being formed all over the island, and the advanced workers are clamoring for revolutionary literature of all sorts, by Marx and Engels and other writers on Communism. . . . The government is now seeking to pass a drastic bill imposing heavy penalties for the mere possession of radical, far less revolutionary literature.[58]

This, of course, was standard practice in Cuba and would be in Guyana a few years later. According to James, "These workers almost at a single bound placed themselves in the forefront of the international working class movement."[59] This is exaggerated praise, for Trinidad had not adopted a Marxist line, but James is correct in perceiving that the workers were charting a new direction. As early as 1932, Hubert Nathanial Crichlow, the father of trade unionism in the British Caribbean, visited the Soviet Union and on his return recognized that "From the cradle to the grave, from the time you born 'til you dead, politics dey with yous."[60] Crichlow also perceived the socialist path as the new direction for the Caribbean.

In 1935, the Cuban Communist Party was the most developed one in the Caribbean. Its secretary general, Blas Roco, attended a meeting in Moscow of Latin American communist parties. But by 1939 the party was a strong ally of Batista and had repudiated its Marxist position on imperialism and class struggle. However, the Cuban Constitution of 1940 included advanced ideas for social legislation, "influenced," as it were, "by the socialist currents of our time."[61]

Max Roumain and Jacques Roumain, the poet who published the first Marxist analysis about Haiti, organized the Haitian Communist Party in 1930; Norman Manley formed his People's National Party in Jamaica following the pioneering agreement with the United Fruit Company in 1937, called it socialist and proceeded in that direction; and in St. Vincent, the leader of the 1935 riots kept a picture of Stalin in his druggist shop until the day he died. It is not to be argued that these countries entirely understood Marxist or Communist doctrines, followed them fully or that the masses totally embraced this new ideology. However, a new class awareness perceiving resistance in yet another manifestation was alive in the Caribbean. The Caribbean would take a new direction which would culminate in the Cuban revolution of 1959, the Castle Bruce experience of 1974, and the Grenadian revolution of 1979 under Maurice Bishop.

Resistance continued in the Caribbean with Guyana the next significant phase. Like other Caribbean territories, Guyana was shaped by colonialism, slavery and a plantation economy in which the sugar monoculture prevailed. Guyana had her share of rebellions beginning with the Kofi revolt, changed masters between the Dutch, British and French, then came into British hands in 1803.

Two points differentiate Guyana's growth (and incidentally account for the brutal repression against Jagan from 1953 until his defeat in 1964) from that of other Caribbean countries: the destruction of a vigorous peasantry and the forceful repression of the labor union movement. The growth of a vigorous peasantry in Guyana was evident soon after emancipation. Cheddi Jagan describes it:

> With the abolition of slavery in 1834 and of apprenticeship in 1838, the emancipated Negroes were no longer willing to stay on the plantation. Some migrated to the city, others sought refuge on land adjoining the plantations. Only four years later, over twenty thousand ex-slaves were residing in their own houses in villages. With money saved from wages earned during apprenticeship, they had purchased several abandoned sugar estates. They paid 25,000 guilders [a guilder was worth 1s.5d in the 1840's] for Ithaca; 25,000 for Victoria; 125,000 guilders for Buxton; and 200,000 guilders for Friendship. These plantations were divided into lots and given to the shareholders. In Demerara alone, 14,127 persons occupied 2,943 lots. By 1851, the Negroes throughout the colony had erected 11,152 houses, and the property owned by them was worth nearly £1 million sterling. Of the 60,000-odd Negroes and mulattoes then in the colony, about two-thirds had migrated to the villages. This was a great achievement on the part of the Afro-Guyanese. They not only sacrificed and saved, but worked co-operatively and initiated the establishment of a system of local government.[62]

Ex-slaves refused to work full-time for low wages on the plantations when they could enjoy prosperity by cultivating their own crops of cassava, tanias, and eddoes. In order to depress wages, the English brought in East Indians ("strike-breakers" as Jagan calls them) to work under conditions that could only be described as "legal slavery." The Negroes now had to depend entirely on their plots for a livelihood. By this time, the Portuguese, who monopolized the retail trades imported inexpensive foodstuffs and drove down the price of peasant produce, thus creating the ultimate destruction of the Guyanese peasantry. In the resulting riots of 1856 and 1889, the Portuguese felt the full wrath of the Negroes. Caught by cheap immigrant labor and cheap imported food, once prosperous peasants were crushed and relegated to "private compounds in which the worker was dependent for almost all of his needs on management."[63] This intense corporate structure had ominous implications for Guyanese life. Jagan gives us a description of that world:

> The plantation was indeed a world of its own. Or rather it was two worlds: the world of exploiters and the world of the exploited; the world of the whites and the world of the non-whites. One was the world of managers and the European staff in their special mansions; the other a world of the labourers in the logies in the 'niggeryard' and the 'bound-coolie-yard.' The mansions were electrically lit; the logies had kerosene lamps. It was not unusual to hear it said that mules were better treated than human beings, for the stables had electrical light. . . . Between these white and non-white worlds there were distances—social (inhabitants of these two worlds did not associate) and physical (the mansions were out of bounds). There was also a psychological distance. I recall vividly my great curiosity about the manager's mansion. I wanted to know what it felt like to be inside the gate. I wanted to know what was going on inside. The opportunity came at Christmas time. I must have been about eight or nine years old. I joined the creole gang and went to share in the largesse of the manager. The manager's wife, Mrs. Gibson, stood at the window of the top floor of this imposing mansion. She threw coins down to us and enjoyed seeing the wild scramble for the pennies. This is the way our manager's wife offered gifts to workers' children at Christmas time on a sugar plantation.[64]

This massive economic power was used to frustrate efforts to form a labor union movement in Guyana. While other Caribbean territories experienced vigorous labor union growth in the thirties, in Guyana there was still "a primitive class struggle in company estates where trade union activity was virtually forbidden."[65] Two years later, in 1937, when the Moine Commission began investigations in Guyana about the previous strikes, the workers were afraid to testify about repressive conditions on the plantations in particular and in the country in general, for the class that controlled the economic life of the country controlled the political life as well. But resistance grew and eventually resulted in armed intervention.

In Haiti, power resided more in the hands of local governors and military chieftains than at the national level. Therefore, local governors and military chieftains would march into the capital, overthrow the ruling clique and remain in power until they in turn were overthrown. In Guyana, an opposite phenomenon prevailed, for power lay in the hands of one central enterprise (Bookers). This enterprise, an outgrowth of the plantation system, controlled the entire fabric of national life, employed eighty percent of the population, and was the *de facto* government. Thus, it is no coincidence that Guyana and Haiti are not only the two poorest countries in the Caribbean but also are among the poorest countries in the world. Any political leader concerned with the problems of his people would have to deal with this colonial anachronism. Jagan did, and this set the stage for intervention by both the United States and Britain.

In 1953, Guyana gained universal suffrage. Cheddi Jagan, who had been fighting for his people since he entered the Legislative Council in 1947, together with L.F. Burnham, brought people together under the People's Progressive Party (P.P.P.). Jagan, a self-proclaimed Marxist, had a program aimed at destroying the "colonial economic-political alliance that dominated the territory" and freeing the country's resources from the Bookers.[66] A general strike broke out 133 days after Jagan was democratically elected under his Socialist platform. The British, claiming that Jagan's cabinet was Communist, moved combat troops into the country, suspended its constitution and deposed the elected government of the people. The British armed forces remained in the country for four years (1953–1957), and a number of citizens were imprisoned.

What was Jagan's crime? Jagan had introduced a Labor Relations Bill that would have ousted company unions, thereby allowing better working conditions for the workers. Jagan stated that the "main cause . . . for the suspension of the Constitution was the pressure of the United States of America."[67] Writing in 1966, Jagan suggested that the United States pressured Britain to overthrow him. He cited the hysteria created by the United States press when he was elected, the fear of a "communist" takeover of the country and the strategic importance of Guyana's bauxite deposits (the second largest in the western hemisphere at the time). President Kennedy's campaign to persuade the British not to grant Guyana independence and the funds provided by American trade unions in 1962–1963 to cripple the Jagan government after its third electoral victory seems to confirm Jagan's charge.

While Jagan was fighting British colonialism, Fidel Castro was fighting General Batista's repressive government. Although Jagan declared himself a Marxist-Leninist, Castro quoted Martí, Maceo, Locke, Rousseau, Milton, Thomas Acquinas, Martin Luther and others to support his struggle against what he considered one of the most tyrannical powers ever to govern in the Caribbean, a government supported by one of the most repressive governments of the time, the United States of America.[68]

Following a general strike that crippled the country in 1933, the tyrant Machado, popularly termed "the Butcher," was forced to leave the country, and the United States made the weak and ineffective Carlos Manuel de Cespedes (a descendant of the 1868 leader) head of government. A month later, A Sergeant's War, out of which Fulgencio Batista emerged, toppled de Cespedes, and a revolutionary government under Antonio Guiteras came to power. Three months later, General Batista overthrew that government and became the head of Cuba.

Batista's entry into Cuban politics ushered in "nightmares of repression, assassination, gangsterism, bribery and corruption."[69] In fact, Batista was so corrupt that he retired to Miami with close to four million dollars when he was defeated in 1944. Meanwhile, American interests were growing substantially. Whereas in 1896 ten percent of Cuban sugar was produced by American owned companies, by 1926 sixty-three percent was produced by American owned mills. By 1941 America's total investment in Cuban sugar cane came to 733 million dollars. As the record shows, Cuba became one of the best investments for Americans:

> American participation exceeds 90 per cent in the telephone and electric services, about 50 per cent in public service railways, and roughly 40 per cent in raw sugar production. The Cuban branches of United States banks [are] entrusted with almost one-fourth of all bank deposits. . . . Cuba ranked third in Latin America in the value of United States direct investment in 1953, outranked only by Venezuela and Brazil.[70]

By the end of 1950, Cuba had the same gigantic plantation economy as other Caribbean countries. It also faced the same resulting poverty as Jamaica, Haiti, Guyana and other islands where the United States controlled the economy. The two presidents who followed Batista were more corrupt than he so that while their governments looted the public coffers and the United States exploited the people and their resources, the peasants at the bottom continued to suffer.

In March, 1952, ten weeks after the Orthodox Party had won the general elections, Batista seized power once more. This time, however, he underestimated the idealism of the Cuban people and one other factor: Fidel Castro. A few weeks after Batistia's *coup d'état*, Fidel Castro appeared before the University Court in Havana and declared that Batista had violated six acts of the Code of Social Defence involving a prison term of 108 years. No one listened. One year later Castro was training an army of three hundred men and two women to resist Batista's tyranny.

On 26 July, 1953, Castro and his followers attacked Fort Moncada, the second largest military fortress on the island, and were defeated. Some guerrillas were killed and others were tortured, but Castro escaped. When brought to trial seventy-six days later, he gave his address, *History Will Absolve Me*, which will remain a masterpiece of Caribbean literature.

This unsuccessful attempt by Castro led to a new wave of brutality in which more than twenty thousand persons were killed before Batista was overthrown. Although ten persons were executed for each soldier lost in the attack on Fort Moncada, the attack on Fort Moncada

> . . . was not entirely a failure. For though the fort had not been captured, the attention of the people had been won. Fidel Castro and the July 26th Movement had become known. In Oriente, if nowhere else, the spirit of resistance to Batista tyranny was aroused.[71]

The Cuban people were renewed and ready for struggle.

Castro was sentenced to fifteen years in prison, but as political agitation grew, Batista was forced to release all political prisoners including Castro and his comrades on 15 May 1955. The tremendous reception that greeted Castro on his way to Havana proved him to be Batista's greatest threat: Castro was constantly watched and, like his spiritual predecessor, Martí, had to plan his revolution from abroad.

After a tour of United States Cuban communities, Castro returned with more than $50,000 to Mexico where his men were training. November 30, 1956, was set for the invasion of Cuba. Despite hardships in which most of his men were killed, Castro reached the island with eighty-three men and eventually the Sierra Maestra, with twelve men.* At this point in time Batista's army consisted of thirty thousand soldiers who had modern U.S. equipment, but this did not daunt Castro, for his guerrilla army only represented the nucleus of a Rebel Army which consisted of the Cuban peasants and workers whose revolutionary origins went back to the dawn of Cuban history. Castro began to mobilize his people:

> By far the most important class that joined the rebels was the peasants. At the beginning, the *campesinos* merely hid the rebels; before many months had passed, the *campesinos*, as a class, were *backing* the rebels. They changed from passive onlookers to active participants. They became one with the revolutionary army.[72]

Castro supporters did not consist only of the peasants. He was supported also by the city workers who led double-lives. For while they appeared as

---

* The question is posed always: How could Fidel Castro who began the Cuban Revolution with a group of twelve men eventually defeat an army that was well armed and equipped with modern weapons; or, how could three hundred armed guerrillas defeat a battalion of over twelve thousand men with modern arms? What is not understood generally or appreciated readily by such questioners is the fact that in a people's war it is not the technical nor military superiority of the enemy that is the decisive factor but the heightened consciousness and the political awareness of the people who are subjected to aggression.

normal city workers during the day, at night they became revolutionaries and actively supported the work of the Rebel Army.

For a year Castro and his men educated the people by explaining the revolution's objectives in over thirty rebel schools. Castro provided a field hospital and printed "freedom bonds" which raised thousands of dollars. This demonstration, on the part of Castro, showed that he was capable of running the country, and it impressed the peasants very much. Batista's repression increased with Castro's activity and success.

From February, 1958, Radio Rebelde began broadcasting from the Free Territory of Cuba in the Sierra Maestro. On 12 March 1858, Castro announced in his *Manifesto from the 26 of July Movement to the People* that the revolutionaries would wage intensive war against Batista's regime beginning 5 April. On 5 May, Batista announced an all-out campaign to crush the revolutionary army. There were great military odds against Castro with twelve thousand of Batista's men to three hundred of Castro's. But Castro's men had three distinct advantages: they were fighting in a known terrain that fitted their methods; they were fighting for their freedom, which they held to be precious; their exemplary behavior inspired the people's confidence.

By 20 July, various radical groups had joined together, forming the National Front Movement. The fighting became more intense as the war opened up on three different fronts. On 2 January 1959, when Castro's army marched into Santiago and accepted Batista's unconditional surrender, the struggle ended precisely where it began, at Fort Moncada. Castro, like Toussaint, was humane in the aftermath of victory and never employed executions for callous revenge. The people went wild as he drove through the country; the Caribbean had entered a new era.

The last phase of the Cuban revolutionary struggle ended with the predominant role played by a "peasant army" ("three-fourths to four-fifths of the soldiers who participated in the final campaign in 1958 were peasants").[73] When the United States tried to thwart the people's revolution with its CIA-operated Bay of Pigs fiasco in April, 1961, even

> . . . the American press itself was forced to mention the heroism of the peasant militiamen who had alerted Castro's army and who had strenuously held out until its arrival on the battlefield. It was they who had spoiled the surprise effect and had prevented the invaders from establishing a bridgehead in that marshy and sparsely populated part of Cuba.[74]

We should note also that in the Cuban situation, the workers had "a long record of unionism and militant labor action,"[75] which undoubtedly aided Castro's revolution. When, therefore, the authors of *Cuba, Anatomy of a*

Revolution comment that "the Cuban peasantry is a remarkable revolutionary force," they were not just discussing the Cuban people in particular but the Caribbean people in general.

The Cuban revolution arose out of a language and experience that is particularly Caribbean. Comparing other Caribbean territories to Cuba, Walter Rodney comments:

> The tremendous transformation in Cuban society must, it seemed to me, be a model in the sense of our being able to utilize some insights which the Cubans gained, gaining from their mistakes as well as their achievements. What clearly cannot be overlooked is that pre-revolutionary Cuban society was not fundamentally different from, say, Jamaican society—that to the extent that it was different, it had gone further along the road of integration into international capitalism, especially new forms like tourism. So how on earth do we really imagine that if the massive tourism of pre-revolutionary Cuba had done nothing but create misery, when we follow along *that* path, we could succeed? If we have been unable to solve the problems of unemployment within the old social structure, that is, within our present capitalist structure, and the Cubans have done so—they have done so to the extent that Cuba is badly in need of labor. They have so expanded social production in all spheres that they are terribly short of labor while we are experiencing the problem, which I mentioned earlier, of a tremendous growth in the unemployment rate. When those objective factors are brought into being, it seems that any reasonable person—any honest person in the rest of the Caribbean—should try to understand what has been going on in Cuba.[76]

George Beckford puts it this way:

> Ultimately, social change must be directed to creating a "good life" for all the people. Once the basic necessities of life of all the people are met there is room for debate as to what constitutes the "good life" and how that is to be achieved.
>
> My conception of the good life for Caribbean peoples is one where exploitation of man by man is removed from the entire social scene; and where man can enjoy life, totally.
>
> The first point demands a social framework which is non-capitalist. For capitalism is based on exploitation. Some kind of socialist framework, therefore, is the *sine qua non* for achieving the longer-term objective. The particular pattern of socialist organization must fit into the traditional value system of Black people. That implies communal efforts—in areas such as land ownership, labour mobilization and capital accumulation. For that is indeed consistent with the tradition of independent development inherited from our forefathers.[77]

Even Lord Valentino, a singer of the impoverished masses, articulates the problems of capitalism and the direction of socialism in his calypso,

"Dis Place Nice."[78] As Huberman and Sweezy said in 1960 soon after the Cuban revolution, " . . . the Cuban Revolution, which at first might appear to many a local incident in a small Caribbean island, is in reality an event of world-shaking significance."[79]

The Cuban revolution ended the second and ushered in the third period of Caribbean development, which included the attempt to construct a socialist state in Cuba, the formation of a cooperative republic in Guyana, and rumblings about a socialist state in Jamaica (which, incidentally, is a misnomer or a studied misuse of the term "socialist"). This is a period fraught with many socioeconomic and sociopolitical changes with important ramifications for restructuring society.

For instance, today we see Caribbean resistance taken to a further degree in Castle Bruce, Dominica. Faced with exploitation by the Colonial Development Corporation, the workers of Castle Bruce Estate decided to take over the estate and run it themselves. As Allan Williams puts it:

> The people of Castle Bruce have always been farmers. Since the time when Captain Bruce established his own castle and slave plantation in this valley, the people have been involved in two basic activities, a. working on the plantation, b. tending to their little provision plots. Even after emancipation, farming activity persisted as a means of survival. This time it was more concentrated on the little gardens, situated sometimes near to their homes, other times miles away in the forest. Labour was offered to the main estates whenever their owners extended the opportunity. *The Castle Bruce Village became a typical Caribbean village.* It comprised a large sector of subsistence farmers on the steep inclines, eking out a miserable existence and an estate on the good flat land, taking people from and tossing them back into this sector almost at will.[80]

Faced with the prospect of further unemployment and poverty, the Castle Bruce Estate's workers decided to buy the estate from the Colonial Development Corporation. After eighteen months of severe pressure and brutality, they purchased the estate from the government, which had bought it from the C.D.C.; they established the Castle Bruce Farmers Cooperative where workers controlled decision-making and all levels of production. The goals of the cooperative were described in a position paper, *A Chance for Change*, of which Mr. Williams comments:

> The most widely expressed goal continued to be the enhancement of the social and economic security of the workers through their control of the means of production. This appears to be a logical extension of the correct analysis of the history of these workers. Under C.D.C. their social and economic security was continually jeopardized because of their lack of control of the production unit. The performance of the peasants around them would also demonstrate the

weakness of private peripheral production activity. The cooperative structure was therefore adopted because it turned the hierarchical decision-making structure of estates on its head, making workers equal controllers of the welfare of the enterprise and consequently *in* themselves. "A Chance for Change" continually speaks of changing the relations of worker to land, i.e., from cheap hired labour to worker controller. The cooperative law structures this concept to the extent that it gives the residual decision-making power to the body of members en masse, and specific administrative powers to committees elected at will by that body.[81]

The Castle Bruce Farmers Cooperative workers seek to promote the lesson of Castle Bruce experience in Dominica. Students of the area are watching the experiment with increased interest, and the fact that Paulo Friere traveled to Dominica to study it testifies to the revolutionary nature of the enterprise. Even though there is still little literature about the experiment and its results are not yet conclusive, it still holds great consequence for the Caribbean.

Caribbean resistance struggles, particularly in the 1930s, have always moved towards a socialist way of life or its nascent underpinnings. In Guyana, Jagan carried out a moderate program of social reform that had little real socialist ideology. Most of his reforms, including the Labor Reform Bill patterned after the Wagner Act, reflected American trade unionism. Although Jagan was called a communist, United States economic and political pressure led him to embrace Marxist-Leninist ideology as the only way of reforming his country's social structure. The United States and Britain, fearing for their investments, crushed him. It was the same with Castro, with perhaps the one difference that the United States tried to crush him and failed. In both cases the United States did not understand the dynamics of Caribbean life.

The Cuban Revolution was the culmination of national liberation in the Caribbean. Trinidad, Guyana, Barbados, and Jamaica all became sovereign territories in the 1960s, and agitation in Martinique, Surinam, and most of the French-speaking Caribbean islands shows that the Caribbean people are still resisting. It is against this history and the central role played by resistance that one must view Caribbean literature. This is not the only way to look at it, but it is one of the most instructive.

Although it is tempting to deal with this third phase of Caribbean history (1960 to the present), that period should be seen within the context of the area's political economy. The need to limit this work to literature and history takes precedence, and thus we must leave this subject for other writers.

IV

RESISTANCE AND LITERATURE

We, a revolutionary people, value cultural and artistic creations in proportion to what they offer mankind, in proportion to their contribution to the revindication of man, the liberation of man, the happiness of man. . . . Our evaluation is political. There can be no esthetic value where the human content is absent. There can be no esthetic value in opposition to man. Esthetic value cannot exist in opposition to justice, in opposition to the welfare or in opposition to the happiness of man. It cannot exist![1]

—Fidel Castro

IN Chapter II we defined resistance as "any act or complex of acts that are designed to rid a people of its oppressors, be they slave masters or multinational corporations." We further differentiated between cultural, socioeconomic, and political resistance, seeing revolutions as but one manifestation of resistance. The point of view that resistance served as a fundamental aesthetic-political quality in the structuring of Caribbean literature reflects neither a foreign, anti-historical, nor anti-dialectical approach; rather, the synthesis of culture, socioeconomics and politics provides the necessary milieu through which, and out of which, an aesthetic-political interpretation of the literature can be made. As is characteristic of any holistic or scientific analysis of literature, be it Caribbean or others, this type of aesthetic-political analysis yields a much richer and more multi-faceted response from the literature.

In order to understand fully resistance as an aesthetic-political element of Caribbean literature, it is necessary to draw on history. Contrary to what many critics believe (and even promote), art, one of the most complex acts of man's being, is not and should not be separable from life. Art can be perceived as the chronicler of human history, the reflector of the spiritual dimension of human experience, and the camera eye (the capturer) of social transformations, manifesting human history in all its rich and variegated hues. We get a better glimpse of Paleolithic man because of his cave paintings and other works of art which depict man's condition at that time in all of its richness. Boris Suchkov puts it this way:

Throughout their existence, art and literature have registered with the sensitivity of a barometer all the changes in the course of mankind's stormy development. The collapse of the humanistic ideals of the Renaissance, which were trampled underfoot with the emergence of bourgeois social relations, was reflected in Shakespeare's later tragedies, in the wise sorrow of *Don Quixote*, and gnomic philosophy of Calderón's tragedy *La vida es sueño*, which sounded the death knell for the vital, optimistic world of Renaissance culture.[2]

The capacity to portray the sense of an age is not limited to literature and the graphic arts but includes music, as seen, for instance, in the "tragic motives that burst into the bright ethereal element of Mozart's symphonies"[3] or in the rousing music of Pëtr Ilich Tchaikovsky's overtures. Indeed, Tchaikovsky's *1812 Overture* celebrates the victorious resistance of the Russian peasants against Napoleon's armies. Written and played against the background of real cannons and church bells, the Russians' advance is marked by the martial theme while the French advance is depicted by the French *marche*; the Russian folk dance is used as a symbol of the uprising of the peasants to defend their country against the French invaders while the glorious pealing of church bells and the firing of cannons proclaim Russian victory.

The Marxist-Leninist aesthetic, which brings to bear upon any analytical and critical analysis of the arts a partisan, class-minded approach, takes the position that

> . . . the artist will be really free to create only when he correctly understands the trend of historical development and is consciously prepared to unite his own will, thought and desire with the progressive movement of the time—the revolutionary creative effort of the masses.[4]

Mr. Grigory Oganov, the author of this statement elaborates: ". . . emotions and creative aspirations are insufficient; they must accord with the need and the spirit of the times. It is the combination of genuine talent and historical perspective which produces real art."[5] It is evident that literary sensitivity and the literary aesthetic emanate from the socio-economic and historical conditions of the life of a people and reflect Karl Marx's pronouncement that "the mode of production of material life conditions the social, political, and intellectual life process in general. *It is not the consciousness of men that determines their being, but, on the contrary, their social being that determines their consciousness.*"[6] [Italics mine.]

This link between resistance and literature is illustrated with particular clarity in the works of the leaders of the liberation movements in Africa where, in the struggle for freedom, poetry became one of the main tools of resistance. Introducing a selection of poems from the area, Margaret Dickinson comments:

> Despite the isolation imposed on them by censorship, the intelligentsia of the Portuguese colonies were profoundly affected. They were still, however, unable to risk overt political action and as a result it was in literature that the radicalism of the late forties found its chief expression. Poetry above all flourished, perhaps because it could more easily evade the censor, perhaps because, being the most concise form of writing, it could be read and hidden more easily than prose work.[7]

However, as the struggle for liberation intensified, the ideological content and artistic form of poetry also changed. Margaret Dickinson compares earlier poetry with that from later stages of the struggle and notes:

> This weakness [of the earlier intellectual poetry] can be seen in many of the poems which, compared to those written later under the influence of the armed struggle, tend to be abstruse, full of allusions which only the highly educated would recognise; the effort to identify with Africa sometimes seems self-conscious; the talk of resistance is often theoretical, suggesting protest rather than action: "voices," "songs," "drums," "hope," and "progress" are celebrated, rather than "hard work," "unity," or "weapons," the things which eventually enabled the liberation struggle to become a reality and which colour later writing.[8]

It is not coincidental that Agostinho Neto (1922–1979), recognized by Margaret Dickinson as perhaps Angola's greatest living poet, led the fight for independence and became the first president of Angola, or that Marcelino dos Santos, the president of Mozambique, is one of Mozambique's finest poets. In fact, most of the revolutionary leaders in South Africa have been poets. When resistance is the chief preoccupation of a country, the aesthetic must become political. Since these men are fighting a struggle to the death, poetry and literature become the conscious unity of will, thought, and desire coalesced with revolutionary activity. As Oganov puts it,

> . . . the artist's heart and mind must be filled with anticipation of the creative action, called forth by the desire to convey some important point which needs to be conveyed, and to do this in one's way, through the prism of language, style, and specific vision of the artist in question.[9]

But as Ms. Dickinson points out, when an artist is working under revolutionary conditions, the theoretical perspective of resistance as an aesthetic gives way to the concrete perspective of resistance, calling for a different collaboration between content and form—the content virtually fashions its own form which is shaped by the new dialectics created by the revolutionary conditions.

It is to be noted that the artist is not necessarily consciously aware of the ramifications of his verse or the nuances of form which he utilizes to express the content of the particular phase of struggle. The writer writes as he must and, in the process, expresses the content of the age which has affected the form. Agostinho Neto's poem "the blood and the seed" reflects the nature of this literary sensibility before the impact of struggle begins. Indeed his poem is almost a psalm of love, a hymn of hope, and a yearning for eternal brotherhood. It is a paean to peace. Listen carefully to this dreamer:

```
We
              from far flung Africa
and above the treachery of man,
across the majestic and unconquered forests
across the flow of life,
which runs anxious, eager and abundant in the
       rivers' roar,
through the melodious sound of muted drums
through the eyes of youthful multitudes,
multitudes of arms, of pain and hope
from far-flung Africa
              beneath the claw
we bleed from grief and hope, from sorrows and
       from strength,
bleeding on this earth disembowelled by hoes,
bleeding with the sweat of forced labor in the
       cotton fields,
bleeding hunger, ignorance, despair and death
in the wounds on the black back of a child, on a
       mother, on honesty
the blood and the seed
              from far-flung Africa
black
and bright like mornings of friendship
desirous and strong like the steps of liberty.
Our cries
are drums heralding desire
in the tumultuous voices, music of nations,
our cries are hymns of love that hearts
might flourish on the earth like seeds in the sun
the cries of Africa
cries of mornings when the dead grew from the seas
chained
the blood and the seed
```

—see, here are our hands
open to the brotherhood of man
united in certainty
for the future of man
for right, for peace, for friendship.

From our toes, roses grow,
perfumed with the river Zaire's tenacity
and the grandeur of Maiombe's trees.
In our minds
is the road of friendship for Africa,
for the world,
Our eyes the life-blood
are turned towards hands beckoning love in all
    the world
hands in the future—inspiring faith in the vitality
of Africa, the human land of Africa
        of far-flung Africa
regenerating under the sun of hope
creating bonds of brotherhood in freedom from want,
from the yearning for peace,
the blood and the seed.

      For the future—here are our eyes
for peace—our voices
for peace—our hands

from Africa, united in love.[10]

Contrast that poem with Marcelino dos Santos' "to point a moral to a comrade," written in the course of struggle:

FIRST PAMPHLET

It isn't that things are easy,
nor is it being easy
that's essential.

The sunflower circles with the light
and that isn't easy but is beautiful.

It is time to understand
that macala and malapa
grow on strong trees
in firm ground

and not in mud.

To go on studying or not to
is neither your nor my problem,
it's ours.

A hospital for the people,
a school for the people,

it's not true

in our land it's not possible
without digging the soil of Revolution.

To expect rice
without sowing it
is not the history of man.

The second step
comes after the first
we live today
not yesterday nor tomorrow
and the mission of us all

       is.

REALISE THE PROGRAMME OF FRELIMO
COMPLETE NATIONAL INDEPENDENCE
AN END OF EXPLOITATION MAN BY MAN

Today's task,
comrade,

is, dig the basic soil of Revolution
and make a strong people grow
with a submachine gun, a bazooka, a 12.7
in Muidumbe, in Catur
and to the south again
in Nampula, Macequece and Inhambane.

And a strong people,
comrade,

will move mountains

create hospitals
create schools.

As the first young shoots proclaimed
in Cabo Delgado and Niassa Province
We are FRELIMO soldiers

accomplishing our task
digging the basic soil of Revolution.

.   .   .

FOURTH AND LAST PAMPHLET

FINALLY

The time of Revolution

is the time of certainty
of hopes realised

and it is for us TODAY

No one is responsible
for being born when he was born
neither before nor afterwards

We grow up,
it's true,

Some before, some afterwards

Walking the earth apart
Each with his own past
But now
The Revolution rules our senses
We are a million voices, a million hands united
and what matters
Is not what I or you want

BUT WHAT WE WANT
and this is how the road is

Engraved on the mountainside
rising and falling

Carved into the plain
through wild grass and dense bush
even through maize higher than our own heads

The effort we make
is neither great nor small
It is what it has to be
        A guerrilheiro
        cultivating the earth
        carrying ammunition
        or medicine

        Building a hospital, a school
        or studying in a distant land

        My place
        is there, where FRELIMO decides

        The line of battle
        is where the Revolution takes me

WE ARE FRELIMO SOLDIERS
ACCOMPLISHING THE PARTY'S TASK
DIGGING THE BASIC SOIL OF
   REVOLUTION
OR AN END OF EXPLOITATION MAN
   BY MAN
TO BUILD COMPLETE NATIONAL
   INDEPENDENCE[11]

Agostinho Neto's "the blood and the seed" is about planting a seed of love, of hope, and of brotherhood in spite of "bleeding hunger, ignorance, despair and death." It is about the future and projects resistance as ideal, metaphysical and tranquil. It and "Mussundo my friend," shaped in nostalgia and hope, bemoan the past in a sculptured and symmetrical form.

However, "to point a moral to a comrade" is a manifesto about every colonized person's unquestioned duty to

REALISE THE PROGRAMME OF FRELIMO
COMPLETE NATIONAL INDEPENDENCE
AN END OF EXPLOITATION MAN BY MAN

The first imperative is to "dig the basic soil of Revolution/ and make a strong people grow/ with a submachine gun, a bazooka, a 12.7 in Muidumbe." The content closely speaks to the present needs of the people, and the very urgency and demand of the ideological content fashion the artistic form. The terseness of the verse structure and the precision of the poetry minimize the possibility of content missing its mark.

The poems quite consciously reveal a kind of organic growth of form. The earlier poem reflects a level of resistance projected as ideal, metaphysical and tranquil, shaped as it is in nostalgia and hope, literally bemoaning the past, with its perfectly sculptured and symmetrical form. This is to be contrasted with the urgent, didactic, and imperative message of the contemporary historical condition which is expressed in the poem "to point a moral to a comrade." In literature, caught up in the struggle, words must be like bullets: sharp, straight-shooting and to the mark. To miss is literally to lose one's life in the process. With the crushing urgency of the revolution, literature becomes functional in that it has a very real task to perform. After the independence of these countries has been won, the content and form in the literature changes again to reflect the dynamics of forging a nation and to express the confidence of newly acquired independence which allows the writer to see the oppressors of his country with detachment and objectivity. Roberto Fernández Retamar's poem, "Epitaph for an Invader" evaluates the former aggressor:

Your great grandfather rode through Texas,
Raping copper Mexican girls and stealing horses
Until he settled down with Mary Stonehill and set
   up house
With oak furniture and 'God Bless Our Home.'
Your grandfather landed in Santiago de Cuba,
Saw the Spaniards defeated, and took home
The waft of rum and a dusky nostalgia of brown girls.
Your father, a peaceful man,
Only paid the wages of twelve Guatemalan youths.
True to your kind,
You took it upon yourself to invade Cuba in
   autumn, 1962.
Today you fertilize the cotton trees.[12]

Here victory is complete; the political struggle for liberation is ended, and the task of social and economic construction begins.

In the literary process the most important concern of the writer is the dialectical interrelationship which takes place between the content (the what) and the form (the how) of any literary work. Indeed the literary critic must clarify this vital interrelation and interconnection between form and content if we are to move our analysis towards any recognizable and logical syntheses, and a better understanding of the aesthetic-political nexus that is to be found in Caribbean literature.

The literary process, which we outlined in the examples of Neto, dos Santos, and Retamar, reflects the relationship between content and form. Speaking of the "indissoluble unity" between form and content, A.

Bushmin in a remarkable article titled, "Analytic Approach to a Work of Art," says,

> Content and form have no separate existence; they are always "together," in an indissoluble unity as two aspects that mutually penetrate each other, forming a single whole. The borderline between them is a logical notion, not a spatial one. The relation between content and form is not that between a whole and its parts, between a kernel and its encasing, the internal and the external, quality and quantity; *it is a relation between two opposites, each of which is transformed into the other.* 'Content is nothing else but a *transition of form* into content, while form is nothing else but a *transition of content* into form.' Such is the philosophical formula that cautions us against any gross or simplified understanding of the complex, mobile and dialectical unity of the categories of form and content in general, and in the sphere of art in particular.[13] [Italics mine.]

Such is the dialectical interrelationship between form and content. This is especially pertinent when we try to understand the particular dynamic of Caribbean literature and when we make the case for the role of resistance as an aesthetic-political quality and structuring element. Content must be encased in and interrelated to form. One must guard against the emphasis of one at the expense of the other and avoid "sociologism" (content at the expense of form) and "formalism" (form at the expense of content). This is the position that seems to be well expressed by A. Bushmin when he says:

> The Marxist student of literature is interested in both the *what* and the *how*, because they are intimately interlinked; what he is after is the cognition of a work of art as a unity of the relations of subject and object and to reveal the social genesis and function of that work. This is a far more complex task than any one-sided sociological, formalist or finally, formally sociological and eclectic approach to phenomena in art.[14]

Yet in literary criticism, the emphasis of one or the other does exist, and, as Bushmin is quick to add,

> . . . it would be pedantic to insist, in all instances, on a simultaneous analysis of form and content. The researcher is entitled to concentrate either preferably on form, without, however, forgetting that he has to do with a form that is involved in a definite content, again without losing sight of that content being artistic . . . priority to one or another is not only permissible but often essential.[15]

It can be argued that this critic is more interested in analyzing content that is artistic. Resistance is that ideological content that is embodied in the artistic form, creating the political aesthetic of Caribbean literature.

Cultural resistance also had important ramifications for Caribbean history, for Caribbean resistance was very much the cultural reaffirmation of the people. Speaking on the issue, Amílcar Cabral comments, "At any moment, depending on internal and external factors determining the evolution of the society in question, cultural resistance (indestructible) may take on new forms (political, economic, military) in order fully to contest foreign domination."[16] The persistence of political, socioeconomic and cultural resistance in the Caribbean was nothing less than the struggle of the masses to retain their way of life within terms that they understand, which constitute the conditions that they thought desirable in order to function as creative and liberated people.

The rise in cultural expression plays a pivotal role in the struggle for liberation and emerges at each critical moment of the struggle. Cabral again points out:

> The study of the history of national liberation struggles shows that generally these struggles are preceded by an increase in expression of culture, consolidated progressively into a successful or unsuccessful attempt to affirm the cultural personality of the dominated people, as a means of negating the oppressor culture.[17]

It is not surprising that in the earliest revolts in the Caribbean, *Obeah* played a significant role. In the Haitian Revolution, not only did *vodun* play an important part but the initial revolts were led by the voodoo priest, Boukman; and in the period prior to the Morant Bay Rebellion (1832–1865), there was a resurgence of African cults, and "myalism," a Jamaican mystical cult, became very important.

As one looks at the later manifestations of cultural reaffirmation that accompanied the resistance of the masses in the twentieth century, one sees the Haitian cultural responses to American occupation in 1915 and the prominence of the Afro-Cuban resurgence from 1920 to 1945 in Cuba. In the British Caribbean, coincidental with the strikes-turned-riots that shook the area in the thirties, there was the rise of cultural activity in all of the islands, especially the rise of literary activity. Richard Price was to discover as late as 1973, after spending two years studying one of the largest surviving groups of Maroons, the Saramake "Bush Negroes" of Surinam, that "Saramakas, recounting to me their ancestors' battle with the colonial troops, made quite clear that as far as they were concerned, it was their gods and *obeahs* that spelled the ultimate difference between victory and defeat."[18]

In the Caribbean, then, resistance is synonymous with the cultural reaffirmation of the people. As Cabral shows:

. . . in keeping their *culture* and *identity*, the masses keep intact the sense of their individual and collective dignity, despite the worries, humiliation, and brutalities to which they are often subject.[19]

Cabral has reminded us further that the masses are those who retain the culture of the people, almost invariably remaining untouched by the culture of the colonizer. In the Caribbean, where the colonizer rules from abroad, the masses of the people formed a syncretistic, African-based culture which provided resistance to the attempted imposition of the colonizers' foreign culture. This manifestation of the resurgence of *cultural expression* must be differentiated from *cultural renaissance*, which is always the responsibility of the elite or the exile, never the masses. The masses of the people in a colonial society are at the bottom of that society. At the top, there is the colonizer, who seeks to impose his culture on the lives of the masses in order to ensure greater control over them.

The greater crystallization of capitalism in the Caribbean, as opposed to Southern Africa, for example, created a well-defined intelligentsia sandwiched between the colonized and the colonizer. Intellectuals were caught between the culture of the masses, which they knew partially but shunned, and the culture of the colonizer, which they longed to acquire. Humiliated and rejected daily by the colonizer, they were unable to rationalize the injustices they saw perpetrated upon the masses and were forced to perceive the ambiguity of their position.

Within the intelligentsia we usually find the all-important urge to return to the source and the first important impetus towards organizing the masses for the struggle against colonial power. From this group come the novelists, some university trained, some not, but all having acquired rudiments of the colonizer's language and literature. Within this group we see the first need to articulate the contradictions and conflicts in a colonial society.

The writer coming from this alienated, petit bourgeois stratum has a particular vantage point from which to perceive these conflicts and contradictions. He is in touch with the aspiration of the masses, with which he is in close contact by virtue of his knowledge of and proximity to them. He is aware of the humiliations he suffers from the colonizer, or the injustices that he sees perpetrated upon the masses. Thus, it is this particular vision and perspective that he brings to bear upon the colonial situation that readily illuminates the situation of his people, pointing out their multifaceted relationship with the colonizer. It is as if within his own person the crisis of the colonial dilemma is mirrored.

The link between resistance and literature is important on a more dialectical level. If one perceives resistance as the extreme in the spectrum of political activity, then one can postulate that resistance occurs when there is a complete breakdown in normal politics. Resistance is politics taken to another dimension when peaceful means are no longer possible. But "both politics and literature," we are told " . . . seek to express the same thing . . . liberty, since both claim to 'liberate' man,"[20] and even though their methods seem to contradict each other, it is only because they are seen from different vantage points. This is so because "what literature says originates in language and the possibilities of language and what politics says originates in the world and its possibilities. World and language thus limit each other reciprocally."[21] World and language are outer poles of the same reality. The world is cognized only through language, and language bridges the gap between noumenon (essence) and phenomenon (the manifestation of essence).

There is, therefore, a dialectical relationship between the two processes, both speaking in the name of liberty but approaching it from different "vantage points" and using different methods, yet both attempting to arrive at the same end. Because man communicates by language, and because man also initiates the political, he is in fact the agent who possesses and controls both processes. Literature and politics therefore complement each other. If further, as Sartre says, "writing is a way of wanting freedom"[22] and "wanting freedom" is essentially a political act in a colonial situation—an act of resistance—writing then becomes a political act fraught with all the urgency and necessity within the context of the Caribbean. In a colonial society emerging from political dependence, struggling for national liberation and searching for national identity, the fusion of both processes (politics and literature) is not only indistinguishable, it literally becomes indissoluble. In the extreme or critical stages of national liberation, one becomes almost analogous to the other, and, as a consequence, the political becomes the ideological content of many novels.

It must be pointed out that this is no fanciful notion. One of Cuba's finest novelists, Cirilo Villaverde, is to the point when he testifies in *Cecilia Valdés* about the alternate use of the "word" and the "machete" as the occasion demanded. He says:

> After the new uprising in Cuba from 1865 to 1868 came the revolution of the latter year, and a bloody war for the next decade, accompanied by tumultuous scenes of Cubans emigrating to nearby countries, especially in New York. As before, and as always, I exchanged literary pursuits for militant politics, that being the way that the pen and the spoken word display here the same vehemence as were displayed there by the rifle and machete.[23]

This is the dialectical relation between politics (resistance) and literature in the Caribbean. It is, therefore, no wonder that the majority of novels from the Caribbean have as their focus the political and sociological concerns of the area.

Within the colonial world, then, it necessarily follows that literature has yet another function in that it becomes one of "the agencies which articulate history."[24] In fact, literature virtually becomes a process in which man is injected into his past world, and acts to come to grips with that past reality before he can come to terms with his present. To write is to historicize reality; that is, to concretize that past. To write perceptively is to understand the possibilities inherent in the past, and this has been the major concern of most of our writers. "The colonised man who writes for his people ought to use the past [history] with the intention of opening the future, as an invitation to action and a basis for hope."[25]

As posited before, the consciousness of the Caribbean peoples has been fashioned by a history of enslavement and foreign domination, and their consequent resistance to that domination. Leon Trotsky reminds us that ". . . the majority of artists form their relation to life and to its social forms during organic periods, in an unnoticeable and molecular way and almost without the participation of critical reason."[26] The consciousness of novelists is formed at this critical level of reality. Novelists begin to form their relationships with society when they unconsciously absorb the dichotomized influences which begin to create conflicts and contradictions within them. Trying to come to grips with opposing pressures usually results in spiritual alienation which the novelists need to articulate. However, to the degree that a writer "concretely understands the trend of historical development," he can unite his spiritual alienation with progressive impulses within society to the same degree. Correspondingly, it is to that same degree that one can anticipate a successful work, keeping in mind that *to know* is not necessarily *to be able.* And this is where I believe that the amorphous, unknowable "artistic sensibility" makes the difference.

Alienation can be regarded as a "direct result of people's social activity conditioned by the specific historical relations of private property."[27] In the final analysis, the kind of human servitude found in a colonial society engenders social consequences directly conditioned by the existing social relations of production in a particular society at a particular moment. In Caribbean society, slavery, poverty, exploitation, racism and all the various negations that alienate the Caribbean people from themselves fashion social relations.

Each work of art, and therefore each piece of literature, must not only propose a concrete liberation from these alien and destructive forms of oppression, which lead to physical and spiritual death, but must also

69

produce a symbiotic and synthetic unity between man's essence and his existence, thereby allowing for the less intense and gradual elimination of alienation and the subsequent enhancement and development of the human personality. This must be the task of the Caribbean writer.[28]

To speak in terms other than the contradictions or conflicts which arise from historical background only leads to confusion and to an incorrect analysis. It leads to the kinds of statements that assert:

> Sociology and Politics have been the chief concern of the Caribbean novelists and have caused most of the major failures. Most of the novelists are middle class Western educated intellectuals who see the Caribbean social world from the perspective of liberal left-wing oriented humanities text books.[29]

The critic, R. M. Lacovia, goes on to name works including V. S. Naipaul's *A House for Mr. Biswas* and concludes that the novelists named

> . . . have all placed their emphasis on sociological and political explorations. The explorations are essential for any developing country or area, but in several cases these explorations fail. It is not the topic which caused these failures (although one must admit that it is the most difficult in literature to deal with), rather it is the orientation.[30]

The critic has not told us which of the books he cites are the failures and which are not. We only know there are several among the group. He holds to the imperative that the only true preoccupations of the Caribbean writer are African concepts such as time (Chronos) and rhythm, which, of course, are only aspects of artistic form. To suggest that books such as *A House for Mr. Biswas* are failures because they do not inculcate these forms counters all reasonable critical appraisals, some of which have acclaimed that "*A House for Mr. Biswas* (1961) established him [Naipaul]as the author of a major twentieth century novel on the increasingly rare scale of *Middlemarch*, *Anna Karenina*, or *The Rainbow*."[31] Such criticism as offered by R. M. Lacovia is untenable.

Mr. Naipaul is the case of a particular kind of success against the background of a much greater failure of vision. Here the notion of the qualitative aspects of the critic's professional apparatus comes into play. The questions that must be asked are: What is the nature of Naipaul's success? By whom has he been acclaimed? More important, is Naipaul's vision about the affirmation of life, about the possible human aspirations, or the richness of the Caribbean people's historical, political and cultural achievements? Or is it about the glorification of death and the depiction of man as a helpless creature incapable of achieving anything, a position analogous to the bourgeois notion about the absurdity of man's condition. Are we acclaiming humanism or nihilism? How are we to understand Naipaul's masterpiece?

Naipaul himself says that "the history of the West Indian islands can never be satisfactorily told. Brutality is not the only difficulty. History is built around achievement and creation; and nothing was created in the West Indies."[32] Neither Ramchand nor Lacovia articulates the issue of nihilism versus humanism. Gordon Rohlehr's analysis of V. S. Naipaul's novels in his article, "The Ironic Approach" is much more "critical" and presents a much better critical approach to literary analysis. Rohlehr's comment that "it is only when one reads *The Middle Passage* that one realizes how completely Naipaul has accepted anarchy and absurdity as the norms of his society"[33] places any discussion of Naipaul's vision in its correct perspective.

Lacovia, however, makes an analytic error because he sets up impossible *a priori* African guidelines which the novel must fit. While Caribbean culture is African-based, it is suffused with many other elements (East Indian, Indian, Chinese). Therefore, it is irrational to set up guidelines based on a static concept, tying all elements of the form to a single cultural base. Further, while the concepts of time and rhythm do provide valuable insights into Caribbean literature, Lacovia overlooks the fact that "without some form of social or political conviction [i.e., ideological content]great literature cannot be written at all."[34] Even if one believes the novelists' orientation was wrong because of their education, this in no way negates the importance of social or political conviction and subject matter in achieving a successful novel set in the Caribbean or anywhere else.[35]

In the same article, however, Mr. Lacovia lauds Vic Reid:

> With his novel, *New Day*, Victor Reid in 1949 opened new possibilities for the usage of dialect and history in Caribbean Literature. The narrator, an old man, spans in his memory 1865–1944, he spans the loss of potential self rule in 1865 to the *new day* in 1944 when self rule is regained.[36]

This tells us little, for it asserts the obvious since many Caribbean writers prior to Reid used history. But, Reid's *New Day is* an example of the successful integration of content and form. Its content, the heroic struggle of a people, mirrors the panorama of Jamaican life in a history that affirms the vision of a people's resistance, their vitality and creativity of life. Its form, on the other hand, is strategic and presents the struggle through the eyes of a participant, thus bringing the action of the story closer to the reader. Second, we see the language of the masses which creates spontaneity and registers certain nuances of the people's responses to and participation in the struggle. Third, a rhythmic throbbing in the dialect speaks to the struggle's urgency, yielding a rich tension and interrelating the external form that holds the novel together. Even though the sophisticated interrelationship of ideological content and artistic form is responsible for the novel's considerable success, the novel has some failings and weakens at its denouement.

With all this in mind, we note that the importance of Caribbean history must be understood within the context of any analysis of a piece of Caribbean literature. Literature can still be treated as an autonomous entity, but an understanding of history insures a richer reading and a more meaningful intellectual experience. Richard Greeman's comments are important in projecting resistance as the stellar element in shaping the Caribbean writer's consciousness. He argues:

> There is nonetheless something curious in the fact that revolutionary politics alone, of all world-views, is seen as so "alien" to literature. No one would dream of questioning the legitimacy of Dante's Christianity as an expression of *his* age. Catholic "ideology" is universally recognized as the structuring element in the *Comedy*. Why not apply the same standard to Serge and the writers of our age? . . .
>
> Rarely in these debates is it understood that there is such a thing as a political and historical imagination which can . . . produce works combining free creativity and political significance; works where political vision is the basis of literary structure.[37]

This is particularly true for Caribbean writers since daily violence—be it political (the attempt to impose foreign control over the people), economic (the attempt to exact the largest amount of labor at the lowest cost) or cultural (the attempt to foster a foreign way of life)—has led to resistance, a necessary and permanent condition in Caribbean culture. Any literary consciousness rising from this cultural/socioeconomic/political milieu must of necessity be violent and political. Political vision becomes the basic literary structure and aesthetic sensibility in Caribbean literature.

Even though he goes back to the Tupac Amaru uprising of 1780 in Peru, Retamar, who includes the Caribbean in Latin America, comments on the importance of revolutionary activity in shaping culture and literature:

> Our culture is—and can only be—the child of revolution, of our multi-secular rejection of all colonialisms. Our culture, like every culture, requires as a primary condition our own existence. I cannot help but cite here, although I have done so before elsewhere, one of the occasions on which Martí spoke to this fact in the most simple and illuminating way. "Letters, which are expression, cannot exist," he wrote in 1881, "so long as there is no essence to

express in them. Nor will there exist a Spanish American Literature until Spanish America exists." And further on "Let us lament now that we are without a great work of art; not because we do not have that work, but because it is a sign *that we are still without a great people which would be reflected in it*." Latin American culture, then, *has become a possibility in the first place because of the many who have struggled, the many who still struggle, for the existence of that "great people" which, in 1881, Martí still referred to as Spanish America but which some years later* he would prefer to name more accurately, Our America."[39] [Italics mine.]

More particularly, Sylvia Wynter comments about the Caribbean situation, "To write at all was and is for the West Indian a revolutionary act. Any criticism that does not start from this very real recognition is invalid."[39]

In making this connection between history (in particular, resistance) and literature, one must not make any *a priori* judgments on the aesthetic problems of the literature or decide whether one work using history is better than another. Not even Engels could set up such *a priori* judgments, and Trotsky would later affirm that literature had its own independent laws. However, in analyzing Caribbean literature, an understanding of history in general and the role of resistance in particular becomes indispensable.

PART II

V

THE BEGINNING:
The Incas, the Tears
of the Indians, Enriquillo
(The Cross and the Sword)

We will not forgive them for they know
what they do
They lynched John who worked to organize the people
They chased him through the woods with dogs
like a gaunt wolf
Laughing they hung him to the trunk of the old sycamore
No, brothers, comrades
We will pray no more
Our revolt is rising like the cry of a bird of the storm
above the rotten sloshing of the swamp
We will no longer sing the sad hopeless spirituals
Another song rises from our throats
We unfurl our red flags
Stained with the blood of our people
Under this symbol we will march
Under this symbol we march
Rise up damned of the earth
Rise up prisoners of starvation

Jacques Roumain, "New Negro
Sermon."

IN any analysis of the Caribbean one must understand that the coming of
the Spaniards brought a violent breakup of the traditional Indian societies.
The Toltecs, Mayas, Aztecs and Incas had achieved highly developed
cultures in Central and South America while the Indian societies in the
Orinoco and Amazon basins and in the Caribbean existed at various stages
of primitive development. Nevertheless, social and cultural intercourse
took place between the relatively advanced Inca and Maya civilizations
and the Indians of the Caribbean and as a result they shared many common
attributes.

The pre-Columbian civilization of which the Caribbean was a part was a well-developed society in which the arts and sciences reached relatively high levels of sophistication. As early as 1609, Garcilaso de la Vega, the son of an Inca princess and a Spanish conquistador, recorded a narrative vision of contemporary Inca civilization and its historical development in *The Incas: The Royal Commentaries of the Inca*. This work is important not only because it depicts highly developed societies but also because it refutes myths about the "savage" Indian. When contrasted with Bartolomé de las Casas' *Tears of the Indians*, it provides a much more balanced perspective from which to analyze Caribbean society and literature. *The Incas* is the first narrative we have, written by an inhabitant, about the lives of the Indians.

The pre-Columbian societies of Latin America had many typological similarities in terms of political, social, and religious organization with ancient African societies including Egypt, Napata, Meroe (Sudan) and Ethiopia. While the Indian civilizations in America developed independently, as did their counterparts in Egypt and Mesopotamia, "the consciousness of the self-aware individual"[2] appeared in a limited form and was held back by the sacral character of governmental institutions which dictated a slow rate of economic development.[3] This civilization depicted by Garcilaso is not idyllic for it had deified despotic rulers and expansionist tendencies, and used a monotheistic religion to solidify its dominant culture. The Indian civilizations of the New World did, however, make their contributions to world knowledge. The Incas had a legal system and an understanding of science, could tell the time of the equinoxes and had an

amazingly accurate knowledge not only of the revolutions of the sun and the moon, but even of the synodic revolutions of the planets Jupiter, Mercury and Venus. . . . As in Central America, . . . the initimate details of the calendar were kept secret by the astronomer-priests, which explains the very superficial note of the chroniclers on the subject. Montesinos is the only author to assert that the Incas had a year of 365 days. He relates that an Inca named Yahuar Huquiz, who was a great astrologer, was endeavoring to determine how many days should be added to 365 every four years. True, says Nordenskiold, Montesinos' statements should be treated with caution. Another Inca, according to Montesinos, introduced the system of dividing the year into weeks of ten days, with five days only in the last week. Nordenskiold also quotes Molina, according to whom the *quipus* were used traditionally to count the years and the months until the reign of the Inca Yupanqui, who introduced the system of counting by winters and summers.

As Nordenskiold remarks, such a degree of scientific knowledge on the part of people who had no form of writing, even hieroglyphics, is one of the most original features of the Peruvian civilization. (I, p. 85)

This excerpt, taken from a note in the work, emphasizes the Incas' tremendous knowledge of astronomy. The Incas also practiced "trephining" and knew how to use herbs for medicine; they understood geometry, and their bridge-building and temple-building skills were amazing. Inca Indians had their own cosmogonic myths (they were not ignorant of the fact that there existed a universal creator, whom they called Pachacamac); this worship of a monotheistic god testifies to the level their civilization had reached. Garcilaso wrote his historical narrative to immortalize this great civilization. As he testifies, his work was

> . . . actuated by the desire to conserve the heritage of my native land, and to secure the little that remains of it before it should disappear entirely, I, the Inca Garcilaso, began to write this history of the former kings of Peru, which I shall pursue till the end, even though it be an immense undertaking. (I, pp. 261-262)

The knowledge that imminent disaster would befall his civilization made Garcilaso aware that the only way he could provide an eyewitness account of his civilization for future generations was to place it on paper. He gave his life to this effort and said at its conclusion, "I have thus paid the debt that I owed my country and my maternal ancestor"; and with 100,000 amens he thanked God for helping him to complete his work. (I, p. 426) The need to record this history came from Garcilaso's realization that Spanish rule meant complete destruction of all this civilization had accomplished through its one thousand years of existence. Unlike the Spaniards, who captured and destroyed the Indian civilizations, the Incas, who expanded and conquered also, did at least bring prosperity to their conquered territories initially,[4] for as Garcilaso explains, after conquering, "the Inca visited his new acquisition of territory and worked to increase its development by constructing canals, granaries, bridges and roads." (I, p. 69)

But given the strength of these Indians, with the capacity of their rulers to raise at any given time twenty or thirty thousand warriors, how were the Spaniards able to defeat these powerful civilizations with so few men? The answer was not exclusively the military superiority of the Spaniards or the internal rivalries of the tribes, but because of their religious beliefs, which led to their enslavement. But let Garcilaso explain:

> I remember that one day, while speaking of the arrival of the Spaniards in Peru with the old Inca, who was a relative of my mother's, I asked him the following question:
> "Inca," I said, "how does it happen that powerful and numerous as you were and, in addition, being the masters of a country composed of steep mountains

which are naturally so difficult of access, you let yourselves be conquered and dispossessed by a handful of Spaniards?"

The Inca had told me a few days before about Huaina Capac's prediction. He told it a second time, then, showing a certain irritation, as though my question implied that the Incas had lacked courage, he said: "You must know that the words spoken by our king were more powerful than all the weapons carried by your father and his companions, and that they, it was that subjected us to foreign rule and dispossessed us of our Empire. (I, p. 344)

Foreign rule and dispossession did not enter the New World on the wings of a dove. They came like a whirlwind, and in their wake more than 20 million Indians were slaughtered cruelly. As the son of an Inca princess who had access to the oral tradition of his people, Garcilaso was able to give us an eyewitness description of his civilization and recount the culture of his people. But it would take a Spanish bishop to document fully and to describe the brutality committed against the Indians. Writing in 1553, las Casas described the Indians in the following manner:

This infinite multitude of people was so created by God, as that they were without fraud, without subtelty or malice, to their natural Governours most faithful and obedient. Towards the Spaniards whom they serve, patient, meek and peaceful, who laying all contentious and tumultuous thoughts aside, live without any hatred or desire of revenge; the people are most delicate and tender, enjoying such a feeble constitution of body as does not permit them to endure labour, so that the Children of Princes and great persons here, are not more nice and delicate than the Children of the meanest countryman in that place.

. . . To these quiet Lambs, endued with such blessed qualities, came the Spaniards like most cruel Tigers, Wolves, and Lions, enrag'd with a sharp and tedious hunger; for these forty years past, minding nothing else but the slaughter of these unfortunate wretches, whom with divers kinds of torments neither seen nor heard before, they have so cruelly and inhumanely butchered, that of three millions of people which Hispaniola itself did contain, there are left remaining alive scarce three hundred persons. And for the island of Cuba, which contains as much ground in length, as from Valladolid to Rome; it lies wholly desert, untill'd and ruin'd. The islands of St. John and Jamaica lie waste and desolate. The Lucayan Islands neighboring toward the North upon Cuba and Hispaniola, being above Sixty or thereabouts with those Islands that are vulgarly called the Islands of the Gyants, of which that which is least fertile is more fruitful than the King of Spain's Garden at Sevil, being situated in a pure and temperate air, are now totally unpeopled and destroyed; the inhabitants thereof amounting to above 500,000 souls, partly killed, and partly forced away to work in other places; so that there going a ship to visit those parts and to glean the remainder of those distressed wretches, there could be found no more than eleven men.

Other Islands there were near the Island of St. John more than thirty in number, which were totally made desert. All which Islands, though they amount to such a number containing in length of ground the space of above Two thousand miles, lie now altogether solitary without any people or Inhabitant. (TI, pp. 1-3)

Las Casas described this unheard of brutality which laid bare the Caribbean Islands and annihilated their original inhabitants as the Spaniards plunged madly on in their quest for gold and silver. But it was in Hispaniola where the destruction of the Indians first began and where one of the most important Caribbean novels based on resistance of the Indians to the Spanish is set. Las Casas describes some of the most wanton brutality of the Spaniards:

. . . They took away their women and children to serve them, though the reward which they gave them was a sad and fatal one. Their food got with great pain and dropping sweat, the Spaniards still consumed, not content with what the poor Indians gave them gratis out of their own want; One Spaniard consuming in one day as much as would suffice three families, every one containing ten persons. *Being thus broken with so many evils, afflicted with so many torments, and handled so ignominiously, they began at length to believe that the Spaniards were not sent from Heaven.* And therefore some of them hid their Children, others their Wives, others their Victuals in obscure and secret places; Others not being able to endure a Nation that conversed among them with such a boisterous impiety sought for shelter in the most abrupt and inaccessible mountains. For the Spaniards while they were among them did not only entertain with cruel beating them with their fists, and with their staves, but presumed also to lay violent hands upon the Rulers and Magistrates of their Cities; and they arriv'd at that height of impudence and unheard of boldness, that a certain private Captain scrupled not to force the Wife of the most potent King among them. From which time forward they began to think what way they might take to expel the Spaniards out of their Country. (TI, pp. 4-5) [Italics mine.]

After studying "a stupefying array of evidence," las Casas concludes the Indians "were . . . no whit less rational than the Egyptians, Romans, or Greeks, and are not much inferior to the Spaniards. Indeed, in some respects, they were even superior to the Spaniards."[5] Although many scholars have tried to ridicule this position, all subsequent information has proved las Casas and Garcilaso to be correct in their analysis of the Indian civilization.

The Indians did not accept Spanish rule placidly. After welcoming the Spaniards in peace and friendship, the Indians soon realized that the Spaniards were wolves in lambs' clothing and girded their armor to resist.

When Viceroy Francisco de Toledo was sent to Peru to lay the basis for Spanish domination over the Indians, his first act was to execute the Inca, Lord Tupac Amaru, the Indian leader who refused to accept Spanish rule. Although Toledo and his associates acquired an immense amount of information on Inca history and customs, which was designed to prove conclusively that Spain's rule in Peru was just by contrasting it with the injustice of Inca rule, the attacks of las Casas served as the spearhead of the attack on Spanish rule in America. Toledo and others could not refute the testimony of conquistador Mancio Serra, who on his death bed said:

> That the Incas had ruled so wisely that in all their realms there was not a single thief, vicious or lazy man, or adulterous woman; that immoral persons were not countenanced; that every man had an honest and profitable occupation; that the mountains, mines, and lands were all so administered that everyone had enough; that the Incas were obeyed and respected by their subjects and considered very capable rulers.[6]

The resistance begun by the Indians continued sporadically throughout the Caribbean. But the three factors outlined earlier (Spanish military superiority, Indian internal rivalry and especially Indian religious belief) led to their eventual defeat. Brutal as it may have been, Spanish victory imposed a higher socioeconomic order into which the Indians were absorbed. In fact, so brutal was the destruction of Indian civilization in Hispaniola that by the nineteenth century, very few Indians were left on the island.

The destruction of the Indians, the advent of Negro slavery, and the rise of nationalism forced Caribbean writers to look back at that glorious period when a great civilization flourished and when their ancestors struggled bravely for their freedom. While the immediacy of slavery focused the novelists' attention upon the present condition of the slave, a need for perspective, a need to understand what that present meant on the larger canvas of historical time, made writers look backward. That there were heroic ancestors who had resisted enslavement became important; increasingly novelists drew on a particular kind of past, one that Sylvia Wynter describes:

> The fact of the past, opposed to the lies of the past is not the important fact; it is the creative myth of the past inherent in the cultural dynamic by which a people transform the colonial reality into genuine nationhood. It is this creative myth which lies at the heart of all cultures.[7]

Most of the important creative writers in the Caribbean turned to this creative myth of the past.

Initially, the literary movement of "Indianism" provided that cultural myth for Caribbean writers. G. R. Coulthard attests to the fact that during the nineteenth century

> . . . identification with the Indians supplied roots in the past and answered a deep-rooted psychological need: that of belonging to a country. The Indian, after all, was the only true *American*. . . . Indianist literature, then, was a literature of protest and affirmation; protest against Spanish rule and affirmation of a strictly national, *American* spirit.[8]

Essentially Coulthard is correct in his analysis, even though it seems to me that the word "protest" within this context should be changed to read "resistance." Whereas the former evokes negative connotations, the latter is more positive in its application and much more correctly identifies the phenomenon that was taking place. The Indians and the Africans were not so much "protesting" as they were actively "resisting" the imposition of a foreign culture. The burden of nineteenth century literature was to manifest the nature of that resistance; it did both in poetry and the novel.

Some of the best poetry in the Indianist movement came from Cuba and Santo Domingo, and one of the most important novels, *Enriquillo*, written by Manuel de Jesús Galván, came from Santo Domingo. The first part of the novel was published in 1879, the second in 1882. In 1954, Robert Graves translated and published it under the title, *The Cross and the Sword*. *Enriquillo* is one of the first Caribbean novels to return to the past and take as its central theme the resistances of the Indians to Spanish enslavement.

Enriquillo, "a true West Indian" as Galván calls him, retreated to the Bahoruco mountains in Santo Domingo and successfully resisted the Spanish forces for fifteen years (1518–1533) until Charles V was forced to grant him the right to choose an area to settle his people. *Enriquillo* successfully recreates the drama of resistance which, as Galvan points out, seemed

> . . . a prelude to all the reactions which in the last three centuries have denied the conquerors their title the lordship of the New World. We do not know whether or not the Spanish statesmen of those times, who gave Enriquillo's rebellion the importance it deserved, had a sense that history must eventually take this course, but were discreet enought to keep it to themselves. (CS, p. 338)

The novel is presented as an historical legend but is an almost literal retelling of the resistance of the Indians in precise historical details. The author so creatively marshalls and rearranges the evidence with such impressive detail that *Enriquillo* is one of the best novels of the Indianist movement. (CS, p. ix)

But Enriquillo is important for other reasons. First, the action takes place in Santo Domingo, the first European settlement in the New World, and recounts the resistance of the Indians in 1509 soon after the Europeans arrived. Second, it dramatizes the early philosophical arguments waged at the Court of Valladolid in Spain about "just and unjust wars" to colonize the Indians and a way of bringing the "light" of Christianity to the benighted people.[9] Third, it presents the exploration and colonization of the Greater Antilles (Jamaica, Cuba, Puerto Rico and Hispaniola) and intrigue at the Spanish Court and in the Caribbean. Fourth, it describes the constant brutality to which the Indians were subjected and their resistance in this early period of exploration and exploitation.

In one notable account Galvan recounts the bravery of the Higuey Indians of Cuba who hurled themselves down gorges, preferring death to enslavement by the Spanish. This very episode becomes the central legend that George Lamming treats in his novel, *Of Age and Innocence*, where the "Tribe Boys" (the Indians) confront the "Bandit Kings" (the Europeans) in an outstanding act of defiance and resistance to create the historical legacy of the people of San Cristobal, who, in Lamming's novel, are the Caribbean people.

Enriquillo begins with an encyclopedic and panoramic view of the entire Caribbean and places the Caribbean against the larger background of Europe, very much as Carpentier does in his *Explosion in a Cathedral*. If Galván is more meticulously historical, then Carpentier is more intensely political. Both novels follow recorded history, capture its essence and apply it to the present. As Galván himself asserts in the preface to this 1894 edition, "the conclusions which are deduced in *Enriquillo* from past events, are advanced there as applicable to present conditions—conditions which had already been foreseen in those days with the seal of historical necessity." (CS, p. xviii)

Enriquillo begins when Guaroa descends from the mountains to take Enriquillo, a young prince, to where Guaroa has "chosen a place of refuge for all my race from the cruelty of the white race." (CS, p. 7) Enriquillo (as a child, named Guarocuyo) is taken to the hills and revered as the "true and only lord, the Cacique of Bahoruco." (CS, p. 16) The Spanish pursue the Indians, who hold out for a month before surrendering to las Casas. The Spaniards take Guarocuyo (Enriquillo) to a Franciscan convent where las Casas baptizes him and changes his name to the formal Enrique ("Enriquillo" being his nickname). The Spaniards kill off the Indians who remain behind. Guaroa, who prefers to take his own life rather than trust the Spaniards again, plunges a dagger into his heart, saying, "I die a free man" (CS, p. 39) and forcing the narrator to comment, "thus died Guaroa, defiant to the last; bequeathing to his race an example of indomitable courage and liberty which was not to pass unheeded." (CS, p. 39)

At the Franciscan convent, Enriquillo is taught the Holy Bible, the Latin classics and the benefits of Spanish civilization. He is particularly entranced by the insurrection of Viriatus, the Lusitanian shepherd who revolted against the Romans. The author reminds us that "no attention should be paid to learned historians who held that the strict education which the lonely young cacique received at the convent must have aggravated his unhappiness; the truth is exactly the reverse, as I have been at pains to point out. (CS, p. 53) Education makes Enriquillo what Don Diego Velázquez calls "the happy result of our combined endeavours." (CS, p. 74) Don Diego Velázquez, Father Remigio, who teaches Enriquillo the civilizing effects of Spanish culture, and las Casas, who teaches him Christianity, become the three most important influences in Enriquillo's life. Later this education illuminates the contradictions of Enriquillo's condition and causes him to rebel.

Enriquillo experiences his first confrontation with the colonial authorities when the Vicereine asks him to tell a lie and, then, to be a page. Enriquillo sees his fellow Indians working like slaves and explodes: "That I should be a page? That I should serve her as a lackey—hold the train of her dress with reverence—fetch and carry chairs and stools for her? That is what I saw the other pages doing, and I do not think that such things are consonant with the honour of anyone who has learned to handle a sword." (CS, p. 103) Enriquillo's dignity is affronted once again when Velázquez, his protector, asks him to serenade his love only two months after Enriquillo's aunt has died. Enriquillo protests. Velázquez reproaches him:

> "So this is what happens! I take immense pains to have you well educated and make a success of you, yet the very first time I ask you to do anything to please me, you dare to refuse! What better occasion could you have to show your affection and gratitude? . . .
>
> "Go away, boy, said Velázquez bitterly. And do not return: I have wasted my time, my care and my money on you." (CS, p. 125)

Enriquillo is enslaved more than he knows, for his entire life is controlled by his protectors. Yet he must realize this himself, for as kind as his spiritual advisor, las Casas, is, he only advises Enriquillo to "be wise and long suffering." (CS, p. 134)

Enriquillo's recognition begins when an attempt is made to post his betrothed, former princess Mencia, as a serf. He recognizes his vulnerability and sees how truly his race is enslaved. But once more his Christian friends keep his resolution and anger in check. As his marriage to Mencia approaches, Enriquillo suffers other humiliations and realizes that

> . . . though highly esteemed and carefully protected since infancy, he was still a poor cacique, a member of the unhappy race whom the invaders treated worse even than the lowest animals. He was about to take possession of his betrothed's estates and manage them himself; but although he lacked for nothing, he was in effect an orphan without patrimony. None of his rich ancestral lands in the Bahoruco had been assigned to him, nor, despite his empty title of cacique, did he enjoy anymore jurisdiction over the Indians of those mountains than the orders of the Distribution of Serfs conferred on him; he was himself a serf, though a cacique of serfs. (CS, p. 206)

When his marriage to Doña Mencia is stopped because she is of Castilian family, and it is not customary for women of her class to marry Indians, Enriquillo, an Indian, recognizes his position and its implications. But he had been taught to be "wise and long suffering," and it will take further humiliation before he acts. (CS, p. 216)

Enriquillo's vulnerability shows more clearly when his protector, Don Francisco De Valenzuela, dies. Since Don Francisco's son, Andrés, hates Enriquillo, shortly after his father's death, a decree annulling Enriquillo's and other Indians' freedom comes down from the Courts. Enriquillo understands: "It has gone, Mencia—my dream, my illusion, the life in which I believed. Nothing remains but the bleak reality. I dreamed that I was free, but now I am no more than a wretched serf. (CS, p. 286)

Andrés considers Enriquillo "the dung of the market square," a phrase that rings throughout Caribbean literature. In *Tears of the Indians* (1552) las Casa accuses the Spaniards of looking upon the Indians as "if they had been but the dung and filth of the earth [who after receiving them as] angels sent from heaven" were turned upon with such cruelty that the Indians were forced "to take Armes against the Spaniards." (TI, p. 10) Jacques Roumain's most important poems, "New Negro Sermon" and "Sales Negroes," refer to the people as "the damned of the earth,"[10] and Frantz Fanon used a similar phrase in the title of his major work, *The Wretched of the Earth* (1963).

Enriquillo's final humiliation comes when Andrés secretly presents Enriquillo's wife, Mencia, with a document stating that Enriquillo has ill-treated her. This is the only way Andrés feels he can win Mencia, who has spurned his affections. When the ploy fails, Andrés tries to rape Mencia, but she is rescued. Still trying to obtain justice from the Spanish, Enriquillo goes to court. When his requests fail, Enriquillo takes his cause to higher authorities and is thrown into prison. All avenues of justice are closed to him; his only recourse is to fight. Enriquillo and his men head for the Bahuroco mountains where they mobilize other Indian leaders to prepare for the expected Spanish attack. All swear allegiance to Enriquillo. Andrés Valenquela leads the first Spanish attack against the Indians and, quickly defeated, returns to town in shame.

When news of the defeat reaches the Spanish, Don Pedro Badillo, lieutenant governor of La Maguana, attacks Enriquillo. He, too, is defeated, and Enriquillo and his men capture more arms and horses. More Indians join Enriquillo, who is resolute and magnanimous, whereas his lieutenant, Tamayo, is reckless and cruel. Enriquillo reminds Tamayo "that this is a war of freedom, not [one] of purposeless cruelty. (CS, p. 328) The difference leads to their temporary separation.

On five different occasions the Spanish, realizing that Enriquillo is more formidable than expected, send emissaries asking him to surrender. Enriquillo rejects the first offer which would free only himself and his chief officers by saying he will not lay down his arms "while a single Hispaniolian Indian remained in serfdom." (CS, p. 333) Hostilities begin once more, and Enriquillo again defeats the Spanish.

The war enters a new phase in which the Spanish try to lure the Indians from their impregnable defenses. The truce had given Enriquillo the necessary time to organize his kingdom, to cultivate food and to set up defences. When Enriquillo and his men capture a Spanish ship and take its gold, the deadlock has to be broken. Enriquillo's former teacher, Father Remigio, is sent to discuss a peace settlement. Enriquillo informs him that he will continue the struggle until Spain decrees freedom for all Indians in Hispaniola.

At this time Bishop Don Sebastián Ramírez arrives from Spain to be the new governor of the island and advises the Spanish crown that Enriquillo and his people "should be compensated for their former deprivation of liberty and for the wrongs they had suffered to their persons and possessions, by the widest possible concessions. Only by such peaceful means would they be persuaded to lay down their arms." (CS, p. 344) Hernando San Miguel is sent to make an agreement with Enriquillo. He promises Enriquillo that lands will be given to his people and that all the Indians in Hispaniola will be given their complete liberty. Enriquillo, convinced of Spanish sincerity, leaves his mountain home after fifteen years and marches into La Maguana, a hero. Choosing his residence at the foot of the Caibo mountains, Enriquillo founds his town, Santa María de Boya, "a sacred place of refuge where the surviving natives of Hispaniola could enjoy peace and liberty," and rules over his people as a true lord and king. (CS, p. 351)

Enriquillo, or *The Cross and the Sword*, recounts the successful resistance of the Indians against the Spanish. Great as this victory was, the Indians were unable to rout the Spanish completely and in the end submitted to Spanish rule. Galván's sensibilities were split since he owed allegiance to the Spanish way of life yet identified with and appreciated the people's struggle for independence—the classic dilemma of the colonial intellectual. In spite of this double allegiance, the nobility of the people's struggle against the foreign colonizers and their indomitable spirit comes through in the novel. Although Galván also believed that the Spanish made contributions to the island, one cannot help but see that their contributions pale before the gallant struggle of the oppressed Indians.

Kenneth Schwartz, for example, claims that "to interpret the work as a defense of the Indian and his freedom seems difficult in view of Galván's ambivalent attitude toward the unfortunate people."[11] Of course, even the language here is patronizing. Only one observation, however—Galván's sympathy seems to lie with the Indian, in spite of his attitude towards them. It must be remembered that even though Galván left the country after the Spanish were driven out of the island after the War of National Liberation in 1854, he continued to serve his country in many capacities. More on the mark, a much more valuable assessment of his work comes from José Martí, who was tremendously impressed by the "political intention" of the work. That the novel should try to come to grips with political problems had very important ramifications for the Caribbean novel.

That Galván should use the resistance of the Indians as the central theme of his work at a time when G. R. Coulthard contends that there was a "widespread feeling that there existed an identity of cause between the ancient inhabitants of America and the new revolutionaries"[12] in Latin America and the Caribbean seems to be indicative of the profound link that existed between the literature and the revolutionary struggle that was taking place. There was a conscious attempt on the part of the author to present the resistance of the Indian as the most important phase of the historical development of Caribbean people, certainly the most inspiring. Further, by using the past to comment on the present, the novel served to show the relation of the past struggle of the Indians to the struggle that was taking place at that time for national liberation, during which the Dominican people successfully defeated the Spanish, causing them to withdraw from Santo Domingo. It was used also to remind the people of the constant need to resist foreign oppression.

The Cross and the Sword, as our first representative novel, is to be seen within the context of classical literature, with Enriquillo possessing most of the typical characteristics of the classical hero. Indeed, he is an idealized and refined character; in this case, he is still a prince (i.e., an extraordinary figure who will increasingly become the center of focus as the novel develops). There is in his actions a certain heroic dimension. Enriquillo embodies the essence of classicism, and his is "the expression of civic consciousness that makes the concept of social duty an absolute one."[13] For Enriquillo his social duty is absolute; he must liberate his people. As for the novel, its lofty tone is the presentation of a beautiful moral art that demands that the novel be both instructive and uplifting. However, the novel succumbs to the central sin of classical art that pictures life as inherently static. The notion of history as a process, changing spirally and rising to new levels of development and awareness, is not to be seen in this classical art. Basically, once Enriquillo has defeated the Spaniards, he returns to live among them, not really being cognizant that the very dynamic of the socioeconomic and sociopolitical aspects of Spanish colonization must mean the annihilation or the total absorption of one way of life by the other. That which was superior was sure to triumph. Hence that which is depicted as the resolution of the conflict (i.e., living side by side with the colonizers) in point of fact becomes the necessary prerequisite for the triumph of Spanish colonization.

Yet within the work there are certain elements of liberal romanticism that would make themselves manifest: the fact, for example, that Enriquillo believed in the "illusions of bourgeois [in this case feudal] liberalism while being opposed to the more unpleasant aspects of bourgeois progress [and was] of the opinion that the new social order merely required certain minor improvements."[14]

This of course would be his downfall. The ultimate recognition that liberation involves more than "reformism" will be made explicit as the element of historicism is introduced and the Caribbean novel becomes more fully developed.

VI

THE LIBERATION MOVEMENT:
Cecilia Valdés, the Early Life of the Negro Poet, the Autobiography of a Runaway Slave

THE French Revolution of 1789 not only had a colossal impact upon European spiritual and social life but its ramifications were to be felt in the Caribbean as well, particularly in the Haitian revolution of 1792–1804. In the United States, Congress in the same year passed one of its most important pieces of legislation, the Bill of Rights, that allowed for freedom of speech, freedom of the press, and upheld the inviolability of the individual, giving to him many other progressive rights.

The social awakening created by the French and American bourgeois revolutions had a tremendous impact on the social consciousness of the age. Where the proponents of classicism saw history merely in a state of completion, staunchly frozen in time, and simply to be used for decorative purposes in the literature, the age of romanticism that was ushered in by these titanic forces of social progress saw history not as fixed, but as a continuing process and sought to examine very concretely "history's movement in time." History, then, was seen as a process in a constant state of development. This, however, was not merely intellectual, for history was a very immediate part of one's consciousness, in the Hegelian sense. Suchkov put it this way:

> The heightened interest in history observable in social thought of the early 19th century was by no means due to purely intellectual causes; history itself burst into people's lives, for the new century did not descend on the world lightly as a dove but to the thunder of cannon, the beating of drums, and whiffs of grapeshot. The rhythmic march of soldiers' feet shook the continent from the Pyrenees to the Volga, and the bloody fields of Austerlitz, Borodino and Waterloo marked the course of Napoleon's cruel star, its zenith and its nadir.[1]

And so it was, too, in the Caribbean where Toussaint and the national liberation movement blunted Napoleon's cruel star so that in 1792 the

Haitians pulled the Caribbean people into the contemporary world and made them participants in world historical changes. In 1816, sixteen years after Toussaint and the Haitian revolution, Simón Bolívar and his national liberation movement did the same thing for Latin America.

The medium best equipped to capture the new social consciousness produced by unleashing these titanic forces was romantic poetry. In his work, *A History of Realism*, Boris Suchkov, quotes Schlegel as making the following observation: "Only romantic poetry, like the epos, can be the mirror of the whole surrounding world, the reflection of the age." (p. 56) Because of this specific capacity, romanticism enriched world art and literature with a sense of history. As an integral part of the international currents, Caribbean poets and novelists turned to romanticism, using their own characteristics and idiosyncrasies to depict Caribbean reality. The early Caribbean novel, like its Latin American counterpart, became steeped in a romanticism that identified very strongly with individual freedom and nationalism. Jean Franco describes Latin American literature:

> The new literature was thus identified with political and social reform in the minds of young intellectuals who held on to these ideals during dark periods of oppression, dictatorship and civil war. In such periods, literature was sometimes the only form of activity left open to them, so that the novel and even poetry came to be regarded as instruments for attacking injustices, and for creating a sense of patriotism and civic pride.[2]

But the use of literature as an active tool of liberation and force to create a national identity was more acute in the Caribbean than in Latin America. Jean Franco underlines this point:

> Nowhere was Romanticism associated with the struggle for freedom more fervently than in the Caribbean, and particularly in Cuba where the struggle for independence endured for the whole nineteenth century. As in Argentina, literature and politics were linked and the novel, more than any other genre, became the vehicle for nationalism.[3]

Romanticism, whose chief characteristic was inflation of the individual ego with little or no causal relationship to social environment, became identified with the struggle for freedom because it used history as process.[4] Even though Peru, the last colonial territory in Latin America, was liberated in January, 1826, Cuba and Puerto Rico still remained colonized, making the struggle for liberation more immediate in the Caribbean. This inevitable and inexorable urge for social progress made romanticism, as an artistic form and method, a vehicle for depicting progress and showing the essence of historical development.

There is quite another reason for the appearance of the specific kind of romanticism that presented itself as an artistic vehicle at that time. In his work, *A History of Realism*, Boris Suchkov differentiates between three types of romanticism: *conservative romanticism*, in which authors adopt a stoic non-acceptance of life and the new society, e.g., Alfred de Vigny; *liberal romanticism*, in which authors believe in the illusions of bourgeois liberalism while opposing the more unpleasant aspects of bourgeois progress and feeling that the social order only required certain minor improvements, e.g., Lamartine; and *revolutionary romanticism*, in which authors to a greater or lesser extent connect romanticism with the rise of the proletarians and the democratic revolutionary movement, e.g., Heinrich Heine, Moreau.[5]

The specific kind of romanticism written in the Caribbean context is revolutionary romanticism, which includes elements of realism and encompasses a society basically divided into two parts: the master and the slave. The essential task of the masses was to free themselves; therefore, the major task of revolutionary romanticism as applied to the Caribbean situation was its interconnection with the rise of the antislavery movement.[6] The movement inculcated the very ideas of such revolutionary romantics as Voltaire and Rousseau which were designed to reveal the contradictions within a slave society. The application of the systems analysis of literature illustrates that the two-sided nature of romanticism was able to act as a vehicle for transmitting the tumultuous ideology of the age.[7] In "Systems Analysis in Literature," M. Khrapchenko points out that

> . . . the widespread inner resistance to new bourgeois relations between people was an opposition that existed in various strata of society in the initial stages of capitalism. At the same time it is important to characterise the noble and lofty ideals and hopes for the renovation of humanity concurrent with great social changes. *Both the resistance and the hopes were not homogeneous. Hence the heterogeneity of romanticism itself that continually amazes scholars and at times baffles them.*
>
> . . . In considering romanticism as an aesthetic system one takes into account first of all the artist's concentration upon the individual and the complicated collisions within the individual, the individual's private and social aspirations; the artist "liberates" man from a temporal, concrete historical context to better reveal his constant, "eternal" features.[8] [Italics mine.]

This heterogeneous nature of romanticism may at first seem inconsistent with a literature that describes the struggle for freedom, but as a vehicle, romanticism was two-sided: one side spoke of resistance to legitimate changes and the other of hopes for the renovation of the social order. In Caribbean slave experience there was collision within the individual's private and social aspirations as found in the artist in bourgeois society in Europe. In the slave society of the Caribbean, the writers' inner world— their aspirations for freedom—and the social conditions of slavery were in dialectical contradiction to each other. Hence artistic individual aspirations and the objective necessity of transforming the social reality existed simultaneously in a synthetic unity. Indeed, it was precisely the duty of revolutionary romantic authors to liberate the Caribbean in its darkest hours of oppression by depicting constant eternal features of man's human right for liberation and dignity.

Revolutionary romanticism in the Caribbean had as its essence the ideological content of the antislavery movement and saw its major task as the revelation of the contradictions and cruelty of this particular mode of production and the conditions of the oppressed as seen through the eyes of the representative individual slave, whether Maroon or freed man. In looking at the presentation of the romantic novel in the Caribbean, the total conditions of the slave experience, i.e., the psychological, moral and economic are seen through the eyes of a freed slave (e.g., *Cecilia Valdés*). In a slave narrative, the collective revolutionary consciousness of all the slaves is manifested in their readiness to seize the time when the occasion arose (e.g., *The Early Life of the Negro Poet*). The life of the Maroon depicts the continuous quest for liberty and the actual participation of the slaves in the liberation struggle (e.g., *Autobiography of a Runaway Slave*).

In all three works we see the contradictions inherent in the society. Excepting the author of *Cecilia Valdés*, the artists are unable to give an integrated picture of the society or to use their material in such a selective manner that it proposes a concrete liberation to man's alienated and unfree conditions, for in a slave society it was by definition virtually impossible for a critical realist to exist. However, the works do reveal revolutionary solidarity in the face of oppression and reflect the dialectic of the struggle for liberation.

Caribbean revolutionary romanticism, then, depicts the collective slave condition through the individual and particular eye of representatives of the slave classes. As a literary trend, one can define Caribbean revolutionary romanticism as "a definite period in the development of Caribbean literary unity conditioned by the development of Caribbean life and literature itself with a certain community in the approach to reality, its aesthetic perception, and the creative method employed. This literary trend begins with the romance, *Cecilia Valdés*.

Cecilia Valdés, sometimes subtitled "A Romance in Old Havana," is usually presented as the classical work in Cuban literature.[9] Whatever the work's defects, the author, Cirilo Villaverde, captured the conditions of urban slavery and dramatized its central concerns by developing the philosophical arguments presented on behalf of slavery to justify the exclusive economic conditions of the institution and then in turn showing the fallacies in these views. It is almost as if Villaverde's slaveholders present the same arguments to enslave the Africans that were used at the Court of Valladolid to enslave the Indians. Doña Rosa presents the arguments in defense of her husband, whose fortunes have been built by trafficking in African slaves. We hear about the advantages slavery should accrue to the "savages" through Christianizing the heathens. When upbraided about the evils of the institution, Doña Rosa says:

> Don't talk to me about your first principles or your beginnings or your ends or your Roman laws! They may say what they please; the truth is that what your father is doing and what Don Pedro Blanco is doing are not the same at all. He is over there, in the land where the savages live. He is the one who receives them in trade; he is the one who takes possession of them by barter or by luring them with some trick or other; he captures them and brings them here to be sold in this country. If there is any crime or wrongdoing, it is he who does it, not your father. And when it comes to that, far from doing anything bad or wicked, Gamboa does them a kindness, something for which he ought to be praised, because if he receives them and sells them, savages you understand, he does it so that they may be baptised and to give them a religion, which certainly they never had in their own country. (CV, p. 133)

This super profitable economic trade of human flesh has led to these spurious arguments in its defense and superhuman efforts to continue it. Slavery's horror does not begin only where the slaves are bought, for the horror and brutality of the middle passage must be reckoned with. Apart from rendering only the philosophical implications of the trade, the author goes back to that horrible journey and links the institution to its source. Don Cándido is a slave trader, and we see the machinations of the trade and a vision of the middle passage with its cruelty. For example, the slave ship, *Veloz*, bearing human cargo for Don Cándido and other Cuban slaveholders is intercepted by the English, and they throw 80 to 100 Africans overboard to prevent the slave ship's capture. Don Cándido reveals his loss:

> "Carricarte saw at once that only a miracle would prevent capture, so he determined to risk everything to save his ship. He gave the order to clear the decks so as to lighten the ship and allow it to work more freely. No sooner said than done. In a twinkling the casks of fresh water, quantities of tackle, rigging and cordage were heaved overboard and all the bales that were on deck."
>
> "The Africans, you mean?" cried Doña Rosa, throwing up her hands in horror. "Why, how frightful!"
>
> "Why, of course," continued Gamboa, with no loss of composure. "You

don't suppose the captain would risk capture of himself, his crew, and the rest of the cargo just to save 80 or 100 blacks, do you? By sacrificing them, he saved three times that number. He acted according to orders; save the ship and its papers at all costs. Moreover, he had to clear the deck to lighten the ship, as I told you. There was no time to lose. It was the only thing to do! Carricarte said so, and I believe him because he is an honest chap and has a high rating. When the brig was in the greatest danger, he had only the very ill or weak ones on deck, those who would have died anyway, and would have died sooner had they been returned to the hold, where they were packed like sardines, because they had to lock the hatches."

"The hatches!" repeated Doña Rosa, "you mean the lids which cover the openings in the deck leading down into the hold? So those who were down below were smothered to death. Poor innocent people!"

"Rubbish!" said Don Cándido, with exquisite scorn. "Nothing of the sort, my good woman. I'm beginning to think you've developed the notion that those sacks of coal feel and suffer like we do. No such thing. No indeed. How do they live in their own country? In caves or swamps. And what kind of air do they breathe in those places? Foul air or none at all. And do you know how they're brought here? All wedged together, each one seated between the legs of the one behind, two rows together with a space between each two rows, so that there is room to bring them food and water. And that doesn't kill 'em. Nearly all have to be handcuffed and quite a number have to be put in irons."

"What are irons, Cándido?"

"Well, I never! Are you just beginning to wake up? Stocks, woman, of course."

"I expect I didn't want to understand you, Cándido."

"All this and a lot more is the direct result of the unjust opposition of the English. Carricarte's only regret is that, in all the excitement and in the hurry to clear the decks, the sailors threw overboard a bright little black girl of twelve. She had already begun to say a few Spanish words. The king of the Gotto tribe gave her to him in exchange for a keg of Vich sausages. The queen gave him two kiddies of seven and eight for a sugar loaf and a case of tea for her private table."

"Angels in heaven!" exclaimed Doña Rosa, unable to contain herself. "And to think that perhaps they weren't baptised," she added. "In any case, those poor souls—"

"Fancy believing that those sacks of coal from Africa have a soul and that they're angels. Why, Rosa, that's blasphemy," interrupted her husband brusquely. "That's just how all these erroneous ideas start. One of the pretexts the English use to justify their efforts to stop the slave trade is just what you're saying. Once the world realizes that Negroes are animals and not human beings, we shall have eliminated their excuse for persecuting us. A similar situation occurred when the government in Spain prohibited the buying and selling of tobacco. A man who makes his livelihood in this business is chased by the *carabineros*. He drops his contraband cargo and gallops away, thus saving his horse and his own hide. Do you think the tobacco has a soul? I wish you'd realize that there's no difference between a bale of tobacco and a Negro, at least insofar as any capacity to feel is concerned. (CV, pp. 210-212)

The concept of the African as a "thing" was not new, but the vivid dramatization of this barbarity—the way the Spanish saw the Africans and the absolute inhumanity of the system—was new and important at the time. If the trade were super-profitable to the Spanish, it was the bane of the Africans. Hence there is both a strategy of open revolt and connivance. We hear Señor Uribe counseling José Dolores about a strategy of patient waiting.

> Conceal your feelings and be patient. Do like the dog when the wasps buzz around his head; show your teeth so they'll think you're smiling. Don't you see that they are the hammer and we the anvil? The white people came first, and they're eating the choice cuts; we, the coloured people, came later, and we gnaw the bones. Let 'em alone, my boy, and some day it'll be our turn. It can't last forever like that. Copy me. Don't you see me kiss many a hand that I'd like to see chopped off? Do you think it comes from my heart? Don't get any such notion, because the honest truth is that for a white man's word I wouldn't give a centavo, not even for the paper it's written on. (CV, pp. 146-147)

The novel also presents us with a very good account of both the internal and external aspects of slavery, and the economics of the institution and its fashioning of the superstructural relations of the society. All of the characters are controlled by this infernal system either for good or for evil; that is, either to oppress or to struggle against oppression. All of the baser instincts of the oppressing group (i.e., Don Cándido, Doña Rosa, Leonardo, et al.) are determined by this infernal institution. It is only the liberation struggle of the oppressed slaves that will reclaim the humanity of the Cuban and Caribbean men alike. Indeed, the noblest character in this whole drama of slavery is the African "Pedro the Carabalí," who is not only "the personification of pride," as he is called, but the living embodiment of that fierce determination to be free on the part of the African and the symbol of the struggle to retain one's humanity, in spite of all the attempts to destroy it. (CV, p. 412)

Apart from the sucessful integration of the economic aspects of slavery into the novel, Villaverde was able also to capture some of the superstructural aspects of slavery. The psychological trauma created by slavery is well depicted in the plight of Maria de Regla, who, having to nurse the baby of her slave mistress, is denied the normal human pleasure of nursing her own infant. Moreover, she is banished to the much harsher form of slave life in the country when she is found cuddling her own infant one night. It is in the recital of this episode by Maria to the polished recipients of the benefits of this system that one gets a glimpse of the traumatic nature of the slave experience:

"So you see, *Niñas*, what bad luck I had. I, a loving mother, forced to nurse the daughter of my *Señorita*, while the child of my own body, my first child, I was prohibited from nursing or even from taking in my arms to kiss her and warm her at my breast. God knows I have always liked children. If I nursed Cecilia well, I would nurse your Ladyship even better, for I loved you as if you were my own. But put yourself in my place, Niña Adela, and just think how I suffered, when I saw your Ladyship healthy, rosy, roly-poly, clean, lace caps, embroidered clothes, many little shirts of fine cambric, lace underclothes, little linen stockings and little silk shoes, sleeping in a mahogany cradle that the Master had ordered from the North, as a present.

"I saw your Ladyship in my arms or in *Señorita's* or in those of *Niña Antonica*, even in the Master's arms. When you would cry or complain of something, they turned the house upside down, and there weren't enough masters, friends, and slaves to run for the doctor, go to the pharmacy and attend to the child, until your little pain stopped and you were all right. Usually it was my fault, according to *Señorita*, when you cried, because your clothes pinched, because the water in the tub in which I bathed you was either too hot or cold, because I put a pin in wrong and it scratched you, and a thousand other things besides.

"Meanwhile, what about my daughter Dolores? Imagine how it broke my heart to see her thin, sickly, snivelly, dirty, nearly naked, crawling on the ground among the chickens in the patio, or between the horses' legs in the stable, or beside the stove used to heat the laundry irons, or in the kitchen with drops of hot lard falling on her, chewing on a chunk of bread or sucking rice moistened in milk that the woman who nursed her had wrapped in a dirty cloth to relieve her hunger. If she cried, Jesus! Instead of comforting her, *Señorita* would say: 'Take that little pickaninny into the kitchen! I can't stand her shrieks.' Dionisio didn't know how to take care of children, and he had his own work to do. Mamerta, who had charge of Dolores, was an old maid; she had no idea how to take care of children, never having had children of her own. She didn't know what a mother's love was. (CV, pp. 448-449)

This replacement of natural instincts with unnatural demands creates psychological displacement in the minds of so many slaves. In this subtle juxtaposition, the inhumanity of the system tramples upon the slave humanity and calls for Herculean strength to maintain sanity.

As depicted by Villaverde, a long intellectual tradition complements that of resistance in the society. Famous names from Cuban cultural history parade before the reader's eyes. The reader is impressed by the fact that Cuba has produced a long list of progressive thinkers who have had a profound impact on revolutionary ideas. Since many slaves who took part in the revolutionary process also helped shape intellectual life, it makes sense that the slave Juan Manzano is aware of Rousseau's and Voltaire's ideas.

In light of the argument made for revolutionary romanticism, it is interesting to observe that Villaverde does confess that "the only models I have been able to follow in sketching the various scenes of *Cecilia Valdés*, have been Scott and Manzoni."(CV, p. 16) In other words, Villaverde followed the historical scenes and customs of the period 1812–1831. Even though the basis of the work is historical and is closely fashioned "d'après nature," as he calls it, the major strength of the work is in the author's capacity to depict the essence of his time. This capacity to depict the slave experience with such tremendous force and vitality allows him to reveal with so much clarity the corresponding superstructural relations of the time.

It is in understanding the historical romances of Sir Walter Scott that we begin to perceive the beginnings of revolutionary romanticism in the Caribbean novel, whose major function, as we stated earlier, was to reveal or depict the major contradictions inherent in slavery, without necessarily suggesting any alternative or integrated vision of society. As a romanticist, Villaverde was able to present and portray in minute detail and great richness the historical color of the age of slavery. However, it would be erroneous if we saw only elements of romanticism in *Cecilia Valdés*, for there were also elements of "realism," as Villaverde himself tried to point out.

In speaking of the elements of realism in *Cecilia Valdés*, a knowledge of Sir Walter Scott's transition from romanticism to realism will help us to understand the process, as Villaverde saw it, and also help us to understand the presence of realism in his work. Speaking of Scott's transition, Suchkov comments:

> Walter Scott went through the same stages in his creative evolution as many other romantic writers. From an early interest in gathering and studying folklore material, he went on to investigate the history of the periods in which it was produced. But unlike the other romanticists, he did not rest content with admiring the mysteries of the folk soul as revealed in ancient beliefs, songs and tales, but analysed the objective conditions, both social and spiritual, that influenced the life of the people. Child of a tempestuous and fierce age, Walter Scott combined analytic study of the past, great erudition and a vast knowledge of the life, manners and customs of the past with a keen sense of history, presenting man in his novels not simply as a member of society but as a participant in the historical process. This represented a tremendous step forward.[10]

It is precisely this combination that Villaverde was able to capture in Cuba himself; that is, the life of the slave and slavery itself are presented and simultaneously submitted to a subtle, yet stinging criticism of the horrendous nature of the institution. This is done by juxtaposing the life of the slave with the life of the slave owner; by presenting the philosophical underpinnings of slavery as argued by the slavemasters with the nobility of the slave under oppression as he struggles for freedom and resolutely moves forward to emancipation through resistance. The characters in *Cecilia Valdés* are integrated into the "real" world, rather than, as in the traditional romantic novel, the spiritual world of the romantic hero, which had little or no relationship to the "real" world. It is this integration of a hero within this world—that is, the presentation of historical man (realistic), and the presentation of the life and customs of a people (romantic)—that we see the blending of the two worlds of realism and romanticism in *Cecilia Valdés*. Like the Scott hero, therefore, the Villaverde hero acts as historical man.

In this sense, *Cecilia Valdés* is closer to realism than Villaverde asserts in his introduction when he says:

> Far from inventing or pretending imaginary and unrealistic characters and scenes, I have carried realism *as I understand it*, to the point of presenting the principal characters of the novel with all their "hairs and ear-marks," as they vulgarly express it; clothed in the dress that they wore in their life time, the majority under their true Christian surnames; speaking in the same language they spoke in the historical scenes in which they appear, copying as far as possible, *d'après nature*, their physical and moral features, in order that those who knew them in the flesh or by tradition should recognize them without difficulty and should at least say: "The resemblance is undeniable." (CV, p. 16) [Italics mine.]

These comments seem more the formula of naturalism than realism. This very emphasis on naturalism causes one of the work's major weaknesses, for at the end of the novel the reader is left feeling that Villaverde has not changed the African from "thing" to "person," a transition we do see in Richard Wright's *Native Son*, in which Bigger Thomas, regarded as "thing" throughout the novel, later affirms his personhood:

> "I didn't want to kill!" Bigger shouted. "But what I killed for, I *am*! It must've been pretty deep in me to make me kill! I must have felt it awful hard to murder. . . ."
> Max lifted his hand to touch Bigger, but did not.
> "No; no; no. . . . Bigger, not that. . . . " Max pleaded despairingly.
> "What I killed for must've been good!" Bigger's voice was full of frenzied anguish. "It must have been good! When a man kills, it's for something. . . . I didn't know I was really alive in this world until I felt things hard enough to kill for 'em. . . . It's the truth, Mr. Max. I can say it now, 'cause I'm going to die. I

know what I'm saying real good and I know how it sounds. But I'm all right. I feel all right when I look at it that way. . . . "[11]

Throughout the course of the novel Bigger becomes aware of himself, through certain acts of violence. However, one does not get the same effect in *Cecilia Valdés*, for at its end, José Dolores, an angry rival, kills Leonardo; Cecilia is incarcerated in Paula Hospital for a year; Dionisio is condemned to ten years in penal servitude for killing Tondo; Don Cándido, the slave trader, apparently goes away scot-free; and we do not know what happens to Doña Rosa. Nothing is resolved except that we are left with a kind of Byronic romantic pathos—an essentially tragic process at the end of which the conflicts and contradictions are not resolved; instead one is left with chaos, unpremeditated rashness and a certain amount of meaningless violence.

We do know that Villaverde followed true-to-life incidents and people, and we are indebted to him for an accurate and vivid presentation of Havana and plantation slavery. But real-life characters and incidents do not always make a good novel. What does make a good novel is the marshalling of all of these elements into a creative work in an attempt to resolve some of the contradictions or paradoxes extracted from the real life situation, to propose some concrete liberation for the oppressed characters and to convey a positive and important point arising from the creative confluence of historical data. But *Cecilia Valdés* leaves us with unresolved contradictions and the feeling that nothing has happened to the novel's most despicable character, i.e., the slave trader. The novel's end sounds like a legalistic summation brought together in half a page that reminds the reader that all has not been lost.

The ending violates the Fanon principle which states that: "The colonised man who writes for his people ought to use the past with the intention of opening the future, as an invitation to action and a basis for hope."[12]

The virtues of *Cecilia Valdés* are many, for it is an indispensable document of the period, but we must consider the significant failure cited above as we look at the organic development of Caribbean literature. Wheras *Cecilia Valdés*' presentation of slavery is generalized against the larger banner of historical time, in Juan Francisco Manzano's *The Early Life of the Negro Poet*, which was written in 1840 and takes place in Cuba, we see slavery through the eyes of a slave himself. The narrative moves from the depiction of Juan from a "faithful slave . . . an humble, submissive being . . . to the most discontented [being] of mankind." (ELNP, p. 86) And even though he vacillates in his behavior to the point where he throws himself at the feet of the mistress, he says, once "the idea of

freedom took possession of my mind . . . I thought myself already free."
(ELNP, p. 87) The narrative moves towards the eventual liberation of the
slave in spite of any repercussion that might occur if he were caught.

The narrative opens with the possibility of the "coatacion" liberating
Manzano's parents and Manzano enjoying a pleasant life amidst the
surroundings of his kind mistress. His mistress soon dies, and Manzano is
treated with the same cruelty as other slaves. This new state gives a specific
picture of slavery since even in his childhood life of privilege, Manzano
experiences cruelty. He recounts:

> . . . I led a life of so much misery, daily receiving blows on the face, that
> often made the blood spout from both my nostrils; no sooner would I hear
> myself called than I would begin to shiver, so that I could hardly keep on my
> legs, but supposing this to be only shamming on my part, frequently would I
> receive from a stout Negro lashes in abundance. (ELNP, p. 61)

Manzano tells of this grief and shame at seeing his mother, on orders
from the master, "stripped by the negroes and thrown down to be
scourged." (ELNP, p. 66) Accused of stealing a capon, Manzano is sent to
the mayoral, who chastizes him. Manzano describes the occasion:

> With sad forebodings, and an oppressed heart, being accustomed to deliver
> myself up on such occasions, away I went trembling. When I arrived at the
> door, I saw the mayoral of the Molino, and the mayoral of the Ingenio,
> together. I delivered my message to the first, who said, "Come in man," I
> obeyed, and was going to repeat it again, when Señor Dominguez, the mayoral
> of the Ingenio took hold of my arm, saying, "it is to me, to whom you are sent,"
> took out of his pocket a thin rope, tied my hands behind me as a criminal,
> mounted his horse, and commanded me to run quick before him, to avoid
> either my mother or my brothers seeing me. Scarcely had I run a mile before
> the horse, stumbling at every step, when two dogs that were following us, fell
> upon me; one taking hold of the left side of my face pierced it through, and the
> other lacerated my left thigh and leg in a shocking manner, which wounds are
> open yet, notwithstanding it happened twenty-four years ago. The mayoral
> alighted on the moment, and separated me from their grasp, but my blood
> flowed profusely, particularly from my leg—he then pulled me by the rope,
> making use at the same time, of the most disgusting language; this pull partly
> dislocated my right arm, which at times pains me yet. Getting up, I walked as
> well as I could, till we arrived at the Ingenio. They put a rope round my neck,
> bound up my wounds, and put me in the stocks. At night, all the people of the
> estate were assembled together and arranged in a line, I was put in the middle
> of them, the mayoral and six negroes surrounded me, and at the word "upon
> him," they threw me down; two of them held my hands, two my legs, and the
> other sat upon my back. They then asked me about the missing capon, and I

did not know what to say. Twenty-five lashes were laid on me, they then asked me again to tell the truth. I was perplexed; at last, thinking to escape further punishment, I said, "I stole it." "What have you done with the money?" was the next question, and this was another trying point. "I bought a hat," "Where is it?" "I bought a pair of shoes." "No such thing," and I said so many things to escape punishment, but all to no purpose. Nine successive nights the same scene was repeated, and every night I told a thousand lies. After the whipping, I was sent to look after the cattle and work in the fields. Every morning my mistress was informed of what I said the previous night. (ELNP, pp. 69-70)

This account corresponds to the horror of the American slave experience, an account of which is given by Theodore Weld in *American Slavery As It Is,* which sold over 100,000 copies in its first year of publication. One of the 1,000 eyewitness accounts by Sarah Grimke, which corresponds roughly to this same period, reads;

A handsome mulatto woman, about 18 or 20 years of age, whose independent spirit could not brook the degradation of slavery, was in the habit of running away: for this offense she had been repeatedly sent by her master and mistress to be whipped by the keeper of the Charleston work-house. This had been done with such inhuman severity, as to lacerate her back in a most shocking manner; a finger could not be laid between the cuts. But the love of liberty was too strong to be annihilated by torture; and, as a last resort, she was whipped at several different times, and kept a close prisoner. A heavy iron collar, with three long prongs projecting from it was placed round her neck, and a strong and sound front tooth was extracted, to serve as a mark to describe her, in case of escape. Her sufferings at this time were agonizing; she could lie in no position but on her back, which was sore from scourgings, as I can testify, from personal inspection, and her only place of rest was the floor, on a blanket. These outrages were committed in a family where the mistress daily read the scriptures, and assembled her children for family worship. She was accounted, and was really, so far as alms-giving was concerned, a charitable woman, and tender hearted to the poor; and yet this suffering slave, who was the seamstress of the family, was continually in her presence, sitting in her chamber to sew, or engaged in her other household work, with her lacerated and bleeding back, her mutilated mouth, and heavy iron collar, without, so far as appeared, exciting any feelings of compassion.[13]

American Slavery As It Is was published in 1839 and *The Early Life of the Negro Poet* in 1840. These graphic firsthand accounts of the system's barbarity should dampen revisionist works that through econometrics or sloppy scholarship try to depict the slave condition as attractive.[14] *The Early Life of the Negro Poet* poses an important point vis-à-vis the nature of the slavery and the ideological underpinnings of the Cuban revolutionary struggle in particular and the Caribbean resistance in general. The following episode illustrates the essence of the experience:

> The second time that I was at Matanzas, there never passed a day without bringing some trouble to me; no, I cannot relate the incredible hardships of my life, a life full of sorrows! My heart sickened through sufferings, once after having received many blows on the face, and that happened almost daily; my mistress said, "I will make an end of you before you are of age;" these words left such an impression on my mind, that I asked my mother the meaning of them, who quite astonished, and after making me repeat them twice over, said, "my son, God is more powerful than the devil." She said no more about it; but this and some hints I received from the old servants of the house, began to unfold the true meaning of her expressions. On another occasion, going to be chastised, for I do not remember what trifle, a gentleman, always kind to me, interceded for me; but my mistress said to him, "mind, Señor, this boy will be one day worse than Rousseau and Voltaire, remember my words." These strange names, and the way that my mistress expressed herself made me very anxious to know what sort of bad people they were; but when I found out, that they were enemies of God, I became more uneasy, for since my infancy I was taught to love and fear God, and my trust in him was such, that I employed always part of the night praying God to lighten my sufferings, and to preserve me from mischief on the following day, and if I did anything wrong I attributed it to my lukewarmness in prayers, or that I might have forgotten to pray; and I firmly believe that my prayers were heard, and to this I attribute the preservation of my life once, on occasion of my running away from Matanzas to Havana, as I will relate hereafter. (ELNP, pp. 76-77)

This episode postulates the nature of religion as opposed to the contemporary ideas of bourgeois democracy as a justification for slavery. Religion as a natural and metaphysical support for slavery is counterpoised against the mistress's conscious attempt to break the slave's will. This counters Enlightenment ideas implicit in Voltaire where rational notions were to "transform heterogeneous egoistic interests and instincts that still guided human actions into some organic harmonious whole."[15]

Advocates of Voltaire had to be enemies of God since they opposed religious unreason, which included slavery's philosophical and ideological underpinnings. That Manzano knew "these strange names" and was "anxious to know what sort of bad people they were," suggests their effect. Having a mere notion of the ideas of either Voltaire or Rousseau, Manzano would have been forced to pose the questions of liberty in quite a different light, which would auger well for another interpretation of the system of slavery. Indeed, his automatic recoil from the ideas of Voltaire and his excessive denunciation of them coupled with his almost *unreasoned*

103

attempts to affirm his fealty to God doesn't seem to ring quite true to a perceptive reader, for there is, in the passage quoted before, just a tinge of unbelief that gives the reader a clue to quite another kind of impression that Voltaire and Rousseau had made upon Manzano.

But if Voltaire argued for the inculcation of the rational as opposed to the irrational and the metaphysical (religion), Rousseau argued for the natural freedom of man in a society that preserved many inequalities. Rousseau's words, "Man was born free, and he is everywhere in chains." must have had as strong an impetus for Manzano as Abbé Raynal's words had for Toussaint and as Viriatus' insurrection had for Enriquillo. Following the bourgeois revolutions in France and the U.S.A., Rousseau's cry rang out as a "tocsin" of the age. As Suchkov puts it:

> This powerful formula proclaiming freedom to be the natural right of natural man expressed the very essence of the age, and was born of the revolutionary ferment sweeping Europe on the eve of the French Revolution. It demanded emancipation from the suffocating fundamental spiritual principles of feudalism that were bringing people so much misery, and recognized the need to change the structure of society.[16]

Indeed the serf stood in the same relation to his feudal masters as the slave did to the slave master, allowing, of course, for some differences in the two modes. In reading about the misery and pain of the millions of European serfs in Rousseau's world, Manzano needed only to substitute "serf" for "slave," "slavery" for "feudalism" and "feudal lord" for "slave master," and Rousseau might have been talking about Manzano's situation. The call to revolutionary action must have entered Manzano's mind. It is difficult to be exposed to these ideas as Manzano was and not be influenced by them, but, still, it is natural to recoil and return to the safe mantle of religion. Perhaps Manzano's need for publication and the need for further emancipation had something to do with his lukewarm response to Voltaire and Rousseau in *The Early Life of the Negro Poet*.

Manzano's intense boyhood desire to pursue ideas seems to support this position. The following passage reveals the passion with which he studied:

> As soon as day dawned, I used to get up, prepare his [master's] table, armchair and books, and I adapted myself so well to his customs, and manners that I began to give myself up to study. From his book of rhetoric I learnt by heart a lesson every day, which I used to recite like a parrot, without knowing the meaning. (ELNP, p. 78)

Not satisfied only with reading, Manzano spent "the hours from five to ten every evening, exercising my hand to write and in daytime I used to copy

the inscriptions at the bottom of pictures hung on the walls." (ELNP, p. 79)
This is not the action of a man who recoils from an idea that holds his mind,
least of all when forbidden by his masters, who

> advised me to drop that pastime, as not adapted to my situation in life, and that
> it would be more useful to me to employ my time in needle-work, a business
> that indeed at the same time I did not neglect. In vain was I forbidden to write,
> for when everybody went to bed I used to light a piece of candle, and then at my
> leisure I copied the best verses, thinking that if I could imitate these, I would
> become a poet. (ELNP, p. 79)

In the presence of the mistress who has been cruel to him, Manzano first
affirms his new awareness by asking for "paper and ink in order to advertise
for a new master."[17] This is a new level of critical activity, the conscious
awareness of a man who intends to use newly acquired talents to liberate
himself. Such a man would not have recoiled from the ideas of Voltaire and
Rousseau.

Manzano's reference as a slave to Rousseau and Voltaire has important
implications for later Cuban and Caribbean revolutionary thought. The
intellectual heritage depicted in *Cecilia Valdés* and Montejo's
revolutionary activities and his respect for Marti and Maceo all anticipate
Castro's *History Will Absolve Me*, the culmination of this trend of
Caribbean revolutionary thought. For it is important to point out that
when Fidel Castro began his revolution, like Manzano and Montejo, he
was not a Marxist-Leninist, but a national-democrat, as his speech,
History Will Absolve Me, attests.[18]

The last four lines of Manzano's narrative contain one of its most
important points. When all the people are in church, a free servant advises
Manzano, who has been subjected to more cruelty: "Juan, my friend, if you
suffer it is your fault; you are treated worse than the meanest slave; make
your escape and present yourself before the Captain General at Havana,
and he will do justice." (ELNP, pp. 90-91) Even with the assistance of the
free servant, who provides spur and saddle, Manzano is uneasy at leaving
his brothers. At midnight on a cold and rainy night, Manzano thinking
himself alone, attempts his escape, only to be greeted with words of
solidarity:

> When I was going away, I heard the sound of a voice saying, "God bless you,
> make haste," I thought that nobody saw me, but as I knew afterwards, I was
> seen by several of the Negroes, but nobody offered any impediment to my
> flight. (ELNP, p. 92)

The narrative ends here. Manzano is helped in his escape by the free servant and the Negroes who reinforce his courage. It is this solidarity of the oppressed classes—slave, free servant and Maroon—that will provide the cohesive front for liberation. The ideological and philosophical underpinnings for a new society were already at work, and given the combination of the two, the road towards the liberation of the society was being carefully forged.

The Early Life of the Negro Poet shows us the plight of a slave, who, freed, becomes a Maroon. However, *The Autobiography of a Runaway Slave* (as told to Miguel Barnet) shows the life of a Maroon. When Miguel Barnet confesses that he has paraphrased Esteban Montejo's recollections, he *mediates* between Montejo's *immediate experience* and the *recorded or presented* account of Montejo's life. One must keep this antipathy between the interpreter (Barnet) and the author (Montejo) in mind while reading the autobiography and examine the motives ascribed to Montejo. For example, when Barnet talks about the poetic "surrealistic slant" of Montejo's vision, we must be on guard. Montejo's experiences during his 105 years were in no way surrealist, for those years contained constant struggle for liberation.

The reader must be on guard against the subtracting of revolutionary content and the addition of anti-ideological form as happens when Barnet, studying a struggle for human dignity, concentrates on things "like agricultural methods, ceremonies, fiestas, food and drink?" (ARS, p. 68) As valuable as these details might be, this takes a deliberate ideological stance in the interpretation of the story.

Barnet continues, "The Ten Years' War was a failure for the Cubans, *but at least slavery had been abolished* (Italics mine)." This sentence is curious. A failure for which class of Cubans? Certainly the Ten Years' War was an unqualified success for the freed slaves. The reader must guard against Barnet's ideological bias and seek the authentic Montejo, who comes through in spite of Barnet.

The Autobiography of a Runaway Slave continues the gnosiological version of the Caribbean life presented in *Cecilia Valdés* and *The Early Life of a Negro Poet*. Montejo, a Maroon, perceives the world as material. At one point he calls it nature, but his social consciousness is fashioned by the natural world; in this context one can understand his rejection of the imposed Spanish religion and the time of his rejection of slavery. Continuing the political tradition that will climax in Castro's *History Will Absolve Me*, he opens the work with the following observation:

> You see, I know it all depends on Nature, everything comes from Nature, even what can't be seen. We men cannot do such things because we are the subjects of a God, of Jesus Christ, who is the one most talked about. Jesus Christ wasn't

born in Africa, he came from Nature herself, as the Virgin Mary was a señorita. (ARS, p. 13)

Montejo asserts that everything has its basis in Nature—that is, the material world—even though we cannot fully explain everything within this world. He dispenses with metaphysical speculation by asserting that Jesus came from Nature and that even the Virgin Mary was a woman, a *señorita*. Montejo continues:

> I used to dream a good bit in those days, but I never dreamed visions. A dream comes through the imagination. If you think hard about a certain plantain tree and look at it, tomorrow or the day after you will dream about it. I dreamt about work and women. Work is a bad thing to dream about. It frightens you, and then the next day you think you are still dreaming, and that is when you catch your finger in a machine or slip. (ARS, p. 69)

Here Montejo holds that social consciousness (imagination, as he calls it) has its basis in the material conditions of life, that even our dreams are related directly to the conscious stuff of the material world and reflect the compendium of real images to which we are exposed every day. This point would have important implications for the philosophical basis of Cuban economic liberation.

This world view, which sees everything as emanating from Nature, corresponds to an analogous notion prevalent during the French Enlightenment and is even referred to by Manzano. According to Maria Petrosyan,

> The French enlighteners believed that the world should worship man, if only because man alone possessed self-awareness, awareness of joy and grief, of the just and the unjust, the ability to conceive of life and death. This alone warranted the greatest possible concern for the individual.
>
> *Rejecting the religious, spiritualistic explanation of the origin of man, the French enlighteners laid special emphasis on the idea that man is part of nature and there is nothing supernatural or mystical about him. The standards of moral conduct are, therefore, to be deduced from the laws of nature and not from "divine principle."*[19] [Italics mine.]

This rejection of the "religious, spiritualistic explanation of the origin of man" explains Montejo's hatred of religion and of the priests' role in Cuba and explains the way he affirms his unequivocal political position. It is common knowledge that religion and priests played a significant and inglorious role in maintaining the colonial and slave systems. Montejo's sentiments and testimony give unequivocal support to this contention. He gives numerous examples of the priests' cruelty, distortions of the Master's teachings and ways religion is used as a rationale for oppression:

> The priest came in the morning and started praying and kept it up for hours. I hardly understood a world and didn't pay much attention to it. To be honest, I have never cared for priests. Some of them were the next thing to criminals. They flirted with pretty white women and slept with them, they were lecherous and pious at once. If they had a child they would pass it off as a godson or a nephew; they hid them under their cassocks and never said, 'This is my son.'
>
> They kept tags on the Negroes, though, and if a black woman gave birth she had to send for the priest within three days or she would be in hot water with the plantation owner. This was how all the children came to be Christians. (ARS, p. 66)

The actions of the priest in this description correspond to Ferdinand Oyono's portrayal of their behavior in *Boy!*, set in French Africa. This suggests that religion played a significant and analogous role as an instrument of oppression in Africa and the United States, as well as in the Caribbean. Two episodes from *Boy!* will suffice. The first portrays the skillful manipulation of religion to ensure obedience of enslaved Africans:

> The new Commandant needs a boy. Father Vandermayer told me to report to the Residence tomorrow. I am glad because I have not been able to bear life at the Mission since Father Gilbert died. Of course it is a good riddance for Father Vandermayer as well . . . .
>
> I shall be the Chief European's boy. The dog of the King is the King of Dogs.
>
> I shall leave the Mission this evening. From now on I shall live with my brother-in-law in the location. A new life is starting for me.
>
> O Lord, Thy will be done . . . .
>
> At last it has happened. The Commandant has definitely taken me into his service. It was midnight, I had finished my work and was getting ready to go back to the location when the Commandant told me to follow him into his office. It was a terrible moment for me.
>
> After he had looked at me for a long while, he asked me point-blank if I were a thief.
>
> 'No, Sir,' I answered.
>
> 'Why aren't you a thief?'
>
> 'Because I do not want to go to hell.'
>
> He seemed taken aback by my answer. He tossed his head in disbelief.
>
> 'Where did you learn that?'
>
> 'I am a Christian, Sir,' I told him, and proudly showed him the St. Christopher medal I wear round my neck.
>
> 'So, you are not a thief because you don't want to go to hell?'
>
> 'Yes, Sir.'
>
> 'What is it like, hell?'

'Well, Sir, it is flames and snakes and the Devil with horns. There is a picture of hell in my prayer book . . . I . . . I . . . can show it to you.'

I was going to pull the little prayer book out of the back pocket of my shorts but the Commandant made a sign to stop me. He watched me for a minute through the wreathes of smoke he was puffing into my face. He sat down. I bowed my head. I could feel his eyes on me. He crossed his legs and uncrossed them. He signalled me to a chair opposite to him. He leant towards me and lifted up my chin. He gazed into my eyes and went on.

'Good, good, Joseph, we shall be friends.'

'Yes, Sir. Thank you, Sir.'

'But if you steal, I shan't wait till you go to hell. It's too far. . . .'

'Yes sir. It's . . . Where is it, sir?'

I had never asked myself the question. My master was amused to see my puzzlement. He shrugged and leant against the back of his chair.

'So you don't know where this hell is where you're afraid you'll go and burn?'

'It's next to Purgatory, Sir. It's . . . . in the sky.'

'My master smothered a laugh. Then, serious again, he pierced me with his panther eyes.

'Well done! There we are then. I think you see why I can't wait till "small Joseph go burn in hell".'

The Commandant imitated the pidgin used by native soldiers. He put on a strange voice. I thought he was very funny. I coughed hard so as not to laugh. He went on, not noticing.

'If you steal from me I shall skin you alive.'

'Yes, Sir, I know, Sir. I didn't say that just now, Sir, because I took that for granted, Sir. . . .'

'All right, all right,' said the Commandant, impatiently.

He got up and began to walk round me.

'You're a clean lad,' he said, looking me over carefully. 'No jiggers. Your shirt is clean. No scabies.'[20]

The second episode puts the case against barbarity, Christianity and enforced slavery more succinctly, and their consequent rejection in more forceful terms: after watching the cruelty to which his companions are subjected, Toundi reflects sadly

M. Moreau is right, we must have hard heads. When Ndjangoula brought down his rifle butt the first time, I thought their skulls would shatter. I could not hold myself from shaking as I watched. It was terrible. I thought of all the priests, all the pastors, all the white men, who come to save our souls and preach love of our neighbours. Is the white man's neighbour only other white men? Who can go on believing the stuff we are served up in the churches when things happen like I saw today. . .

It will be the usual thing. M. Moreau's suspects will be sent to the 'Blackman's Grave' where they will spend a few days painfully dying. Then they will be buried naked in the prisoners' cemetery. On Sunday, the priest will say, 'Dearly beloved brethren, pray for all those prisoners who die without making their peace with God.' M. Moreau will present his upturned topee to the faithful. Everyone will put in a little more than he had intended. All the money goes to the whites. They are always thinking up new ways to get back what little money they pay us.

How wretched we are.[21]

This was in Africa. The same case can be made for the United States, where another Maroon, William Wells Brown, describes the alliance between church and state and how church ideology legitimizes the political position of the state and maintains the social order. In Brown's *Clotel*, the Reverend Hintz Snyder delivers his regular Sunday morning sermon to slaves on a typical plantation, taking his text directly from the Bible:

> "All things whatsoever ye would that men should do unto you, do ye even so unto them; that is, do by all mankind just as you would desire they should do by you, if you were in their place and they in yours."[22]

He informs the slaves that God placed their masters and mistresses over them and that they should obey their earthly masters as they would their heavenly master. He continues:

> *Take care that you do not fret or murmur, grumble or repine at your condition; for this will not only make your life uneasy, but will greatly offend Almighty God.* Consider that it is not yourselves, it is not the people that you belong to, it is not the men who have brought you to it, but *it is the will of God who hath by his providence made you servants, because, no doubt, he knew that condition would be best for you in this world, and help you the better towards heaven, if you would but do your duty in it.* So that any discontent at your not being free, or rich, or great, as you see some others, is quarrelling with your heavenly Master, and finding fault with God himself, who hath made you what you are, and hath promised you as large a share in the kingdom of heaven as the greatest man alive, if you will but behave yourself aright, and do the business he hath set you about in this world honestly and cheerfully. . . . Riches and power have proved the ruin of many an unhappy soul, by drawing away the heart and affections from God, and fixing them on mean and sinful enjoyments; so that, when God, who knows our hearts better than we know them ourselves, sees that they would be hurtful to us, and therefore keeps them from us, it is the greatest mercy and kindness he could show us. . . .
> . . . Besides, you really have a great advantage over most white people, who have not only the care of their daily labour upon their hands, but the care of looking forward and providing necessaries for tomorrow and next day, and of clothing and bringing up their children, and of getting food and raiment for as many of you as belong to their families, which often puts them to great

difficulties, and distracts their minds so as to break their rest, and takes off their thoughts from the affairs of another world. Whereas you are quite eased from all these cares, and have nothing but your daily labour to look after, and, when that is done, take your needful rest. Neither is it necessary for you to think of laying up anything against old age, as white people are forced to do; for the laws of the country have provided that you shall not be turned off when you are past labour, but shall be maintained, while you live, by those you belong to, whether you are able to work or not. . . .

Lastly, you should serve your masters faithfully, because of their goodness to you. See to what trouble they have been on your account. Your fathers were poor ignorant and barbarous creatures in Africa, and the whites fitted out ships at great trouble and expense and brought you from that benighted land to Christian America, where you can sit under your own vine and fig tree and no one molest or make you afraid. Oh, my dear black brothers and sisters, you are indeed a fortunate and a blessed people. Your masters have many troubles that you know nothing about. If the banks break, your masters are sure to lose something. If the crops turn out poor, they lose by it. If one of you die, your master loses what he paid for you, while you lose nothing. Now let me exhort you once more to be faithful.[23]

The priests who minister these explicit injunctions upon the slaves knew they had to provide the necessary psychological and intellectual *raison d'etre* for the slavery system wherever it existed. It is important to observe that where Manzano was forced to recoil from the liberal doctrines of Voltaire and Rousseau, Brown used their doctrines of the natural rights of man to argue for the freedom of the slaves and to contest what he considered the false doctrines of the church.[24]

Whereas Manzano accepts the religious underpinnings of the system in *The Early Life of the Negro Poet*, in *The Autobiography of a Runaway Slave* Montejo vigorously rejects such a religious base to slavery and exposes religion's function in a slave society:

The priests interfered in everything. If they said a Negro was troublesome, he had to watch out, otherwise he would find someone ready to dispose of him at the first available opportunity.

Religion was strong at Ariosa. There was a church nearby, but I never went because I knew the priests *were the real supporters of the Inquisition in Cuba*; I say this because the priests were known to do certain things. They were devils with women. They turned the sacristy into a brothel. Anyone who has lived in Ariosa knows the stories, they even got to the barracoons. I know quite a few, and some things I saw myself.

The priest put women in dungeons, in holes where they had torturers ready to murder them. Other dungeons were full of water and the poor wretches drowned. This has been told me many times.

I saw priests with loose women who slept with them and afterwards said,

"Father, a blessing." They also talked at Ariosa of what life was like in the churches and monasteries. The priests were like other men, but they had all the gold, and they didn't spend it. I never saw a priest enjoying himself in a tavern. They shut themselves up in their churches and there they wasted away. They made collections every year for the church, for the saints' vestments and flowers. (ARS, p. 68)

A more vivid picture than Montejo's of the priests' reactionary role cannot be given, in spite of Barnet's interpretation. Not only were the priests viciously cruel but also they thwarted the people's drive for full independence. These are very revealing statements by someone who was perceived to be anti-ideological. Montejo is careful to state that "Negroes were never any of these things, least of all priests. I never saw a black priest. The priesthood was for whites of Spanish descent. You had to be Spanish before you could even become a watchman, although a watchman does nothing but keep an eye on things." (ARS, p. 66) After establishing that blacks were never permitted to be priests, Montejo continues by relating the cruelty of the Spanish priests and their participation in the oppression of the blacks. But the perspicacious reader sees elements of distinctions between oppressor and oppressed classes coming through in Montejo's analysis. Montejo does recognize that one had to be of Spanish origin to be a priest, lawyer or even a watchman. One must be other than of Negro origin to gain privileges in the society. It is in his resentment against religion that Montejo establishes his fealty to the oppressed classes.

Another consideration must be taken into account in reading Montejo's autobiography, for one can argue that Montejo was more political than Barnet presented him. We know Barnet paraphrased the work; according to Barnet's own testimony, his particular concern was "a story" from an "anti-ideological standpoint," (ARS, p. 7) yet in spite of Barnet, the autobiography is full of ideological and political content. Any analysis of Montejo's thoughts establishes him as an intensely political man. He was a great patriot, a lover of liberty and of a free Cuba. The reader who overlooks this misreads the autobiography. The keenness of Montejo's political vision gives the work its rich tonal qualities and underlies the structure of the novel. Montejo is revealed as a man of decided views, including disgust with Americans and an intense dislike of his oppressors. He is the link between Manzano and Castro and presents the pulse of the masses before revolution when he reveals the intense feelings of the people for their national liberation:

People can't imagine how inflammable the country was during those years. Everyone was constantly talking of rebellion, war was approaching, but I think most people were not sure it would begin. A lot of them were saying that Spain didn't have much longer to run, the rest kept their mouths shut or hid their heads in a piss-pot. I didn't say anything myself, although I was glad about the revolution and I admired the brave men who were risking their lives for it. The most popular of them were the anarchists, who received their orders from Spain, although they were fighting to free Cuba. They were something like the *nañigos*, very united, and did everything together. They were immensely brave. People were always talking about them. After the war the anarchists became very important in Cuba, but I stopped keeping up with them then. One thing none of us knew about was this annexationism you hear about nowadays. *What all of us wanted, as Cubans, was the freedom of Cuba. We wanted the Spanish to go and leave us alone. 'Freedom or Death,' people said, or 'Free Cuba.'* (ARS, pp. 87-88) [Italics mine.]

This sentiment runs throughout the autobiography. Montejo's desire to be free, his unbounded admiration for those who fight for liberty and his unrelieved damnation of those who oppose it permeate the autobiography. For him, "Martí, the patriot of Tampa and the finest man in Cuba" (ARS, p. 90) was perhaps the only one who stood one notch below Antonio Maceo, for whom Montejo has unparalleled praise and admiration. It is difficult to believe that Montejo wrote only a line or two about Martí and yet so much on the bandits, who performed Robin Hood-like roles, and on people like Manuel García, who contributed handsomely to the War of Independence.

One never ceases to be amazed by Montejo's acute political and social awareness and his implicit understanding of the issues. He relates religion and politics in what at first seems an astonishing insight for a slave until the reader understands Montejo's development. He tells the following story:

The raffles always took place during Holy Week, with the support of the priests themselves. Even today raffles are a giant fraud, especially when organized by the Church. About ten years ago I went with all the old veterans on parade to a church near Arroyo Apolo where there are lots of honey-berry bushes. We were invited by the priests. One of them, the one who said mass, *tried to win over the old men with the words of Christ and stuff like that.* He actually said right in the middle of mass that all communists should be exterminated and that they were the children of Satan. This put me in a rage, *because I had been a member of the Popular Socialist Party* (the name of Cuba's Communist Party until the reorganization of the Revolution) *for many years on account of its plans and ideals, particularly the welfare of the workers.* (ARS, p. 118) [Italics mine.]

Here a runaway slave, a member of the Socialist Party, recognizes at a glance the workers' and liberation fighters' arch enemies. Montejo takes his stand by counterposing his enthusiastic support for the Communist Party with the opposition that the priest demonstrated against them.

Montejo's greatness is his incisive understanding of his duty to his country and to himself. There are many incitements to patriotism and pride, any one of them a gem with Montejo's concept of duty equalling or surpassing the patriotic sentiments of Martí, Marceo or Castro. He articulates a man's duty to his country and to his fellow man:

> The fact is, the war was necessary. The dead would have died anyway, and this way they were dying for a purpose. I stayed alive by chance, it seems my time hadn't yet come. The gods send different tasks to each of us. I talked about all this now and I can laugh about it, but in the thick of the fighting, with dead bodies all over the place, bullets and cannon balls and all hell let loose, it was different. The war was needed. It was wrong that so many jobs and privileges should fall into Spanish hands, or that women should have to sleep with Spaniards to get work. None of this was right. You never saw a Negro lawyer, because they said Negroes weren't good for anything except the forest. You never saw a Negro school master. It was all kept for white Spaniards, even the white creoles were pushed aside. I saw this happen. A watchman with nothing to do except walk up and down, call the hour and put out the lights had to be a Spaniard. It was the same everywhere. There was no freedom. I realized this when the leaders explained it all to us. This was why we had to go to war. (ARS, p. 132)

This profound call for social justice emanates from the experiences of Montejo's life. The autobiography's components form a web that includes a dynamic and revolutionary content and creates a tension forcing ideological content and artistic form to bristle with concrete images of social injustice. The verbal fabric of the work gives its ideological content a tonality and emotional coloring and holds these two aspects in dynamic tension, creating a synthetic unity of overwhelming cohesion. It is impossible to read Montejo's lines without being immediately captured by the sense of communal solidarity (like that found at the end of *The Early Life of the Negro Poet*) and without recognizing Montejo's passionate desire for freedom:

> Whenever I see one of those Negro elders in my mind, I see him fighting. They didn't talk about what they were fighting for, or why, they just went and did it. It was in defence of their lives, of course. If you asked them how they felt, they said, 'Free Cuba, I'm a liberator.' None of them wanted to continue under Spanish rule. You can swear on your mother's grave that's true. None of them wanted to be shackled again, or eating jerked beef or cutting cane at dawn. So they took up arms. (ARS, p. 131)

Montejo found his greatest measure in this perceptive understanding of the dynamics of an oppressed society, which led to a tradition of resistance that grew into the national liberation movement in the Caribbean. This legacy of the early Caribbean/Spanish literary experience would yield to the French in the next phase of the development of the Caribbean experience.

VII

THE TRANSITION:
Ainsi parla l'oncle,
Batouala, Banjo, Masters of the Dew,
Pigments, Return to my Native Land

ALTHOUGH writing of the Spanish Caribbean dominated Caribbean literature in the nineteenth century with its antislavery and Indianist focus, by the late nineteenth and early twentieth century, literature of the French Caribbean predominated with a theme of racial equality. Whereas the American Indian was taken as the symbol of patriotism in the Spanish Caribbean, Africa and African things became the symbols of national pride in the French Caribbean.

Haiti's revolution, the first and only successful slave revolution in the New World, released many creative impulses in the nation, allowing the artist to re-evaluate his heritage—what it meant to be Haitian and hence Caribbean. This re-evaluation stimulated the literary phenomenon, Negritude. The famous Haitian poet, René Despestre, reminds us:

> During all of the nineteenth century there were men in Haiti who, without using the term Negritude, understood the significance of Haiti for world history. Haitian authors such as Hannibal Price and Louis-Joseph Janvier were already speaking of the need to reclaim black cultural and aesthetic values. A genius like Anténor Firmin wrote in Paris a book entitled *De l'égalité des races humaines*, in which he tried to re-evaluate African culture in Haiti in order to combat the total and colorless assimilation that was characteristic of our early authors. You could say that beginning with the second half of the nineteenth century some Haitian authors—Justin Lhérisson, Frédéric Marcelin, Fernand Hibbert, and Antoine Innocent—began to discover the peculiarities of our country, the fact that we had an African past, that the slave was not born yesterday, that voodoo was an important element in the development of our national culture.[1]

Written in 1885, *De l'égalité des races humaines* sounded a theme that would attract writers of African descent all over the world for the next sixty or seventy years. Its author, Anténor Firmin, argued passionately that the

Egyptians were black people of Ethiopian descent who made notable contributions. He commented further that "every imaginable subtlety has been brought to play, every quibble has been built up into sound argument, every possible erudite subterfuge has been accepted, all in order to make out that the ancient Egyptians were white."[2] At the very time the European powers divided Africa at the Berlin Conference (1884) and Joseph Gobineau claimed European racial superiority, Firmin argued for recognition of the Africans' highly civilized past with its important implications for blacks. Since Haiti was the major oasis of Africanism in the New World, Firmin argued that Haiti should serve as an example for the Caribbean people.

In 1900 Hannibal Price's *De la réhabilitation de la race noire par le peuple d'Haiti* explored the same theme and stressed "even more strongly the part played by Haiti in restoring the dignity of the Negro in the world."[3] Price described the stirring battle scenes of the Haitian War of Independence and called Haiti the country where the Negro first became a man:

> I am a man of Haiti, the Mecca, the Judea of the black race, the country where are to be found the sacred fields of Vertières, la Crète à Pierrot, la Ravine aux Couleuvres, le Tombeau des Indigènes [scenes of battles in the Haitian War of Independence], and a hundred others where every man with African blood in his veins should go on a pilgrimage at least once in his life, for it was there that the Negro became a man: it was there, that, breaking his chains, he condemned slavery in the New World for ever.[4]

The American Occupation of Haiti (1915–1934) became a decisive landmark in the literary and cultural history of the country in that the people resorted more strongly to cultural resistance and used their African traditions to fight American imperialism and the Haitian bourgeoise, which accepted everything foreign and rejected all things Haitian and African. As Naomi M. Garret observed:

> Chief among the events upon the national scene that have affected Haitian writers of the present age are the social unrest and economic and political instability of the country in the early years of the present century, the intervention of the Government of the United States in the affairs of Haiti, the ethnological studies of Dr. Price Mars, and the dissatisfaction of the young poets with the past generation.[5]

As a consequence, the poetry which emerged during this period was perceived as "an instrument of knowledge,"[6] in an epoch in which the people "were striving for spiritual liberation."[7]

117

One of the most important works of this period was Dr. Jean Price Mars' *Ainsi parla l'oncle* (the uncle of the title referred to the traditional storyteller in Haitian folklore) published in 1928 in which he urged the Haitian writers to inculcate their traditional African elements and Haitian folklore into their works and to utilize the collective ethos of the people in order to rehabilitate Haitian man. For Dr. Price Mars it was necessary to remind the writers of the important role that Haitian folklore and mythology had played in the psychology of the Haitian people. As he stated so eloquently in such rich and symbolic language:

> For a long time we have nourished the ambition of restoring in the eyes of the Haitian people the value of their folklore. . . .
>
> It is they [the white world] who have been the artisans of black servitude for four centuries, because they, having at their service force and science, have magnified the adventure [of slavery] in contending that the negroes were the refuse of humanity, without history, without morals, without religion to whom it was necessary to instill, no matter how, new moral values, [and to make] new human investiture. And when in the fervor of the crises of transmutation, which stirred up the French Revolution, the slave community of San Dominique rose up in insurrection to reclaim the titles that nobody until then dreamed of recognizing, the success of their reclamations was for them an embarrassment and a surprise simultaneously: embarrassment, unacknowledged moreover in the choice of social discipline; surprise of the adaptation of a heterogeneous flock to the stable life of free labor. . . .
>
> Moreover, our presence on a point of this American archipelago that we have "humanized," the breakthrough we have made in the process of the historical events in order to assure our place among men, our manner of using the laws of imitation in order to try to make ourselves an assumed soul, the pathological deviation that we have inflicted to the *bovarysme* of the collective in conceiving ourselves other than what we are, the tragic incertitude that one such bearing imprinted on our evolution at the moment when the imperialism of all others, disguised their convetousness beneath external philanthropy, gave certain relief to the existence of the Haitian community. Before the night comes, it is not useless to gather the facts of our social life, to fix the gestures, the attitudes of our people to scrutinize their origins and to locate them in the general life of man upon the planet. They are the witnesses whose deposition cannot be neglected in judging the value of a part of the human species. (APO, pp. i-vi)

By digging deeply into the available scientific evidence of the time, Dr. Price Mars alerted the writers to the fact that ancient Africa contained great centers of learning and had all the prerequisites of culture that were found in all other civilizations. Therefore, Haitians had nothing to be ashamed of, if only they would draw upon their own culture and folklore. As he reasoned:

". . . if by civilization of a country, of a people, of a race, one understood the social and political organization, the intellectual culture to which this people or this race has arrived; if one comprises the ensemble of their institutions, their beliefs, their customs and their races, if all these things reveal in this people a sense of life, collective and private, a law from which arise rights and morals, there have been, in a given moment, on the African continent, centers of black civilization where not only do we find the ruins, but of which the explosion has extended over the limits of the steppe and the desert. (APO, p. 64)

In describing these centers of culture and recounting their grandeur and their artistic achievements, Dr. Price Mars showed Haitians the importance of their African past and the culture that their people had given to the world.

Of greater importance than the descriptive and historical details which he gave Haitians about Africa was his advice to Haitian writers that they should use the vast store of their literary and cultural heritage as the basis for their literary production. Since most of these writers came from the educated or elite stratum of the society they needed to identify more closely with the culture of the black masses at the bottom of the society. For as Dr. Price Mars demonstrated in his work, Haitian folklore was both rich and diversified and provided the formal literary structures from which a truly national literature could grow. Only by so doing could these writers make an original contribution to Haitian and Caribbean literature. As Dr. Price Mars concluded from his studies:

Stories, legends, songs, proverbs, beliefs flourish with an exuberance, a generosity and a candor which is extraordinary. Magnificent human matter which solidified the warm heart, the unnameable conscience, the collective soul of the Haitian people. Better than the accounts of the great battles, better than the descriptions of great facts of official history always slanted by constraints of only saying a part of the unassailable truth, better than the theatrical posing of the men of State in attitudes of command, better than the laws which can at best only be borrowed laws, badly arranged for our social state where temporary holders of power condense their hates, their prejudices, their dreams and their hopes, better than all those things which are most often artificialities of fate imposed by contingencies and adopted only by a segment of the nation—the stories, the songs, the legends, the proverbs, the beliefs are the works or products spontaneously picked out, in a given moment, from a sparking thought, adopted by all because they are loyal interpreters of a common feeling, becoming dear to some one and turned finally, into original creation by the obscure process of the subconscious.

Because of this original contribution to Haitian thought—"a literary landmark"[8] as Edmund Wilson called it—Haitian writers were awakened unto the new possibilities of the richness and diversity of their literary heritage.

Yet not only did Dr. Price Mars have an enormous influence on his generation of writers, he became the major impetus for the indigenous movement that was emerging in Haiti at the time. Carl Brouard, one of Haiti's most original poets, concluded that Dr. Price Mars was the only writer who had an influence upon a whole generation of Haitian writers.[9]

This generation of writers, who were influenced by the American Occupation and fashioned by the studies of Dr. Price Mars, became known as "the school of La Revue Indigène."[10] Founding the journal, *La Revue Indigène* as their literary mouthpiece, these writers set out "to encourage respect for the values native to Haitians and to black people."[11] The avowed aims of the movement were nationalistic. As Philippe Thoby-Marcelin, one of the founders of the movement, explained:

> One of this movement's basic characteristics was its frankly nationalistic orientation: its will to assert our national idiosyncrasies, reacting against the influence of the United States, which had put our country under its tutelage, and to arm our countrymen against any attempt at absorption by making them see that our cultural heritage could be the principal weapon of resistance. But we also started out with the idea that Haitian authors could only achieve an honorable place in world literature to the extent that they wrote as Haitians, speaking the language of their own country and their own times.[12]

The major writers of this movement were Normil Sylvain, Emile Roumer, Jacques Roumain, Philippe Thoby-Marcelin, Antonio Vieux, Daniel Heurtelou and Carl Brouard.

It is this generation of writers—drawing on the contributions of Anténor Firmin, Hannibal Price and Dr. Jean Price Mars and strengthened by the confluence of new racial (as opposed to racist) concepts of their black selves from the neighboring countries—who gave to Haiti its first truly nationalist literature.

Therefore, the achievement of *La Revue Indigène* lay precisely in the fact that "these poets put no limits upon their verse except that it should grow out of their own culture and mirror the traditions, aspirations, joys, and sorrows of their people."[13] According to Naomi M. Garret, of the 1,400 selections from the 75 poets whom she studied in her work, *The Renaissance of Haitian Poetry*, most of the writers were motivated by the themes of resistance:

> they feel that a poetry of their country must take into consideration the plight of the long-suffering peasants who form, by far, the mass of the population. Stemming from this idea, much of their verse is a condemnation of the former slavery of their ancestors and a protest against the present exploitation of the

Haitian masses, against racial prejudice, and against man's inhumanity to man. It lauds the patience and forbearance of the downtrodden, extolling the simple beauty of their beliefs and traditions; it pleads for justice, for tolerance, and for human brotherhood.[14]

One must not conclude that the literature was narrowly nationalistic, for some of these writers reached beyond the boundaries of Haiti to include their counterparts in the Caribbean, Latin America and America. Jacques Roumain and Norman Sylvain sought to bring the literature of the Caribbean and Latin America to the attention of the Haitian readers, while in 1932, Dr. Price Mars wrote a series of three pioneering articles on the Harlem Renaissance in the review *La Relève* in which he noted the extraordinary influence that negro art and literature were having on the American community. Not the least importance, among the works that spoke to the growing awareness of race identity, was the contribution of Maurice Delafosse's splendid work *Les Noirs de l'Afrique* (1922) which opened up innumerable possibilities for Caribbean literature in French.

Out of this ferment of influence emerged works by a number of Caribbean writers which carried on the tradition of cultural resistance in literature which had begun with the slave songs and the patriotic poems of the post-slave epoch. These sterling beginnings gave way, for the most part, to a much less intense kind of national literature in which the writers imitated the French colonial masters. The poetry of the Haitian Renaissance attempted to reproduce and integrate the rhythmic patterns and the throbbing sensibilities of the emotional and social life of the Haitian people, to capture the literary images that were peculiar to Haiti and to use the creole dialect, a unique creation of African and French language, as an important means of communicating their poetic sentiments.

At this historical period in the French Caribbean, the novel began to share the stage with the poetry. Two important novels emerged to expand the dialogue which the poetry had begun. Both of these novels challenged the presumed superiority of European civilization and examined the ill effects of colonialism: *Batouala: A True Black Novel* (1921) by René Maran and *Banjo: A Story without a Plot* (1929) by Claude McKay.

These novels cannot be called Caribbean in a thematic sense because *Batouala*, set in Africa is about Africans, and *Banjo*, set in Marseilles, is about West Indians and the common black condition. But they are important for any study of Caribbean resistance in literature because they attack European colonialism and white superiority. Because both writers came from the Caribbean and understood colonialism, their works contributed to further resistance and had important implications for Caribbean literature.

Born in Martinique of Guyanese parents, René Maran (1887–1960) spent most of his youth in France. In 1910 he accepted a post in Central Africa with the French colonial administration. Africa had a profound psychological impact upon Maran. According to F. A. Irele, it served "to change the course of his literary pre-occupations and to transform to a considerable extent his own social and human awareness."[15] His prior concern for symbolic poetry changed to the intense and meticulous observation of his African brothers from which *Batouala* came.

As Donald E. Herdeck points out in his introduction to *Batouala* (1921), "it was not only an event of major literary importance, but also a turning point in both the intellectual and political history of contemporary Africa. . . . *Batouala* was the first great novel about Africa by a Black writer." (BT, p. 9) The novel, which won the prestigious Prix Goncourt, leveled one of the most strenuous attacks against French colonialism in Africa and "helped prepare the intellectual ground work for the anti-colonial revolt which was to sweep the post-World War II World." (BT, p. 13) Blacks in Paris and in the colonies read the work which created violent reactions in white France. *Batouala* was an important precursor of Negritude with Maran acknowledged as "the first black man in France to have dared tell the truth about certain methods of colonization and to have revealed the true mentality of blacks and what they thought of European occupation."[16] *Batouala's* subtle castigating of French activity in Africa is rivaled only by Ferdinand Oyono's novel, *Boy!* As Maran describes Europe's exploitation, one realizes that slavery was replaced only by a more subtle method of socioeconomic exploitation. Batouala speaks with intense anguish:

I will never tire of telling, . . . of the wickedness of the 'boundjous.' Until my last breath, I will reproach them for their cruelty, their duplicity, their greed. What haven't they promised us since we have had the misfortune of knowing them! 'You'll thank us later' they tell us. 'It is for your own good that we force you to work. We only take from you a small part of the money we force you to earn. We use it to build you villages, roads, bridges and machines which move by fire on iron rails.' . . . Moreover, instead of taking only a part of our gains, they steal even our last sou from us! And you don't find our lot unbearable? . . . Thirty moons ago, they still bought our rubber at the rate of three francs per kilo. From one day to the next, with no explanation, they paid us only fifteen sous for the same quantity of 'banga.' . . . And it's just at that moment that the government chose to raise our poll tax from five to seven or even ten francs! . . . We are only taxable flesh. We are only beasts of burden. Beasts? Not even that. Dogs? They feed them, and they care for their horses. Us? We are for them less than those animals; we are lower than the lowest. They are slowly crushing us. (BT, pp. 86-87)

This terrible exploitation and human depravity on the part of the Europeans characterizes *Batouala*.

During his thirteen years working for the French colonial administration in the Ubangi-Shari region, Maran patiently observed French treatment of Africans and African reaction to enslavement. *Batouala* was so painful and maddening to the French that Maran was forced to leave his job. Yet, after Maran received the Prix Goncourt, Paul Souday wrote in *Le Temps* that "Maran's indictment of colonial administrators was so formidable that every Frenchman, and every European too, would blush for shame."[17] The novel, important for its indictment of the African colonial system, had a tremendous impact upon Martinican literature in particular and upon Caribbean literature in general. F. A. Irele contends in his monograph, *Literature and Ideology in Martinique*, that before the appearance of *Batouala*, "literary expression [in Martinique] conformed in its themes and formal patterns to the French norm. . . . René Maran brought a new development into the outlook of Martinican writing, in an indirect but decisive way."[18] Caribbean novelists such as Claude McKay, Aimé Césaire and Léon Damas all attest to its influence upon them.[19]

McKay was so impressed with *Batouala* that he used it in *Banjo* to indicate the degree of alienation that the educated Caribbean felt from the roots of his culture. In an exchange between Ray and a student from Martinique, the student presents Empress Josephine's birth on Martinique as an index of the island's importance yet sniggers that the "sale of *Batouala* had been banned in the colony." (BJ, p. 199)

In *Batouala*, Maran tells of the African's continual flight from the whites: As soon as the Africans moved to a new settlement, the Europeans would swoop down on them. The African eventually submitted to European ways with the following results:

Since we have submitted to them, we have no more right to bet any money at all at the 'patara.' We have no more right to get drunk either. Our dances and our songs disturb their sleep. But dances and songs are our whole life. We dance to celebrate Ipeu, the moon, or to praise Lolo, the sun. We dance for everything, for nothing, for pleasure. Nothing is done or happens, but we dance about it forthwith. And our dances are innumerable. We dance the dance of the water of the land and of the water of the sky, the dance of the fire, the dance of the wind, the dance of the ant, the dance of the elephant, the dance of the trees, the dance of the leaves, the dance of the stars, the dance of the earth and of that which is within it, all the dances, all the dances. Maybe it is better to say that we danced them all not long ago. Because as far as these times are concerned they allow us to do them only rarely. And still we have to pay a tithe to the government. (BT, p. 84)

McKay also celebrates this pure, instinctual society, "the happy irresponsibility of the Negro in the face of civilization" (BJ, p. 313) in *Banjo*. When McKay protests, "For civilization had gone out among these native, earthy people, had despoiled them of their primitive soil, had uprooted, enchained, transported, and transformed them to labor under its laws, and yet lacked the spirit to tolerate them within its walls," (BJ, pp. 313-314) he takes up Maran's call and transfers it to blacks displaced from their African home. He does this by contrasting the carefree and instinctual Banjo with the intellectual Ray in a world where "it was hell to be a man of color, intellectual and naturally human in the white world. Except for a superman, almost impossible." (BJ, p. 164)

Whereas Maran protested the evils of colonization and registered the effects of white civilization upon black Africa, McKay explained that picture by showing the implications of that civilization on black people trying to live in a white world. Within this context we understand Ray's outburst in *Banjo*, "Civilization is rotten." *Banjo* is important as a Caribbean novel in its attacks on the values of western society, values propagated as superior yet having the devastating effect of keeping the people enslaved.

McKay's answer lay in the glorification of the natural and simple life of the peasant. He rejects middle class respectability, which he calls "that careful touting life" (BJ, p. 288) personified in the life of the chauffeur. McKay chronicles the chauffeur's descent (ascent) from the abyss of society to middle class respectability:

> That chauffeur will marry with a clear conscience from his scavenger money. He may chuck up the chauffeur's job and buy a café—become a respectable *père de familie*—a good taxpayer and supporter of a strong national government, with a firm colonial policy, while you and I will always be the same lost black vagabonds, because we don't know what this civilization is all about. But my friend the chauffeur knows. It took over a thousand years of lily-white culture to make him what he is. And although he has no intelligence, he has the instinct of civilization, Banjo, and you and I just haven't got it.
>
> I can't make out nothing, pardner, about that instinking thing that youse talking about. But I know one thing and that is if I ain't got the stink of life in me, I got the juice." (BJ, p. 289)

The middle class is rejected and the simple life of the peasantry takes its place. Against this background the peasant novel in the Caribbean comes into being. It must be perceived as a form of resistance since it seeks to present the peasants as the major focus of the society, the ones who really matter, even though they suffer at the hands of the colonial power and the rich elites of the society. Perhaps the most important of the peasant novels is *Masters of the Dew*, written by Jacques Roumain and published in 1944. *Banjo*, however, had important ramifications for Caribbean literature and a definite impact on some of our best writers. Madame Kesteloot has said of *Banjo*:

> *Banjo* was the first novel to articulate the Negro problem fully and clearly. Blacks in Paris could not remain indifferent to so many revolutionary ideas. But they were also attracted by *Banjo*'s free and easy style, by its human warmth, the reality of its characters. Senghor, Césaire, and Damas can still cite entire chapters.[20]

It is interesting that *Banjo* so profoundly influenced these three writers, who made some of the most important contributions to black letters over the last forty years. Indeed, in an interview with René Despestre, Césaire referred to *Banjo* as "one of the first works in which an author spoke of the Negro and gave him a certain literary dignity."[21]

Maran's celebration of the natural and McKay's glorification of the instinctual found their fullest echo in the peasant novels of Jacques Roumain. His *Masters of the Dew*, one of Haiti's best novels, seems to be the logical culmination of the thematic process that was begun by *Batouala* and *Banjo*. Born in 1907, Roumain grew up during the American occupation of Haiti and shared the *crise de conscience*, which Michael Dash asserts "shocked the educated Haitians into an awareness of themselves as members of a post-colonial society whose evolution since 1904 seemed to have been seriously challenged by the fact of the American presence."[22] Roumain was imprisoned for fighting against the American occupation, and some believe that his early death was caused by "brutal punishment inflicted by the police while [he] was in prison." (MD, p. 17) Roumain's militancy and his intense nationalism bear a direct relationship to the presence of American forces in Haiti.

Roumain was superior to Maran and McKay as a novelist and poet since he depicted Caribbean life in its fullest dimension. As the Martinican novelist, Édouard Glissant, points out, Roumain "made himself the champion of Caribbean life."[23] His attention to peasant life was undoubtedly influenced by the emphasis on peasant experiences in *Ainsi parla l'oncle* by the Haitian writer, Price-Mars, his ethnographic training and his membership in the school La Revue Indigène, of which he was a founding member. However, whereas *Ainsi parla l'oncle* celebrates the peasants and their customs, Roumain's *Masters of the Dew* recognizes quite clearly the limitations of such customs and, more important, the negative aspects of excessive cultural emphasis and the crimes that can be committed in its name.

Masters of the Dew is important in the development of the Caribbean novel for its recognition of the close relationship between ideology and literary creativity, a relationship which Edmund Wilson depicts in simple and almost banal tones:

> . . . this is simply the inevitable Communist novel that is turned out in every country in compliance with the Kremlin's prescription. You have the struggle against the bourgeoisie, the summons of the exploited to class solidarity, the martyr who dies for the cause—in this case scientific irrigation. The creole-speaking peasant hero is fired by a social idealism which he is supposed to have learned from a comrade on the sugar plantations of Cuba, but which he expounds with a *Daily Worker* eloquence that would be scarcely possible in Creole.[24]

Wilson does not understand the novel's strategy or the concept of *coumbite*, an African concept of cooperative labor, which is basic to African socialism. Since the actual conditions of Haitian life gave Roumain a ready knowledge of exploitation of the Haitian peasant, he did not need the Kremlin or the *Daily Worker*. A member of the petit-bourgeoisie, Roumain knew the conflicts and contradictions of his particular class in a colonial society. Further, the concept of cooperative economics goes back to the heart of African experience in the Caribbean. If it is rational and feasible to apply scientific investigation to the droughts as Manuel (the novel's protagonist) did, then it is equally logical to apply scientific analysis to society as Roumain did. Roumain uses political vision as the basis of his literary creation by placing the *coumbite* as the central focus of the novel and in one brilliant stroke fuse three categories of resistance.

Roumain proposes the *coumbite*, which "continues the tradition of the Dahomean *dokpwe*,"[25] as the only means of salvation for the Haitian people plagued by a severe drought. By developing around this central theme the subsidiary theme of the struggle of the peasants to free themselves from the exploitation of the economically powerful and to project this struggle in class terms, Roumain is able, with minimum posturing, to present a novel that fully projects the theme of economic cooperation (African socialism), and use it as a political base to bring the peasants together.

Hence Roumain (Mercer Cook believes that Romain *is* Manuel in the novel) (MD, p. 10) is very scrupulous in respecting the traditions of his ancestors, even though he recognizes their limitations. "I respect the customs of the old folks, but the blood of a rooster or a young goat can't make the seasons change, or alter the course of the clouds and fill them with water like bladders." (MD, p. 87) He knows that education will erase the superstitions of the past, hence his first project after he brings water to the village will be to construct a school to educate the people. It is this coming together of ideology and literary creativity that really distinguishes *Masters of the Dew*. *Masters of the Dew* is also very important in that it proposes a concrete liberation from the alienating forces of poverty and despair that have come to dominate the life of the Haitian peasant. It proposes a concrete solution to the negativity that Maran and McKay were fighting against. It makes no sense to argue as one critic has that Maran wasn't black enough,[26] or as another has, by implication, that Roumain was not poor enough.[27] The novel must be seen in human terms. Roumain/Manuel calls for solidarity where divisiveness reigned, for hope where resignation has predominated, and a willingness to accept the ultimate sacrifice (death), for his people to assume themselves—to present man in his noblest aspect: that of giving himself for his brothers, and this concept is part of the triumph of the novel.

The peasant novel then becomes the vehicle for propagating the idea of "rebellion" (Manuel is accused on countless occasions of fomenting rebellion). But the problem of this kind of novel is that it tries either to glamorize the peasant or to expect him to operate at only one level of simplicity incapable of examining problems of ideology in any profound way. Indeed, the very way in which Roumain manipulates the form "beyond mere photographic realism," as Michael Dash puts it, to examine the nature of folk customs, exploitation and the equally strategic projection of the central theme of reconciliation (finally embodied in the love of Manuel and Annaise, and the subsequent pregnancy of Annaise) projects itself with the same deceptive and transparent simplicity of say, Carpentier's *In the Kingdom of This World*. In fact, the simple search for water to irrigate the lands becomes a search for new life; a search which, if it is successful (and it is), could open up many new possibilities for the community, calling upon their cooperation, a scientific understanding of terrain and a new assault upon the forces that retard their progress. Fundamentally, the novel is about the recognition that the country is the peasants and that they must be aware of this basic fact. For as Manuel asserts:

We're *this country*, and it wouldn't be a thing without us, nothing al all. . . .
We don't know yet what a force we are, what a single force—all the peasants,
all the Negroes of plain and hill, all united. Some day, when we get wise to that,
we'll rise up from one end of the country to the other. Then we'll call a General
Assembly of the *Masters of the Dew*, a great big *coumbite* of farmers, and we'll
clear out poverty and plant a new life. (MD, pp. 74-75)

Masters of the Dew is about peace, reconciliation and regeneration. The fratricidal feud that runs through the book yields to an era of forgiveness, mutual cooperation and love. Manuel's and Annaise's child is a symbol of how "life can start all over again," (MD, p. 158) and how ultimately peasants can master their own environment.

Masters of the Dew climaxed a particular era in Caribbean literature. Meanwhile other literary developments took place that would have important implications for the novel. In Puerto Rico, for example, the 1930s produced

> . . . a new generation of intellectual youth that called for an examination of conscience; they wanted answers in order to find their identity. They were concerned with two key questions: Who are we? Why are we? It was a generation with the courage to set down it's preoccupations in black and white.[28]

This generation, which struggled to discover its authentic self, produced periodicals such as *Isla, Indice* and *Brújula* and two works that have been called "the two best books of this century on Puerto Rico":[29] Antonio S. Pedreira's *Insularismo* and Tomas Blanco's *Prontuario historico de Puerto Rico*. *Insularismo* is most important because Pedreira tries to find what he terms the *puertorriqueñismo* or the Puerto Rican soul. Although he misinterpreted Puerto Rican history in attesting, "We are a people alien to violence, and politely peaceful, as our countrysides,"[30] and although others claim he suffered from "an aristocratic—and we might also say racist—conception of our evolution,"[31] Pedreira tried to discover what it meant to be Puerto Rican and therefore what it meant to be Caribbean.

This struggle to define the self within Caribbean experience was not confied to Puerto Rico, for other Caribbean writers came to grips with the same problem. In 1932, an important year for Caribbean literature, young Caribbean students in France published *Légitime Défense*. Although they only published one issue of this important periodical, its influence boomeranged throughout the African world, including Africa itself, the Caribbean and the U.S. Romanticism, which was used to great advantage in Cuba during the previous century, served only as a pale imitation for writers in Martinique and the other French islands. Haiti was exceptional in producing a Firmin and a Price, but even these writers faced rejection when their works were published. Martinique, Guadaloupe and French Guyana, which had never broken from France and was further assimilated into French colonialism than other Caribbean territories, adhered to French literary tradition more than their Caribbean counterparts. So closely had writers imitated their French colonizers that Madame Kestleloot commented rather exaggeratedly and somewhat untruthfully that "prior to *Légitime Défense* there was no originality in West Indian literature in French."[32] However, she argues that the Haitian case must be examined separately.

In its only issue *Légitime Défense* attacked these false imitators with a passion. Its authors criticized the lack of creativity in the French bourgeois society and rejected everything that their educated parents upheld. They rejected French literature and accepted surrealism because, as Madame Kestleloot points out, it

> provided an excellent brake to cultural assimilation and furnished new weapons against the academic style of traditional French West Indian art. Surrealism had the added advantage of shocking bourgeois society and stimulating social revolution . . . [further] . . . surrealism was adopted by West Indian students in France for its revolutionary spirit, its permanent rebellion against art, morals, society.[33]

Surrealism, whose purpose was "shocking bourgeois society" and whose posture was "permanent rebellion against art, morals and society," was not sufficient of itself to produce really great art because it emphasized artistic form at the expense of content. Indeed this first negation of traditional French standards led to a higher synthesis and new forms that grew out of the tremendous revolutionary turmoil in the Caribbean during the 1930s. While surrealism facilitated the break from the past, its nature did not allow Caribbean writers to dissect their own society without Marxist analysis and realism as central literary tools. As Boris Suchkov points out, surrealism

> broke the link between the image and reality, treating the image as a form without objective content and only using it as a vehicle for chaotic feelings and emotions, associations and sensations arising in the poet's soul, which is supposedly independent of the external world and unaffected by its logic.[34]

Most Caribbean writers and their Afro-American counterparts turned to surrealism and Marxism, and in the case of Richard Wright, to naturalism. But social content of the Caribbean experience, pulsating with 1930s violence, provided the necessary "link between image and reality." The negation of the past and subsequent unity of the past with future hopes yielded a new and higher synthesis expressed in the dynamism of Damas and Césaire.[35] On one side was surrealism, which allowed for the emotional and almost chaotic break with past forms, while on the other side was the necessary objective content of oppression and dispossession among other alienating social conditions. Carpentier would reject this necessary aimlessness of surrealism in 1949 in favor of the richness of Caribbean history which he expressed incorrectly in the term "magical realism."

These artists accepted Marxism as their method of inquiry because it offered them a concrete liberation from enslavement by pointing to the real situation in their homelands. Even though a young philosophical method, it showed that poverty, colonialism and dependence were not inevitable conditions ordained by heaven but instead it proposed equality and promised liberation. These Caribbean writers, like their U.S. colleagues, saw communism and surrealism as two indispensable weapons for liberation. No wonder *Légitime Défense* made its harshest attacks against French Guiana* (the French penal colony) and challenged the ban on *Batouala*.

Légitime Défense gave way to the newspaper, *L'Etudiant Noir*, whose goal was to be less Caribbean and more African. As Senghor writes,

> *L'Etudiant Noir* and *Légitime Défense* . . . represented respectively two tendencies shared by the students. Although both reviews had been subject to the same influences, they differed on several points: *L'Etudiant Noir* believed in the priority of culture. For us, . . . politics was but one aspect of culture, *whereas "Légitime Défense" maintained . . . that political revolution should precede cultural revolution, the latter becoming possible only if radical political change had occurred.*[36] [Italics mine.]

This was an important distinction, for it emphasized the importance of resistance in the thoughts of Caribbean writers and presumed, as Césaire had in his work *Cahier d'un retour au pays natal* (1938), the revolutionary background of the Caribbean people. *Tropiques*, the periodical founded in Martinique during 1940 by Aimé and Suzanne Césaire, pointed out that the Césaires had not completely broken with their past and could make important contributions to the liberation of the people of Martinique and the French-speaking Caribbean.

Légitime Défense's emphasis on political revolution becomes even more important when we remember that the French Caribbean remained the most backward political colonies of the Caribbean. In particular, the political situation in French Guiana gives so much prominence and pertinence to Dummerville's contention in *Au seuil d'un nouveau cri* that "decolonization was progressing all over the Caribbean, would you be the only one left behind? . . . Hadn't you [France] taken the first step when you abolished slavery?" (ASNC, p. 204) Revolutionary violence became imperative for a country still under the yoke of colonialism and so tied to the mother country.

---

* Whereas Guyana (formerly British Guiana) is spelled with the "y" instead of the "i," French Guiana continues to be spelled with an "i". Hence *Guyana* and *French Guiana*.

130

Léon Damas (1912–1978) pointed out the backward situation of the French-speaking Caribbean in *Retour de Guyane* (1938), a complete indictment of the colonial system in the penal colony, French Guiana. The French sent convicts to French Guiana and then required that the convicts spend an additional amount of time equivalent to the incarceration in the country before they could be released. During this time the convicts terrorized the native people. As Damas points out in *Retour de Guyane*, "He [the criminal] becomes a tramp, terrorizes us, rapes our children, imposes his customs and morals on our society, degrades, corrupts, and debases it instinctively."[37] Léon Damas, born in Cayenne, French Guiana, contrasts himself with René Maran. Damas is best known for *Pigments*, the first major work of the Negritude movement.[38] The anguish expressed in *Pigments* anticipates Frantz Fanon's work. As Ellen Kenroy Kennedy puts it, "twenty years before Frantz Fanon had organized the concept of the colonized personality into psychoanalytic theory, *Pigments* . . . revealed the anguish of what has come to be known by that term."[39] Indeed, Negritude poets influenced Fanon and the novelist, Bertene Juminer.

As early as 1934 Damas' poems appeared in the French periodical, *Esprit*. In 1937 *Pigments*, in which Damas tried to recover his lost soul and recapture his identity, appeared in full. Damas had been assimilated by education and social position into the French Guiana elite where he accepted all things French and European. Hampered by a frail constitution, he had missed the gay abandon of boys his age and experienced rigidity and artificiality of his world of exclusion. In terse rhythmic and repetitive verse Damas laments his lost past:

> Give my black dolls back to me
> So that I can play with them
> the simple games of my instincts
> instincts that endure in the darkness of
> their laws with my courage recovered
> and my audacity
> I become myself once more
> myself again
> out of what used to be
> once upon a time
> once without complexity
> once upon a time
> when the hour of uprooting came
> Will they never know the rancor in my heart
> opened to the eye of my distrust too late
> they did away with what was mine
>   ways
>   days

life
song
rhythm
effort
foot path
water
huts
the smoke-grey earth
the wisdom
the words
the palavers
the elders
the cadence
the hands
the feet
marking time
upon the ground

Give them back
to me
my black

dolls
black
dolls
black black
dolls.[40]

In the poem, "Their Thing," Damas renounces the civilization that was so brutal to his ancestors and venomously rejects the fruit of assimilation, the false sophistication and the artificial manners that were fostered by his mother. All receive a scathing attack in his poem, "Hiccups." In the end, though, he strives to keep himself pure and his heart inviolate when he affirms in "Good Manners":

And my face gleams with the horrors of the past
and my dreadful laughter would repel
    the specter of the hounds
                            pursuing runaways
and my voice which sings for them
is sweet enough to soothe
the soul saddened by their
    por—
        no—
            gra—
                phy

and my heart keeps watch
and my dreams feeding on the noise of their
    de—
        pra—
           vi—
              ty
is stronger than their clubs besmeared with
    foulness.[41]

Damas' indictment is powerful. In this poem there is a resonance of affirmation that Fanon would later declare in his letter to Juminer about the situation in French Guiana: "have confidence in your people and consecrate yourself to their dignity and fulfillment. For us there are no other ways."[42] To French Caribbean writers imitating the French stylists' rippling, idyllic poetry about the islands, *Pigments* was shocking. As Kesteloot points out, "from its first publication, the new poetry of Negritude revealed itself as revolutionary—and effectively so, because it touched the feelings of the entire black race. The words of a West Indian were inspiring Africans."[43] In fact *Pigments* was so effective that it was banned on the Ivory Coast after soldiers recited Damas' poems when they rejected induction into the armed forces.

In 1938 Aimé Césaire's famous *Cahier d'un retour au pays natal* appeared. A melange of poetry and prose in yet another celebration of the Caribbean's African past and a bitter denunciation of slavery, it had important implications for the entire African world with Césaire continuing where Firmin, Price-Mars and Maran had left off. As Irele points out, "the sense of involvement implicit in Maran's work becomes explicit in the work of Aimé Césaire, who was to give a definite figure to the hesitant social vision of his predecessor."[44] The periodical *Velontes*, published the entire work in 1939, but it was ignored until the French surrealist, André Breton, picked it up in a Martinican haberdashery in 1940 and called it "nothing less than the greatest lyrical monument of this time." (RNL, p. 5) In his introduction to *Cahier* Mazisi Kuene says Césaire and Fanon perform the same task: ". . . the incision of the colonial mentality, the tearing away of the white man's superiority complex and in its place the creation of the ideology of man in his totality as a humane and a civilizing being" (RNL, p. 12) while Kesteloot says, "in a single, violent poetic effort, Aimé Césaire brings together his own experience and the destiny of his race, as to render any further separation impossible."[45] Césaire struck at the very heart of Western civilization, at its ontological presumptions, at its syllogistic reasoning, at its moral and ethical values—all instruments in which Europe had arrogated to herself the right to enslave people whom she preferred to call "prelogical."

Césaire denounced her (i.e. Europe and Europeans) totally and thoroughly:

Words?
Ah yes, words!
Reason, I appoint you wind of the evening.
Mouth of authority, be the whip's corolla
Beauty, I name you petition of stone
But ah! my hoarse contraband laughter
And my saltpetre treasure!
Because we hate you, you and
your reason, we claim kinship with
dementia praecox with flaming madness
with tenacious cannibalism

Treasure? let us count it
the madness that remembers
the madness that screams
the madness that sees
the madness that unchains itself

And you know the rest
That 2 and 2 make 5
that the forest mews like a cat
that the tree pulls chestnuts out of the fire
that the sky smoothes its beard
etcetera, etcetera. . . .(RNL, p. 55)

This is renunciation of the white god of Logic and Reason. Tongue-in-cheek, Césaire accepts European criticism of his people:

I declare my crimes and say that there is
        nothing to say in my defense.
Dances. Idols. Relapses.
I too have murdered
God with my idleness
my words my gestures my obscene songs

I have worn parrot feathers and
musk-cat skins
I have worn down the patience of missionaries
I have insulted the benefactors of humanity.
Defied Tyre. Deified Sydon.
Adored the Zambezi.
The expanse of my perversity confounds me. (RNL, p. 57)

This is a malicious and devastating attack against things European. Having acknowledged the evil of his ways, Césaire celebrates those things black which are vital to his being, and in the process accepts some of the ideas expressed earlier by McKay in *Banjo*. He confesses in order to negate, but what we in fact see is a reaffirmation of the very things that have allowed him to retain his humanity in spite of the trials, tribulations and cruelties to which he has been subjected. It is a time to let innocence, primitiveness, and a lack of complexity reign. It is a return of what Senghor called "the most ancient times, the unity recovered,"[46] a return to peace and tranquility:

> voom roh oh
> let the promised time come again
> and the bird that knew my name
> and the woman who had a thousand names
> fountain and sun and tears
> and her hair like young fish
> and her steps my climates
> and her eyes my seasons
> days without harm
> nights without offence
> stars of confiding
> wind of complicity (RNL, p. 59)

Now was the time not to turn away in shame from the past but rather to face it with pride and elation, a time for celebration to honor those who had remained true to themselves. Therefore Césaire sings out joyfully:

> Heia for those who have never invented anything
> those who never explored anything
> those who never tamed anything
>
> those who give themselves up to the essence
>   of all things
> ignorant of surfaces but struck by the movement
>   of all things
> free of the desire to tame but familiar with
>   the play of the world
> truly the eldest sons of the world
> open to all the breaths of the world
> fraternal territory of all breaths
> undrained bed of the waters of the world
> flesh of the flesh of the world pumping with
>   the very movement of the world
> Warm small hours of ancestral virtues

135

Heia for the reincarnation of tears and the
    worse pain brought back again
Those who never invented anything
those who never tamed anything

Heia for joy
Heia for love (RNL, pp. 75-77)

In the end, *Cahier d'un retour au pays natal* is a celebration of universal love and a plea for recognition of man's universal ties in a world beset by hatred and devisiveness.

The same literary activity which was taking place in the French and Spanish Caribbean replicated itself in the British Caribbean. While the literary movement began in Jamaica in 1920 under the tutelage of Tom Redcam*, its full flowering did not take place until the end of the decade when C. L. R. James and Alfred Mendes published the only two number of their magazine *Trinidad*, at Christmas 1929 and Easter 1930 in Trinidad. In the first volume of *Trinidad*, the short story "Triumph" appeared, and for the first time "the yard life" (the ghetto) of the urban life of the Caribbean was depicted in its literature.

In 1930, the journal *The Beacon* was published in Trinidad and replaced *Trinidad* in the national life of the island. According to its editor, Albert Gomes:

> I had been away in the United States during 1928–1930. While there, someone had sent me a copy of a collection of poems, short-stories and essays by Trinidadians and others that Alfred H. Mendes, another Trinidadian of Portuguese ancestry, had compiled and published. It was elegantly put together, its form suggesting the influence of the 'London Mercury', J. C. Squire's English monthly of the time. I was very excited by Mendes' publication. Did this really mean that a cultural breakthrough was imminent

---

* As Kenneth Ramchand noted, between 1910 and 1920, Tom Redcam launched *The All Jamaica Library* to deal with the literature of Jamaica written by Jamaicans. (Introduction to C. L. R. James, *Minty Allen*, p. 5) According to J. E. McFarlane, Redcam is granted the honor of laying the foundation of formal poetry in Jamaica. As he observes:"
"There may have been—indeed there were—writers in Jamaica before his time whose work possessed some merit as literature; but of the poetry that is undeniably Jamaican in its impulses, that draws its life and colour from Jamaica's sun and air, its streams, its blue skies, its wooded hills, and flower-filled valleys, Tom Redcam is the founder. Through the barren, dreary years he stood almost single handed as its defender and preserver, until a few spirits, touched with a kindred fire, joined him in service." (*A Literature in the Making* [Kingston, Jamaica: The Pioneer Press, 1956], p. 2)

in Trinidad? At 17 or 18 one desires passionately that events should bear witness to one's dreams and hopes.

Back in Trinidad, I discovered that Mendes had gathered around him a small circle of young men who shared his interest in literature and music. They met regularly and informally at Mendes' home where they listened to recorded music, argued way into the night, and read excerpts from each other's writings. This was the tiny oasis of artistic appreciation I found in the vast philistine desert of Trinidad on my return in 1930; and from it arose the movement of the Thirties that played such an important part in the literary development of the island, later extending its seminal influences to the entire West Indies. It was around my magazine 'The Beacon' that this movement grew, the movement, giving 'The Beacon' the initial push forward.

The members of the group to which Mendes introduced me were held together by a common bond of detestation of the hypocrisy, obscurantism and general claustrophobia of Trinidad society and a gallant resolve to lay seige to all these evils. They spurned the values of the society and withdrew from it into the corner of their choice. Here they could better assert their own values, in a dispensation all their own. But they soon lapsed into a self-flattering aestheticism. Perhaps because they were themselves so much the products of the system they condemned they were constrained to this protest of derisive withdrawal. Withdrawn, they developed a sense of their own uniqueness and another form of snobbery. They were, I think, among the earliest romantics of the social reform movement in the West Indies; for such acts of protest as they later engineered consisted in the main of adolescent cocking-the-snook at the mildewed Victorianism then prevalent. Significantly, only two of them, C. L. R. James and R. A. C. De Boissiere, rose from this comfortable armchair aestheticism to affirmation of political views. The others, in time, either gravitated towards the status quo and ceased to protest, or continued to find solace from its humiliations in dilletante devotion to the arts, or, embittered, derived a masochistic comfort from endless sterile protestation.[47]

Like the publications of the French and Spanish Caribbean, *The Beacon* set itself up as the "debunker of bourgeois morality, obscurantist religion and primitive capitalism,"[48] and in its second number, the editor in his article, "Black Man," painted what he described as, "a depressing picture of racial persecution of the Negro in the Southern United States."[49] Immediately, he was visited by a senior officer of the Trinidad Police Force (a white Englishman) who wanted to know where he received such information and whether he realized that "this sort of writing was dangerous in Trinidad."[50]

In 1933 *The Beacon* ceased publication, but out of the movement arose writers and thinkers such as C. L. R. James, Alfred Mendes and Ralph De Boissiere who continued to agitate for the liberation of their countries. In 1933 James published *The Case for West-Indian Self Government* in which he called for self-government in the West Indies, and in 1936 he published his novel *Minty Alley* in which he elaborated upon his yard (ghetto) theme which he broached in "Triumph."

Yet it was Alfred Mendes who first expanded upon James' depiction of the yard theme when he published *Black Fauns* in 1934. This led Kenneth Ramchand to conclude that "it was Mendes and James, not Roger Mais who first looked as artists at the despised West Indian proletariat."[51]

In *Black Fauns*, Mendes drew upon the folklore of the people (particularly the people's belief in *Obeah*) to describe the manner in which life was lived in the early ghettoes of the Caribbean. For example, Mendes described the ghetto in the following manner:

> Sunlight poured from the skies and a light wind went rustling through the large leaves of the breadfruit-tree. From the gutter that ran diagonally across the yard rose a strong stale stench. A few picoplats and semps darted among the branches of the breadfruit-tree, uttering their staccato notes ecstatically. The heap of bleaching stones in the centre of the yard was completely covered over with the washing jobs of the women, and on the lines hung sheets and dresses and underwear of every description. For this work the women earned between ten and fifteen dollars a month, out of which they paid their rent of three dollars and got food, supplemented, of course, by what their men gave them. The rooms were about twelve feet by twelve, and in this particular barrack, built on land standing away from the street, all the doors and windows gave onto the yard which was seventy-five feet wide by thirty feet deep; so that the two rows of rooms, extending along the width of the yard, faced each other.[52]

In spite of the poverty that existed in the yard, the reader is captivated by the solidarity of the people in the face of poverty and an almost ritualized celebration of life in the face of dispossession.

While Mendes, James, Boissiere and Gomes participated in this movement of self-discovery and self-government, James was painfully aware that within the society there were color differences which separated those who were white from those who were black. Thus with the rise of the yard (or the urban dispossession) there became the painful awareness that not only was the society broken down along economic lines but it was also broken down along internal racial lines. As James recognized later:

> Albert Gomes told me the other day: 'You know the difference between all of you and me? You all went away; I stayed.' I didn't tell him what I could have told him: 'You stayed not only because your parents had money but because your skin was white; there was a chance for you, but for us there wasn't— except to be a civil servant and hand papers, take them from the men downstairs and hand them to the man upstairs.' We *had* to go, whereas Mendes

could go to the United States and learn to practise his writing, because he was white and had money. But we had to make our money.[53]

Because of this racial demarcation of the society, James recognized that he and Césaire possessed the same education and, as writers and West Indians, had much in common:

> In the 1930s there were a number of us in the West Indies who were to become writers—in Trinidad, myself and George Padmore (we were boys together, and used to bathe in the Arima River, underneath the ice factory); in Martinique there was Aimé Césaire. We hadn't the faintest idea that the time would come when we would be in the forefront of the revolution for African independence. Now Aimé Césaire, I believe, had much the same sort of education in the Victor Schoelscher school in Martinique Then he went to Paris and something happened to him which is very notable about all of us—he joined the Communist Party. George Padmore joined the Communist Party. I joined the Trotskyite movement. We were educated not only in the literature and material life of Western civilization, but we also became Marxists and were educated by Marxism. To the end of his days Padmore remained a Marxist.
>
> There were some of us who were not black men. There was Carpenter the violinist. There was Alfred Mendes. There was a tall, handsome boy, a very able boy, called Frank Evans, a white boy. There was Daly who had an extremely sharp wit, and was lightskinned. There was De Boissiere. There was Albert Gomes. We went one way; these white boys all went the other way. We were black and the only way we could do anything along the lines we were interested in was by going abroad; that's how I grew up.[54]

James might have mentioned the name of Leon Damas who received his high school education in Martinique at the same school as Césaire with whom he was a class mate and with whom he shared the same colonial education and suffered the same racial antagonism. As Professor Daniel Racine has observed:

> It was at the Lycee Schoelcher, mostly attented by 'bekes' or white Martinicans, that Damas first became aware of racial differences as a result of their humiliating remarks and attitudes, although as a Guyanese he was admitted to the beke society and had white bekes as friends when black Martinicans were really introduced in that society.[55]

Products of the same education, they would suffer the same fate and resort to the same literary means of coming to grips with their being and examining the nature of their society. Thus in 1938 James published *Black Jacobins* (an examination of the Haitian revolution), Damas published

Retour de Guyane (which "exposed the social plague that blighted Guyana"[56]), while Cesaire published his now famous *Return to My Native Land*: three Caribbean artists coming to grips with the problems of their individual countries from different angles of vision.

One year later, Eric Williams, Prime Minister of Trinidad and Tobago, finished his doctoral dissertation, "The Economic Aspects of the Abolition of the West Indian Slave Trade and Slavery," later published as *Capitalism and Slavery*. The influence of C. L. R. James on this work is unmistakeable in that James examined "the economic basis of slavery emancipation as it was in France"[57], while Williams examined the same subject in British slavery. As James comments: "I sat down and wrote what the thesis ["The Economic Aspects of the Abolition of the West Indian Slave Trade and Slavery"] should be with my own hand, and I gave it to him [Williams] . . . I saw the manuscript quite often, I read it about three or four times. The facts themselves and the road he was to take, I wrote that for him."[58]

The departure of some of these gifted minds did not stop the growth of the literary movement in the British Caribbean. Instead, it moved to Barbados where, in December of 1942, Frank Collymore (b. 1893) published his magazine, *Bim*, which has played a central role in the literary life of the British Caribbean. Indeed, some of the finest Caribbean writers first had their start in *Bim*. One year later, Edna Manley, wife of the former Prime Ministers of Jamaica published *Focus* in Jamaica, whereas *Ky-Over-Al* was published in Guyana two years later in 1945.

We have seen in Villaverde's novel that there are elements of realism and, in Esteban, a man who is perspicaciously aware of his own reality and his relationship to the sociopolitical conditions. Historically we also know that realism was born out of the emanation of one from the other. The works offered in this period, however, are all realistic novels. Like the romantic novels, realism had the "same historical task, that of presenting the real substance and direction of historical progress."[59] Moreover, realism complemented the one-sided view of romanticism.

How then did romanticism differ with realism? It differed in three important respects. First, although romanticism revealed the contradictions in slave society and pointed to its demise, early realism pointed out the contradictions inherent in colonial society in its early phases but could only describe the barbarity of the social order. Secondly, although romanticism "liberates" man in a particular way from his temporal, historical context, realism locates man more precisely within his historical and social context and forces him to deal with that given reality. Third, although romanticism dealt with—and was set primarily in—the slave mode of production but was unable to reveal the contradictions of the capitalist mode of production, it could attest to some of the psychological mechanisms that were used to buttress this "property-owning" system.

So much for the differences of romanticism and realism within the content of Caribbean society. The next question that must be asked, however, is why realism was better able to capture the social relations of another order (i.e., capitalism) when romanticism was unable to do so. The answer lies in the fact that romanticism

> did not fully understand social contradictions in their entirety and exaggerated the role of the individual, making his inner world universal and severing his links with the objective world. In tackling the same problems as romanticism, realism differed from it in seeing reality as an integrated whole, within which relations and causes were mutually conditioned. It investigated the objective prerequisites and conditions of historical relationships and their material and social bases.[60]

Bearing in mind the nuances that directly related to the slave condition, herein lay the fundamental distinction between romanticism and realism. As a method, then, that had as its primary aim and major task the "comprehension of the essence of objective reality by artistic means,"[61] realism had as its main task the attempt to comprehend the nature of colonialism and the mechanism of white superiority by way of artistic means. Moreover, it was through social analysis and in the study and portrayal of man in society that the realist sought to discover the causal relationship between man and his social condition. It was precisely its capacity to depict this causal nexus of reality that made realism render the vision of Maran, McKay, and Roumain in such a very profound manner. There was in the works of Maran the very implicit understanding that colonialism was the cause of Batouala's unhappiness, and that it was European greed and exploitation of the colonial world that had brought so much misery to Batouala and millions of other Africans. It is Batouala's understanding of the socio-economic causes of his misery that really makes him cry out, "I will never tire of telling of the wickedness of the 'boundjous.' " Indeed, the cited passage on page 133 shows the explicit connection between the rate of rubber and the raising of the poll tax: "We are only taxable flesh," he says. "We are beasts of burden." The interconnecting link between his misery and the economics of exploitation is made manifest.

This is the major reason why Maran was so viciously attacked when his work came out, for what he did was to show the real "cause" of misery in a colonial society. It had not been done before. This was the great strength of realism: its method of critically analyzing a society that had been transformed from slavery to colonialism.

With the growth of a colonial society and the consequent crystallization of capitalist relations the inevitable fragmentation, i.e., the alienation of personality, begins to be revealed much more clearly. This complex conflict between the individual and his society, in which man's existence is separated from his essence, will be revealed also in the study of the realistic novelist. It is this disorientation, this sense of alienation, that black people felt as they existed in a white world; it is this "spiritual collapse of the hero concerned only with his private self-interest" that becomes the subject of analysis. The individualism of Banjo, who is bent on fulfilling his own pursuits, reflects some measure of the disorientation-fragmentation of the society. It is in an age of crisis that the artist McKay is able to depict the conditions. Muddled somewhat as he is, Banjo is still able to criticize what he calls middle-class respectability (even though he doesn't quite understand all of its ramifications). What, of course, is interesting is that McKay, who began as (or should I say, had pretensions to be) a Marxist, like his major character Banjo, wound up debunking white civilization— uncritically one may add—in its entirety.

But if both Maran and McKay were merely content with debunking the colonial and white racist order, or, in some cases, with merely describing its objective reality, Roumain went a step further. As a realist writer, he too criticized but, more important, he offered alternatives to the dispossession of the peasant, and therein we begin to see elements of the *critical realist*. For there is in his writing an understanding of the social and class forces at work, including the peasants as a group who recognize that they are "the masters of the dew." There is also the fundamental understanding that modern history is about the replacement of one group by another; i.e., when the peasant workers who have an historic mission recognize their power they will "rise up from one end of the country to another" and take their rightful place in history. This position would be the task of an even more penetrating analysis by the critical realist writers.

Leon Damas and Aimé Césaire anticipated both the literary techniques and thematic arguments found in the novels of Bertène Juminer. But this is only indicative of the progression and development of ideas in Caribbean literature. Indianism had given way to what one might call the "incipient" Negritude of Firmin and Price, which was further developed and expanded by Damas and Césaire. Meanwhile, the English Caribbean was beginning to stir. Strikes-turned-riots had plagued the entire Caribbean for the whole decade of the thirties, and, as a consequence, particularly in the English Caribbean, there was the growth of an important literary movement. As G. R. Coulthard has contended:

> There was definitely a connection in the British Caribbean between the awakening of a national consciousness and a desire for independence and the

burgeoning of a new national literature, which set itself higher standards than those hitherto accepted. Writing in the first number of the magazine *Focus* in 1943, Mrs. Edna Manley said, "Great and irrevocable changes have swept this land in the last few years and out of these changes a new art is springing."

And this 'new art', this new impulse found its first outlet principally in the literary magazines *Focus*, published in Jamaica, and *Bim*, published in Barbados. Many writers who have subsequently become known throughout the English-speaking world, and indeed have been translated into French, Spanish, German, Portuguese and other languages, tried their wings in the pages of these magazines.[62]

It is these two contiguous currents—the awakening of a national consciousness and the subsequent realization of the disparities in their society and the cross-fertilization of their literary outpourings—which led to the further development and consolidation of Caribbean literature.

VIII

TOWARDS SELF-GOVERNMENT:
New Day
The Hills were Joyful Together
Brother Man
The Ripening

THE French Caribbean writers from Firmin right down to Césaire were mostly concerned with restoring a sense of personal dignity to the Caribbean man and projecting his identity. This they did by reminding the world of the contributions of the blacks, vehemently rejecting the props upon which Western civilization was built and condemning to the hilt their colonial status. They were in the nationalistic phase of development when to salvage their personhood from the onslaught of Western propaganda was the most important thing to do. Firmin referred to the past greatness of the race; Hannibal Price saw the rehabilitation of the race through the Haitian experience; Maran considered the evil of colonialism; McKay glorified the instinctual nature of the African people, considering it superior to the technically oriented white society; Damas cried "give me back my black dolls"; and Césaire asserted with pride, "Heia for those who never invented anything."

From this national phase of self-assertion, Caribbean writers went on to call for self-government and independence—a call that came on the wave of violent resistance that took place in the Caribbean in the 1930s. For the question must have been asked, "How can one assert this independence, this selfhood, when all the other critical levels of life are controlled by the 'other'?" It is at this level that we can begin to understand the Caribbean in the 1930s. Writing in 1933, C. L. R. James, the Caribbean novelist and scholar, made two important observations. First he examined the schism which existed between the predominantly Negroid group of the society (that is, the darker-skinned negro people) who clung steadfastly to their culture and the colored group of Negroes (that is, the lighter-skinned negroes) who acted as the puppets of the dominant class.[1] The second question to which James addressed himself was the dichotomy between the stated principles which the English preached at home and the actual manner in which they conducted themselves in the colonies: a contradiction which led them to label all people "revolutionary" and "subversive" who did not agree with the manner in which they treated the people in "their colonies": Thus did James argue:

> It is not surprising that the famous English tolerance leaves him entirely [in the colonies.] At home he [the Englishman] was distinguished for the liberality and freedom of his views. Hampden, Chatham, Dunning and Fox, Magna Carta and Bill of Rights, these are the persons and things (however misconceived) which Englishmen, undemonstrative as they are, write and speak of with a subdued but conscious pride. It is no accident, the Whig tradition in English historical writing. But in the colonies any man who speaks for his country, any man who dares to question the authority of those who rule over him, any man who tries to do for his own people what Englishman are so proud that other Englishmen have done for theirs, immediately becomes in the eyes of the colonial Englishman a dangerous person, a wild revolutionary, a man with no respect for law and order, a self-seeker actuated by the lowest motives, a reptile to be crushed at the first opportunity. What at home is the greatest virtue becomes in the colonies the greatest crime.[2]

Because of this contradictory attitude and the intense desire on the part of the British (and all the other foreign colonizers) to prevent the colonized man from governing his own country, there existed a great chasm between the government and those who are governed. As James observed:

> Governors and governed stand on either side of a gulf which no tinkering will bridge, and political energy is diverted into other channels or simply runs to waste. Britain will hold us down as long as she wishes. Her cruisers and aeroplanes ensure it. But a people like ours should be free to make its own failures and successes, free to gain that political wisdom and political experience which come only from the practice of political affairs. Otherwise, led as we are by a string, we remain without credit abroad and without self-respect at home, a bastard feckless conglomeration of individuals, inspired by no common purpose, moving to no common end.
>   "Self-government when fit for it."
>   That has always been the promise. Britain can well afford to keep it in this case, where evidence in favour is so overwhelming and she loses so little by keeping her word.[3]

It was this contradiction between the governors and the governed, this inability of Caribbean peoples to assert their independence at all critical levels of their lives, that led Caribbean writers to discuss the question of self-government. But while the writers of the 1930s and early 1940s concentrated on the role and importance of the peasantry and emphasized the peasant's "fierce attachment to the land . . . [and his] violent denunciation of the exploitation to which the peasant [was] subjected,"[4] the writers of the late 1940s and the early 1950s shifted their attention from the peasantry to the urban dweller and the evils which he suffered in the new conditions of urbanization. (The literature continued to use the tradition of active historical resistance but focused upon the urban conditions of Caribbean peoples.) While Vic Reid (1913-   ) in his novel *New Day* (1949) emerges as one of the earliest novelists in the British Caribbean to continue in the tradition of the peasant novel, Roger Mais (1905-1955), in his novels *The Hills Were Joyful Together* (1953) and *Brother Man* (1954), examines the slum of Jamaica and presents it as a microcosm of the growing urban condition of the Caribbean countries. In Édouard Glissant's novel, *La Lézarde* (1958), translated in 1959 as *The Ripening*, we see an attempt to augment and modify the concerns which the novels of Reid and Mais examined.

If in Galván's *Enriquillo* we see a rejection of the forced imposition of an educational, political and social apparatus of the colonizer on a subjugated people, struggling to maintain their identity, it also must be understood that they signed a treaty that allows them to live side by side with the colonizer (which means, in fact, that the colonizer still controls the political, economic and social relationships of the island). Having, therefore, established a certain degree of autonomy, they must still deal with the alien forces that exist around them. Although it is true that many of the superstitions about the invincibility of the Spanish are gone, the veneration of Spanish contributions to the life of the island still remains a dominant factor in the life of the people. The double vision of Galván is sufficient testimony to the ambiguous role that Enriquillo must still play in the society.

But if Enriquillo was able to rule over only one town on his island, the aim of Reid was much larger: it was the vision of total independence of the subject people, even though his portrayal is marred by severe limitations. Despite these limitations, however, the novel draws a much fuller portrait of the relations of a colonized people, who, through their active resistance and constant struggle for self-government (different from total independence), seek but a limited goal. As Reid himself explains,

> What I have attempted is to transfer to paper some of the beauty, kindliness, and humor of my people, weaving characters into the wider framework of these eighty years and creating a tale that will offer as true an impression as fiction can of the way by which Jamaica and its people came to today. (ND, p. viii)

146

To do this, Reid had to depict the way that resistance fashioned a people's consciousness and sensibilities, and this was his strength. Inherent in Reid is a capacity to internalize the sentiments of the peasant and project them with a new vigor, freshness and integrity. Lamming contends, for example, that one needs to know Reid in order to have a better and fuller understanding of Caribbean life. He says,

> Writers like Selvon and Reid—key novelists for understanding the literary and social situation in the West Indies—are essentially peasant. I don't care what jobs they did before; what kind of grade or education they got in their different islands; they never really left the land that once claimed their ancestors like trees.[5]

It is this kind of vision that allows Reid to go back into the gut of the people to delineate the struggle for self-government and eventually independence.

New Day is about the agitation and resistance of the Jamaican people in their struggle for self rule. The author begins by locating the action in the Morant Bay Rebellion (1865) using the rebellion as his point of departure. The story is told through the eyes of Johnny Campbell, a participant in the Morant Bay Rebellion. He has lived to see the dawning of this "new day," which is brought to fruition in 1944 by his "son-son" Garth Campbell, who is a direct descendant of David Campbell (brother of the narrator, and the only councilman of Bogle who survived Governor Eyre's brutality). The resistance of the people is charted at various stages, but the author commits a fatal blunder in depicting the subjugated people in virtually the same role prior to the rebellion as that which they maintained after self-government. Self-government, according to the author, is merely something that "Mother England" has given her children or prepared them for; hence, the master-slave relationship of 1865 only gives way to an owner-employee relationship (or a mother-England/thankful-children) of enlightened capitalism in 1944. Since there was no conception on the part of the author that before one could talk about self-government, there had to be a fundamental reordering of the social order—that in negating the effect of Bogle's revolt in the acceptance of the peaceful acquisition of self-government—he unconsciously perpetrates the myth that liberty and identity are things given rather than things inherently the right of all people, neither to be given nor to be taken away by any power.

Bogle's fight for independence and Davie's establishment of a fully independent community on the Cays are not perceived as the correct goals of a colonized people but merely aberrations in the body politic achieved the wrong way: through violence. Because Garth achieves self-government (what in the author's mind is a more lasting form of political arrangement) by peaceful means—because he doesn't commit the "excesses" of Bogle—the stamp of legitimacy is given to the peaceful achievement of independence in the Caribbean but does not correctly assess the role of Caribbean resistance. Lamming has shown in his works that "independence" (a further stage along the road of self-government) is almost meaningless if it is merely the changing of a flag, the establishment of a prime ministership, and the singing of a new anthem.

The vision of Reid is therefore limited. It recognizes the need of a people to control its destiny; and it recognizes the importance of resistance in the formation of national identity. Nonetheless, it fails to perceive the traumatic reorganization in political and social relations that must take place if self-government is to mean anything at all. It is this very relationship of subservience, structured and built into the very language of colonized-colonizer relationships that Lamming begins to attack. It is "our way of seeing" that needs to be fundamentally altered. In fact, Lamming would have preferred that people from the Caribbean not even be educated by the master (remember, both Enriquillo and Garth are educated by the colonizer), for to be educated in another language, to some degree at least, begins to constitute a vision of other possibilities.

The attempt to go back into the history of resistance as a point of departure, the use of dialect throughout the novel (the first novel in the Caribbean to do this) as a means of presenting the story, and the image of a peculiar Caribbean sensibility that animates the book mark it as an important contribution to the Caribbean novel. Like Galván, Reid uses actual historical incidents. He begins by evoking the names of all the past heroes who have contributed towards this vision. Calling on the names of these men, he begins to recount the suffering of the masses over these crucial years prior to 1865. In setting up the historical ambience for the entire novel in the first chapter, Reid is presenting the action through the eyes of someone inside the rebellion who is able to see and interpret the action from within rather than, as in the case of Galván, narrating the events of the rebellion with the hindsight of an authorial voice editorializing the action.

It is important to note that Bogle, when the novel opens, is calling for total liberation. "Secession! Secession!" Total freedom is his cry. The father, on the other hand, who is not a "Stoney Gut man," as he proclaims, and who identifies with George William Gordon, is the chief foreman of Gordon. (There is no man that Gordon likes as much as his father.) It is from this line of belief that Garth descends—a belief in the colonial notion that if all legal ramifications were observed, then "Mother England" would act with fairness to her people. It is precisely this miscalculation that leads to the death of Pa Campbell who, in defiance of Davie's warning that

Ramsey is killing anyone who has signed the petition, resolutely affirms, "I will go down. Mr. Gordon can no' die in vain. I will ask to see Governor Eyre. I am no' Stoney Gut man. The English will not make war on Christians," and singing, "Onward, Christian Soldiers," he marches right to his death, shot in cold blood by the English. (ND, p. 8) Little does Pa Campbell realize that the Church of England, as opposed to the local Baptist Church that practices their African rites, is fully on the side of the colonizer, and its only function is to indoctrinate the colonized into a form of subjugation preaching, "Servants, be obedient to them that are your masters according to the flesh, with fear and trembling, in singleness of your hearts, as unto Christ." (ND, p. 39) On the other hand, it is the native Baptist Church that mobilizes the population against the cruelty of the English. Symbolically it is Brother Aaron, a member of the native Baptist Church who invites Pa Campbell, in spite of the fact that they are longtime foes, to attend Bogle's meeting at Stoney Gut.

> "We want you to come to Stoney Gut, he told my father with humbleness. "You are 'most *buckra* white, but more than that, a man o' influence in our district. *Tough you be Church o' England, we know you are no' blind to what is happening to poor people.* We want you to come and sign a Petition to Governor Eyre 'fore next Vestry meeting." [Italics mine] (ND, p. 33)

It is within this context that the struggle for independence is taken up. The rich buckra (white) against the poor peasantry; the Church of England against the people, struggling desperately to free themselves from this injustice. To hear Pa Campbell describe them is sufficient to understand their status as the buckra drive up in their coaches and their silks to church while the poor people merely watch the show. And in this intricate link between God, the king and the obedience of the people, all is set in motion to esnsure their enslavement. Hear Pastor Humphrey:

> Saint Paul was a man of the world. He knew what terrible punishment could be inflicted on those who did not submit to constituted authority. He himself had been once an instrument of this authority. He knew that, rightly or wrongly, such authority had the power to flay, or even slay the malingerer. So he said: 'Servants, be obedient . . . with fear and trembling in singleness of your heart unto Christ,' 'Then he is a—look down his nose at us.' 'Let the malingerer beware of the might of constituted authority.' (ND, p. 44)

Here is the might of the Church aligned with the power of the state to enslave the people, but there is in Reid the staunch conviction that somehow a revolution must proceed in an orderly way, which, of course, is a contradiction of terms. Given the centuries of suffering, little could be done once passions, restrained for years, explode. Yet Reid finds it prudent to counsel through Lucille,

> My grandparents were with Toussaint L'Ouverture and took part in the fight for freedom. My parents used to tell me of it, and what is happening here seems to be the beginning of another Haiti. So you see, you musn't be afraid to trust. I am on your side, but I don't want our side to move along too fast.
>
> *   *   *
>
> My people knew the suffering of the poor Haitians and sympathized with them. But when the Revolution came, the poor people forgot who had been their friends and simply killed anyone who appeared to be a white. That was why my grandparents and their family fled to Jamaica. If the Revolution had come slowly, it might have come without bloodshed. I am a friend of Deacon Bogle, but I am afraid he might move along too fast; and what happens when a wagon moves too fast? (ND, p. 62)

It is important that it is Lucille who is giving this warning. For it is Lucille, white, who would marry Davie and be his helpmate when he moves to the Cays.

But if Pa Campbell is of the Church of England, he is also a very proud and dignified Jamaican. He is willing to have his son brought before the *Court of Justice* when he hears that he is charged with "disturbing the peace," but when he learns that his son is to be whipped "like a yam-hill thief" it becomes too much for his dignity. If he is found guilty of "disturbing the peace," a questionable charge under the circumstances of drought and starvation and on an occasion while he is petitioning for their rights—a form a civil disobedience—this is something that Pa Campbell could understand. But to be whipped, is a thing that could not be countenanced for his "second-born." Initially, he had not agreed with the demands of Bogle and his Stoney Gut men, but Stoney Gut people are his people and the tide of events causes him to change his mind:

> I say, sympathy is no' in my heart for law-breaking, but Stoney Gut people, are my people all the same. Yesterday I said I would not sign their petition. Things have happened today, things which must make a man think. Hear me now. (ND, p. 82)

On the following day he signs the petition, and at the urging of a few friends, Pa Campbell agrees to be the peacemaker. But his efforts are almost too late, for Bogle and his men have already released the constables taken the day before and have decided to march on Morant Bay to see the Custos (magistrate) at the Vestry meeting. Bogle and his men are ready for war as they begin to moblilize men from other parts of the country and hold meetings with the maroons in order to gain their support. When Dr. Creary asks the Custos whether he will see Bogle and his men, his retort is, "They will see the muskets of the militia." Bogle has come to Stoney Gut to seek "justice for the poor" but all he sees is the feasting of the rich, the plenitude denied the hungry cry of his people as the vestry men feast off the richness of the land. (ND, p. 104)

"We hungry! We want to see Custos Aldenburg' Bring out the fat-belly German-man! You are in there a feast on poor people's money while we out here a-starve." (ND, p. 109)

When the constables try to arrest Brother Abram, the ensuing riot begins, the custos begin to read the Riot Act and simultaneously the militia men shoot into the crowd. But the urge for freedom is too strong, the humiliation and suffering and the injustice of the people too intense. Bogle and his men take refuge in the church from where they begin their retaliation, and where Bogle solemnly reminds his men: "Men o' Stoney Gut, hear me! War is here today-today." (ND, p. 119) Drawing on the history of the Jamaican resistance movement, he recounts the early beginnings of the Maroons in 1655 and recounts the use of Jamaicans in American in the War of 1812.

How your Jamaican men died there! Remember the roll o' musketry in the night? That night when five thousand Americans came out o' New Orleans town and fell on you and your English redcoat allies? Well did your Jamaican men fight, Old Hickory Jackson said afterwards; but General Andrew Jackson did no' know that you failed because your voice was no' created to howl against men who go into battle for their rights. Wartime, hunting-time, hear the shells talk! Much glory and much shame ha' you seen. Sometimes against one, sometime against t'*other-human you are. Bullhorn*." (ND, p. 121) [Italics mine.]

And it is at this point that he reminds them of the injustices of Pastor Humphrey.

"Stoney Gut people, we did no' want war: We come to Morant Bay to seek justice. You know we can get no justice from the Bench. You know the taxes buckra English has asked us to pay is more than we can bear. How many o' you have no' got blood relations in lock-up right now because they can-no' pay their taxes?" *Yes, yes, is true that! True, that, Deacon.*

"Is true, yes? Tithes me brethren.Don't we know how Pastor Humphrey managed to build a great house for himself? Don't we know say even our

Baptist Chapel must pay tithe to Humphrey's Anglican Church? So that his stipend will pay for carriage and servant and no' that only is not plain and straight to all o' we that rascality was in Humphrey when this pastor took the contract himself to build this said church in which we stand now." (ND, p. 121)

It is a history mixed, as it were, with fidelity to the "mother country," even fighting against those who sought their liberation; but, more important, it is a history of a people fighting at every turn to achieve their own freedom. This is the history that Bogle presents to his people. Today they must fight for their own liberation against a system whose very oppression is personified by the Anglican Church in the island. No wonder that when the final assault is made against their oppressors it is to the church to which they run. It is from the Anglican Church that they burn not only the courthouse but the school for the rich as well. The rebellion thus begins with bullets that are "flying from the courthouse to the church," two symbols of oppression. In the courthouse are the Custos and his men; in the church are Bogle and his men. The courthouse symbolizes the laws that oppressed the people and the church symbolizes the way in which religion repressed the people, yet through which the people have maintained their culture, from whence came their strength to resist. Some of Bogle's men have been killed; he wants to retaliate; "forty for forty", and it is at this point that he seeks to get some ammunition for his men.

Nonetheless, the strength of the English is too much for men who were not fully prepared for war, and Governor Eyre and his men have ruthlessly fought and bullied Bogle and his men. The only surviving councilman, Davie, escapes to the Cays with Lucille and there begins his experiment with independence.

It is important to note that before Davie escapes, at the crucial moment of the onslaught, he is in disagreement with Bogle's tactics of revenge—"forty for forty," as Bogle puts it—and is angry at the killing of the Custos and his men:

> "I told Deacon we should no' kill, but take them to the Gut, where they would be hostages if war comes. But is that what he does? No. Stoney Gut men get mixed up with Morant Bay rabble and do as the rabble would. Will this no' turn even our friends from we? Is what Mr. Gordon and the other will say now? Think say the Maroons will come to we when they hear we ha' mixed with the Morant Bay people? Think say those proud fightermen will want to march side-by-side with riff-raff? Is that it that makes Deacon Bogle such a dam' fool?" (ND, p. 129)

This, of course, is where I believe that Reid goes wrong. He chastises Bogle for retaliating fully only because it will alienate the better classes of people.

He implicitly chastises the "Morant Bay rabble" as being riff-raff and is really more concerned with the reaction of the better classes than he is with the people. This mistake, of course, was the one that Toussaint made when he shot his nephew Mosie in his effort to placate the French, failing to recognize that at a time of rebellion or resistance the need is to draw on the masses of people for support, rather than to avoid offending the sensibilities of the few. In fact, whether Mr. Gordon and the others were right or wrong, they were hanged by Eyre anyhow, without regard to whether they were the better classes or not. Their cardinal sin was that they were involved on behalf of their people.

Reid, then, is suggesting moderation. Davie is the only voice of moderation in the Bogle camp and it is to him the privilege of beginning a new society is entrusted. He takes Lucille Du Bois, who is a guest at the Custos house to the cays, at the time that the rebellion begins. It is he who captures her moments before Bogle and his men move to burn down the Custos house, and it is to Pa Campbell's house that she is taken to be protected from Bogle and his men. Davie even tries to rescue Gordon from Eyre and his soldiers but he fails. To the Cays Davie must go to fashion out his new republic. The reader must remember for all practical purposes that Davie is the most moderate of Bogle's councilmen, the one who is concerned with the sentiment of the so-called "better classes" of people.

Part II of the novel tells of Davie's experiment in the Cays. To Lucille and him a son, James Creary Campbell, is born. They become a self-sufficient community in the industry of collecting guano and bird eggs and shipping them to Jamaica. Living on the Cays they begin to prosper. It is in this new land that we are presented with a vision of the new order of things.

"Is a new land, this, you ha' come to, Morant men", he said, "where what you get for your bellies shall be no' gauged by the colour o' your skin or the weight o' your pocket. Work, we must work for what we must eat. A new land . . . this, where only Mas'r God is king. It is perhaps no' known to you this Cay is no' owned by the Queen although her governor in Jamaica has since 'Sixty-three been granting leases for guano rights. So, till it is taken over by Queen Zion it will be to us. The Sixty-fifth Psalm tells us: 'Praise waiteth for thee, O God, in Zion and unto thee shall the vow be performed." (ND, p. 204)

There is, of course, a heavy taint of religion in Davie's new land, but it is a land that is founded on the principle of liberty and equality. It is one that demands hard work and dedication and one in which Davie, carried away by his vision of this new prosperity, fails to see life in its fullest dimensions. It is this problem of freedom and ideology, which Lamming explores in *Natives of My Person*, that Davie fails to come to grips with and which is personified in Lucille's outbursts.[6] One must also remember that she asks for moderation when the Rebellion breaks out, drawing on the Haitian example as an analogy. Here Lucille is complaining about the change that has come over Davie. She talks about the fact "these poor people have never known better—there is food in plenty—security for they and their children—they will not ask for more; but surely . . . you know there is something missing . . . something that's out there . . . something we've left behind." (ND, pp. 210-211)

She complains:

> I came here a woman, with the man I loved to make life with him—to make life, not living death. To work, to fight, but yes—to live and love and laugh also. He wanted to work and fight, and I have done so because he wanted me to. But has he given me what I wanted, Johnny? Has your bro'?". . . Lucille said with aloes: "He is not my husband. He is my overseer. No flowers. No singing except old hymns. No books, except the Bible and *Pilgrim's Progress*. Do you know that last night he more than hinted that I should destroy the books which Captain Grantley bought me? And do you think I do not know that he must have destroyed the bottle of brandy? (ND, p. 211)

Davie fought valiantly for freedom from oppression and control over his life. Yet, he has applied, with characteristic dedication, the same drive to make the island fecund as he did to control his woman. She confesses, "He is not my husband. He is my overseer." Even his brother, who has been with him since the beginning, has to confess:

> Her eyes are searching my face for answers, but how can I tell her that before times he could no' stand being governed, and yet now he is up in the saddle and riding us all the way he wants to go? Yet I must answer. My bro' has got his two hands to the plough and has taken to the Book while he waits for time to be full. Time, we must give him time to forget what 'Sixty-five did to him. (ND, p. 212)

Davie is unrelenting. He is striving now to impose a way of life on his people at the cost of their happiness, personified in the unhappiness of his woman. The crucial element of explaining to his people what he is about and how he is striving to reach his goal is perhaps the most important task that he omits to do. For the first time he will have to choose between the narrow limits of his liberty, i.e., all work and no play—all economic pursuit as opposed to the equally important aesthetic elements of life that he has neglected—personified by Lucille's longing for nicer clothes and some release from the thralldom of work. When the hurricane comes on the day that Captain Adams arrives, not only does Davie lose his life when a tree trunk falls upon him but Lucille is taken to Cuba during the Cuban War in 1868, living eight years later as a prostitute in Kingston.

In a way Davie has squandered this opportunity to build a new world. His death and the prostitution of Lucille could be read as symbolic of the prostitution of that opportunity. When, in 1882, the island is given back to the English it is the only logical step for this squandered opportunity, and the complete retrogression from Bogle's dreams. Sammy, for example has joined the West Indian Regiment and dutifully hoists his Union Jack at sunup and lowers it at sundown. Ruth, his sister, is the wife of an English soldier and eventually settles in the Transvaal in South Africa. Naomi, the younger sister, has married a sugar proprietor in Kingston, and the aspiration of Bogle emerges as that of a dream betrayed.

In James Creary we see the further prostitution of the dream of full independence. He becomes a full-scale businessman and eventually marries an English woman. He imitates all of the ways of the colonizer that Bogle and his men fought to destroy, and his son Garth is saved only by the timely intervention of another natural disaster, a smallpox epidemic, and Johnny Campbell.

Garth grew up with Johnny Campbell, who observes that "there's no *aloes* in him, for we ha' taken the thorns from his path." (ND, p. 249) He goes to Cambridge University and Gray's Inn, returning to Jamaica as a lawyer. Garth, however, is painfully aware of his bourgeois origins. He says:

> I grew up a buckra boy who wore shoes and had his daily quart of milk as a matter of course. When I played, there was no fear of destroying my only suit of clothes. Really I grew up *among* my poor friends, but not *with* them. (ND, p. 252)

He asks his Uncle John,

> "Tell me, Uncle John. You have often spoken of the old things but you have never given me an opinion. We have been taught in our history class that Gordon and Bogle were devils while Eyre was a saint who only did what he did because it was necessary. You knew both Gordon and Bogle. Were they as bad as painted?"
> Well, answer, I must answer now.
> I tell him: "I do no' know. A small one I was then, no' knowing right from wrong. If Mr. Gordon or Deacon Bogle did wrong, it was because the times we lived in were no' right to them. Worse was the poverty then than now, with hunger riding men for three years. *But, right or wrong, no good came of it.* Secession was what Bogle asked for—and what he got. Constitution taken away and the Crown a-rule from Whitehall. And *that happened 'cause we went too far too quick.*" (ND, pp. 252-253)

This is a striking confession from one who has seen all of the struggle from

Bogle's time to Garth's. To suggest that "no good came of it" and that "we went too far too quick" is a striking manifestation of the distorted vision that Reid gives to Garth. He maintains that a people ought to remain within the Empire "but our energy for life should be guided into ways that would spell progress for our people." (ND, p. 254) But his is an inherently false notion. For a people who have been colonized, it is necessary to break every last shackle of colonialism and begin all over again. Johnny pleads with Garth to use his "safety valve" (i.e., his education and his knowledge of the law) to carry the people forward to a new day. But it is precisely this education and its values which would keep the people enslaved forever. Apparently he doesn't understand the legacy of Gordon and Bogle, who both fought for the emancipation of their people.

Garth must take over from where Davie left off, but he must not make the same mistakes that Davie made, leading to a further watering-down of Bogle's call for full independence. There is seen in Garth the full glorification of the English, as Johnny admires him standing "tall and straight in his gown and wig," the very symbols of oppression against which Bogle fought.

Garth begins to turn his attention to the problems of the poor, to the plight of the working man who must exist on meagre wages. He is painfully aware of the problem of illiteracy, the need for education and the need for men to grow free and strong, "fearing no man." Giving himself to the dream of a new Jamaica, Garth realizes that his main task revolves around organizing the workers, "The time has come for trade unionism. We must have collective-bargaining with employees. A fairer share in the profits. Otherwise no profit at all." (ND, p. 258) Garth therefore forms a union in Kingston in order to test his strength against the "fat capitalist." The first test comes when the Corporation street-building program begins. The workers refuse to work for "starvation wages." The confrontation, however, comes on the first day of hiring, when the men are confronted by riflemen who are intent on serving the interests of the corporation. When Garth attempts to push his way through the police line to reach a high point in the office building to address the men, he is pushed back by the officers, and the riot begins. Suddenly, riflemen are shooting into the crowd. Garth and his followers are shot. When the firing subsides, three men are dead and a dozen are wounded.

In this first encounter Garth comes out the loser, but in order to free himself from a manslaughter charge and prevent more than one hundred men who supported him from going to jail, he has to go "through musty old books, seeking for the marks what generations o' freemen ha' made for us to walk by; marks that tell us why we are free who live under the Jack. Every time he stumbles on a mark I see him nod his head like he is saying *thankie* to the men o' ancient times." (ND, pp. 277-278)

The mark, however, that he goes back to is English Law, the Magna Carta. By turning to the Magna Carta and sanctioning the legal means provided by the English, Reid has moved us much further away from Bogle's dream and presented us with a diluted version of an English approved means of forging our way to freedom. The men win their case and Garth emerges as their "heroic leader." Stunned, however, by his first labor loss, Garth retreats into the safety of his family's business and later begins to live among the people in the fields of the sugar estates. In an effort to foster a greater sense of the importance of unionism, he encourages the men on his estate to form a union; he hopes this will go on to influence men on other estates to form their own unions. By way of example, Garth tries to create a sense of what the rights of workers should be on the other estates by giving each family on his estate an acre of land to grow their crops; he provides their homes with water and electricity and raises their wages. By so doing, he is able to create in the men some notion of their rights, which quickly spread to the workers on the surrounding estates.

With the organization of the workers on the other estates, the estate owners and managers get together to protect their own interests, to hold down wages, and to provide as few services as possible to the workers. First, the workers are characterized as "a dam' group of Bolsheviks," (ND, p. 300) but through the influence of Garth, the owners, with the exception of one, Mr. Garfield, accept the union and begin to accept some of the demands of the workers. But in spite of the liberalism of Garth, all he is asking for is an enlightened or advanced form of capitalism. Garth himself is a landowner and this brings in the whole question of paternalism on his part. With the formation of the union, Garth moves into politics, but from the inception, his analysis of the political situation is wrong. For example, he sees the destiny of his people solely within the ambit of the British Commonwealth,

> "The scene is changing, Uncle. We are growing up. We are getting out of the chrysalis."
> "We? We Who?"
> "The Colonial Empire. Once it was the British Empire, now it is the British Commonwealth and the Colonial Empire. Soon it will only be the British Commonwealth—each of us with our own pair of wings. But flying together." (ND, p. 311)

It is with this patronizing view that Garth sees the destiny of his people. In spite of all the humiliations, in spite of all the cruelty, in spite of all his people's intense resistance for independence, the only relationship that he can perceive for his people is that of "mother country" to "dependent country," from master-slave to owner-worker. The relation is one of dependency and respect with the explicit presumption that in order for independence to be allowed in a successful way we need to be within the fold of "Mother England." This complex is the dependency one that Juminer condemned so strongly. Garth can see no other relationship outside of this hierarchical order of things, and this is the most serious flaw of the novel. Bogle set out to achieve full independence—so did Davie, but with the death of Davie the island became a protectorate of "Mother England," and by the time we reach Garth, he has retreated as far as possible from the original position of Bogle. Using an analogy of wings as symbolic of liberation, he asks:

> "And how will we get our wings?"
> "We will ask for them, but first we must learn how to use them."
>
>   *   *   *
>
> "We had them once, you know, Uncle."
> I nod me head. "Yes, true that."
> "We lost them. We flapped too heavily, so mother-bird clipped them. For our own good, she said. She was probably right. They would have flapped us into trouble." (ND, p. 311)

This is an incredible position for a potential Caribbean leader to take. He doubts the capacity of his people for self-rule, even though a segment of his people have been ruling themselves for more than two hundred years. Further, to suggest that "mother bird clipped our wings" because "they would have flapped us into trouble" is to endorse a paternalistic and defeatist attitude that the whole history of the Caribbean categorically denies.

Garth begins his political career by launching a number of political groups. Finally, however, when the British send its commission to investigate the earlier riots, Garth demands self-government from the British with the following plea:

> "Full self-government within the orbit of the British Commonwealth! Universal Adult Suffrage! Give us a chance to shape our own destinies! Let us stand beside you, Mother England, but free and self-respecting not as whining children, but as adults, with full respect to the obligation we owe our parents! Get rid of imperialism! Let us have no decline and fall, but a permanent institution that will stand as long as free men live! Implement the four freedoms—do not allow them to drift down into the Atlantic! Get rid of these horse-and-buggy concepts, Mother England, before the rest of the world speeds out of sight leaving you wallowing in the mire of prejudiced tradition. . . ." (ND, p. 337)

The context within which Garth has demanded self-government is ridiculous. He begs for a chance to shape his destiny, and at the end of the novel he still perceives some sort of filial relationship that exists between the two countries and talks about some obscure respect and obligation that a child owes a parent—a complete contradiction of all that the history of his people has stood for, and a plea for the right to remain dependent. Even the United Nations Charter on Human Rights demands much more than this. The novel ends with Garth's last statement—"give us liberty to walk as Jamaicans, and we will walk up the same road as you, England." (ND, p. 338)

In his pamphlet, *The Case for West-Indian Self-Government*, C. L. R. James came close to making this same observation when he wondered aloud:

When will British administrators learn the lesson and for the sake of future cordial relations give willingly and cheerfully what they know they will have to give at last? How do they serve their posterity by leaving them a heritage of bitterness and hate in every quarter of the globe? Solution of the problem there is but one—a constitution on democratic lines. This does not necessarily mean a form of government modelled plastically on the English or Dominion systems. Ceylon shows one way, Malta another. The West Indian legislators have their constitution ready. That is not a matter for debate here. But there will only be peace when in each colony the final decisions on policy and action rest with the elected representatives of the people. Hard things are being said today about parliamentary democracy, but the West Indian Colonies will not presume to reject it until England and the Dominions show them the way. The high qualification for membership of the Council must go. The high franchise for the power to vote must go. That tight-rope dancer, the nominated member, must vanish forever, and the representatives of the people thrown back upon the people.

No one expects that these Islands will, on assuming responsibility for themselves, immediately shed racial prejudice and economic depression. No one expects that by a change of constitutions the constitution of politicians will be changed. But though they will, when the occasions arise, disappoint the people, and deceive the people and even, in so-called crises, betray the people, yet there is one thing they will never be able to do—and that is, neglect the people. As long as society is constituted as it is at present that is the best that modern wage-slaves can ever hope to achieve.[7]

It is in this sense that one could understand the plea which Reid made to Mother England: a plea to give Caribbean peoples a chance to shape their own destiny.

But the problem of self-government and independence did not examine only the *external* relations of the colonized and the colonizer, it had also to examine the *internal* relations of the colonized and the manner in which the legacy of colonialism shaped their internal communities. Therefore, while Reid examined the historic struggle of the Jamaican people and zeroed in on the rural response of the peasantry up to the point where they are transformed into workers, Roger Mais examined the internal lives of the urban dwellers, the astounding degree of poverty and squalor which has emanated when the peasantry moved from the rural to the urban areas. Thus in Roger Mais novels, *The Hills Were Joyful Together* (1953) and *Brother Man* (1954) we see the movement from what has been essentially a peasant novel to the appearance of a novel which is concerned primarily with the urban dweller. Here the novel is placed within the context of the city and the exploration of urban life becomes the major concern.

In examining the novels of Roger Mais certain aspects of his life become important for an understanding of the text. Imprisoned for six months for agitating for self-government for Jamaican people, Roger Mais was able to draw upon his prison experiences, his intimate knowledge of the urban condition and his close involvement with the national liberation movement of Jamaica to dramatize the plight of the dispossessed urban masses who lived in the slums of Jamaica. For him, the Jamaican slum experience became a microcosm of the urban condition in the Caribbean. In introducing the novels of Mais, Norman Washington Manley, an elder statesman of the Caribbean, made the following observations:

> I knew Roger Mais intimately, and I lived and had my being in the National Movement from its birth until its ultimate success. *I firmly believe that Roger was a product of that moment of history and drew from it the direction and power and purpose which his writing reveal. . . .*
>
> No Jamaican writer working in those early days of our National Movement could do a greater service for us all than to interpret that other world to which the majority belong for the rest of us to see and understand. No Jamaican writer was better equipped to do that job than was Roger Mais, and it is impossible to imagine a more vital and human and arresting exploration than these books made.[8] [Italics mine.]

In many ways therefore, the novels of Roger Mais were able to enlarge and to carry forward the thematic concerns which were raised by Vic Reid.

The Hills Were Joyful Together is a mosaic of the various aspects of slum life which is experienced by countless Jamaicans who live in the "yard." The tremendous underdevelopment of colonial societies is paid for in unemployment, poverty, diseases, moral degeneracy and most of all, the tremendous violence which emanates from the people. It is this turning inward of colonial violence that one finds in the urban centers of colonial countries. As Barrie Davies says of *The Hills Were Joyful Together*, "Mais is giving us the spiritual annihilation underlying the economic degradation through the jagged insistence of the prose and its rhythmic repetitions."[9]

Basically, the novel centers around the lives of a number of couples: Surjue, who is caught stealing and who eventually is killed in trying to escape from prison to see his woman Rema; Rema, who goes insane because of Surjue's imprisonment and burns herself alive; Bedosa, the husband of Charlotta, who was killed by a train; Shag, a hardworking man, who eventually kills his wife Euphemia when he finds her in bed with Bajun Man; and the prostitute, Zephyr, who has a heart of gold, and "whose stable income and basic generosity provide a center of order in the yard."[10] Yet the novel is fraught with a basic violence which seems to brutalize the peoples' sensibilities and drives them into greater depths of degradation. The chaplain, a character in the novel, wonders aloud:

> What happens to people when their lives are constricted and dwarfted and girdled with poverty . . . things like that and that and that come out of it . . . moral deformity, degradation, disease . . . heaven help us all, for all are guilty before heaven. . . . God forgive us all, for all of us stand, with these, in need of forgiveness . . . (HWJT, p. 197)

Yet all is not poverty and want. Struggling to assert itself of this condition of dispossession is the sense of community and the warmth and tenderness which touch the lives of the inhabitants of the slum:

> That evening they built a big fire and set big stones about it in the middle of the yard, and they sat around on chairs and benches and stools and upturned boxes and anything they could sit on, and the women fried fish and johnny-cakes, and the big fire lit up the darkness and sent up showers of sparks, and they sang songs and told stories and cracked jokes and forgot their worries and their fears and their jealousies and their suspicions and the occasion took on all the aspects of a picnic, and they were like children again.(HWJT, p. 39)

There is also the sense that since they only have each other that they need to help each other in order to overcome the terrible loneliness of the ghetto. This seems to be best exemplified when Rema, in gratitude for the assistance that Zephyr gives her when Surjue was caught, retorts:

> "Thanks Zephyr, gee, you're the best friend I have in the world, it seems."
> "Don't talk about it, honey, *we got to help one another; in things like sickness an' trouble it's just natural for people to help one another, it seems to me*." (HWJT, p. 122) [Italics mine.]

Yet it is the prison-setting of the novel (which takes up parts one and two of the novel) around which the central political arguments are made.

Indeed, Mais utilizes the subject of penology as a measure by which one can examine the general humanity of a society. First, he argues that imprisonment makes animals of us all and speaks to the final degradation to which it plunges man:

> Walls, walls, and all that passed between them . . . a man unmanned, un-countenanced, given over to the naked stare of self-pity . . . society, and the cankering, unyielding sore . . . enclosed within these walls a man was shut from light, like a seed struggling toward the sunlight from between damp stones . . . shut away like this a man lost his manhood and became a cypher, and lost his spirit and became insensible stone . . . shut in like this, with the rats scampering in the ceiling, and the stale smell of human waste and offal, and the vultures circling eternally in the sky, a man became at last lost to himself utterly and to the world . . . shut away a man like this and all you had was his skin—stretched tightly against his body that knew the pang and torture and bitterness and degradation of whip and bludgeon and ankle-chain, and his shame, and the shame of others with him, all . . . all of the man that you shut in here was one with the bricks that went into the hideous walls, never to come out again, like the bricks that held together the hideous cells in darkness, and the mould that grew and ripened on the damp and reeking walls.
> All of the men enclosed within these deadening walls, within this sightless, unfeeling darkness stayed here with the generations of lost men that were brought here damned to insensible negation out of sight of the world . . . the lost generations came here, were taken up, caught up, lost without memory of the living world . . . lost without end in darkness, the spiritless, succeeding generations upon generations, the murderers and rapers of young girls, the spoilers of others, the arsonists, the cut-throats, their manhood slowly squeezed from them, to be drunk up at last by the screaming murderous walls. (HWJT, pp. 208-209)

For Mais, it is from the system of prison that one can get a fairly accurate view of the general standards of the society. And as the chaplain makes clear to the superintendent of the prisons:

> I have not made a study of penology. But I tell you this, we make criminals out of men and women and children in the kind of society we are satisfied to put up with. We are just as much criminal, in a sense, as they. (HWJT, p. 239)

The chaplain emerges as the moral spokesman in the novel. By implicating his society for the outrage that they have committed against colonial peoples, he is subjected to the full fury of the superintendent. Thus as the conversation between the two continues, the chaplain is accused of being a communist:

'Excuse me, Padre. That is not fair. You use words extravagantly. Forgive me if I must say it, but you talk just like one of those Communists.'

The Padre gathered himself and stood up. He was taut, and shaking with anger deep down.

'Fools!' he said, his voice quivering slightly. 'We are all fools. We are smug and satisfied, and let the Communists beat us to it every time.'

The Superintendent fidgeted uncomfortably in his chair.

'No, get this straight, I am not a Communist,' said the Padre, 'but I can tell you a thing or two. Why do you think Communism grows and thrives among underprivileged people? You sit back in your swivel chair and shake your fist at it, can you answer that?'

He sat down as suddenly as he had got up, and passed the back of his hand across his brow.

He said in a gentle voice: 'Forgive me. I am a little upset today. I should not have lost my temper. Here,' he felt in his pocket, took out a little crumpled pamphlet, it was titled THE UNIVERSAL DECLARATION OF HUMAN RIGHTS. He held it up and thumbed its leaves, his hands still shaking slightly. 'Ever seen one of these? It is issued by the General Assembly of the United Nations. Date, March 1949. Already it has come to mean nothing to us but more words in a book. But here it says, on page 6, Article 22, "Everyone, as a member of society, has the right to social security and is entitled to realization . . . of the economic, social and cultural rights indispensable for his dignity and the free development of his personality." That is what it says. And that is the crux of the whole question here, the basic approach to penology in a civilized state. The population of our prisons is made up almost wholly of people who had no other alternative but to commit these crimes for which they are being punished, and what is more shocking still, they will be forced to commit them again and again, each time they are outside. For they have no other means of putting food into their hungry bellies, let alone all consideration of dignity and the free development of their personality. In this country of less than 50 per cent literacy about one-third of the population is unemployed.'(HWJT, pp. 239-240)

Here, the authorial intrusion may have been too insistent as it might have been too heavy-handed. Yet it serves to dramatize the author's point that the very nature of the social order is so structured that the persons who find themselves living in the slums of the Caribbean have no choice but to commit antisocial acts against the society; the very social order which was responsible for its condition in the first place. Secondly, it is the poverty and the illiteracy of the society which account for the brutality and the violence within the society, which in the final analysis, is reflected in the make-up of the prison population. The elaborate system of prison, therefore, becomes the only way in which one is able to contain the legitimate demands of the society.

This analogy between the prison system and the society was not, it would seem, a fortuitous selection on the part of Mais. There was an historic precedent in 1862, when Governor Eyre was sworn in as lieutenant governor. The first correspondence which George William Gordon sent to him dealt with the "administration of justice in connection with Prison regulations."[11] Thus Mais was not particularly inaccurate when he sought to locate this analogy in the history of the society. Therefore when next we see the chaplain after his heated argument with the superintendent, we see him going into the chapel to pray, amidst an atmosphere which takes us back into the long and dark age of slavery:

> He went in, drew the blinds, threw open a window from the bottom. He stared across the tops of some trees to the scarred roof of the old church in the distance . . . behind it, towering, the sheer prison wall.
>
> On a little ledge behind him there stood a heavy crucifix, and before the crucifix an ancient prayer stool. There was some old tapestry hanging against the wall. The crucifix, the stool, the tapestry, most of the things inside this attic, reached back into the past, to the grim old days of slavery. The place haunted him with all its austere beauty and its ugliness. He came here often, alone, to pray.
>
> He stood at the window a long time, looking out across at the ancient, historic church. The wind blew his untidy hair about his head. He put his hand up, automatically, to smooth it down.
>
> Some thin, starved-looking, ragged children came running up the street, laughing, shouting, swearing, skylarking. They had their slates and books with them, coming from school. His lips moved as though he would say a prayer for them; bless them. He shook his head, hesitating, as though the sense of his own helplessness, unworthiness rose up like that terrible wall between him and heaven. (HWJT, pp. 241-242)

This is the legacy of slavery: a history of exploitation and poverty. But the children coming from school with their slates and their books represent one level of hope; one manner in which the descendants of the slaves may escape the fate of their parents.

Throughout the torturous course of the novel there is yet another character who represents the symbol of hope and pleads for the recognition of the reader. His name is Ras, a member of the Rastarafian movement which preaches the gospel of peace and love, and who, in his dignity and pride, pleads to the noble instincts of his people. Thus when Puss-Jock, the father of Ditty, returns to the yard after a long absence, his daughter runs away from him and seeks the protection of Ras. Puss-Jock with a new sense of haughtiness, attempts to thrust Ditty upon Ras. The response of Ras is distinct for the quality of its nobility:

'You can have her if you want, Ras.'
Ras said: 'Howdy brother. Peace an' love.'
'Say you can have her if she tek you' fancy. High time fo' she to get a man.'
'Yuh words are wantin' in wisdom an' elegance,' said Ras quietly, as though he was speaking a sermon. 'They flow from de mout' of a fool. They not deservin' an answer. But brother, don' try to draw me anger. Go-long yuh ways befo' yuh tongue trip you. Peace an' love.' (HWJT, p. 250-251)[12]

It is to this quiet message of salvation, the formal proclamation of an alternative social and cultural vision of the society, to which Ras speaks. It is this attempt of the Rastafarians to offer a new vision to the society that becomes the thematic center of Mais' second novel, *Brother Man* in which Ras becomes John Power (Brother Man), the central character, who offers to his people the gospel of peace and love and instructs them to direct the search for their spiritual sustenance to their African origins.

Thus while the Anglican Church (that is, the official Church of England) is depicted as an oppressive force in collusion with the colonial order in *New Day*, the Rastafarian movement is depicted as a positive and progressive force, concerned with the welfare of the dispossessed masses in *Brother Man*. Indeed, the Rastafarian movement emerges as the direct descendants of the native Baptist churches of George William Gordon and Paul Bogle and the race-first doctrines of Marcus Garvey. *Brother Man* is a member of the Rastafarian movement and aligns himself with the poor down-trodden people of the island. Yet Mais seems less concerned with the physical poverty of the urban dwellers than he is with the need of the people to recapture their sense of dignity and worth in spite of their condition of poverty and squalor. Because of these concerns, the novel becomes a parable of love and devotion to one's people and an attempt to speak to the spiritual regeneration of a colonial people.

Like *The Hills Were Joyful Together*, the novel is set in Orange Lane in Kingston, Jamaica and the lives of the people are filled with poverty, brutality and violence: Papcita, the lover of Girlie, is eventually killed by Girlie for deserting her; Corelia, whose husband was jailed for six years for selling ganga (marajuana) eventually goes insane, kills her three-year old son and hangs herself, while Bra' Ambo, the Shango man, is depicted as a sinister force in the novel.

Basically, however, the story revolves around the goodness of Brother Man, who "belonged to that cult known as the Ras Tafarities," (BM, p. 74) and, became a symbol of peace and love in the slums of Orange Lane. As a member of the Rastafarians, Brother Man believes that the "black people are God's chosen people."

'De spirit of de Lawd went over into Ethiopia when Israel was parted among the nations. De twelve tribes were scattered an' lost. But *de spirit* of de Lawd passed over into *Ethiopia, after the Queen of Sheba came to Solomon and learned all his wisdom, an' passed over back to her own land. So it was black men out of Africa who became God's chosen people, for they had learnt de Way.'* (BM, p. 121)

In the goodness of his heart he goes among the wretchedness and poverty of the Lane and manages to rise "above and beyond the petty envies, and convetousness, and hates, and desires, and all the gossip that went about them from day to day." (BM, p. 121)

Among the people therefore, he preached a gospel that advocated the power of understanding over judgement, and so he judged no man. As the narrator pointed out, "Understanding to him came after judgement, and with the getting of understanding of that kind, man ceased to pass moral judgement, whether of approbation or condemnation." (BM, p. 180) He believed that the acquisition of knowledge was more important than the acquisition of money and so he preached: "If you will seek after knowledge as men seek after silver you will get it, and if you lift up your voice for understandin' it will come." (BM, p. 90) Above all however, he advocated the sentiments of peace and love among his brethren.

Yet, in spite of his goodness, the hate which most Jamaicans had for the wild men with the beards (the Rastafarians) eventually contaminated their love for Brother Man even though this hate appeared to be a temporary phenomenon. Thus when he is unable to heal Codelia's son, in her grief and insanity, she causes him to be arrested by falsely placing a number of counterfeit coins in his money jar.

At about the same time that Brother Man was arrested for possessing counterfeit coins, a brutal rape and murder took place along the lonely Palisadoes Road. The young woman who was raped identified the rapist and murderer as "a black man, wild, unkempt . . . [and] wearing a beard." (BM, p. 170) In the belief that the rapist was a member of the Rastafarian movement, all of the old hatred against a movement that attempted to issue an alternative to the society, came out in full vengeance. Gradually, it would seem, the entire community in the Lane began to vent their hate upon Brother Man:

About three days after the Palisadoes incident, a wave of resentment swept through the city. It was directed against all bearded men. The leading newspapers played up the angle that a community of bearded men in their midst, formed together into a secret cult, was a menace to public safety.

People began writing letters in the press. All bearded men should be placed behind barbed-wire. They should be publicly washed (?) and shaved! They should be banished to Africa. They should be sterilized. They should be publicly flogged. They became identified with a certain political party. They should be denied the vote. They were, in fact, potential rapists and murderers all.

One broad-minded citizen wrote a letter pointing out that all men, whether they let their beards grow, or shaved every morning, were in a sense potential murderers and rapists. It was never published.

But the wave of resentment and anger and intolerance against a minority spread, and was carefully fanned to a nice conflagration by political opportunists and a partisan press.

Within a week bearded men were being assaulted and mistreated in the streets. Many members of the Ras Tafarite persuasion were forced to shave their beards in secret, or suffer publicly humiliation of another kind.

Brother Man went about his affairs undisturbed by what was happening around. (BM, pp. 173–174)

The frenzy and the hate which gripped the crowd was soon directed towards Brother Man and eventually he became a victim of the people's hate.

'Down de ole Ras Tafarite! Murderers dem. . . .'

'Nutt'n but chop man, an' rape woman, an' scuffle an' pass bad money, an' t'ief!'

'Way wid dem, lick dem down, kill dem!'

'Ole Ras Tafarite dem!'

The clamour and shouting behind grew louder, coarser, shriller, women and children mostly.

He said, 'Only hear me a little, hear me out. . . .'

But his voice was drowned in the shrieks and curses of the mob.

'Lick him down, kill him! What, oonu 'fraid him? Oonu move over gimme pass, mek way.'

He raised his arms again, tried to address them. A woman shouldered her way to the front of the crowd, a half-brick in her gnarled fist.

As he raised his hands, she flung the brick. It caught him a glancing blow on the side of the head.

As he pitched and fell he put his hand to the side of his head. It came away covered with blood.

Blood spouted freely from the gash in his head, it ran down his cheek, and spattered on his shirt.

A great blood-thirsty cry went up from the crowd.

Like a pack of wolves they surged in upon him.

A woman on the outskirts, screamed, rushed forward, threw herself on her knees beside him, tried to shield him with her body. They tore her clothes and roughly threw her aside. She was an old woman, with scarcely any strength in her body at all. They kicked in her ribs, trampled her. She lay in the gutter bleeding.

The reeking wave of humanity surged over and over him, fighting each other to get at him, like a jackal-pack, when one of them is down. (BM, pp. 185-187)

Later, however, ashamed of their actions, the neighbors dropped in to ask after him, which in a manner proved to be a vindication of his position.

Yet it would seem that what the people feared was not the unkempt and disheveled nature of the Rastafarians but the content of their doctrine which called for the complete reevaluation of their ways of life. Indeed, as early as 1933, C.L.R. James had observed that there was a schism between the brown man and the black man of the Caribbean. He argued that:

The Negroid population of the West Indies is composed of a large percentage of actually black people, and about fifteen or twenty per cent of people who are a varying combination of white and black. From the days of slavery, these have always claimed superiority to the ordinary black, and a substantial majority of them still do so (though resenting as bitterly as the black assumptions of white superiority). With emancipation in 1834 the blacks themselves established a middle class. But between the brown-skinned middle class and the black there is a continual rivalry, distrust and ill-feeling, which, skilfully played upon by the European people, poisons the life of the community.[13]

It was this dichotomy, exemplified by Brother Man, to which the Rastafarians addressed their religio-political doctrine. They emphasized the need for Caribbean peoples to return to their spiritual and cultural origins and posited Africa as the centrality of that origin. It is this doctrine which the people, by beating Brother Man so ruthlessly attempts to reject. Indeed very early in the novel we are alerted to just this fact when Brother Man tries to explain his doctrines to a young boy:

He tried to explain to the eager boy something of his own cult, and of the cult of the Nazarites, and what it meant to them not to shave their hair.

But it was a bit too much for a boy to understand, and after a while Bra' Man stood up, and the boy stood up with him, under the glow of the street lamp, and Bra' Man stretched out his hand and laid it on the boy's head, and said: 'Now you go home, son, and try to understand all the things I have told you, an' God walk wid you, son, peace an' love.' (BM, p. 75)

John Power joined the Rastafarian movement in 1938. From its inception in the thirties to the present time, the teachings of the Rastafarian movement has had a tremendous impact upon the people of Jamaica and the people of the Caribbean. Reporting on the growth and importance of the Rastafarians in 1970 Rex Nettleford pointed out that:

Yet the role of the Rastafarian movement has been a dynamic one in the wider society of which it is really a part. Many of the ideas and much of the mood of this group have seemingly passed on to the younger generation at large. What would have been regarded as peculiarly Rastafarian in 1959–60 was to be assimilated ten years later into the mainstream of thought on black power and majority control. . . . By the late sixties there was much more widespread embrace of Rastafarian attitudes, ideals and even practices among bona fide members of the wider society. The symbolic expressions of long and carefully unkempt hair and the wearing of bright garb believed to be 'African', the open defiance of 'the unjust law' against the smoking of ganja which is still prohibited by the rules of the wider society but remains the holy and wisdom-giving weed to the Rastafarians, the unashamed commitment to Africa and a yearning for knowledge of the African past, the conscious reference to the self as *black man* rather than as *negro*, the unfaltering expressions of wrath against an oppressive and what the Rastafarians regarded as a 'continuing colonial society', the campaign against police brutality suffered by the poor presumably because of their poverty and the mal-administration of justice, the expressed hatred for the humiliating 'white bias' in the society though not necessarily for white people, the deprecation of the agonizing logic of a history of black slavery and white domination—all the above were to be appropriated by many Jamaicans during the 1960s in a growing awareness of the need to define their existence or by those who, according to one Rastafarian, had been 'liberated from the obscurity of themselves'.[14]

Writing in 1969, Walter Rodney, after living and working among the Rastafarian community could report that:

In our epoch the Rastafari have represented the leading force of this expression of black consciousness. They have rejected this philistine white West Indian society. They have sought their cultural and spiritual roots in Ethiopia and Africa. So that whether there is a big flare up or not, there is always the constant activity of the black people who perceive that the system has nothing in it for them, except suppression and oppression.[15]

It is very clear then that the Rastafarian movement has made a very tremendous impact upon the social and cultural development of Jamaica and the Caribbean and that Roger Mais, in his prescience, was able to anticipate the impact of the movement upon the society and to make an important contribution to the literature of resistance in the Caribbean.

Technically, Roger Mais added a very special dimension to the literature of resistance. By using African oral prose forms (the riddle, the proverb, etc.,) and the rituals of the people, he was able to locate the literature more specifically within the context of the Caribbean and to create the sense of rhythmic repetitions to which Barrie Davis refers. Moreover, Mais's use of these forms gives his works a tropical freshness, a flamboyant cadence, a dynamic urgency and an especial nativity, just as the sixteenth century prose of the King James Bible, which informs Jamaican Creole speech gives a kind of majestrial tone to the language of his novels.

But while Vic Reid locates his beginnings in the historical past of the Morant Bay Rebellion and carries his narrative up to the new day of universal adult suffrage, and Roger Mais examines the squalor of the urban areas at the time of the new day and offers the religio–social and cultural doctrines of the Rastafarians as his point of departure, Edouard Glissant (1928–) goes further back into slavery, argues for the fusion of tradition and modernity into a new synthesis and offers his concept of what the new Antillian (that is, Caribbean man) ought to look like. Such is the burden of his novel, *La Lézarde* (1958, translated as *The Ripening* in 1959.

For three and a half centuries Martinique has been subjected to the colonial domination of the French. The novel itself, which is set around the Martinician elections of 1945, goes back into the rebellion of 1788 in which the "the count who was commander-in-chief of the army did a good bit of killing and deported the survivors to the northern island. Later in the same year, 1788, great cargoes of newcomers were shipped in from Guinea, and many of them took to the woods." (R, p. 217)

When the novel opens we find that the country is "only now awakening to the new and violent ways of the world, which after a long silence had dawned upon it and made it cry aloud." (R, p. 20) Papa Longoue, the old *quimboiseur* and maroon, through his knowledge of the past represents the historical continuity of the country's social and cultural development. On the other hand, the present destiny of the country seems to be placed in the hands of a group of adolescents. Within their group Mathieu, one of the leading characters of the novel who represents modernity has undertaken the factual, analytical research of the past: "His job was to dig materials out of the town archives and weave them into a local history." (R, p. 26) Counterposed to Mathieu is Raphael Targin (Thael) who represents tradition. He is a young man from the mountains who knows "the old legends, who cares for the mysteries and who speaks like a prophet." (R, p. 23) Other members of the adolescent group are Marie Celat (Mycea), Paul Basso (Pablo) Margaurite Adole (Margarita) and Luc. Collectively, the historic task of this group is to vindicate the promise and spirit of freedom for which their ancestors stood, even though it entails the elimination of a local renegade who has been sent by the French government to stifle subversive movements in the island.

Throughout the land the river Lizard flows fecundating the land and symbolising the irreversible flow of knowledge from "our primitive magic, to the dawn of true knowledge." (R, p. 33) The characters, in their struggle to transform the conditions of their lives, were perceived at one level as actors in the drama of the life of the country playing their fated parts in its historic destiny. Thus Thael, Mathieu and all the other characters, find themselves acting not as

> mere men, but instruments of their country's fate, subjects of future legend. Their steps wove the cloth with which the land was to be covered, and yet nobody knew it. They did not know it themselves, or how would they have kept on living? (R, p. 104)

It is this inevitablity of man's function in the transformation of his reality that looms as one of the important considerations of the novel.

The second and more important consideration of the novel revolves around the continuity of tradition and modernity, and the degree towards which legends, as a means of knowing, are able to reveal a part of the country's truth. For it is the narrator's contention that "legends, which reflect like mirrors a man's search, are in this land accepted, without either glorification or denial. Hence they are at the same time significant and yet doomed to decay." (R, p. 60) Because legend, which is partial truth, is doomed to decay, it must be augmented by factual reality, which itself is partial truth. The search for the correct combination of these two modalities of truth, becomes the key to unlocking the future of the country's direction.

Thus as Thael (tradition) and Mathieu (modernity) proceed through the country, their perceptions are refined by the nature of the reality which they see before them:

> Comparing the monotony of this flat bridge and the buildings of the distillery with the landmarks of the earlier road, with the three trees which had marked the successive stages of his journey (the flamboyant, the plum, the silk cotton; symbols of glory, abasement and legend in their red, yellow and gray); considering the dullness of the present scene and the splendor of the recent past, Thael came to the conclusion that he had left the realm of myth and entered the wasteland of the everyday, that he was about to learn not the boundlessness of suffering but the stifling confinement of commonplace misery. (Mathieu was right. He was no longer living in the fiery circle of a volcano, he had relinquished its burning splendor. Now he was retracing the steps of the island's history, noting facts, like a scholar. Suddenly accuracy became his ruling passion, and dead men told him the true course of events in the past.) He ran down an alley between two fields of densely growing cane, in order to know at first hand this prison, to feel, between its whistling walls, the full weight of its tyranny. (Mathieu was right again. *He* had no need of direct experience. Sitting in his study, he understood the significance of the symbols and knew reality by intuition.) (R, pp. 70-71)

So as they struggle together to discover the truth of their condition they both recognize that an understanding about the true direction of the country could only be achieved through an interpretation of the recorded history of the people (that is, through dates, graphs and historical records) and their legends (that is, their myths and stories and mysteries). It is the understanding of this truth which led Thael to observe that "history does to him [Mathieu] what the old legends have done to me." (R, p. 80)

It is this knowledge which becomes the flame (the title of the first part of the book) and which prepares Thael and Mathieu to act in unison to accomplish their deed (the title of the second part of the book); that of eliminating the renegade, Garin. The one is really the alter ego of the other and thus their dialogue:

> "When I confirm a date, I confirm the power and the glory that I feel within me. . . . But we're not the mere vehicles of a protest, an outcry . . . "
>
> "Did I say anything about an outcry?"
>
> "We're not just exponents of violence, of poverty, or the memory of days gone by. When we dream, Thael, who is to say that our dream is vain, unless he too has fermented in the same everday suffering, the same stifling air? . . . I fought a solitary battle and lost it; now I am thrown back among the wandering ghosts of the past. It's your turn, Thael. You will do the deed and win the prize. . . . "
>
> (I'm not saying anything, Mathieu. How can you know what you know unless you have cause for weeping?)
>
> "Yours is the widom and the power of decision. . . . For you've come to decide; yes, you are here to join the ebullient past to the bitter present. Yours, Thael, is the joy. Don't say a word; I know it. I must stay here, where I am, proclaiming your power. You will need me, and the mists in which I am enveloped. Out of this vast, ignorant monotone we shall make a song of joy. Yes, everything is still nebulous. But soon we shall have the deed. The river runs with a new purposefulness to the sea, the Lizard, or whatever other river you like, equally propitious, one of the creeks where a whole people comes to splash about and rejoice. On a future day the delta will no longer be dirty. This is the only way that, in the past, the Lizard betrayed us. We shall master the technique of making dikes and canals, and suddenly the Lizard will arrive crystal clear at its destination, just as our people will step out with new confidence in front of the rest. . . ." (R, pp. 80-81)

The deed being done, or in the process of being accomplished, they must now turn to the future, the promise of which is contained in the electoral/platform ("The Elections" is the title of the third part of the book) of the People's Party.

In a land where there is government oppression and the presence of poverty, disease, malnutrition and death. A sensible program which attempts to alleviate such conditions must give serious considerations to the provisions for which the People's Party called:

> "more efficient exploitation of the island's natural resources and for the employment of day laborers rather than indentured, "living-in" plantation hands, who had no freedom to move from one place to another. They asked that agricultural workers should enjoy the same rights as their counterparts in the town, and that local representatives have greater power. The matter of the relations between town and country was one currently under debate in party circles." (R, p. 130)

As was to be expected, the program of the landowners' party demanded the continuance of their "multiple subsidiaries . . . [and continued to] look on the town as the danger spot" (R, p. 130) of the nation.

Despite the deceptive slogan of the land owners' party which promised "a bigger and better place in the sun" (R, p. 130) for all, the People's Party outlined the problems of the country and from that standpoint offered a vision of possibilties for the future:

> The speaker called for attention. In the course of the evening, he said, every detail of our woes had been mentioned: malnutrition, starvation pay, excess crops of sugar and no demand for them on the world market. The picture was pitch-black, with no ray of light to relieve it. But in the midst of their suffering our people had given a new meaning, all their own, to the word "liberty." Along with the people of adjacent islands we must combat the sterility and inertia in which we were living. We wanted light and air and communication with the world outside. The country itself was rich in possibilities, but its oppressors had thrown a mantle of death around it. Ten years ago they had killed one of the best and strongest of our brothers. Once he was gone, they had had a free hand. But now we were awakening; like Lazarus we were rising from the tomb. But no one must expect a miracle. Vigilance and combat must be the order of the day. (R, pp. 132-133)

It is for the achievement of these possibilities that these young people have given their energies and now, on the first Sunday in September of 1945, the people go to the polls to decide whether they want a new order or not. As Professor Wilbert Roget notes, the Second World War served as a watershed in the island's history in that "the blockade of the island of Martinique by the allied marines led to the isolation of that island. The economic hardships endured were superseded only by the Antillians' painful encounter with the blunt racism of the occupying French forces."[16] For a country which was traumatized by a war and prior colonial neglect, the elections of 1945 in the city of Lambrianne, was an extremely important affair:

Emerging from the black hole of the war and the train of shadows it had left behind, the people were eager to affirm their rebirth. The election of a Representative was not the only thing at stake; the important question was whether the dark night was really over and a new day was at hand. Was the wide world open to those who longed to explore it? Could the ideal of brotherhood, so long dormant and inefficacious, finally make its way? (R, p. 191)

With the certainty of victory came thoughts of the political unity of the Caribbean area. As Pablo shouted: "Sometimes I dream of islands, all the islands around us . . . It seems absurd that they should have separate existences, all alike. They ought to be joined together." (R, p. 199) With victory assured and the hopes for a new future rekindled, new conceptions for a new day arose in their minds. But before that new day could issue forth, one needed to go back into the past. For as Pablo contends: "We must go back to Papa Longoue, to the lore which we have so long forgotten. To Africa. We must go down to the sea [which is the future] and sail out over it." (R, p. 199)

The victory of the People's Party caused the adolescents to take a more searching look at the relation of the past to the present and the need to understand that the present generation was but one link in the continuous chain of liberation that spread from the maroons to their generation and which would continue beyond their own generation. As Mycea explains to Mathieu:

"Is there really a barrier, a barricade, between ourselves and the generation that went before us? Must we be punished for having striven to perfect a technique, to know the truth about ourselves and act accordingly? We weren't the ones to take the initiative, really. The people carried us, their children, along. For what were we? Boundary lines, buoys borne by the flood; not helmsmen, but watchful passengers." (R, p. 215)

Indeed, their actions, in the last analysis, must become legend and merge into the cultural history of the islands and thereby shape the future generations of Martinicans.

For Glissant, however, the legacy of the Caribbean struggle is large and contains many elements. Although Mais argues for a predominant African heritage of the Caribbean, Glissant argues for a diversified Caribbean (he calls it Antillian) heritage that includes the vast spectrum of people that go to make up the Caribbean. Thus he argues for a diversified Caribbean man who has a special relationship to the world:

Our people have a special significance. Almost all the races of the world are represented here, not just since yesterday, but for centuries now. The end result is the 'Antilles man.' A mixture of our African forebears, sailors from Brittany, Hindus, Chinese merchants. . . . They wanted to make us forget Africa. But of course we haven't forgotten. Very good. But does that justify our having such an inflated opinion of ourselves? Our people have no such conceit."

"Very well; it's only an overgrown village. We're only a dot on the map. But what we have done, we have done with our own hands. Remember how you said to me: 'You came here of your own free will.'? The reason for our pride is that we have at last made our voice heard in the great world. Our people, confined to this tiny island, scorned and forgotten, have been born into the family of nations." (R, p. 225)

It is this conception of Caribbean man that becomes one of the chief concerns of *The Ripening*. For having postulated that most of the races of mankind are represented in our Caribbean lands,[17] the concept of what constitutes Caribbean man takes a much different hue for Glissant than it does for most of the other writers whom we have been studying. For him, Africa ought to be the base of Caribbean culture but the rich contribution of the other cultures ought not to be neglected. For as Wilbert Roget has argued:

Africa is a constant source of reflection in Glissant's works. But what this writer presents is neither the "traditional" Antillais image of Africa—that negative stereotype as analyzed by Fanon—nor the nostalgic and pacifist (Senghorian), or else the strident and combative (Césairian) proclamations one encounters in the various voices of the *Négritude* movement. Glissant's evocation subordinates all African references, or rather, he utilizes these references in furtherance of a more urgent, though perhaps less immediately glamorous, project. This project is to develop in the Antillais complete rootedness in his land and his history so that he may be equipped to interact on equal footing with peoples of different cultural proveniences.

The African component of the Antillais make-up is consequently to be viewed as a contributing element, not the determining element. And given the historical precedence of an ideology which extolled the supremacy of the African features (*Négritude*), Glissant finds it necessary to resist such a tendency. He wishes to ascribe to Africa its just measure in the composite Antillais identity.[18]

This wish to broaden the concept of the Caribbean identity seems to have become a prominent concern among many writers. Gerard Pierre–Charles, in his article on Caribbean cultures has suggested that:

The history of the Caribbean is as complex and volcanic as its geography. The numerous Caribbean societies were born of historical and geographical coincidences, of Indian and black populations encountering a motley of colonists who ploughed these waters and exploited these lands. Hence the violence always characterizing social conflicts in the area, and hence its ethno-cultural wealth and diversity.

From a mosaic of races, languages, rhythms, temperaments, and religious beliefs emerge a culture and a civilization mirrored in intellectual creativity of incomparable value in music, dance, literature and religion and in terms of struggle: all marvelously synthesized, by the way, in the Cuban revolution.[19]

It is such a diverse society, such a mosaic of races, languages and culture, yet subjected to the same kind of historical subjugation of which Reid, Mais and Glissant speak. For the young adolescents of *The Ripening*, however, the *true* Caribbean man will emerge out of the coming together, or at least in the recognition of the diversity of Caribbean history.

In a review of *La Lézarde*, a young person named Nyunai argued that the novel demonstrated that "the slow germination of national consciousness [accrues] through the misery, exploitation and humiliation" of the people of the country. Because of this, he continues, *La Lézarde* should be considered as "the epic march of a whole people, I'd say of an entire race, from slavery to freedom."[20] Before the publication of *La Lézarde* Glissant offered some thoughts about what a novel should do:

It seems that a novel that has as its goal to "reveal" a reality, should accost this reality from all sides at the same time, in its positive and negative elements. In brief, this novel [that is, the novel of the black writer] *should carry out the research* to find the essential qualifications of this reality [the reality of the black, colonized world], and *should reveal* the short comings from which it suffers. The condition perpetrated upon Negro peoples by colonization is such that the patient research of its riches and its flavor is almost impossible. Black reality is still a tributary of colonization, *it is not a reality free unto itself*; the novel is enjoined to abandon this fortuitous quest for riches to denounce that lack of liberty. From that moment, it becomes a cry, an indictment, an appeal to the future, and no more an attempt to perpetuate the riches of the present.[21]

According to Glissant, the purpose of the novel is therefore two-fold; to denounce the brutality of colonization and an appeal to the future. It is to these two realities that Glissant writes: the exploitation of colonization and the future of these Caribbean states.

As we examine *New Day* we see it as an almost perfect example of a novelist's vision trapped in that peculiar relation of dependence on the master's or the colonizer's values. Independence, yes, but with you, "mother England." The strength of the novel, however, lies in the understanding by the author that it is resistance which has shaped the destiny of the people and has signalled the unquenchable need for freedom. In *The Hills Were Joyful Together* and *Brother Man* we see the attempt to examine the present (a result of the past conditions) and to suggest an alternate reality for the people: a reality which is structured within the context of the people's reality and indigenous to the culture. Here *dependence* gives way to the *independence* of the people's vision. It is in *The Ripening*, however, that we see the force of the argument that the past and the present are only in service of the future, and that the novel, apart from denouncing the present is called upon to become a cry for the future order of things.

But *New Day* is not quite critical realism even though it goes beyond mere *realism*. This is found in the fact that history, although not used primarily for *decorative* purposes, serves primarily for *descriptive* purposes and does not evaluate the history of the people in a critical manner. While there is an attempt at social analysis (inadequate, though it is,) the novel does depict the continuity of events and at least show some casual relationships between these events.

The Hills Were Joyful Together, on the other hand, while it depicts the conditions of the urban poor, the work tends to border on naturalism, in that one almost gets a photographic reproduction of the condition of the slums. There is an attempt to depict the causal connection of the reality in a critical manner, but the analysis is imposed from without by authorial intrusion rather than depicted as arising from the inherent action of the novel itself. Moreover the fragmentary or episodic nature of the novel prevents that concentrated effort of character and plot-development that is necessary for such critical analysis. In *Brother Man*, Mais seems to mar, what is an otherwise important work, by an excessive amount of melodrama. In this sense, Kenneth Ramchand is correct when, in commenting on a particular scene in which Mais tries to attribute certain Christlike qualities to Brother, he argues that "no other West Indian writer could have created a scene like this without comic intention."[22]

In Glissant we find a ponderous prose style with a highly contrived artistic presence that tends to diminish much of the urgency of the content of the work. While this tortuousness seems to inhere in the language itself, it makes it difficult to convince one of the evils of colonialism if it is couched in language and inundated with symbols which seem to speak more to an artistic game than to the "revelation" of reality. Neither purely realistic, naturalistic, or melodramatic, *The Ripening* seems to be more allusive and exhortative. Because the author poetizes his prose, the critical capacity of his endeavor is lessened tremendously.

In the end these novels waver between critical realism and realism and in a way serves as a good transitional point from the realism of Maran and

McKay to the in depth socio–psychological realism of Lamming and Juminer. Because these writers understood, no matter how narrowly, the importance of the past, the possibilities inherent in the present, the need to present an alternative vision of society, and the need to channel our energies into the future, they demonstrated that the masses of Caribbean people were ready for independence. It would be left to Lamming, Juminer, V.S. Naipaul and other writers to examine this new condition of our being in a powerfully different way.

IX

TOWARDS INDEPENDENCE:
Of Age and Innocence
Season of Adventure
Water with Berries

IF the characters' fundamental limitation in Manuel de Jesus Galván's *Enriquillo* and Victor Reid's *New Day* is their inability to perceive the mother country as other than guiding dependent people, then George Lamming's characters in *Of Age and Innocence* and *Season of Adventure* surmount this. Although Aimé Césaire develops the theme of the colonizer and the colonized in *Discourse on Colonialism*, Lamming is the first writer in the British Caribbean to explore seriously the relationship between them at the psychological level.

What occupies Lamming's major characters' minds regarding colonial reality locates them in time and space and becomes the central issue in Lamming's novels. Lamming uses the peculiar psychology of the Caribbean mind to illustrate certain sociopolitical problems inherent in colonialism and the struggle for independence. Because it is impossible to "understand the spiritual life of a people as a whole without first understanding the spiritual and moral essence of each person," the critical examination of one particular individual's mind becomes of utmost importance; thus, layer by layer, Lamming removes the complexities that motivate each character, thereby revealing an important basis for understanding the psychological problems of the transformation from thinking in colonial terms to thinking independently.[1] The careful spinning out of the characters' inner world reveals their purposes and weaves them into the social fabric of the society.

Of *Age and Innocence* uses the legend of Prospero and Caliban, in which Prospero and Caliban are seen as being linked inextricably in the drama of colonialism in which the fate of the latter is dependent on that of the former. Here, Prospero represents the European colonizer and Caliban the colonized. Lamming takes William Shakespeare's *The Tempest* as his point of departure "to grapple with that colonial structure of awareness which has determined West Indian cultural values,"[2] contending that *The Tempest* is essential to his literary purposes. In his important work, *The Pleasures of Exile*, Lamming says:

> I cannot read *The Tempest* without recalling the adventure of those voyages reported by Hakluyt; and when I remember the voyages and the particular period in African history, I see *The Tempest* against the background of England's experiment in colonization. Considering the range of Shakespeare's curiosity and the fact that these matters were being feverishly discussed in England at the time, they would most certainly have been present in his mind. Indeed, they must have been part of the conscious stuff of his thinking. And it is Shakespeare's capacity for experience which leads me to feel that *The Tempest* was also prophetic of a political future which is our present. Moreover, the circumstances of my life, both as a colonial and exiled descendant of Caliban in the twentieth century, is an example of that prophecy.[3]

That Lamming, one of the first Caribbean writers to handle what I will call socio-psychological realism, should turn to Shakespeare is understandable since Shakespeare was one of the first international writers to examine the psychological conflicts engendered by man in a property-owning society. When Shakespeare wrote *The Tempest* he was influenced by two major works: Michel Montaigne's essay, "Of the Caniballes" and William Strachey's "True Report of the Wreck and Redemption of Sir Thomas Gates upon and from the Islands of the Bermudas." "Of the Caniballes," written in 1580, presents the savage or the cannibal in a noble and ideal light. Of the savages Montaigne said:

> Now (to returne to my purpose) I finde (as farre as I have beene informed) there is nothing in the nation that is either barbarious or savage, unless men call that barbarisme which is not common to them. As indeed, we have no other ayme of truth and reason, than the example and Idea of the opinions and customes of the countrie we live in. There is ever perfect religion, perfect policie, perfect and compleat use of all things. They are even savage, as we call those fruits wilde which nature of her selfe and of her ordinarie progresse hath produced: whereas indeed, they are those which our selves have altered by our artificiall devices, and diverted from their common order, we should rather terme savage. In those are the true and most profitable vertues, and naturall properties most lively and vigorous, which in these we have bastardized, applying them to the pleasure of our corrupt taste. And if notwithstanding, in divers fruits of those countries that were never tilled, we shall finde that in respect of ours they are most excellent, and as delicate unto our taste; there is no reason, art should gaine the point of honour of our great and puissant mother Nature.[4]

But these savages of whom Montaigne spoke lived in a state of peaceful bliss, in a society where there was not the individual ownership of property and where all articles of production were shared by all members of the society. In this society true virtue reigned and, as Montaigne explained:

> there was never any opinion found so unnaturall and immodest, that would excuse treason, treacherie, disloyaltie, tyrannie, crueltie, and such like, which are our ordinary faults. We may then well call them barbarous, in regard of reasons rules, but not in respect of us that exceed them in all kinde of barbarisme. Their warres are noble and generous, and have as much excuse and beautie as this humane infirmitie may admit: they ayme at nought so much, and have no other foundation amongst them, but the mere jealousie of vertue. They contend not for the gaining of new lands; for to this day they yet enjoy that naturall ubertie and fruitfulnesse, which without labouring toyle, doth in such plentous abundance furnish them with all necessary things, that they need not enlarge their limits. They are yet in that happye state as they desire no more than what their naturall necessities direct them: what soever is beyond it, is to them superfluous.[5]

The picture that Mointaigne presents is one of *primitive communism*; a society that is ideal in the fulfillment of its wants. Shakespeare had undoubtedly read the above translation of Montaigne's work. "Of two volumes of Florio's Montaigne in the British Museum, one bears the autograph of Shakespeare as its owner; another that of Ben Jonson."[6] In those happy days utopia was possible.

But then came the victory of the British over the Spanish Armada in the English Channel in 1598 and feudalism gave way to capitalism and with it came expansionism and colonialism. The colonization of Virginia provided the other episode for Shakespeare's *The Tempest*. The second source of the play comes from William Strachey which tells of the wreck of the eight ships which set out to people and make strong the colony of Virginia. In 1611 William Strachey wrote his manuscript about the colonization adventure (even though it was not published until 1625) as G. B. Harrison suggested, "a number of phrases in Strachey's report seem to have been caught up into *The Tempest*; it is possible that Shakespeare saw it in the manuscript."[7]

By what strange twist then was the noble savage or caniballe of Montaigne transformed into such a heinous primitive by Shakespeare in the form of Caliban. First, Shakespeare, who wrote from the insights that were formed at the dawn of English colonialism, could not but have seen that the savage of Montaigne was in need of the Christian-colonial light. Thus Marinda's complaint against Caliban:

Which any print of goodness wilt not take,
Being capable of all ill: I pitied thee,
Took pains to make thee speak, taught thee each
hour
One thing or other: when thou didst not (savage)
Know thine own meaning; but wouldst gabble, like
A thing most brutish, I endow'd thy purposes
With words that made them known: but thy vile race
(Though thou didst learn) had that in 't, which good
natures
Could not abide to be with; therefore wast thou
Deservedly confin'd into this rock,
Who hadst deserv'd more than a prison.[8]

The savage, endowed with the purposes of the colonizer, must be transformed by the principles of a Christian-colonial society and taught to know his/her meaning as the colonizer so prescribed he/she should.

Second, and yet more important, was the nature of social consciousness and psychological motivation which had taken place in the Western world between the time that Montaigne had written "Of the Caniballes" (1580) and the moment when William Shakespeare wrote *The Tempest* (1611). The transfer of power from feudal Spain to capitalist England which was imbued with the desire for the further conquest of foreign lands provided for a radically new way of seeing the world. This resulted in a changed social consciousness and and a different sense of psychological motivation. Thus Montaigne wrote primarily to satisfy his own private needs and saw his internal being as the measure of all reality ("I look within myself; I have no business but with myself . . . I write, not my gests, but myself and my essence."[9])

Shakespeare's vision in the age of dawning colonialism was directed outward of necessity. Because of the new demands of his age, Shakespeare saw the need to understand the relationship between the inner self (i.e. the psychological dimensions of man's inner being) and the outward dimensions of the new social world that was developing. And hence, as Lamming suggested, his capacity for experience.

Many of the leading writers of the time understood the nature of these new and interrelated phenomenon which they depicted in their literary works. William Shakespeare emerged as the most astute writer in the English language to understand this phenomenon. Boris Suchkov, in his historical analysis of the development of realism, presented a very perceptive understanding of this literary problem:

> Renaissance art and philosophy were the first to recognise the integral
> connection between being and consciousness and the need for an analytical

study of reality as the basic requirement of the new age. This concept was formulated by Francis Bacon, the main principle of whose philosophy, to quote Herzen, was to proceed from the particular to the general in the study of both the external and the internal world of man.

Analysis was becoming the main feature of realistic art. It is present in the work of the great Renaissance writers Rabelais, Cervantes and Shakespeare. Breaking through the mythologised narrative of *Gargantua and Pantagruel* it allowed Rabelais to convey the social outline of papistry, scholastic ideology and the feudal state, and in the figure of Panurge certain features of the new man beginning to acquire bourgeois characteristics, whose way of life turned out to be incompatible with the utopian humanism of Thélème. In Cervantes's novel the analysis is even more evident enabling him to give a more profound picture of his age and a more penetrating description of its main conflict: the tragic incompatibility of the Renaissance ideas of humanism with the concrete development of society. At the same time as glorifying goodness, Cervantes was destroying the illusion of its eventual triumph in the conditions of a gradually developing bouregois world order. In the case of Shakespeare, who generalised the standing features of the social psychology of a property-owning society, the central conflict of Rabelais's and Cervantes's novels lost its conventional fantastic nature, and assumed a concrete, historical form showing his realistic understanding of the interrelation between man and society. For Shakespeare the social medium in which his characters acted provided the mainspring for their moral conflicts and struggles.

By portraying society as the sphere of conflict between material and social interests Shakespeare laid the foundation of realism as a new artistic method.[10]

It is this rather complex literary phenomenon which leads Lamming to see *The Tempest* as his logical point of departure for his exploration of the socio-psychological realism of Caribbean literature.

In his article, "Caliban, Notes Toward a Discussion of Culture in Our America," Roberto Fernández Retamar discusses the historical explanation of the Carib/Cannibal/Caliban myth of the Caribbean people[11] and perceives it as "the typically degraded vision offered by the colonizer of the man he is colonizing."[12]

Lamming picks up this historical myth relationship and develops it—but with serious limitations. First, he fails to transcend the dependency cycle of the colonized upon the colonizer that Manoni depicts in *Prospero and Caliban* (1950). Lamming states:

Moreover, I am a direct descendant of Prospero worshiping in the same temple of endeavour, using his legacy of language—not to curse our meeting—but to push it further, reminding the descendants of both sides that what's done is done, and can only be seen as a soil from which other gifts, or the same gift endowed with different meanings, may grow towards a future which is colonised by our acts in this moment, but which must always remain open.[13]

Whereas in 1960 Lamming wishes to leave open room to construct a dialogue "using the legacy of language—not to curse our meeting—but to push it further," by 1975 Retamar rejects this position and comments, "What else can Caliban do but use the same language—today he has no other—to curse him [Prospero], to wish that the 'red plague' would fall on him."[14] A radically different way of seeing occurs only fourteen years later.

The second limitation, some may call it an error, in Lamming's analysis comes when he calls Caliban "a child of nature," a kind of primordial innocence, presuming that in giving Caliban language, which is a conceptual tool, that Caliban existed in no important sense as a person. If this is true, then Caliban is not a person; he is a "project" and assumes only symbolic dimensions in this experiment. If he is a person (Lamming does see him as a person when, for example, he devotes a whole chapter, "Caliban Orders History," for his book *The Pleasures of Exile*), then it is erroneous to presume that the "impact of language" did not have to be tempered by the conception of self which Caliban himself possessed until his encounter with Prospero.

Aimé Césaire saw this particular problem more clearly than George Lamming. In an interview with the Haitian writer, René Despestre, Césaire explains how he utilized the technique of surrealism to plumb the soul of his being to arrive at his original self:

A.C.: I said to myself: it's true that superficially we are French, we bear the marks of French customs; we have been branded by Cartesian philosophy, by French rhetoric; but if we break with all that, if we plumb the depths, then what we will find is fundamentally black.

R.D.: In other words, it was a process of disalienation.

A.C.: Yes, a process of disalienation, that's how I interpreted surrealism.

R.D.: That's how surrealism has manifested itself in your work: as an effort to reclaim your authentic character, and in a way as an effort to reclaim the African heritage.

A.C.: Absolutely.

R.D.: And as a process of detoxification.

A.C.: A plunge into the depths. It was a plunge into Africa for me.

R.D.: It was a way of emancipating your consciousness.

A.C.: Yes, I felt that beneath the social being would be found a profound being, over whom all sorts of ancestral layers and alluviums had been deposited.[15]

Contrary to Lamming's assertion, Caliban was not simply a "project." Even though he might have been essentially simple and innocent, Caliban possessed personhood. Prospero's enterprise consisted solely of trying to fashion that innocence to his own exploitative and imperialist purposes. While language invested Caliban with possibilities for the future, it was circumscribed by his original self-concept; herein lay the risk which Prospero would take in his experiment, for Caliban might reassert himself. Indeed, it took four hundred years for that assertion to happen successfully.

In *Of Age and Innocence* (1958), Lamming goes back before Columbus' arrival to the resistance of the Higuey Indians of Cuba and creates the legend of the Tribe Boys' (past Indians and African blacks) conflict with the Bandit Kings (European). The voice of memory and age (Shephard's mother) tenaciously preserves and transmits the history of the Caribbean (San Cristobal) to innocence (three young boys: Bob, a black; Lee, a Chinese; and Singh, an East Indian). It is the boys, the next generation who must deal with independence and the new relationships it involves since the present leaders who are struggling for independence are so closely connected with the bitterness and the animosities which the colonial experience engendered.

The Society which the boys formed represented a new hope for San Cristobal. This hope is counterposed to the People's Communal Party which their elders have formed and which is led by John Isaac Shephard, Aly Singh, a former cane cutter on the Baden Semper sugar estates (and father of the boy Singh) and Joseph Lee, a retired school master who became a merchant (and father of the boy Lee of the Society). In their struggle for independence, the Party attempts to achieve freedom as Lamming perceived it. As an anonymous contributor to the Barbados paper, *Manjak*, puts it: "Lamming defines freedom as the ability of the West Indian to overcome those aspects of the colonial experience that militate against political sovereignty, cultural authenticity and the true fulfillment of the person."[16]

But the boys felt that they had indeed achieved the promise for which their elders were fighting and saw themselves as the shining example of San Cristobal's future. For as they contemplated:

> This was San Cristobal. And they were thinking of the wish which had lately aroused the island to a sudden frenzy of rumour and promise and expectation. Last night they had listened again to the speakers in the public square, and they were reminded that they too were a part of the promise which everyone had heard. They too were together, and in a sense which was more immediate and intelligible than the wailing excitement of the crowd. They had come together as a little Society which worked in secret, and the unity which the speakers were urging San Cristobal to achieve was for them a fact. It seemed that they had, in some way, surpassed their elders; so that they behaved, during these

expeditions, as though they were no longer dependent on the decisions which others were making for them. It had made their age irrelevant, compared with the wasted experience of those who were so much older. Sometimes they felt that the others would have to catch up on what they had already accomplished. (OAI, p. 115)

Thus the novel becomes an attempt to bridge the gap between the *promise* which the boys perceived and the *reality* with which their elders must contend. Only a piercing look into the past, both real and legendary, can give the Caribbean people that sense of identity which is necessary to come to grips with the problems of autonomy. Only a sense of dispassionate detachment from the present can allow them to achieve the genuine promise which independence offers.

Of Age and Innocence, set on the eve of San Cristobal's independence, examines the relationship between the colonized and the colonizer and suggests a perception of the new attitudes which are necessary for independence. The novel examines the attitudes of three generations. First we observe the attitude of Mother Shephard (John Shephard's mother) and Mrs. Crabbe (Mr. Crabbe's mother), which represent the old order of seeing. Secondly, we see John Isaac Shephard and his followers (the nationalists) on the one side and Mr. Crabbe and his men (the colonizers) on the other side. The younger generation (Bob, Lee, Singh, and Rowley Crabbe, Crabbe's son), the descendants of Prospero and Caliban, are in the center.

In this work we see Lamming working out the ideas that are found in *The Pleasures of Exile*. For it is in the unity of the boys that we see the use of language and experience used "to push our meaning further," and to examine the whole act of colonization (Prospero's enterprise) through the discourse and dialogue of the descendants of both sides. It is Lamming's contention that this is the soil . . . the soil from which other gifts may grow. It is a future that will be colonized by the acts of Bob, Singh, Lee and Rowley, all descendants of Prospero and Caliban. But this is precisely the problem for the descendants of Prospero and Caliban. Before they can come together, there must be the ritual purification of their acts, in which Lee, Bob and Singh (the descendants of Caliban) come into themselves, i.e., know themselves and reject the whole act of colonization (Prospero's enterprise) and opt for a new beginning. This is inevitable with Prospero's descendants since they must reside in the same world, but with a changed relationship to that of equals not as "adults with full respect to the obligation we owe our parents."

As the book opens, we see people aboard a plane returning to San Cristobal. Rowley Crabbe (a European, of approximately ten years), who is going to meet his father, asks his grandmother, "Why does Daddy choose to live out of England?" (OAI, p. 19) Rowley wants to know the reason for his father's choice of vocation, for leaving England as well as his relationship to the Caribbean people. John Shephard, a native of San Cristobal, is on the same returning plane. He commandeers the plane and demands that all explain their reasons for going to San Cristobal. For a few moments the future of the plane, a world unto itself, is in the hands of "an armed man of uncertain and perplexed mind," (OAI, p. 54) who seeks the truth of their intentions. During the questioning, Shephard says to Rowley, " 'You have a good, sensible face,' he said, 'courageous and strong. That is good.' . . . 'I hope you shall escape the poison of your forebears' breeding.' " (OAI, p. 56) It is a most important warning, for only if Rowley can escape the "poison of his forebears' breeding" will he be able to fertilize new relations among the island's people and build a better San Cristobal.

We see San Cristobal as a place where

"Africa and India shake hands with China, and Europe wrinkles like a brow begging every face to promise love. The past is all suspicion, now is an argument that will not end, and tomorrow for San Cristobal, tomorrow is like the air in your hand. I know San Cristobal. It is mine, me, divided in harmony that still pursues all its separate parts. No new country, but a land inhabiting new forms of men who can never resurrect their roots and do not know their nature. Colour is their old and only alphabet. The whites are turning whiter, and the blacks are like an instinct which some voice, my voice, shall exercise. San Cristobal so old and yet so new, no place, this land, but a promise. My promise, and perhaps yours too. . . ." (OAI, p. 58)

Shephard thinks that past suspicions can be wiped away only by reordering relationships, so that he has Prospero release the privilege he exercises over Caliban.

Part II opens on the island with the three boys (Bob, Lee and Singh) and Ma Shephard making gifts to propitiate the sea's thirst. Rowley Crabbe joins them, asking Ma Shephard, " 'Can I call you Ma, too?' And the three boys were astonished when they saw the old woman embrace the stranger and sat him down beside them." (OAI, p. 64)

Ma Shephard realizes that San Cristobal's destiny lies in the hands of these four boys: "I talk to you like a duty tell me the four must be part o' any prayer my lips make concernin' San Cristobal." (OAI, p. 71) With Ma Shephard and the boys, age joins innocence. Before Ma Shephard sends the boys plunging into the future, she must plumb the depths of her past, which is the island's past. She tells the boys about the hurricane that covered the land with water and recounts the legend of the Tribe Boys (the original Indians) who, using guerrilla warfare to retrieve their island from the Bandit Kings (the Europeans), suffered a terrible defeat.

The Tribe Boys who remain walk out like they surrender, an' the Kings wait for them to kneel an' beg, 'cause they was goin' to let them serve if they only kneel in surrender.

'But they won't' said Bob, 'they swear in whisper one to the next never to take defeat from the Kings, never to be victim complete. An' they walk without stoppin,' and the kings only watch them walk like they join a trance, right to the top o' Mount Misery. And there they kiss on the cliff forever, an' then lean their heads down in a last minute dive to their own funeral.' (OAI, p. 99)

She also describes the fire that raged before emancipation. Now on the eve of independence, the island breathlessly awaits a future fraught with danger.

Bob, Lee and Singh begin to relive the history of resistance in its telling. When Ma Shephard describes the blacks' resistance prior to emancipation, she may be referring to the 1831 Jamaican rebellion or to the Haitian revolution. Whatever the illustration, the boys' history is one in which arson played a major part:

'Twas a malice on every side that start disaster. The men who make that fire fret how their labour went robbed in a lan' which refuse to make them brother an' sister, or feed them with a right reward for the sweat they drip night an' day. The lan' come to look like a tyrant in their eye, an' they decide to burn whatever memory hol' them to the plough. An' they burn every blade, young an' ol', ripe or not ready, it matter no more, an' they promise to burn an' burn for ever till those who conquer San Cristobal an' own it from afar relax their will, or choose some next han' to labour with the lan'. 'Cause they had no more home to go to. San Cristobal was the only home they know, an' it was no home. So time seem a waste in their eye, an' they put their livin' to a fearful purpose in those fires that make every workin' nerve shudder the night the silence take possession o' the hills. (OAI, p. 69)

The Indians refused to bow down and worship the colonizer, and the blacks retaliated with arson, eventually achieving emancipation. When the Africans no longer wanted to work the land, other races were brought to San Cristobal:

'Twas even in my time I see a new race o' labour voyage in an' come to stay, makin' all kind o' mixture here in San Cristobal. Now it was India, an' later China, an' more too I cannot recollect, from east an' west, whatever nations outside had power to sell or len' mankind, they come, an' time take whatever memory come with them, 'cross the sea, an' their habit make a home right here, you an' me an' all who now stay for good or evil till eternity take them off, one by one or all together. (OAI, pp. 69-70)

The Caribbean became a cosmopolitan land of different hues with the colonizer (represented by Crabbe and his men) on one side, the colonized (represented by Shephard and his followers) on the other. Crabbe and Shephard and their sons must shape a new relationship out of a history of brutality and manipulation dating back to the resistance of the Tribe Boys and the blacks.

By examining the attitudes of the two major protagonists' mothers, Mrs. Crabbe and Ma Shephard, we see the relationship between the colonizer and the colonized. Mrs. Crabbe's outrage is complete when she is inconvenienced by electricity and oil strikes, as this exchange between her and Ma Shephard illustrates:

'I call it an outrage,' she said, 'depriving us of electric, and then refusing to sell oil to those who need light. The inconvenience of it and the injustice.'

'It is bad, I know,' Ma Shephard said. 'Bad to undo the wires, an' bad not to sell oil to those they call enemy.'

'And they want to lead this country,' Mrs. Crabbe shrieked. 'You know what would happen if they had their way.'

'They mus' learn to forgive,' Ma Shephard said quietly.

'Forgive.' Mrs. Crabbe exclaimed, 'but what have we done? We've tried to teach what we know. We've brought a civilized way of life they never knew, and then this is what we get in return. Just hatred and prejudice. Can you imagine what would happen if we weren't here? Can you imagine the disorder that would follow if we had to leave? Now, tell me, can you?'

She seemed to expect an answer, but Ma Shephard held her head down as though she wanted to forget the charges which were being made against her son and Singh.

'What we call justice is only a way of seein' right an' wrong.' she said, 'but no man can see if his eyes ain't open, and their eyes ain't open, theirs nor the ones they hold enmity 'gainst.' (OAI, pp. 264–265)

This is the symbolic Prospero imposing order in the willed belief that darkness will follow should he depart. Yet, the symbolic Caliban reorders reality by taking away light (the electricity and oil strikes) and imposing darkness. As Ma Shephard informs Mrs. Crabbe, "What we call justice is one way of seeing." The moral order (light), which Mrs. Crabbe thinks her people have given Caliban, can be perceived as light or darkness, depending on the point of view. What is light to Mrs. Crabbe is darkness to the San Cristobal people, and what is inconveniences and ingratitude to her is the people's way of assuming their independence and identity.

Returning from England, Shephard brings new hope to San Cristobal's people, who see him as a savior while the whites think him a lunatic. When Shephard delivers a speech, thus giving his people speech on the Day of Deliverance, the results are overwhelming:

> 'Was like a new day o' deliverance,' someone said, 'the day he announce that speech when the music stop.'
>
> 'Tis words make him work his magic,' a woman said, 'when a man got words he can open any ear.'
>
> 'An magic don't take no time to work,' said the man, 'before your eye clap twice you in the spell.'
>
> 'He move my heart that mornin,' the woman said, 'an' if I could have lay my han' on them who say he was mad, only if I could have lay my han' on the lyin' tongue that try to slander his brain.'
>
> 'They didn't want him to do the work he start,' the man said, 'but he choose the right day to make that speech, the mornin' we celebrate San Cristobal. 'Tis a next day o' deliverance he goin' bring.'
>
> 'An' he ain't talk no lies,' the woman said, 'he ain't let his tongue slip a single lie when he say that San Cristobal is his an' mine, an how he goin' make it belong to everybody who born here.'
>
> 'Tis why they say he mad an' make that disturbance on the plane,' said the man, 'the spirit must have tell them what plan his min' was makin'.'
>
> 'Those who born here come first,' said the woman, 'he make it plain as scripture that we got to come first. An' for that they call him mad. But if 'tis mad, 'tis a madness we been waitin' for God only knows how long. (OAI, pp. 76 77)

Here we do not have Reid's concern for the mother country. All are invited to participate in the new experiment, but if they do so, it will be on Caliban's terms. Shephard, the new giant, awakens "San Cristobal unto a new conception of itself." He wants to rule, "a new ambition," which his mother says will "hold him in bondage." Opposed to Reid's Garth whose knowledge of the law provided a safety valve, "Shephard is a engine without any room for brakes. They can talk 'till their tongue run out o' saliva, nobody ain't stoppin' him now.' " (OAI, p. 164) People from all over the country journey "to swear their allegiance to Shephard," (OAI, p. 170) for "he had become a frontier which they could follow without fear, a faith which had made their future certain." (OAI, p. 171)

Shephard becomes San Cristobal's future, for through him San Cristobal's people hope to find their identity. But what is the identity

Shephard hopes to shape? He confesses to Penelope, who resembles a woman who deceived him in love, "I have played no part at all in the making of that meaning which others use to define me completely," a meaning which Shephard confesses "applies equally to millions." (OAI, p. 203)

Lamming uses Penelope's uncontrollable lesbian longing for Marcia (as contrasted with Mark's incessant search to identify with his people), which she cannot express because of the alienation sure to result, as a metaphor for the colonial's predicament:

> They will all begin to reconsider me, and this is the kind of alienation which I could not bear. Is this the fate of the abnormal? It is not their difference which is disturbing. It is the way their difference is regarded which makes for their isolation. Their status is altered for others as though they had undergone some malevolent conversion. They must carry always a mark which denotes the measure of their fall from some general order. . . . It would be better to lose one's status completely and be seen wholly as a new thing; much better than to have one's status granted with a certain reservation. It is the reservation which occupies the mind of the other, until one feels it like a scar, or a defamation. I believe this is what those people who are called inferior experience and find resentful and intolerable. If their difference, whether it took the form of colour or religion or occupation, were regarded as their whole condition, all would be well. They could settle comfortable in their status, knowing that they were, in fact, their status. The Negro, the homosexual, the Jew, the worker . . . he is a man, that is never denied, but he is not quite ready for definition until these reservations are stated, and it is the reservation which separates him from himself. He is man in spite of . . . I shall be Penelope in spite of. . .(OAI, p. 151)

The colonizer's refusal to grant identity and autonomy to the colonized, is the colonial's tragedy, for even if identity is granted, it is "in spite of . . ." This reservation separates the colonial from himself and marks him as different. How does one remove these reservations and reorder relationships? To reverse the relationship, the colonizer, who limits the colonized's identity, must be placed in the opposite position and learn a whole new set of relationships.

Shephard wants no lies and no suspicions. When Bill Butterfield (a white) comes to warn Shephard about a plan to assassinate him, Shephard is suspicious of Bill and drives him away before he can deliver the message. Later, when Bill sent him a note through Thief warning him of Crabbe's plan to assassinate him, he felt guilty that he had turned Bill away because of the fear and suspicions which he and his comrades felt about the intentions of the stranger:

But he was thinking of the boys and his warning against suspicion, and he recalled the evening in another room when he had met with his colleagues to discuss the strike. It was then that he had been reminded of the contagion which distrust could carry to any heart, and he saw Bill Butterfield turning away from the table, rejected and despised by men who were afraid to trust. And he himself was part of the bitterness which made Singh and Lee suspect the stranger's intentions. They had turned Bill away, and they had done so in the certainty that their instinct was right. And he had accepted.

Now his suspicion had turned against him as though it mocked his judgment. His regret had failed to relieve the feeling of guilt which Bill Butterfield had created. It was Bill he thought of when he warned the boys against suspicion, and it was his intolerable sense of guilt which he tried to express in that warning. He would have liked to see Bill, but he knew it would be difficult to tell in words the measure of his feeling, and he wondered what he could do to prove his need of the other's forgiveness. He turned in the chair, bringing his head down to his knees. His mother raised herself feebly from the seat and went beside him. (OAI, p. 289)

Now Shephard is forever in Bill's debt because of this action and the risk Bill has taken. His only hope lies in the new society where the young boys "might find a way to avoid the suspicion which had made a wall between strangers." (OAI, p. 201)

At this point the struggle for a new order in San Cristobal transcends color, for both Bill (white) and Shephard (black) are on the same side of San Cristobal's future against Crabbe (white) and Paravecino (a creole), who are intent on keeping their privilege. The boys—personified by Bob (black), Lee (Chinese), Singh (East Indian) and Rowley Crabbe (white)— must reconstruct society.

Shephard grows almost fanatical with an ambition even his mother begins to fear. On the night before the election that will surely bring independence, Shephard becomes a man in the fullest sense of someone capable of controlling space and time and of bending events to his will. The personification of the independent man, Shephard boasts:

> Tomorrow, respected comrade, I shall hold this land in the palm of my hand, and bend it like a wheel to meet my intention. I shall call on the earth to clap and the water to sing and every living thing shall tell its pleasure in a humble service to my sovereignty on an island that once slept under water. But tonight, Kennedy, I shall walk the water and for a moment consult with my maker (OAI, pp. 316-317)

Shephard thinks of himself in almost Christlike terms while Mark, who thinks that Shephard is responsible for the death of his girlfriend,

Penelope, perceives Shephard as we see him for the last time before he is murdered:

> He had seen that face before in a similar aspect of fantasy: the taut, ecstatic lips and the eyes lost in an eagerness of unnatural vision. Shephard spoke with his eyes. A dark delirium had settled over them. Their gaze contained a terror which Shephard could not control, but a similar occasion had taught Mark their meaning. He understood their warning. Shephard had slipped beyond the normal habit of his reason, and Mark was beginning to feel rebuked by his lack of sympathy. He felt Shephard's hand tightened on his. (OAI, pp. 317-318)

The Christlike characteristic that Shephard felt is transmitted to his followers:

> THIRD VOICE: A most shameful murder they make.

> FIRST VOICE: And of one who was truly call' to lead us into the light. As it was with our Lord and Saviour Jesus Christ, wasn't it?

> FOURTH VOICE: You speak a word, my friend, so it was with our leader, Shephard.

> THIRD VOICE: He would have us see the light, and he die' for it. But they will find out their mistake, the criminals, oh yes, they will. Let's leave everything to God. (OAI, pp. 327-328)

Shephard's strength lay in his ability to transform the people of San Cristobal by giving them a new self-conception, by pulling them together into one strong society and by bringing them in step with the outside world; his greatest contribution to the island came from his capacity to heal and mobilize the people, as one person testifies:

> THIRD VOICE: He make a bond between you an' me an' every race that live with sufferin' in San Cristobal. He heal whatever difference divide them, an' when his real work was 'bout to begin, they snatch his life, an' deprive San Cristobal o' that future which Heaven was preparin.'
> Tis what they do. 'Tis what they do the night his blood cry out all over the sea.' (OAI, p. 347)

Because Shephard fused the dispossessed from every race into a new unity, he became the greatest threat to the colonizer.

Crabbe, on the other hand, is the colonizer who runs the Government Information Service and has controlling shares in Radio San Cristobal, thus affecting the people's self-concept, and who, as police chief, physically controls the people's movements. When we first see Crabbe, he is coming to hear the legend of the Tribe Boys and the Bandit Kings because his son, Rowley, has raved about it. Ever since Shephard returned from England, Crabbe has kept him under surveillance because he understands Shephard's strength. He astutely explains what Shephard is doing to his creole assistant, Paravecino:

> He wanted each group to get an idea of who they were and that must include where they originally came from. When he had planted that in their heads once and for all, what did he do next? He showed them that there was no difference between them, Indian, Negro, Chinese or what you like, in their relation to people like me and the Governor and what he calls the fellows of Whitehall. That's what he made clear, and there isn't a soul in San Cristobal, literate or illiterate, young or old, who didn't understand what he was saying. Whatever difference there was between them, they had one thing in common: a colonial past with all that it implies. . . .
>
> But what the bastard never mentioned . . . was the benefit which that colonial past had also brought them. It is this complete amnesia on the part of all people like Shephard that is a kind of madness. (OAI, p. 167)

Like his mother, Crabbe is trapped by the notion of the colonizer's civilizing mission. He cannot forgive Shephard his strength and plots his assassination. Reginald Paravecino, "the stooge of every governor who had worked in the island during the last ten years, crawling his way like an undetected leper to some future list of royal honours," tolerates Crabbe even though he hates him. (pp. 168) In Paravecino we find an attempt to personify what Lamming calls the "idea" of the metropolitan country as opposed to the "fact" of it. In explaining the dilemma to Crabbe, Paravecino says:

> You gave Shephard an image of yourself, and then circumstances provided him with the opportunity to examine that image. If you had never allowed these colonials to flock to your country as they please, Shephard might not have happened. So they went, and you know better than I what they found. They found you in a state of disorder which was worse than anything they knew in the colonies. And it was their experience of this disorder that suggested to them what could happen when they got back home. In fact they returned for no other reason. It was you, not the colonials, who started the colonial revolution. But you can't have your cake and eat it. You can't pride yourself on liberty and deny them the experiment too. Nor can you go on enjoying the privileges of a lie at the expense of people who have discovered the lie. The image of a superior animal doesn't make sense after these men like Shephard work in a London factory or sleep whenever he pleases with some little progressive slut from the London School of Economics. You treat these men

like children and forget that children have a way of growing up. And what they understand is always different from what the parents had imagined. (OAI, p. 168)

Here Lamming again refutes Reid's image of the colonial as dependent and in need of guidance. Unlike Reid's Garth in the metropolitan society, Lamming's Shephard, when confronted by the contradictions of Britain, immediately becomes aware of both his difference and the tenuousness of white superiority. Also, Crabbe despises Paravecino for the very ideas (love of the colonizer's education, women and honors) instilled in the colonized's psyche to dominate him. The wonder is that Paravecino does not turn upon Crabbe as quickly as Baboo, (the Indian warder and double agent who is spying for both Crabbe and Singh) and Shephard do.

Crabbe and Paravecino find themselves in an unholy alliance against Shephard. The crisis comes when Thief, a natural thief by vocation and hence his name, steals a letter from Crabbe, who has an insane love of black women, while he is having sexual intercourse. The letter, which details the plan for Shephard's assassination, later becomes the major piece of evidence used against Crabbe.

The real nature of Crabbe's relationship with the people is seen when he talks with Penelope, who, because of her lesbianism, is able to empathize with the dispossession of the people of San Cristobal. She challenges him:

> "Has it occurred to you that we are surrounded by people whom we don't understand?" Penelope asked. She was talking to Crabbe as though he were not near and might not hear. "And they frighten us."
>
> "Until we find a way of dealing with them," said Crabbe. "It is then that we feel safe among them."
>
> "But we are never sure how to deal with them." said Penelope. "How can we be?"
>
> "You learn from results," said Crabbe, "you may try the wrong method, now and again, but it's always from results that you learn."
>
> "Have you ever talked with one of them?" Penelope asked.
>
> "No, I've never," said Crabbe, "but in my job I find that the same principle works. You can only try and learn from the results. (OAI, p. 267)

Crabbe controls the island's police and media, yet perceives the people as "projects" and has never entered into dialogue with them. To him only results of the colonial experiment matter. But, as Penelope reminds him, " 'That's probably what frightens us,' she said, 'I mean Shephard's state of mind, as you call it, and his conviction that he is on the side of life. *Shephard feels he, too, is on the side of life*'." (OAI p. 268) [Italics mine.]

Implicit in this discussion is the fundamental way in which the colonizer sees reality. Under further probing, the colonizer's (Crabbe's) real views hit us like an arrow. Notice this dialogue:

> "I don't think Shephard would say that you were mad" said Penelope "He might say that you were doing what was natural, considering who you are, your education, your background, your whole way of looking at the world."
>
> "There may be several ways of looking at the world, but there is only one world," said Crabbe. "It is my world and Shephard's world."
>
> "It exists in different ways in different heads," said Penelope.
>
> Crabbe looked suddenly irritated. "Are you trying to defend Shephard?" (OAI, p. 269)

This implicit arrogance in Crabbe's (Prospero's) views of the world makes anyone who does not see it as he does a mad being who must be eliminated. Crabbe is imprisoned by his way of seeing and cannot imagine that things might change in San Cristobal.

When Shephard is killed on the night before an election he would surely have won, the people, conscious only of their grief and lost possibilities, take the law into their own hands. Crabbe sees "his power shrink to a relic, obsolete and useless as the yellow berries that cried under their feet" (OAI, p. 347) and mobilizes the troops. Just as colonialism began with violence, so it is violence to which Crabbe resorts:

> He was beginning to anticipate the future which would smother them noisily with lead and steel. But it was not enough to exterminate them. They were unkillable until you had found good reason for seeing them dead. Their death would be a waste without some moral justification for the troops. He heard them, loud and inarticulate as the day, deciding the future of San Cristobal, and he knew that his wish was right. Shephard had to die if the future of San Cristobal was to be rescued from chaos. The troops had to come if San Cristobal were to be saved from their savage and passionate hunger for blood. The order for the troops was justified. His duty was beyond any argument. But the letter? How could they proceed without the slander which the letter had caused? (OAI, p. 347)

Crabbe must retrieve himself from a situation in which he is severely compromised. The people know about the stolen letter that testifies to Crabbe's plan to assassinate Shephard. Shephard is dead, and the people demand that his murderer be tried. Crabbe must find the letter, for to allow it to appear in court will seal his complicity in the murder. Worse, if Thief offers the letter to the court, Crabbe's life on the island will come to an end and his imperial honor, the very foundation upon which his privilege lies, will be destroyed. Thief has Crabbe's life in his hand and "by argument or deception, he [Crabbe] had to win Thief without any concession to his rule in San Cristobal." (OAI p. 348)

But Crabbe's rule is already in jeopardy, for Baboo, whom he trusts, betrays him by telling Aly Singh about his plans:

> He had not told Baboo why he had really undertaken to let the men escape, and he wondered how he could safely avoid a scandal if his plan had failed. *But he thought he understood the temperament of men like Baboo* and those who worked the light which charged from the wood across his face to a splintered white edge over the sea. His secret was a burden which reminded him of his role in San Cristobal. *And suddenly he tried to rebuke himself for thinking things might not have happened as he had ordered them.* (OAI, p. 366) [Italics mine.]

Crabbe's blunders are twofold. First, he hasn't taken time to know his "projects." Second, he never considers that events can happen except as he orders them. He watches the complete breakdwon of the old order yet cannot see his relationship with the people in terms other than master-servant, colonizer-colonized, Prospero-Caliban.

Events move fast, and Crabbe cannot control them. Time has passed him by, and "the future was neither part of his certainty nor his suspense. It did not exist." (p. 371) He is trapped by relationships which are no longer appropriate to the changing situation which has arisen. Yet he insists on being in control of events even after his men (the local police officers who have accompanied him to the beach to retrieve the letter that implicates him in Shephard's death) have deserted him. He is now under the control of Aly Singh who has cornered him on the beach. However, he refuses to concede any of his power and authority. Singh, observing the obstinacy and arrogance of the man, can only conclude:

> "Not a year nor a day." said Singh, "but a lifetime I have been waiting for a moment like now."
> "What have you done with my men?" Crabbe asked.
> "To the end," said Singh, "to the very end you will behave like a ruler."
> "I ask you what happened to my men?" Crabbe repeated.
> "And after you see clear as day you have nothing to rule you will be the same," Singh said, ignoring Crabbe's show of courage. "Like the leopard changing his spots. Knowing your life as one thing you cannot feel it different, no matter what change." (OAI, p. 373)

Simultaneously with the struggle for independence there existed a national conspiracy for power. Hence, when Aly Singh (Indian) asked Crabbe, who is now in his power, who killed Shephard, Baboo (Indian), who had been working for both Singh and Crabbe, shot Crabbe before he could answer.

This sudden change of events brought home the awful truth to Aly Singh: Baboo had shot Shephard so that he (Singh) rather than Shephard who was black, would become the first Prime Minister of San Cristobal. As Baboo explained to Singh:

> "Was only for you, Singh, was only for you I do it," he whispered, "from infancy I dream to see someone like myself, some Indian with your achievement rule San Cristobal. My only mistake was to wish it for you Singh, was only for you I do what I do. . . ." (OAI, p. 384)

Joseph Lee and Aly Singh who have captured Crabbe only to see him shot by Baboo, must now destroy Crabbe's body so that they will not be implicated in his death. More importantly and symbolically, Crabbe must die because he cannot perceive the dawning of a new day and remove his mask of imperial dominance. He dies dispossessed, for before he died Singh revealed to him the letter which he had written calling for the assassination of Shephard. Crabbe who represents foreign control beginning with the Bandit Kings' arrival, yields to Aly Singh. Relationships have truly changed.

With the disappearance of Crabbe martial law is proclaimed and the colonizer's troops are now running the island. Aly Singh and Joseph Lee are held by the authorities and tried for murder. With Shephard's death and the trials of both Aly Singh and Joseph Lee the nationalist coalition is weakened. Yet both Crabbe and Shephard have been trapped by their old relationship, the former incapable of imagining himself as anything except master, the latter overcome by ambition to rule. San Cristobal's future depends upon a new relationship among the boys of the next generation.

When we first meet the boys (Bob, Lee and Singh), they have no awareness of color and have confused feelings towards Rowley Crabbe. The little society the boys have formed teaches pride:

> "An' we promise not to beg, remember. No money without something in exchange 'cause the Society teach a pride we want to keep. You don't work, then you don't collect." (OAI, p. 89)

This attitude departs from the dependency syndrome depicted in Victor Reid's *New Day*. When we meet Rowley Crabbe on the plane, his innocence bewilders his grandmother. When he asks Ma Shephard, "Can I call you Ma, too?" he acknowledges feelings of those who participate in the colonial experience. And then Singh asks his other friends:

> "How it is he seem to fit so natural?" Singh said, flicking his fingers over the lighter in his pocket.

"Tis because he, too, different from his father," said Bob. "Like me an' you, he too take the future in his own han'."

"Why you think he so different from his father?" Singh asked. He had tightened his fingers round the lighter, and his hand was emerging slowly from his pocket.

"Tis not a matter for why or wherefore," said Bob. "Seems to me he just different like you an' me different, an' that is that." (OAI, p. 121)

The boys share the sense of difference, yet with a common inheritance and the knowledge that the future is in their hands. As the author explains, in this society we see the promise of San Cristobal:

They had come together as a little Society which worked in secret, and the unity which the speakers were urging San Cristobal to achieve was for them a fact. It seemed that they had, in some way, surpassed their elders; so that they behaved, during these expeditions, as though they were no longer dependent on the decisions which others were making for them. It had made their age irrelevant, compared with the wasted experience of those who were so much older. Sometimes they felt that the others would have to catch up on what they had already accomplished. . . .

But the secret Society which they had formed was different. It was as though they had transformed the myth of the political meetings into some reality which no one could question. In the first place it was, unlike the other games, a secret experiment. They had succeeded in avoiding attention, and they did not have to resort to the artificial roles which the other games required. There was no need to change their names or choose occupations which could only be filled by men. Above all, the secret Society was directly connected with what was happening in San Cristobal. There behaviour was no longer a boy's imitation of his wish to be different, for the Society had achieved the secrecy which each had pledged at the start. Inevitably, it had given them a new sense of power. They were agreed on their own rules of conduct and duty, and they had decided on their own rewards. (OAI, pp. 115-116)

The Society gave the boys a special relationship with their parents. They see themselves as a flattering example of the wish which Shephard and his colleagues had made; they question their parents' values and attitudes:

"But everybody must be different," said Lee, "an' we different already."

"I only listen to my father with one ear," said Bob, " 'cause I talk to myself through the next, an' hear what you say."

"San Cristobal goin' look like what we doin' now," said Singh, "an' we'll be the first to start what the big ones alway talkin'."

"My father say they goin' keep San Cristobal," said Lee, "like how we have the Society, but he don't know 'bout the Society, the way we three different an' still alike."

"They talk 'bout the future like a war," said Singh, "how the future goin' come only with the struggle."

"An' we have the future already," said Lee, "cause we make a little Society for three, an' we see how it work."

"Tis 'cause they live so long before," said Bob, "that the future look hard to reach. But we reach already." (OAI, p. 120)

Now secure in their future and a power and unity of which their elders have only seen possibilities, the boys arrange a meeting with Rowley at their secret place in Paradise Woods. They give Rowley a lighter " 'cause it made in Englan,' . . . he can remember here an' his home at the same time, the Society an' San Cristobal all in one." (OAI, p. 122) The lighter links the home of the colonized and the colonizer, symbolizing the colonized's (Caliban's) returning the gift of enlightenment to the colonizer (Prospero). The lighter, made in England, returns the original light, the colonizing experience.

Although Lamming pushes dialogue between the colonized and the colonizer further than Reid, he is still limited by his inability to perceive San Cristobal's (the Society's) future outside the context of a relationship with England. Whereas Reid believes in the tutelage and guiding hand of the mother country, Lamming sees a relationship of mutual independence based on changed relationships among equals, yet fashioned by a mutual history and trapped by a future in which both societies are inextricably linked. Rowley's trusting interaction with the Society allows him to consider San Cristobal his home, the place where he is later buried.

The lighter symbolizes Rowley's pledge, made by calling upon his forebears, to keep the Society secret. His pledge of secrecy, acceptance into the Society and commitment to the future creates a new and special relationship of colonizer to colonized within the larger society and a new relationship with his father. Rowley Crabbe now possesses a secret not even his father, the police chief, can penetrate. In his initiation,

Rowley clasped the lighter and repeated his pledge, "I'm Rowley, Crabbe's son . . . I swear to keep the Society secret . . . " It had taken him like a guide showing the way to this hiding place. He could never deceive them, or he would have betrayed also the luck which had made this friendship with the boys. Now he would be able to endure the tyranny of affection that ruled his father's house. He was going to put his father's importance in its proper perspective. His secret was a challenge to his father's authority. "He's chief of police," he said, "chief of this and chief of that, but I swear, I swear to keep the Society secret. . . ." (OAI, p. 131)

So strong is the unity of the new Society that Singh Jr., thinking his father wants to murder Rowley Crabbe's father, feels "a sudden revulsion" for his father, yet cannot share this knowledge with Rowley. On the other hand, in Paradise Woods Rowley questions;

> "why he felt he needed the company of Bob and Singh and Lee while his father needed to live at a distance from Singh's father and Lee's father." (OAI, p. 138)

Rowley cannot understand why his father's and grandmother's affection for him should also mean their rejection of Bob, Lee, and Singh. Here Lamming works at a more intimate psychological level than either Galván or Reid as he tries to explore the psychological relationships between Prospero and Caliban while trying to advance new dialogue between their descendants.

Rowley's honoring the Society's secret gives him a certain power over his father while Singh's withholding his secret (his father's wish to kill Rowley's father) creates in him a peculiar kind of sympathy with Rowley that he has never felt for Lee or Bob. Bob also holds a secret from the Society in his first breach of trust with Lee and Singh, and this creates a feeling that Rowley be given greater intimacy than the others. Even though the boys keep secrets from each other, intimacy grows. They are so tightly knit that they are willing to defy orders of the striking nationalist elements to get Rowley's parents oil, which eventually leads to an accidental explosion when the oil is placed in Crabbe's car at the mental institution where Crabbe and his mother have gone to visit Marcia. Rowley, who was in the car when a patient from the mental institution set the car afire, is killed.

The society comes to an end with the fire at the mental institution where Rowley burns to death. Ma Shephard, suspecting a diabolical influence which John Shephard might have over the boys, has grown distant. Her influence over them wanes and she has no awareness of the degree of their implication and knowledge of the fire. Her inability, or reluctance, to accept the knowledge of their participation, and her inclination to perceive them only in their innocence, cuts her off from understanding them. She just can't believe that they might have known something about the fire. When they assert that John Shephard is in no way responsible for the fire, she can only think, "Could it be that these boys are offering to lie in order to save her son? He had caught them young, she thought, and there was no power which could persuade them he was wrong." (OAI, p. 288)

While the town celebrates the souls of the departed, the boys remain over Rowley's grave, asserting their total fellowship and unity and believing fully that the Society would always exist in their hearts:

"To the end I goin' remember him," said Singh, "to the very end, an' when my father let loose from prison, he can fret like that church bell buryin' the dead. I goin' remember him."

"Me too," said Bob. "He hold a place equal to me an' you in the Society, an' so he die. Could be you or me lying dead under where that candle shine."

"He was equal," said Lee, "equal, equal."

"An' dead as we know him dead there," Bob said, "the recollection make him real, real, like he was listenin' from the next side of the grave."

"He was real all right," said Lee, "Different like me an' you born an' raise different, but equal real like you an' me, 'cause never before was my nerves this safe with the dead so near." (OAI, p. 405)

A member of the colonizing people, Rowley is finally accepted by the boys, and Lamming presents us with a notion of the way the new society should proceed. But if this seems inherently shallow because we are not presented with the kind of therapeutic violence necessary to insure a new relationship, then we should note that the last picture we see of the boys is rebellion as they return from Rowley's grave. Cheered by the people, they challenge the established authorities by throwing stones at the troops as they try to enter the court chamber to hear Ma Shephard's testimony against Aly Singh. In the end they perceive themselves as the Tribe Boys in rebellion against the new colonialist elements, the Bandit Kings.

Resistance also appears as a central force in Lamming's novel, *Season of Adventure* (1963). Here Lamming begins to draw upon the collective subconscious so that Haitian Voodoo and the Ceremony of the Souls provide symbol and myth, the necessary tissue for his work. The Ceremony of the Souls should be described:

This Ceremony of the Souls is regarded by the Haitian peasant as a solemn communion; for he hears, at first hand, the secrets of the Dead. The celebrants are mainly relatives of the deceased who, ever since their death, have been locked in Water. It is the duty of the Dead to return and offer, on this momentous night, a full and honest report on their past relations with the living. A wife may have to say why she refused love to her husband; a husband may have to say why he deprived his wife of their children's affection. It is the duty of the Dead to speak, since their release from that purgatory of Water cannot be realized until they have fulfilled the contract which this ceremony symbolizes. The Dead need to speak if they are going to enter that eternity which will be their last and permanent Future. The living demand to hear whether there is any need for forgiveness, for redemption; whether, in fact, there may be any guide which may help them towards reforming their present condition. Different as they may be in their present state of existence, those alive and those now Dead—their ambitions point to a similar end. They are interested in their Future.[17]

This ceremony serves several functions. First, it acknowledges the necessity of communicating with the past; second, this effective myth, filled with innumerable possibilities, gives the work texture; and third, the way in which the upper classes recognize or ignore Voodoo and the relationship between its followers and non-followers manifests the class distinctions and provides Lamming with his particular manner of literary vision. The necessity of reordering and reevaluating these relationships becomes the important focus of Lamming's work.

The relation of these cultural forces is seen in the "downward" movement of Fola, a middle-class young lady thrust into the *tonelle*, (the temple where the Vodun rights are performed) and forced to come to grips with her identity. Fola wishes to escape her past until she is brought to the *tonelle* to witness the Ceremony of the Souls. In the *tonelle*, her backward glance into the world of Voodoo and the steel band fosters a new self-concept and propels her towards self-discovery. As the police chief's daughter, Fola moves from society's upper stratum towards identification with members of its lowest stratum, the world of the steel band and Voodoo. Pregnant with a lower class ruffian's child, she commits the unpardonable sin of crossing from her privileged neo-colonialist status to dispossession.

When the republic's vice-president is assassinated, the banning of the steel band brings the lower classes into the street. They overthrow the Caribbean's first independent republic and assert themselves as the people in the republic who really matter. Lamming understands what independence should mean and the changed relationships of independence, which lead Powell, the Chief Protagonist, to exclaim in the *Season of Adventure*:

> "Change my arse", he shouted, "is Independence what it is? One day in July you say you want to be that there thing, an' one day in a next July the law says all right, from now you's what you askin' for. What change can that be? Might as well call a dog a cat and hope to hear him mew. Is only words an' name what don' signify nothing."[18]

Lamming begins to operate from the recognition that freedom must be more than a flag, more than words, more than a date. As Powell continues to explain "Free is how you is from the start, an' when it look different you got to move, just move, an'when you movin' say that it is a natural freedom that make you."[19] That natural freedom is as real, pure and spontaneous as the steel band music Powell plays. One must experience these qualities to speak about independence; one must assume a new relationship between the self and the other.

Lamming recognizes the need to explore the deep reservoir of what Sylvia Wynter calls the "creative myth" (that is, the fact as well as the legend of history) of the Caribbean past. But Lamming goes a step further in his use of history. Whereas Galván and Reid dealt with the past simply on a one-to-one correspondence of facts, Lamming recognizes the complexity of the past and the need to explore its mythical nature. The facts of the past are so complex, vital and primordial that even though it might appear absurd, as Wilson Harris points out, they

> lie nevertheless like a submerged constitution in the jungle of time, a river of dead souls without race or family: facts to invoke, in curious, even profane recollection, not a conception of the virgin, but a conception of the barren, a visionary trail of "ruin" within "ruin" akin to a profound digestion of metaphysical organs—freedom and compassion.[20]

The restoration of the peasant to dignity and strength is Lamming's important contribution to the tradition of resistance in the Caribbean novel. *In The Pleasures of Exile* (1960), Lamming points out that it "is the West Indian novel that has restored the West Indian peasant to his true and original status of personality."[21] Wynter stresses Lamming's use of that source:

> Lamming looked down, away from the mono-crop export complex and its imported and imitative super-structure of culture to the only living tradition in the Caribbean—that of the peasants. They were now for the writer not a source of labour, but of culture, of a way of life, of an art of social living battered, tormented, assaulted, dispossessed, ignored, despised, but alive—the culture of the peasant, of the landless marginal man, of the indigenous man. For it was only by drawing from, by feeding from him that a truly national literature could begin. As long as the literate class turned its back on the source of its vitality, there was no writing. Writing began when the 'High Tradition' emerging from the popular tradition turned its gaze back; and that complex inter-action which is at the base of all creative national cultures began. The turning back of the novelist to the popular tradition was the movement of return, the long passage back from the exile of alienation. The future of Caribbean literature, and of the Caribbean people, whose psychic journey it structurally parallels, will depend on that disputed and almost impossible passage.[22]

Victor Reid began this process in *New Day* when he turned to the teeming masses that fought the English at Morant Bay, and Lamming continued it when he explored the peculiar problems of the colonial society on the eve of independence.

However, there is reason to believe that by 1971 Lamming had perceived the limitations of his original analysis. Even though Prospero gave Caliban ("language as symbolic interpretation, as an instrument of exploring consciousness,") Caliban at some stage would have to find a way to break that contract, which got sealed by language in order to restructure some alternate reality for himself. Lamming exemplifies this in his last novel, *Water With Berries* (1973), when Teeton (a twentieth-century descendant of Caliban) is forced to kill Old Dowager ("the age and in some ways the impotence of the earlier Prospero") in order to free himself.

After ten years of novelistic silence, George Lamming published *Water With Berries* (1971) in which he returned to *The Tempest* to elaborate upon the relationship between the colonizer and the colonized and to explore the nature of meaning that inhered in that special relation. In many ways *Water With Berries* is a pretentious novel which weaves its magnificent prose in a dulcet manner throughout the work but overwhelms the literary effort by the slimness of the plot structure.

The title of the novel is taken from the violently defiant speech of Caliban in which he reviles Prospero for the harsh and exploitative manner in which he has treated him:

Caliban:
   This Island's mine by Sycorax my mother,
   Which thou tak'st from me: when thou cam'st first
   Thou strok'dst me, and made much of me: wouldst give me
   Water with berries in't: and teach me how
   To name the bigger Light, and how the less
   That burn by day, and night: and then I lov'd thee
   And show'd thee all the qualities o' th' Isle,
   The fresh springs, brine-pits, barren place and fertile;
   Curs'd be I that did so: all the charms
   Of Sycorax: toads, beetles, bats light on you:
   For I am all the subjects that you have,
   Which first was mine own king: and here you sty me
   In this hard rock, whiles you do keep from me
   The rest o' th' Island

Prospero: Thou most lying slave,
     Whom stripes may move, not kindness:
     I have us'd thee
     (Filth as thou art) with humane care, and lodg'd thee
     In mine own cell, till thou didst seek to violate
     The honour of my child.
Caliban: Oh ho, oh ho, would't had been done:
     Thou didst prevent me, I had peopled else
     This Isle with Calibans.[23] [Italics mine.]

This aspect of the historical confrontation between Prospero and

Caliban seems to haunt the literary imagination of Lamming. Thus, where in *Of Age and Innocence* Shephard represents a particular manner of coming to grips with the historical cycle of Caliban's vengeance and his participation in an historical reality which binds his future inescapably with that of the colonizer, *Water With Berries* recognizes the necessity of shattering those former ties of dependence (which inheres in the shared experience of colonialism) and posits the need to work towards the creation of a genuinely independent state. As a consequence, the novel becomes an allegory of colonialism which examines the relationship of the descendants of Prospero and Caliban.

When the novel opens we see Teeton, the major protagonist, preparing to return to San Cristobal to participate in the revolution that would overthrow the neo-colonialist regime in his land. The trouble with the novel, however, is that all of the action takes place in the country of the colonizer.

Yet, while Teeton prepares to return to his country, his central dilemma revolves around the close relationship which has developed between himself and the Old Dowager, his landlady. Unable to find a place to live when he arrived in London after he had escaped from San Cristobal, the Old Dowager offers Teeton a room in her house which starts a relationship of entanglement which brings Teeton increasingly under her control.

> The house was the Old Dowager's; but the room was his; and house and room were in some way their joint creation; some unspoken partnership in interests they had never spoken about. He had changed lodgings nine times during his first year in London. Six years ago he had discovered a home in the Old Dowager's house. But it was time to go. The lump was thawing in his throat. He would have to tell her soon of his plans to leave. (WWB, p. 14)

As the years went by, Teeton and the Old Dowager formed a much stronger bond of friendship. She became the maternal and protective guardian while he became the courteous and reciprocating child. Indeed, the relationship became so close that when the corpse of Nichole (the wife of Teeton's friend Roger who had committed suicide) was found in Teeton's room, the Old Dowager, assuming that Teeton was in serious trouble, readily looked over the body until Teeton arrived.

When Teeton returned to his room he found Nichole's corpse. Automatically the Old Dowager took charge of the situation and assisted Teeton in burying the body in her garden in order to prevent a scandal. But this act of generosity and complicity placed Teeton in an even greater debt to the Old Dowager. When, however, Teeton and the Old Dowager escaped to the stormy island of the Orkneys where the Old Dowager owned a cottage, Teeton realized that not only was her control over him almost complete, but that she had begun to identify him with her late husband Prospero:

> "O course it's his boat," the Old Dowager said, ridding the last chuckle from her smile. "It's his and mine . . . " She was serious, almost grave. "Which means it's also yours while you're here. It's ours. The boat belongs to all of us."
>
> Teeton offered no reply. He couldn't dispute the Old Dowager's generosity; but he recognised her need. She was determined to make him feel an equal part of everything that went with the cottage. He didn't think it appropriate to bring the Old Dowager back to the real point of his interest in the boat. He let his attention drift back to the drama of the fire. But the Old Dowager had started up her chuckle again.
>
> "You remind me so much of him." she began.
>
> "Of him?" Teeton asked, indicating the room overhead where the pilot might have been.
>
> "No, no, not him," the Old Dowager went on. "I mean my husband. So much like him."
>
> She brought her shoulders further back as though she had now relieved herself of some pain. She turned her gaze on Teeton, and let her eyes travel slowly, playfully over his body.
>
> "So much like him," she said again, giving her comparison new emphasis. "That's just how he would have asked about the boat . Is it his or yours? Just like that."
>
> Teeton looked a little embarrassed; as though this association had caused him some offence. But the Old Dowager had been so jealous of his safety, so protective of his interests, that he felt no impulse to show his displeasure. And it struck Teeton that there was a sense, deep and subtle and even dangerous, in which she had achieved some powerful hold on the roots of his emotion. She had trained him to forgive her; to find some reason for diminishing any offence, however wounding it might have been. And he noticed, with a feeling of something like amazement, that he was smiling, claiming his share of the Old Dowager's mischief; conspiring with her, it seemed, at the sacrifice of his own natural response. (WWB, p. 186)

Because of the paradox of circumstances, Teeton is almost totally dependent upon the Old Dowager. At this point in the novel the author takes us into the mythic world of *The Tempest* as he resurrects some of the characters of the play. The Old Dowager is the wife of Prospero and mother of Miranda who we never see in *The Tempest*; Myra is Miranda, the daughter of Prospero; Fernando is Antonio, the brother of Prospero and lover of the Old Dowager; and Nichole, the white American woman who committed suicide and who places Teeton in this dilemma of complicity, is described as "an Ariel of mischief." (WWB, p. 216) In this context, Teeton is the twentieth century descendant of Caliban who is brought face to face with the descendants of Prospero.

As depicted by Lamming, Fernando is the caretaker of the cottage where the Old Dowager spends her vacation each year. When Fernando saw the close relationship which existed between Teeton and the Old Dowager he was consumed instantly with jealousy and demands of Teeton: "Is it her money? Or is it the house you are after?" (WWB, p. 223) A flame with such frenzied passion he could scarcely excuse the treachery and perfidy of the Old Dowager:

> There was a tangle of clouds before his eyes, like burning smoke ascending from a pyre of leaves. He could dimly see Teeton; see, that is, a shape of something; some kind of creature which he had to recognize; some punishing eruption of nature. How could it be true? How could the Old Dowager have punished his heart with such a rival for her love? It was monstrous, monstrous beyond meaning, what this stranger had come to be for her. (WWB, p. 244)

Believing that Teeton had replaced him in her affections, he had no alternative but to kill Teeton, but, as he tried to kill Teeton, the Old Dowager fires her rifle and kills Fernando. Once more Teeton is saved by the Old Dowager who kills Fernando not only to save Teeton's life but to avenge Fernando for not having told her that her daughter, Myra (Miranda), was saved in the storm which took Prospero to Caliban's island. As the Old Dowager affirmed, the reason for her actions were almost inevitable:

> The Old Dowager came slowly down the stairs giving all her attention to the broken head where the ear was leaking blood. She didn't look at Teeton.
> "He is dead," Teeton said.
> "I did what I had to do," she said, resisting any impulse to look in his direction.
> Teeton couldn't grasp her meaning, the incredible detachment which the Old Dowager showed as she stooped to hold the body on the floor.
> "Fernando dear," the Old Dowager was appealing, "why did you say the storm took Myra too? Why did you tell me that she died?"
> Her voice was like a miracle in Teeton's ears. Now she looked calm, almost impartial in her apparent lack of feeling. She didn't speak again, as though some subtle, and dreadful force of enmity was born in her silence. Teeton began to feel his guard go up again. The Old Dowager was capable of any action. The man's body was still alive and fresh with grief for the Old Dowager and her daughter. Teeton looked at the body; then tried to gain the Old Dowager's attention. But she had turned away, walking towards the front window with its view of the pier. (WWB, p. 231)

Yet this very act of complicity places Teeton firmly and almost irrevocably into the Old Dowager's control. But it is precisely this form of dependence which Teeton must break if he wishes to be free from a relationship which so binds him to the destiny of the other (the colonizer.) As a consequence, Teeton can only release himself from the burden of such complicity and dependence by killing the Old Dowager in a very violent and bloodied manner. He must kill the Old Dowager—the age and the remoteness of the earlier Prospero—if he wishes to be freed from the complicity of the past and to sever the psychic dependence upon the colonizer.

In an interview with George Kent, Lamming spoke of the symbolic importance of the relationship between Teeton and the Old Dowager and its implications for colonial dependence:

KENT
On the other hand, he's working out something with the character, the Old Dowager, getting into relationships with her that give him a sense of discovery. Is she part of the Prospero influence?
LAMMING
That's right. She's sort of taken over the role of Prospero, with this difference: whereas Prospero in *The Tempest* is a male force because the world from which he is operating is aggressive, expansionist and conquering, by the time we get to *Water With Berries*, that world has now contracted in a way. It has now retreated; it has aged. And what we see in the Old Dowager is the age, the remoteness, in some ways the impotence of the earlier Prospero. That power—that imperial power, that spirit of adventure, that extraordinary obsession with mastering reality, with turning the earth into one's private garden—is now gone; there is only the Old Dowager there with memories of a great past, of a great ancestral root. Now, Teeton lives as a *tenant* in her house, which is only another way of describing how he and people like him live in that country. He develops a very strong relationship to her. She exhibits a tremendous maternal concern toward him. She is careful about his health, very protective of him against the intrusions and injustices that might come from outside. There is the suggestion that in some part of her she is carrying on Prospero's role, for she does see in Teeton some aspect of her own responsibility. Now, he responds to her in a human way of care and concern; from time to time, images of his mother come to mind. But he also realizes that he is permanently condemned if he does not find the way of breaking this kind of response, of breaking this kind of relationship to her. Finally, he does it by killing her.[24]

It is the need to break with this almost incestuous relationship that becomes the central concern of *Water With Berries*. For as Lamming explained in his interview with George Kent:

The colonial situation is a matter of historical record. What I'm saying is that the colonial experience is a *live* experience in the *consciousness* of these people. And just because the so-called colonial situation and its institutions may have been transferred into something else, it is a fallacy to think that the human-lived content of those situations are automatically transferred into something else, too. The experience is a continuing *psychic* experience that has to be dealt with and will have to be dealt with long after the actual colonial situation formally "ends."[25]

Because the colonial condition is a continuing psychic experience which inheres with violence, the colonized person can only respond with revolutionary violence[26] in order to tear himself away from the psychic prison of enslavement. Revolutionary violence becomes the only manner through which and by which the colonial man and woman can respond adequately to the quality of violence which shapes the colonial experience. Thus Lamming argues:

> I believe that it is against all experience that a history which held men together in that way can come to an end in a cordial manner. That we can say, "Here is the parting of the ways; we will meet up here and continue as though nothing had ever happened; we can put all this horror, all this brutality behind; we are now equal in a new enterprise of human liberation." That horror and that brutality have a price, which has to be paid by the man who inflicted it—just as the man who suffered it has to find a way of exorcising that demon. It seems to me that there is almost a therapeutic need for a certain kind of violence in the breaking. There cannot be a parting of the ways. There has to be a smashing. (WWB, p. 91)

This call for the revolutionary smashing of ties with the colonizer represents a substantive change in the world-view of Lamming in that he seems to feel that the shared-meaning which existed in the relationship between Prospero and Caliban and which could have been negotiated in an amicable manner is no longer possible.

Yet one may argue that the central content of this changed position of Lamming resides more in the literary intention of the novelist's sensibility rather than in the concrete achievement of the work. Wilson Harris in his work, *Tradition and the West Indian Novel*, has argued that *Of Age and Innocence*

> is a novel which somehow fails, I feel, but its failure tells us a great deal. The novel would have been remarkable if a certain tendency—a genuine tendency—for a tragic feeling of dispossession in reality had been achieved. This tendency is fustrated by a diffusion of energies within the entire work. The book seems to speak with a public voice, the voice of a peculiar orator, and the

compulsions which inform the work appear to spring from a verbal sophistication rather than a visual, plastic and conceptual imagery.[27]

If it is true that Lamming did not capture a "tragic feeling of dispossession" in *Of Age and Innocence*, it is also true that even though *Water with Berries* is suffused with the verbosity of language (poetic though it might be in some places), it is bereft of the density and tightness of plot structure that is necessary to carry forward the central content of the work. Yet the novel does examine the importance of smashing the colonial relationship in a violent manner and this becomes the most important concern of the novel. *Water with Berries*, therefore, extends the development of George Lamming's earlier literary concerns and dramatizes the inescapable impact of the changing political ideas upon the literary sensibilities.

The need to smash these psychic ties of colonialism at the actual level of combat becomes the burden of Bertène Juminer's novel, *Au seuil d'un nouveau cri*. While the easy transition from dependence to independence which Lamming presents in *Of Age of Innocence* and *Season of Adventure* is boldly challenged in *Water with Berries*, this transition is still seen within exclusively personal and almost selfish terms. Juminer, however, not only explores the fallacy of the easy transition, but places it within the collective terms of the colonial experience. Moreover, Juminer demonstrates the need for revolutionary violence in actual conflict with the colonizer, at home and abroad, and explores the therapeutic need for revolutionary violence in order to establish an honest sense of national identity and thereby, facilitate a true sense of reconciliation.

X

SMASHING THE TIES:
Au seuil d'un nouveau cri,
Bozambo's Revenge, Guerrillas

Dr. Bertène Juminer's *Au seuil d'un nouveau cri* (1963) epitomizes the use of resistance as a central theme in the Caribbean novel and brings to fruition many of the issues raised by the previous novelists, whom we have discussed. *Au seuil d'un nouveau cri*, which presents another dimension of sociopsychological realism, at perhaps a more complex moment of historical development, has many metaphysical concepts and tries to solve problems based in the psychological implications of enslavement. Juminer, a personal friend of Frantz Fanon, dealt with many of the problems Fanon raised, including revolutionary violence, the relationship between black men and white women, and the problematic colonial relationship between Prospero and Caliban.

Fanon's theories, which arose from his psychiatric work among Muslim men in Algeria, noted that psychological and psychiatric problems in the oppressed came from the social milieu. Indeed, the turning point in Fanon's career came when he and his colleague, Tosquelles, discovered that they

> . . . had committed a cardinal error in automatically assuming that they could impose the techniques of one milieu to another without paying attention to the nature of the one group to which they were applying their methods. The first rule was to conduct a stringent examination of the nature of the community, in this case, the nature of the Algerian male community within the hospital. *In retrospect they asked themselves how is it possible to function on the basis of a theoretical analysis that was not grounded in the particular geographic, historical, cultural and social milieu of the group in which they worked.* Their answers had implications that could not be lost on their colleagues and that determined their own subsequent course of action.[1] [Italics mine.]

Juminer, like Fanon, believed in the therapeutic value of revolutionary violence on the psyche of the colonized man. He believed this violence was necessary to purge his nature of the colonial psychosis of "inferiority" and "unworthiness," and therefore the focus of his work is located in an examination of the psychological state of his characters. Where Fanon as doctor/scientist was almost dogmatic, Juminer as novelist/artist is almost vague and insubstantial. Revolutionary violence becomes, as all symbols in any good work of art, "inexhaustible and infinite in its meaning, when it utters in its secret language (hieratic and magic) of allusion and suggestions something indelible, that is not equivalent to external words."[2] In his clinical analysis of the colonial mind, Juminer is as profound as Lamming yet in many ways much more compelling, and his work presents a more complex form of sociopsychological realism in Caribbean literature.

Au seuil d'un nouveau cri goes back into the maroon rebellion and pits the revolutionary Sonson/Dummerville against the less revolutionary Modestine/Pierre. The novel is divided into two parts: "The Cry" and "The Echo." The first part revolves around the ideas and attitudes of two major characters. As the novel opens, brutality common on the sugarcane plantation forces slaves to seek refuge in the mountains, where they plan their attack against the whites. When the war begins, Sonson, the revolutionary forces' chief, orders Modestine to capture his former slave master, D'Entefoix. Despite orders to the contrary, Modestine kills the younger D'Entefoix when he spits in Modestine's face.

As Sonson clearly recognizes, revolutionary violence is the only means of fully liberating the slaves, for it is "only the revolution, that supreme affirmation of the self, that allows the slave to get back his human condition." (ASNC, p. 31) However, revolution is a collective process, not an individual aberration. As Sonson explains, "to win alone is absurd and it finally amounts to being vanquished through one's own frustrated group and kept apart." (ASNC, p. 31) Sonson chastizes Modestine for following justifiable individual feelings in a revolutionary struggle.

Sonson gives Modestine another chance to join the revolution with the assignment of capturing the older D'Entefoix and bringing him back alive. Modestine finds D'Entefoix at home, but as he is about to capture him, D'Entefoix takes refuge in the home of Delangres, who bought Modestine from his master and gave him his freedom. Because he cannot violate his friendship with Delangres, Modestine must return empty-handed at this critical juncture. To whom does he owe his allegiance? To Sonson, a black who sees the struggle in a Manichaean way, or to Delangres, a white who has defied other slave masters by introducing free labor on his plantation and has proved himself to be a revolutionary in his own way—fighting for the abolishment of slavery. This is Modestine's dilemma, about which "The Cry" (First Part) is built.

Sonson sees the struggle exclusively in racial terms. He feels that, "joined by color, the whites altogether had humiliated and dominated the niggers, aiming at destroying their soul by inculcating into them the horror of being black." (ASNC, p. 46) Total annihilation, then, was the aim of the whites. For Sonson black people cannot regain their humanity in unison with whites. The only alternative, then, is total annihilation of the whites. As Vere W. Knight points out, "Sonson is projected as the ideal type revolutionary leader—a thinker as well as a doer, freely chosen by the people, having himself previously chosen, consciously, the revolution as the way out of his situation."[3] The revolution is "to mobilize consciences by using key words in which the masses would recognize themselves and whereby, in the end, find again a desire for freedom." (ASNC, pp. 55-56)

Anyone who doesn't see the revolution in these terms is immediately judged traitorous. Modestine finds himself in just such a position. He does not think himself a traitor, yet he is faced with the dilemma: tell the truth, give Delangres over and save his own life or lie and risk his own death. Captured, Modestine is brought before Sonson who has him tied, blindfolded, and taken to another cave for trial. Yet Modestine remains convinced that he has not committed a treasonous crime in defending Delangres. In his humiliation he still wonders about the use of violence and is troubled by the paradox of hate. Modestine ponders:

> The white man says that we do not take over a system to destroy it. We introduce ourselves into it and destroy it from the inside. Without knowing one another, Delangres and the Maroons were pursuing the same goals; the abolition of slavery, and even their means of obtaining this were similar. The Maroons sent saboteurs into the plantations and engendered subversion. But he on his own plantation built up a form of opposition which was nonetheless revolutionary. (ASNC, pp. 74-75)

Delangres, who is also against slavery, commands Modestine's respect and loyalty, for he uses free labor on his plantation and to prove his sincerity will suffer beating. Modestine is awed by him. He has never seen a white man like Delangres and marvels when Delangres talks about the French Revolution during which in his view, whites were fighting for the liberation of blacks. Delangres offers Modestine equality with these words: "I am not your master, you are free. I had to shout in order to overcome your voice; shout that new liberty which you were inaugurating by acts of submission." (ASNC, p. 87) Even though Delangres gives Modestine his freedom, Modestine is unable to accept this free condition because of his slave mentality.

Like Sonson, Modestine recognizes the need for cathartic revolutionary violence. However, unlike Sonson, he also recognizes that the struggle must transcend hate and race, that only through love can the unity of man occur. It is because he is dedicated to the principle of love and brotherhood that his cries of self-anguish and self-reflection show so much pathos:

> You promised yourself to preach love; to transform your combat in a crusade of love between man. But you had to kill first; you will have to kill again to quench this inrooted hatred. And this dreamed combat [of love] which was so pure will never come about unless this fire which was burning in you came out. (ASNC, p. 92)

Captured, Modestine is to be judged by six of his brothers. He knows his fate is already decreed, for no one has gone before this tribunal and been found innocent. Having lied to protect Delangres, he knows his only reward will be death as violent as that of Christ, the other traitor, who died for love.

Yet at the prospect of death, "there remained for you one supreme consolation; you had not betrayed the true revolution, the one which was preaching the coming into the world of liberty without hate." (ASNC, p. 111) Modestine is convinced that after the blacks' victory, "tomorrow would rise on a new world, without slaves, but where whites and blacks would not be facing each other, but would be side by side." (ASNC, pp. 111-112) Modestine thinks the revolution's guiding principle should be love; otherwise, if only hate and annihilation of the whites should prevail, a new form of slavery and hatred would not only destroy the blacks but defeat their purpose. Modestine believes people should fight against all forms of slavery. That is the reaon he leaves Delangres' plantation to join the Maroons. For him the struggle should not be seen exclusively in terms of color since he feels that after the victory of the blacks, the whites' importance as a symbol of authority and superiority will diminish. After all, as Delangres has told him, the whites far away are fighting for the blacks' liberation, a position Sonson clearly repudiates:

> The whites say that they wish to liberate us. From whom? Who are our masters but themselves? All that's not very clear. One cannot be liberator and master at the same time. . . . The whites are weak; they know we are going to win, so they want to steal our victory from us by cunning. To give it away before being forced to do so. They are trying to trick us by giving with one hand and taking away with the other. As long as I command, it will be to tear away, not to pick up. (ASNC, p. 114)

Juminer's position is a long way from Galván's, Reid's and Lamming's since Juminer insists that the very nature of colonization demands a violent tearing away before any effort of healing can be attempted and dialogue initiated. Frantz Fanon's *Black Skin, White Masks* (1952) details this same idea in rejecting M. Mannoni's "dependency complex" in colonial people. Neither Galvan nor Reid perceived the therapeutic need for revolutionary violence, and Lamming did not explore it far enough, preferring instead to examine the problem of colonialism on a theoretical level.

Sonson recognizes that freedom must not be given, and that one cannot really enjoy and appreciate freedom that is given, for the psychic ties of dependency are too deeply rooted. Sonson acknowledges that one cannot enjoy a liberty

> for which one hasn't deeply suffered. What is given goes away as it comes, without stirring; but what is conquered doesn't escape without resistance, without despair. For great fights there are great trophies. Apart from that everything else was only a form of charity; picking up crumbs, slavery always. (ASNC, p. 115)

This is precisely Fanon's argument in his classic, *The Wretched of the Earth*.

Modestine's predicament is painful because he recognizes that, given his limitations, Delangres is a sensitive white man who understands the colonial's problems as much as he possibly can. Delangres recognizes, for example, the justice of the Maroons' cause and that their hatred was not in their nature but born of their situation.

Both Delangres and Modestine are condemned to death; Delangres to a physical death, and Modestine to a spiritual death. As Modestine acknowledges, no penalty could be worse than banishment:

> You had wanted to be black to the very bottom of your heart in order to give all of its weight to forgiveness, and to the forgiveness of offences once received to this new fraternity of which you were dreaming. And now a black tribunal was taking away your color and taking away all your hopes. Your brothers were banishing you from their revolution and their race. The word traitor had made you stumble. The word white was consuming you and was dispersing your ashes to the wind. (ASNC, pp. 155-156)

Modestine no longer has even fraternity with those to whom he has dedicated his life. The whites have rejected and humiliated Modestine; now the blacks banish him from their world. Yet Modestine knows that he has triumphed in the real revolution of love. Facing death, he no longer hates old D'Entefoix, and a "great forgiveness illuminated him and filled him with love for his brothers who were going to immolate him. Pure, he was suddenly purity in body ravaged by the sinlessness which would purify, as the nails which nailed him to the Cross. At your contact everything would be purified, [and you will become] the child of the universe." (ASNC, p. 157)

Modestine and Delangres understand the sacrificial nature of their deaths. Modestine wins the real revolution by transcending Sonson's violence while understanding its necessity and cathartic and therapeutic effects at this particular point in the history of colonialism. Sonson's cause, no matter how just in the beginning, will fail in the larger cosmic order because it is tainted by hate, while Modestine's battle is a struggle for "spiritual freedom, self-purification and the creation of a universal brotherhood—these are the ideals for which he gives his life."[4]

The novel's second part, "The Echo," is set in contemporary Paris, and, as Randolph Hezekiah puts it in "Bertène Juminer and the Colonial Problem," ". . . the violent West Indian slave revolt depicted in the first part ["The Cry"] seems to transcend the limits of space and time to become the Twentieth-century revolt against imperialism in the second part ["The Echo"]."[5]

In "The Echo," Dumerville becomes the twentieth-century Sonson, and Pierre, a direct descendent of Modestine, the twentieth-century Modestine. The conflict changes slightly, but the thrust of the message remains the same. Whereas Modestine defies his black brothers to save Delangres, in "The Echo," Io (Veronique), who is white, defies her parents to love the black Pierre. Further, Juminer sees Io and Pierre as allies fighting the same oppressive master. Pierre/Modestine fights against unquestioning violence and hatred whereas Dumerville/Sonson insists violence is the only means of dealing with oppression.

Pierre is a member of a Parisian communist student cell, of which Dumerville is the leader. Dumerville feels enslaved by a foreign culture thrust upon him. Like slaves in "The Cry," he escapes his imprisonment by daydreaming, thinking that very little has changed since slavery. As he watches the more subtle spiritual disintegration that has replaced slavery's physical cruelty, he notes that the slaves possessed an advantage in retaining their speech, myths, and morals. Dumerville realizes he must use the accepted language of the French master instead of the slave Creole dialect in order to function in that society. He revolts passively by refusing to do so.

For Dumerville, the only change that has taken place from the days of slavery is that imperialism has replaced slavery, with the oppressed reacting in negative despair. Dumerville thinks only active resistance can bring freedom and anything less in the twentieth century will fail. Dumerville analyzes his condition:

The imperialists had installed and legalized in our country a caricature of their

217

own society. After slavery came the colonial status; after this colonial status came the so-called total integration which was fatally fragmentary. . . . Never had they sincerely wanted you to join them on the same pedestal of manhood. Never had they consented to play the game. . . . you rebelled once you discovered they were preventing you from becoming a man; in return if they were not threatening you they would get offended by your ingratitude. Your only answer was a refusal—that negative despair, was the only recourse of the oppressed. . . . Your fathers had gained a physical liberty which they (the whites) boast to have given to you freely. . . . Only political liberty can guarantee the liberty of the citizen. This liberty is still to be had and will not come about without combat, without sacrifice. (ASNC, pp. 173-174)

This situation is contemporary, for the struggle begun by the slaves has not ended. Dumerville believes imperialists are weak because they do not have a moral reason to oppress the colonials. Even though with "each act of repression the imperialist was proclaiming that he was only stopping communism," (ASNC, p. 174) the people must continue fighting on for total liberty.

Juminer also believes there is a peculiar relationship between the white woman and the colonial man, particularly the black intellectual, with the white man (master/imperialist) using intimidation and violence to keep each in place, thus making them allies in the same battle for freedom. Paradoxically, when the black male (particularly the black intellectual) begins to adorn himself with his oppressor's attributes, he sinks towards insignificance. The more he is assimilated, the more he is emasculated. However, the more the white woman asserts herself and identifies herself with the white oppressor, the more the white oppressor fears her. Thus, the liberated woman and the unassimilated black male colonial are the colonist/imperialist's most potent threat. Losing control over his woman, the white colonizer begins to cling more tenaciously to his colonies.

These ideas are structured around Io's (Veronique) and Pierre's relationship. They meet in a bar while she is chaperoned (protected) by her intended husband's relatives. Io and Pierre begin to dance. Io finds her responses to Pierre limited by her fiance's family and feels the need to escape. By secluding Io from her fiance, Pierre believes that he is rescuing her from captivity. Io defies her parents (those who have control over her life) to see Pierre, who initially perceives their encounter as just another seduction until a strange affinity created by the oppressions they are heir to floats between them and the problems of sex, race and color recede from his own anguish: "as a consequence, he realizes that as trapped colonized man, he was discovering another identical anguish which relegated sex, color and origin into pure relativity. Io and he were companions in captivity and beyond a common past would survive a stronger more thoughtful solidarity of people conscious of being contested against." (ASNC, p. 216) Pierre realizes that Io (Veronique) is suffering more than he, for she is a slave. He feels that her only recourse is to run away before she is totally subdued, but before he knows it, she becomes a defiant rebel, and the then obvious sexual attraction becomes the trigger to set off the mechanism of repression.

Pierre, who becomes more involved with Io, resents the fact that she is going to marry a white man. He reads about racial violence in the southern United States, where a black man is lynched for allegedly raping a white woman, and he is filled with anger; he becomes a revolutionary once again. But before bitterness consumes Pierre, Io appears, once again raising the conflicts within him:

> and now here you were like the other nigger, your blood bouncing in your veins, you body becoming electrified and crying out in sudden ecstasy at the sound of a white voice, messenger this time, not of violence, but of peace; not of hatred, but of love; by hitting you in the heart, she tore you up, she filled you with exquisite vivifying sufferings. It was her soft liberating voice which at once washed away all my anxiety and my fright. (ASNC, p. 222)

This dilemma is the classic one of the black intellectual of the colonized world torn between his impulse to participate in the revolution and his allegiance to the "other." Pierre's first impulse of anger shared with his brother in combat is correct. However, he succumbs to the "soft, liberating voice" of this white woman, a fellow sufferer, which places him in the schism that tends to plague the black intellectual at all times.

The challenge for Pierre in this paradoxical relationship is the black intellectual's ability to confront his situation and to understand the larger fraternal relationship to which each brings his individual strength and to understand that "her passivity, like your anticipations represented the modalities of the same escape, the coordinates of one same dream and one same defeat." (ASNC, p. 223)

In contrast, Dumerville, the purveyor of revolutionary violence, has a lower profile than Sonson had in "The Cry." Unlike Sonson, Dumerville is not adverse to using white women. As chief of the communist cell, he promotes revolutionary violence to rid his home land of the imperialist. He recognizes the power of the imperialist and wants to see him defeated and his arrogance ended. He see the colonial man rising up in spite of the many set backs he has suffered. And even though he feels the colonial struggle in the French Caribbean was not proceeding as quickly as the colonial struggle in the British or Spanish Caribbean, he sees hope in their struggle in the French Caribbean and reminds his comrades:

. . . we are not alone. All the Third World is with us. The essential thing is to make our fight known; to inform our brothers in Africa and Asia about it, at the same time that we are educating our people. Of course, we are being expelled, we are being killed, but they can neither expel nor kill all of us. Imperialism needs us in order to exist, in order to survive. They can kill strikers, torture others or imprison them and in a way I say, all for the good. On one condition; that we know how to take advantage of these crimes. Each dead man must be taken to the streets in open trunks and shown to the people so that they can see and understand and revenge themselves. (ASNC, p. 239)

At first, believing in the possibility of understanding from the colonizer, Dumerville is nonviolent. But a number of incidents propel him into seeing the need for revolutionary violence and self-sufficiency within the struggle. As he puts it, "it became clear that only violence would be the answer to repression; a violence organized and concentrated on these three words: resistance, urban agitation and external relations." (ASNC, p. 239) National liberation in the twentieth century must not only end oppression but also forge a new link between the masses and their leaders. For Dumerville, the struggle should cultivate a new sense of reciprocity involving the collective will and a collective effort. Dumerville feels very strongly that

confident reciprocity will only come about from a double endeavor: first from a descent into hell in order to look for your nation and burn with her, and melt yourself into her. Then together with those who would have joined you, lift her up upon your shoulders so that you may all together surge upwards, while making all the weight of your collective ardor press upon the imperialist conscience. (ASNC, p. 243)

For Dumerville, one is either for or against the revolution and national liberation. Pierre, however, will work for national liberation, but is not ready to spill blood. For him, "fighting imperialism had never meant hating the whole of white humanity. Everywhere there were good, loving men and hateful men. This distinction must be made between whites and those of your own race." (ASNC, p. 245) When Pierre looks at Io (Veronique), he realizes that she is caught between him, whom she loves, and her people, with whom she must live and who constantly remind her that only a whore can love a nigger. Pierre realizes that to think of the national liberation struggle exclusively in terms of race is wrong.

Pierre is waiting at a bar to meet Io when her future brother-in-law approaches. The brother-in-law is hostile and advises Pierre to leave Io alone. Io appears, upbraids her future brother-in-law for trespassing on her life, takes Pierre's arm and walks out of the bar. Io, the camouflage, dies, and Veronique, the revolutionary, is born. Pierre, who hears the future brother-in-law call "Veronique," learns her real name. Veronique, like Modestine, becomes a "daughter of the universe," and understands she isn't anyone's property. She becomes sacred and exalted.

Pierre decides to take Veronique to her home, where they see her father waiting in front of the gate. Veronique's parents want her to be ashamed of Pierre, the Negro. In a defiant gesture of her new liberty, Veronique kisses Pierre in front of her father, who grabs Pierre, slaps him twice, saying, "You nigger, leave us in peace." Veronique screams, "Enough, enough, Pierre my darling," (ASNC, pp. 271-272) her cry an echo of Modestine's at the end of the first part—a cry affirming solidarity and man's universal love and brotherhood.

Meanwhile, sudden and brutal government repression comes on Dumerville and his followers when an official decision dissolves the organization and threatening letters impair the members' safety. Beaten by the colonial experience, they remain easy prey in exile. Dumerville's choice is simple: he must return home and continue the revolution. Pierre's choice is not so easy: he sees returning to the islands as running away, which would only weaken himself and his ally. Pierre stays in Paris because of Veronique, believing that he will strengthen the struggle for liberation by uniting with her.

It is important to point out that many of Bertène Juminer's ideas are also found in the works of Frantz Fanon. The two were close personal friends, and it was Juminer who correctly diagnosed Fanon's illness and shared the stress of Fanon's last year. Fanon died on 6 December 1961. A few months later, Juminer wrote an homage in *Presence Africaine*; twenty months after Fanon's death, *Au seuil d'un nouveau cri* appeared. Obviously Juminer was either working on the novel during Fanon's year of sickness or began it shortly after his death. Many of the novel's ideas appear in "Hommage à Fanon." Speaking of Fanon in this tribute, Juminer recalls:

Only recently alienated himself, he [Fanon] makes himself into a study and decides to study this great mental malady which both the colonized person has gotten just as much in his deep nature as the Western master. The diagnosis is biting and sorrowful for all of us. At the risk of incurring the resentment of my black brothers, I shall have to say that the black man is not a man. And the white? In order to understand him in his real psychiatric fashion Fanon found himself plunged in the reality of Algeria. He was finished with half-way measures. There is only one way to heal; the Revolution, which will bring the two alienating types to a normal life. By liberating the Algerians it will heal the Europeans. Fanon throws himself into battle for "the victorious road to the liberation of the colonized person." On his way towards liberation he also hopes to help the Europeans to listen to the opinions of fraternal voices of all those throughout the world that are beginning revolutions and who recognize that in the battle a people recognize themselves again.[6]

Here is the idea that explicitly governs the novel: " . . . There is only one way to heal, the Revolution, which will bring the two alienating types to a normal life." Indeed, the revolution brings Delangres (white) and Modestine (black and colonized) together; only when the two are close to death and know the trauma of revolution do they recognize their triumph. Through revolution Modestine truly finds himself. Cleansed by murder of young D'Entefoix, he feels a sense of forgiveness for the old D'Entefoix and so his life affirms the higher claims of humanity. Inevitably, Modestine/ Pierre finds himself in conflict with Sonson/ Dumerville, who affirms only the racial vision of life. The struggle is also a reciprocal process in which by liberating himself from the oppressors, the oppressed is himself liberated by the struggle. This was Fanon's vision. The Algerian Revolution was as important for Fanon as the Cuban Revolution was for Dumerville.

In the same article, Juminer also recalls a dedication Fanon inscribed in *The Year of the Algerian Revolution*, which he sent to Juminer. It reads:

This book is the illustration of a principle. Action is merely incoherence and agitation if it does not restructure the conscience of the individual. In the great battle against the colonial oppressors the Algerian people are displaying the subjective dimension of an intensity, from which the entire Algerian nation can no longer be the same. Have confidence in your people [French Antillean] and consecrate yourself to its dignity and its fulfillment. For us there is no other way.

Last December, I arrived with my dictaphone and asked him for a message for the activist of the *Union of the People of Guiana*. For three quarters of an hour he analysed the Antillean Guiana situation and came out for the 'great movement of decolonization' which the world has supported.[7]

It is obvious that Modestine/ Pierre's conscience has been restructured in the work. When we first see Pierre in "The Echo," he feels stifled by the Parisian atmosphere and wants to return to the Caribbean. When he begins his relationship with Io (Veronique), a mindless flirtation turns into a deeper fraternal union. Interracial love transcends racist rejection. The same case can be made for Modestine.

Like Fanon, Juminer recognized the universality of the Caribbean struggle, specifically, the French Caribbean struggle. Dumerville warns that "only political liberty can guarantee the liberty of the citizen. This liberty is still to be had. It will not come about without combat, without sacrifice." (ASNC, p. 256) Fanon, in fact, was happy that a number of

Martinicans were killed in the Fort de France incident because he felt their death would encourage others to overthrow the colonizer. When Dumerville recounts the Caribbean's problems, he specifically refers to that incident and warns his brothers: "We are not alone, all the Third World is with us. We must make known our battle to our brothers in Africa and Asia while we educate our people." (ASNC, p. 212) It is fairly obvious then, that Juminer draws on the concepts of "restructuring" the conscience of the individual, and places the Caribbean colonial struggle in the larger context of the Third World struggle. The importance of the "therapeutic nature of revolutionary violence" is as obviously Fanon's as is the other question that Fanon tries to answer: whether, in fact, normal human relations were possible between a black man and a white woman. It can be argued with regard to the former, for example, that Juminer went further than Fanon and answered affirmatively. The fundamental positions, however, were basically Fanon's and we seem to be much more aware of them because of Fanon.

Juminer's third novel, *La Revanche de Bozambo* (1968) translated *Bozambo's Revenge* (1968), is an ostensible political novel. Where *Au seuil d'un nouveau cri* finds its beginning in the epic myth of the maroons, *Bozambo's Revenge*, which is more global in scope, takes the European slave trade as its point of departure. Locating the colonial struggle squarely within the context of Europe's early plunder of Africa and the New World, *Bozambo's Revenge* goes on to posit the contemporary urban guerrilla warfare as the necessary response to the contemporary imperialist system of domination.

Thus Juminer develops the theme which he raised in *Au seuil d'un nouveau cri* a little further by suggesting that racism, colonialism, and imperialist oppression can be eliminated only by destroying the imperialist system completely.[8] The initial need for the cleansing effects of *revolutionary violence* must give way to the more purposeful demand of *revolutionary struggle* so that one may be able to eliminate all of the subtle nexus of psychological relationships which are created by the colonialist-imperialist presence.[9]

Strategically, *Bozambo's Revenge* depends upon a systematic reversal of European-oriented symbols and concepts which are used to dramatize the psychological nature of imperialist oppression. Thus "white" becomes "black" and vice versa; "Europe" becomes "Africa" and vice versa, the "white man's burden" becomes "the black man's burden" and the entire European context is transposed into an African context. As Paul L. Thompson has suggested in his introduction to the work, this "scenario of cultural reversal . . . puts the oppressor into a perspective which blows away the cant and mystification of western colonial claims." (BR, pp. XIV-XV) Further, he goes on to suggest that:

The hundreds of uncanny reversals of roles: the historical pomposities, the cliches of prejudice, of fertility goddesses of national monuments, of genocide, and conquest, and the benumbing ferocities of the para-military colonial cadres ought to satisfy anyone needing a laugh or a snicker. But the rhetoric of *Bozambo's Revenge* goes beyond satire: it cauterizes away any possible belief in a system of cultural imperialism, no matter its "glorious" trappings. (BR, p. XVI)

Thus *Bozambo's Revenge* operates as a symbolic narrative in which the author attempts to turn "colonialism inside out" (as the alternative title suggests) in order to explore the complexity of the psychological trauma which colonialism-imperialism entrusted upon colonial peoples and to demonstrate why it is necessary to overthrow the entire system so that the colonial man can recapture his dignity and his wholeness.

In order to achieve its objectives, *Bozambo's Revenge* examines all of the well-worn claims of European colonialism through the author's method of strategic cultural reversals and demonstrate the absurditites of those claims. Primarily, the author examines the reasons advanced for Europe's dominance of colonial peoples and the aesthetic perceptions and sensibilities which were used by the dominating society. It punctures Europe's pretended notions of generosity, dismisses the proverbial ingratitude and childlike consciousness attributed to the natives, and rejects the notion that only chaos would follow if colonial people were allowed to rule their countries. While Juminer calls his work a novel, it can best be described as a political satire—a form of political pamphleteering—ideas are given prominence over the development of plot and character. In fact because there is such little development of plot and characters that the burden of the work revolves around the banned pamphlet, "What is Baoulian Colonialism," which was written by the jailed patriot, Georges-Edouard-Ferdinand Escartefigue, secretary of the Anti-Colonialism Society. We never see him in the novel but in the epilogue he "was brought out of his cell and flown by private jet to Baoul-Bled [Abidjan, the capital of the colonialist-imperialist world], officially invited by Mango Zekodene [president of the colonialist-imperialist world] to discuss the formation of the first autonomous government of the O.B.E., of which he is to assume the vice-presidency." (BR, p. 160) Apart from Escartefigue, there are three other leading members of the revolutionary nationalist group: the Archduke: Edgar Dupont; and his nephew, Anatole Dupont. On the other side we find Inspector General Bozambo, Comandant Adiami and Colonel Sar, who are defending the colonialist-imperialist interests.

When the work opens Anatole Dupont is seen arriving at Bantouville (Paris), "a kind of small paradise which African [European] genius has created from a swamp by the banks of the Sekuana, a lazy and capricious river called the Seine" (BR, p. 160) which is peopled by blacks who rule and dominate the city and the world. As Anatole proceeds throught the streets in search of his uncle's residence, he is greeted by the political slogans of the Anti-Colonialist Movement which bedeck the buildings and the walls of the city. Observing these slogans, Anatole wonders:

> what Europe [Africa] did to bring onto herself the implacable African [European] domination. Decadence? Congenital weakness? Historians and archeologists agree that at one time, Europe [Africa] had reached a certain stage of social organization, but opinions differ when it comes to explaining its importance and nature.
>
> The question is absurd for those who abmit no civilization or culture save the Black [White]. A civilized Europe [Africa]? You must be joking! She was nothing but a wasteland, or nearly; a place of anarchy and bandits, until establishment of the colonial outpost. (BR, pp. 10-11)

A few learned Africans, "officially regarded as dreamers or anarchists," (BR, p. 11) held that ancient African civilizations reached heights of greatness and prosperity and induced their own decline when they began to pursue their own imperialist (that is, expansionist) course. Because Africa was an advanced civilization where monotheism flourished, these wise men claimed that she could boast of having achieved a notable height in civilization.

Continuing through the streets, Anatole was attracted to the huge billboards advertising the latest film of Bora Belkoukoune (Bridgette Bardot) in "wide-screen and Africolor" (BR, p. 12) which demonstrates to him immediately the cultural dimensions of imperialism. At once he is reminded of the manner through which the cultural life of the colonial people is controlled and the way in which their aesthetic perceptions are manipulated and fashioned by the ideas of the other. In an instant, he remembers his childhood and the exploits of Zartan (Tarzan) zooming through the forest to save some unfortunate African and the manner in which the colonizers present themselves as pioneers; "champions of civilization [who] sacrificed their lives to bring the continent out of darkness." (BR, p. 13)

The irony of such absurdities suddenly dawns upon Anatole. As he continues along the streets he sees black men who had been discarded by the colonialists' army, set aside to beg for a living after they had been forced to serve the oppressor. He hears the latest pop music as it assaults the air and wanders into the cafe from whence it came. At the bar he listens to the voices in the cafe;

Bursts of customers' voices discuss current events, such as the struggle of the whites of *ouolove* America to [black Afro-Americans] obtain integration in the schools hitherto reserved for Blacks [Whites]. A few, more civilized, Europeans, [Africans] wearing African [European] dress and speaking the same but with a strong toubab accent (they rasp their r's instead of eliding them properly), reinforce the conviction that, in these places, the African [European] is indeed in conquered lands. (BR, p. 15)

As he ponders the enormity of the scenes which he has just witnessed, as he listens to the conversation of the colonial administrators in the cafe, and as he thinks about the condition of African men and women all over the world, he recognizes that the time for dialogue with the whites is over and that revolutionary struggle becomes almost inevitable:

Europe [Africa] keeps quiet and backs off before Africa [Europe]. There is not, nor could there be, a dialogue between them and this is even in the best interests of the people whom history has condemned to silence. Everything which is happening in here and outside cannot but reflect the difficult confrontation between the African [European] spirit and the backwardness of the rest of the planet, and testify to the Black [White] man's burden. (BR, p. 16)

Leaving the cafe with his suitcase in his hand, Anatole proceeds to his uncle's house. As he walks along the almost empty streets of the city, he is approached by some police officers. It is dangerous for a blackman to walk in a white city at night with a suitcase in his hand at a time of anti-colonialist tensions. He may be carrying a bomb or other destructive device. He feels that he is pursued. He shows a clean pair of heels and never stops until he finds himself in the safety of one of the bars in the ghettoes of Bantouville. He orders a drink and demands a paper. As he browses through the paper his eyes catches the headline: "Two hundred thousand Whites [Blacks] marched on far away in Samoryville yesterday." (BR, p. 26) In bold italics, Anatole sees the quotation of their leader: "We will go as far as we have to, non-violently, to obtain equal rights with Blacks [Whites]." (BR, p. 26) Confronted with such brutality against his people he could not help but ponder the historical roots of his people's condition:

In the four centuries since Africans [European] first set foot in America, the misfortunes of the white [black] race have been multiplying. First there was the slave trade, where Whites [Blacks] were sold by their own people to break their backs under the whip in mean agricultural tasks for ten generations. Then came the abolition of slavery, not without a struggle that shook the entire continent, from the foulbephone United Provinces of America to the Tierra del Hielo in ouolove America. Paradoxically enough for anyone acquainted with the Negro's [White's] innate inhumanity, a few men and women of the black [white] race joined this struggle whose goal was to throw off the yoke of African [European] imperialism. Koumba Couli-Cagou [Harriet Beecher Stowe] did this with his thrilling book *Uncle Jules' Hovel;* [Uncle Tom's Cabin] then Vivi Oumarou [Victor Schoelcher] in the Caribbean carried on after the white hero Laclôture [Toussaint L'Ouverture] died of thirst and heat, deported to the farthest confines of the arid Sudanese savannah, despite which his victorious country became the first white [black] republic of the New World. (BR, pp. 26-27)

Commenting on the nature of racial segregation which existed in the United States, where he felt that dogs lived better than the Blacks, he dismisses the tactic of non-violent struggle by some Afro-Americans who "still volunteer to be loaded onto trucks, hymns on their lips, to be taken off to prison. It appears to be a mania with the race to sing while being martyred," (BR, p. 28) a position that Fanon took himself much earlier.

As Anatole saw it, the answer to the African condition of dispossesion was not racial integration but rather total liberation, "that is, the departure of the Occupier." (BR, p. 28) Given all the evidence, Anatole could only conclude that the phenomenon of racism was to be found in the basic structure of society itself:

> The deep roots of the racism perpetrated by Negro [White] power around the world must be sought in the basic structure of African [European] society. The African [European] has never ceased to try to free himself from the matriarchal yoke and all his expansionist tendencies bear the mark of this obsession. (BR, p. 28)

Thus, in one broad intellectual sweep, Anatole manages to outline the historical depth of the anticolonialist struggle and the magnitude of obstacles that it faces in its "lifelong struggle to recover its identity and shape its own history,"[10] as another Caribbean scholar defines it.

Overwhelmed by the intensity of such thoughts, Anatole is awakened from his revery by the violence of a woman's voice exclaiming:

> "Real bastards, those Blacks [Whites]!"
>
> The woman has just spoken. Anatole starts, then considers her thoughtfully.
>
> "Bunch of sadists," she continues, "I've seen in the newsreels how they treat us: trained dogs, cocomacaques, fire-hoses. . . they beat on women, old people, children singing in their best Sunday clothes, with nice clean gloves, going to church. . . "
>
> "Us Whites, we're fools! As long as we keep singing hymns we don't deserve any better than to get thrown in the can for blocking traffic. (BR, pp. 29-30)

The narrative then shifts to the activities of the colonizers. Inspector

General Bozambo is in charge of the territorial security of the state. He and his colleagues in Bantouville are disturbed by the growing subversive activity of the anti-colonialist movement. In response, they revert to the characteristic behavior of the colonizer by committing atrocities against the natives. However, they are unable to stop the growing acts of patriotism of the colonized people who continue to struggle for their independence.

On the side of the colonialist-imperialist forces in the island is Commandant Adiami, who has been able to rise rapidly in the armed forces of the colonizers because he has blackmailed the minister of state in the metropole. When Anatole was chased through the streets he dropped his suitcase which was found by the police officers. Commandant Adiami, bent on promoting himself, announces that grenades are found in Anatole's suitcase. A note found in Anatole's suitcase, leads the cops to Edgar Dupont, a known patriot, and he is picked up for questioning. Fearing an outbreak of disturbances, Bozambo goes back to his files to study Escartefigue's pamphlet, "What is Baoulian Colonialism." As he begins to read the pamphlet, he is both amazed and infuriated by the content of Escartefigue's perception of the colonial reality. Escartefigue's pamphlet begins by examining the role that received ideas played in the colonialist-imperialist system of domination and the manner in which the colonialists perceived the colonized:

> This is the reasoning of the eternally exploited class which adopts a general superiority solidifying into a simple opposition of colors: the colonized White [Black] is a lazy savage; monogamous and therefore immoral; Christian and therefore ungodly; without a history and therefore without culture. On the one hand, the black [white] elect, born to conquer; on the other hand, the white [black] damned, stricken with a congenital complex of colonializability. Thus, any corrupted culture will ultimately move into a jingoistic era which tolls its death-knell while claiming an apogee. (BR, p. 41)

Because the colonialist-imperialists perceived the colonized person as lazy and incapable of acheiving any social and/or political transformation of his condition, the colonized person must make a choice: will he struggle violently for liberation or will he play the aesthetic games which the "cultural rehabilitators" (the proponents of Negritude) have played? Escartefigue concedes that because "the exploiter knows neither repentance nor pity. . . it is a waste of time to try to appeal to the feelings of the powerful." (BR, pp. 42-43) Therefore the only language that the imperialist understands is violent revolutionary struggle. He reasons further that while the European exploiters have tried to destroy our culture and our history, they were mistaken if they believed that the Treaty of Berlin (1885), in which the European powers carved up Africa among themselves, signaled heir final phase of dominance over Africa. As Escartefigue concludes, "one loes not remain the mightiest forever." (BR, p. 44) The colonized will rise ւp and take his/her rightful place in history.

In light of this truism, the role of the colonial person in the pursuit of iberation demands the following:

> Our role, as Whites [Blacks] dominated by Africa, by her weapons, her wicked economic doctrines, her religion and her culture, is to regroup, to set off and to carry to its conclusion, our struggle for national liberation. It is to my brothers in misery that I speak. I want to reach them all: those who have lost themselves in the African [European] culture to the point of forgetting our own (those are, it certainly seems, the intellectuals); those who have attended only elementary school or no school at all, because they were forced at an early age to go work in the factories (since imperialism has built an industrial and severely vegetarian civilization on the backs of our race); even those who accept the uniform of the native Gallic infantry and put down our revolts; and finally those who have not only converted, but become priests of the Baobabist religion, that religion whose cynically avowed aim is to eradicate our ancestral faith. Everyone must join us, sooner or later, to take an active part in the struggle because no matter how severe the mutilation, the deep roots survive. Our language is one of these roots and the occupiers can tell us as often as they want that it's just an undeveloped tongue, but we will not give it up. And so it is in Gallic that I wish to speak. (BR, p. 44)

While he recognizes the progressive role of the cultural rehabilitators (such as Césaire, et. al.,) at a particular moment in time, Escartefique recognized the need to take the struggle further to organized political resistance against the colonizer. This tremendous surge by the people to struggle for their liberation must be paralleled by a leader who is willing to give his life for his people in struggle. Thus, would he pronounce these truths in the language of his forefathers:

> But I will not only speak. I want to shout, to take up Lamine Zamba's [Aimé Césaire] threat: 'And I will hurl my great white [black] cry so chillingly that the foundations of the world will tremble.' And my ambition is to go further, to bring all the colonized peoples to discover the necessity of going further, collectively, and organized.
>
> Until now we have never had a true leader. Those who spoke for us were not willing to pay the price that our struggle demands. Our mission of liberation must follow a double path: dialectic and action, or it will not be at all; because it is not enought to discover some miraculous keys, even with great clamor; one must also be prepared to use them.
>
> Seen as the only means of liberation, clinging to the phrase white is beautiful, and wringing it dry, dialectic is doomed to failure. Not only does it not set off any profound echo in the masses, it even reassures the imperialist

229

who goes so far as to enter into the game, so as to bury the essence of our demands in his own cultural mystique. And so it is that any conscious colonized person sees the necessity of going beyond a slogan into political action: that is to say that he is ready to accept all the consequences. It is only from that moment that communication with the masses is established and becomes a threat to the occupier. (BR, pp. 48-49)

It is in this unison of "dialectic" (that is, discussion) and "action" that one would find the solution to the problem of colonial-imperialist domination. Such is the ultimate need: to go forward collectively and organized in action.

This, essentially, is the central theme of *Bozambo's Revenge*. Having stated the political tasks of the colonized in so *explicit* and *categorical* a manner, the text does not seek to work out the artistic message within the development of the novel. Instead, the novel reduces itself to a conflict between Inspector General Bozambo and Commandant Adiami, the former exacting his revenge on the latter by having him [Commandant Adiami] sent back to the metropole in disgraced circumstances.

When the thread of the struggle against the colonial order picks itself up, we see the Archduke seeking to complete the task which Escartefigue's pamphlet suggests. As the narrator notes:

Since Escartefigue's imprisonment, the Archduke has become the prime mover of anticolonialist subversion. He gives orders, signs his names to tracts, maintains a veritable legend of invulnerability and messianism around him; his name alone galvanizes the crowds, and all the nationalist leaders, like Escartefigue, who are presently in the can, appeal to him as their authority. As of this moment he has miraculously escaped capture, to the point, that, except for Bozambo, most of the police force consider him a kind of ghost that walks. But Bozambo won't give up. The Archduke exists and must be captured, or subversive activity will only increase and multiply. (BR, pp. 65-66)

Yet at the end of the novel, the liberation of the country is not won by violent revolutionary struggle but by a decree of the colonizing power. Sensing the rising tide of patriotism among the people and feeling the repeated acts of subversion against the state, the imperialist powers are forced to turn over partial autonomy of the country to the leaders of the Anti-Colonials Movement. Hence, there was great rejoicing in the city of Bantouville when the news of autonomy came, and "even most nationalist ones, now convinced that the dark misery which had been strangling the people is about to end, go with the tide and make up compound names, like Mango-Leopold or Manga-Suzanne." (BR, p. 159)

The taking of Gallic names seems to suggest that the colonized people had not been quite freed from their colonial psychoses. Yet the autonomy seemed to affect the comprador-bourgeois class much more harshly than all the other members of the society.

> Most of them are upset at having to give up the numerous material advantages conferred upon them by the colonial life: plentiful, docile and inexpensive servants; astronomical salaries, paid in C.B.E. baouls, plus the hardship allowance that is customary in the colonial world; administrative positions well beyond their capabilities, while in Baoulia they could not hope for the equivalent jobs; annual holidays in the mother country, often extended upon presentation of a signed note from a compliant doctor. For these, the privileged, autonomy is a real disaster. (BR, p. 160)

This class, it would seem, because of their position in the society and their peculiar relationship to the imperialist powers come in for the harshest condemnation by Juminer, for he believed that they were the ones who were most treacherous to the aspirations of the total society.

For Edgar Dupont and the Archduke, autonomy meant the receipt of a ministerial position while Anatole became the chief of staff to the Archduke. Yet one is left with the distinct impression that the entire revolutionary process was aborted because of this smoothe transition to autonomy. As the narrator notes:

> It is characteristic of the process of decolonization that it be accompanied by abrupt changes on the individual level: one activist leaves the chamois and pail of soapy water for a brand new minister's portfolio; another his welfare card for a ministerial's pass.
>
> Since, according to the framework law, the ministers of National Defense and of the Interior, among others, will remain under the jurisdiction of the mother country, Colonel Sar and Inspector General Bozambo are preparing to reorient themselves toward a new career side by side with Escartefigue and the Archduke. (BR, 161)

Even though this potential revolutionary struggle for liberation fails to achieve the complete elimination of the colonial psychoses, *Bozambo's Revenge* advances the analysis of the colonial condition and articulates the necessity for revolutionary struggle in the creation of new state of psychological awareness, dramatises the need to move from "dialectic" discussion to revolutionary "action" and the need to move towards the organized transition from one phase of struggle to another.

But if the rhetoric of *Bozambo's Revenge* carried forward the *political message* of Juminer, the work fails in a partial manner because of the pamphleteering nature of the literature. Warning against the dangers of such writing, the Uruguayan writer, Mario Benedetti, observed:

231

I'm not against the pamphlet. I'm against pamphleteering literature. I think the pamphlet is as legitimate a form as any other and that there are masterpieces in that form, for example pamphlets by Marx, Lenin, Franz Fanon and Ché Guevara.

In the course of my political activity I've written some pamphlets myself, signed or not. But in political literature, politics must appear as an element, in the same way that so many other aspects appear in literary work: history, psychology, anthropology, etc. Of course political literature has to and will appear, in general, in accordance with the political position of the author. But since it is literature, it must be that first. If it doesn't observe literary rules, doesn't exist as literary work, the political message it carries can be lost."

Because pamphleteering literature obscures the intent and urgency of a given work, it diminishes the content of its *political message*. Because pamphleteering literature is unable to depict the complexity of the social, political and cultural forces as they impinge upon the sensibilities of the colonial individual, it is unable to explore the tremendous emotional and psychological condition of the colonial individual and his being in the contemporary world.

But if *Bozambo's Revenge* suffers from a certain lack of literary niceties and dexterity in which the content overwhelms the form, and the insistence of the author's political message (that is, the need for revolutionary struggle to obliterate all traces of the colonial psychology of dependency), then *Guerrillas* by V.S.Naipaul presents the complete opposite of this phenomenon, ridicules and makes absurd the attempt of colonial people to reject the centuries of unjust colonial rule, and presents the thesis that any attempt to overthrow the colonial order is destined to fail because of the inherent incapacities of colonial peoples. Indeed he tries to perpetuate the racist notion that if the colonialists leave, chaos would follow in their path.

Thus where *Bozambo's Revenge* suggests that the colonial struggle should move from dialectical discussion to revolutionary action, Naipaul suggests that colonized peoples are incapable of any meaningful and thoughtful action and thus parodies and caricatures the attempt of colonial man to make any meaningful transformation of the colonial structure of relations.

To understand V. S. Naipaul's response to the nature of revolutionary struggle of Caribbean peoples (and all colonial peoples), one need only understand the major governing theses of his novelistic-aesthetic pronouncements which consist of the suggestion that "history is based around achievement and creation and nothing was created in the West Indies,"[12] and his belief that "these islands, black and poor, are dangerous only to themselves."[13] Against this background, his attempt to analyse the nature of revolutionary struggle in the Caribbean in his novel *Guerrillas* could only reveal itself as a manifestation of the past hostilities and ambivalences which Naipaul feels toward the society from which he comes and a convenient skeleton upon which to hang his antiquated notions.

In the 1960s Michael de Freitas, alias Michael X, alias Michael Abdul Malik, was lionized by English society for his promulgation of Black Power rhetoric. In 1968 Andre Deutsch published his book, *From Michael de Freitas to Michael X*,[14] in which Michael X was personified as the "symbol of Black Power in Great Britain [with the acknowledgement that] the future of race relations of the country depend very much on his thoughts and actions."[15] In 1972 Michael de Freitas was sentenced to death in Trinidad, West Indies for the murder of Joseph Skerritt and Gale Benson, an English woman, and was hung by the neck in 1975 for their murder.

The intense interest which the life of Michael X created influenced *The Sunday Times* to commission V. S. Naipaul to write a story about the life of Michael X. This story took the form of two articles, "The Life and Trials of Michael X," which appeared in *The Sunday Times Magazine* on May 12 and 19, 1974. In the following year, the novel *Guerrillas* appeared as a grotesque, carricatured fictive account of the life of Michael X who was transformed into a revolutionary hero and whose life became the fulcrum around which revolutionary struggle is based.

In "The Life and Trials of Michael X," V.S. Naipaul attempts to make some sense of Michael X's existence. Making it very clear that Michael X was the creation of the people of Great Britain, V. S. Naipaul argued that:

Malik was made in England. England gave him friends, a knowledge of elegance, a newspaper fame which was like regard, and money. England always gave him money; no one, for so many good black causes, needed money so badly. It occurred to him, for instance, late in 1966, when his wife was in arrears with her mortgage payments and receiving solicitor's letters, that West Indians need adequate representation in the courts. He interested people in this cause. *Oz* of February 1967 announced the West Indian legal need, and in heavy type at the top of the page prescribed the remedy: " 'Defense' needs money. Send to Michael Abdul Malik, Leith Mansions, Grantully Road, W9."
England made many things easy for Malik. But England in the end undid him. Malik exaggerated the importance of his newspaper fame. He exaggerated the importance of the fringe groups which seemed to have made room for him. He was an entertainer, a play-actor; but he wasn't the only one. He failed to understand that section of the middle class that knows only that it is secure, has no views, only reflexes and scattered irritations, and sometimes indulges in play: the people who keep up with 'revolution' as with the theatre, the revolutionaries who visit centres of revolution, but with return air-tickets, the people for whom Malik's kind of Black Power was an exotic but safe brothel. Malik though he shared the security of his supporters. One day, half

doodling ("No Money"), half jotting down memoranda ("Letter from Lawyer"), he wrote: "My inheritance is London—all of it."[16]

Michael X's fame in Great Britain didn't last too long. By 1967 he was jailed for one year for an offence which he committed in violation of the 1965 Race Relations Act which was set up exclusively for persons such as Micahel X and others who spoke out against racism.

In 1969 Michael X was given a sum of money by Nigel Samuel, the son of a British millionaire, in order to set up a "Black House" project in which an urban self-help village would be created. Within a year this project was failing and Michael X was preparing to return to Trinidad. V. S. Naipaul describes Trinidad at the time:

> Trinidad in 1969 was moving towards a revolution. The black government of Eric Williams had been in power since 1956; and something like the racial enthusiasm which had taken him to power now seemed about to sweep him away. Political life in the newly independent island was stagnant; intellectuals felt shut out by the new men of the new politics; and American Black Power, drifting down to Trinidad, was giving a new twist to popular discontent. Black Power in the United States was the protest of an ill-equipped minority. In Trinidad, with its 55 per cent black population, with the Asian and other minorities already excluded from government, Black Power became something else, added something very old to national protest: a mystical sense of race, an expectation of imminent. . . revolution without a programme, without a head: it was something Malik might have exploited. But he didn't make much of a political start. He 'marched' with some striking bus-drivers, but he puzzled them when he spoke, not of their cause, but of his obsessions: the need to change the uniform of the Trinidad police.[17]

Speaking about the people who lived in the populous northwest corridor of the island, V. S. Naipaul discarded them in the following manner:

> Trinidad's urban north-west is a great parasitic suburb, through which money is yet magically cycled. Much of the population is superfluous, and they know it. Unemployment is high but is perennially short. The physical squalor, the sense of a land being pillaged rather than built up, generates great tensions; cynicism is like a disease. Race is an irrelevance; but the situation is well suited to the hysteria and evasions of racial politics. And racial politics—preaching oppression and easy redemption, offering only the theory of the enemy, white, brown, yellow, black—have brought the society close to collapse.[18]

Examining the career of Michael X, his rise to power and his relationship to the people of Trinidad, V. S. concludes:

Malik's career proves how much of Black Power—away from its United States source—is jargon, how much a sentimental hoax. In a place like Trinidad racial redemption is as irrelevant for the Negro as for everybody else. It obscures the problems of a small independent country with a lopsided economy, the problem of a fully 'consumer' society that is yet technologically untrained and without the intellectual means to comprehend the deficiency. It perpetuates the negative, colonial politics of protest. It is, in the end, a deep corruption: a wish to be granted a dispensation from the pains of development, an almost religious conviction that oppression can be turned into an assest, race into money. While the dream of redemption lasts Negroes will continue to exist only that someone might be their leader. Redemption requires a redeemer; and a redeemer, in these circumstances, cannot but end like the Emperor Jones: contemptuous of the people he leads, and no less a victim, seeking an illusory personal emancipation. . .[19]

According to V. S. Naipaul, there was no such thing as an economic system geared to serve the interest of the metropolitan country. There was/is no historical relationship between the "lopsided economies" of which he speaks and the economic exploitation of the world's imperialist powers. Writing in 1974, he could not have anticipated the demand for the New World Economic Order which took place at the Seventeenth Session of the United Nations General Assembly in 1975. For V. S. Naipaul there is only deficiency and lack of intellectual means to comprehend this deficiency and the politics of colonial protest.

Words such as "revolution, change, system [were all] London words, London abstractions, capable of supporting any meaning Malik—already reassembling his gang, his commune—chose to give them."[20] For Naipaul, everything was borrowed. Colonized as they were, there was no way in which colonized people could articulate their reality. Hence Michael X became the personification of that reality, and with inescapable consequences:

He was the X, the militant, the man threatening the fire next time; he was also the dope-peddler, the pimp. He was everybody's Negro, and not too negroid. He had two ideas of his own. One was that the West Indian High Commissions in London paid too little attention to their nationals. The other, more bizarre, was that the uniform of the Trinidad police should be changed; and this was less an idea than an obsession. Everything else was borrowed, every attitude, every statement: from the adoption of the X and the conversion to Islam, down to the criticism of white liberals ("destroying the black man") and the black bourgeoise ("they don't know the man from the ghetto"). He was the total 1960s Negro in a London setting; and his very absence of originality, his plasticity, his ability to give people the kind of Negro they wanted, made him acceptable to journalists.[21]

Given the absence of originality and the "plasticity" of his character it becomes easy for V.S. Naipaul to generalize from these abstractions and to accuse all Caribbean and Third World peoples of an absence of originality and plasticity of character. There was no need to examine the complex reality of colonial existence. After all what did it matter: "When everybody wants to fight [and] there's nothing to fight for. [When] everybody wants to fight his own little war, everybody is a guerrilla." (G, p. 95) In the Caribbean and other Third World countries, there could be no grand reality since no one could perceive any larger cause. "Everybody" Mr. Naipaul concludes, "wants to be a guerrilla."

Because V. S. Naipaul saw nothing positive in the struggle of colonial and Caribbean peoples, *Guerrillas* simply became an opportunity, nay an artistic opportunity, for him to express his nihilistic vision and artistic conception. Thus Michael X becomes James Ahmed; Gale Benson becomes Jane; Joseph Sketritt becomes Stephens; Jamal, "an American Black Power man,"[22] becomes Roche, "the great white revolutionary hero from South Africa;" (G, p. 42) Mrs. Skerritt becomes Mrs. Stephens, only she is now in collusion with her son. While other characters are added (e.g. Meredith Herbert and Harry de Tunja) V. S. Naipaul remains faithful to "The Life and Trials of Michael X" and arrives at a number of amazing conclusions about the nature and functions of revolutionary struggle.

The story line of the novel is simple enough. It tells about the return of James Ahmed, a Black Power activist of Trinidad who was made a leader in London, to lead the black masses out of poverty and deprivation. When the novel opens we see Jane and Roche leaving their home in the Ridge (a middle-class area of the island) to drive to Thrushcross Grange, a commune which Jimmy has set up with the assistance of some of the imperialist firms in the country. Like *Bozambo's Revenge*, the novel opens up against a background of revolutionary slogans which are painted on the walls of the city and which reflect the nature of revolutionary turmoil that is gripping the island. As the narrator sees it, the island, in a new stage of decay, is going through what could be called a sponsored revolution to which Jimmy Ahmed was the appointed head.

At Thrushcross Grange, Jane and Roche meet Jimmy and they began to discuss his activity at the commune and (meeting Jane for the first time) describes his origins to them:

It's work, I'm a worker. I was born in the back room of a Chinese grocery. I'm a *hakwai* Chinee. You know what a *hakwai* is? It's the Chinese for nigger. They have a word for it too. And that's what they thought I was going to be when I got back here. 'Oh, he's a big shot in England and so on, but over here he's just going to be a *hakwai*. Let him start up his movement. Let him take on the niggers. Let him see how far he'll get. This isn't England.' They thought they were trapping me. Now they see they've trapped themselves. Eh, massa? They've got to support me, massa. Sablich's and everybody else. They've got to make me bigger. Because, if I fail—hmm. I'm the only man that stands between them and revolution, and they know it now, massa. That's why I'm the only man they're afraid of. They know that all I want in my hand is a megaphone, and the whole pack of cards will come tumbling down. I'm not like the others. I'm not a street-corner politician. I don't make any speeches. Nobody's going to throw me in jail because I'm subversive. I'm not subversive. I'm the friend of every capitalist in the country. Everybody is my friend, I'm not going out on the streets to change the government. Nobody is going to shoot me down. I am here, and I stay here. If they want to kill me they have to come here. I carry no gun." He raised his bare arms off the chair and held them up, showing the palms. The short sleeves of the drab-colored tunic rode down his pale, firm biceps and revealed the springs of hair in his armpits. "I have no gun. I'm no guerrilla." (G, pp. 22-23)

Yet the society that Jimmy has returned to is one of monotony and sameness; a society that has been shaped by the culture of the colonizer. In spite of his rhetoric, however, Jimmy's life has been reduced to a sense of fear and desolation in his new environment. As the conversation among Roche, Jane and himself continued, he began to feel "unsupported" and "separated" from his words. With the separation of his words and his acts "he had a vision of darkness, of the world lost forever, and his own life ending on that bit of wasteland." (G, pp. 36-37) A revolutionary, it would seem, who is scared and contemptuous of his own people and afraid of his separation from his adopted English home.

It is to words that Jimmy turns in order to make his world complete. Writing performs a creative function in Jimmy's life and gives him a sense of coherence and order. Bereft of the word, all was darkness and void.[23] Thus where Escartefigue uses Gallic words (i.e. the words of his original tongue) to regain himself and his heritage (that is, to reclaim himself through language), Jimmy uses words to restore a sense of authenticity to his being. Thus in his writing about himself, he makes the following discovery:

He had begun without conviction, simply putting down words on the pad. But then excitement had possessed him; the words became more than words; and he felt he could go on for a long time. Now, out of that very excitement, he stopped writing and began to walk about the room. As he walked he became aware of the night and the bush; and he was undermined again. Melancholy came over him like fatigue, like rage, like a sense of doom; and when he went back to the desk he found that the writing excitement had broken and was impossible to reenter. The words on the pad were again just like words, false. (G, pp. 39-40)

In his conversation with Roche and Jane he discovers the separation between his words and his acts. Usually he writes "out of disturbance, out of wonder of himself," (G, p. 36) yet once the spell is broken, he can not continue and the chasm of loneliness fills his soul. Now, faced with the melancholia that this active separation has created, words no longer fill the void:

> He broke off. The charm did not work. Words, which at some times did so much for him, now did not restore him to himself. He was a lost man, more lost than he had been as a boy, in his father's shop, at school, in the streets of the city, when he saw only what he saw and knew nothing. (G, p. 42)

It is into this darkness and desolation of James Ahmed's world that Jane, the personification of white liberalism, comes. A world of impermanence that contrasts very sharply with her former world of privileges and security.

The world that Jimmy reenters is one which had just gained its independence. It was a society which had no tradition; "a place that had produced no great men, and its possibilities were now exhausted." (G, p. 59) Such a society has no place in the community of nations; for it is an anachronism in time and space. In this society, therefore, the sense of impermanence is strong and the terrifying truth of the society could be exemplified by Jimmy's epigram: "When everybody wants to fight there's nothing to fight for. Everybody wants to fight his own little war, everybody is a guerrilla." (G, p. 95)

All then is ultimate chaos and despair. Not even the appointed leader is able to understand the chaos. What began as a sense of outrage against the colonial order is reduced to chaos and undirected outrage, and each class of the society faces the same abysmal gloom and despair: For those who live in the urban centers, all is chaos:

> It was a community now without rules; and the area was now apparently without municipal regulation. Empty house lots had been turned into steelband yards or open-air motor repair shops; cars and trucks without wheels choked the narrow lanes. Where garbage dammed the open gutters, wrinkled white films of scum formed on the black water. The walls were scrawled, and sometimes carefully marked, with old election slogans, racial slogans, and made-up African names: *Kwame Mandingo (Slave Name— Butler).* There was something competitive and whimsical about the slogans and the names. Humor, of a sort, was intended; and it seemed at variance with the words of threat and anger. (G, p. 114)

For those who live in the Ridge and represent the well-to-do, middle-class of the society, their lives are characterised by instability, which the separation of Harry de Tunja from his wife, Marie-Therése, highlights with much clarity. For this class of people, life reduces itself to a scramble to escape from the perpetual chaos of their lives:

> There was little sympathy for Harry, because with the breakup the even more unsettling news had come out that the de Tunjas had been establishing their status as Canadian "landed immigrants." Harry had been the complete Ridge man. Now, to many people on the Ridge, his news was like a double confirmation of the instability in which they all knew they lived.
>
> Something of this instability, of an order suddenly undermined, extended to the beach house, so that, independently, both Jane and Roche understood they had come to the end of the last pleasure they shared on the island: Sunday at Harry's beach house. The furniture in the porch was the same; the striped hammocks were the same; Joseph was busy in the kitchen; yet the day had been reduced to its routine and the house was already like something vacated. (G, p. 138)

For those who live in the villages, the same fate awaits them for they are all caught up in the same dramas of their compatriots. For these villagers there will be no possibility of a future:

> Children played in some yards. Sometimes, on a veranda, a bare-backed man, face and hands blacker than his chest, as though scorched by a fire, sat in a hammock made of an old sugar sack and held a naked baby. Father and child: the tedium of Sunday in the bush. This was a busy road. The crowded city was just over two hours away. Yet these villages seemed insulated from the weekend holiday traffic: charmed villages, stranded in time, belonging to another era, an era that contained no possibility of a future. (G, p. 176)

With such instability, chaos, voidness and desolation, not only is the society without hope, but it resides in another era of human history.

The climax of the novel occurs, however, when one of the guerrillas, Stephens, is killed in the hills. As a consequence, a state of emergency is declared, a number of riots ensue, and Herbert Meredith, a celebrated radio-interviewer is recalled to the government as minister without portfolio. Everything is reduced to chaos, and Harry, in his telephone conversation with Jane, describes the conditions in the following manner:

> He said, "It's bad, girl. They say the police cracking up. Guys taking off their uniforms and running away. But I don't know. The police are still at our station. And Joseph is still taking food down there. . . ."
>
> "I don't see how you can blame the police. They don't know who they fighting or who they fighting for. Everybody down there is a leader now. I hear there isn't even a government. You hear about Meredith? He went out braver-danger, you know, to try to talk to them. They chase him." (G, p. 212)

At this point of the novel, the author reduces the entire conflict of the people to a crude and absurd joke. No one is capable of understanding or mastering the situation, and, as the conversation of Harry and Roche reveals, ignorance prevails supremely:

> Harry said, "I don't think so. I don't think anybody knows what is happening with the police down there. I don't think even our local police people know. They're just sitting tight and eating our food."
>
> "What about Jimmy?" Roche said. "Any more about him?"
>
> "Jimmy kinda drop out of the news. At first it was all Jimmy Ahmed and the Arrow of Peace. Now you hearing about all kinds of guys popping up everywhere. Peter, tell me. Before Sunday, did you ever hear about the Arrow of Peace? How did I miss a thing like that?"
>
> "I'm the last person to ask. I miss everything. I never thought Jimmy had it in him to start anything like that. I always thought that Jimmy was the kind of man who would disappear at the first sign of trouble."
>
> "That's probably what he's done. Events move too fast for him. And for Meredith too. The two of them wanted to play bad-John, and the two of them get licked down." (G, p. 215)

Thus the activity of the people is reduced to absurdity, the people are depicted as being incapable of self-government and independence, and the society stands bereft of any human possibilities. The guerrillas are then hunted down with American-made helicopters, Jimmy's commune fails, and Meredith and Roche make some significant observations about the society when they participate in an interview over the local radio station. First, Meredith suggests that the major problem with Caribbean and colonial peoples is the fact that "we are too vulnerable to other people's ideas. We don't have too many here;" (G, p. 235) an echo of Juminer's concept of "received ideas" of the colonized. Roche in his turn suggests that the society "isn't organized for work or for individual self-respect." (G, p. 236) To which Meredith concludes that:

> "We're a dependent people, Peter. We need other people's approval. And when people come to us with reputations made abroad we tend to look up to them. It's something you yourself have been complaining about. But I have another problem here. You know the position of black people in England. You know the difficulties, the campaigns of hate. Yet some of us get taken up by certain people and are made famous. Then we are sent back here as leaders." (G, p. 237)

Such people, it would seem, cannot be capable of meaningful and a purposeful struggle for liberation. All their activity could be reduced to the meaninglessness of gang warfare; that is, the ability only to inflict and turn violence *inward* rather than the capacity to organize themselves and turn violence *outwards* thereby organizing human activity and energies in a meaningful and purposefully directed manner.

In the end, Bryant (metaphorically, the other side of Jimmy), a tormented and dejected character, turns his cutlass upon Jane and kills her. Jimmy, unable to truly separate himself from his ties to the metropolitan culture and his sense of dependency upon the white (wo)man's ideas, is completely lost by Janes death:

> Jimmy, responding, tightened his grip around the neck. He scarcely felt the neck; he felt only his own strength, the smoothness of his own skin, the tension of his own muscles. He concentrated on that smoothness and tension until she began to fail. She grew heavy; his strength became useless; and as he felt her fail a desolation began to grow on him. And then there was nothing except desolation.
>
> He was squatting on the ground, beside the dry pit of the septic tank and the heap of dug-out earth, looking at the earth and not the face, and not seeing the earth. He saw a day of sun at the beach, sea and sky bright beyond the coconut grove, the girl bleeding on the fender of the car, accepting water from his cupped hands, and love coming to her frightened eyes. But the eyes below him were closed. They knew nothing; they acknowledged nothing; they had taken away everything with them. He entered a void; he disappeared in that void.
>
> Then he was lost, lost since the beginning of time. But time had no beginning. And he was disembodied. He was nothing more than this sense of loss that grew deeper and deeper as he awakened to it; he would have liked to scream, for the relief. The world cleared up, time defined itself. He was himself, in a stone room, full of incense, with stone coffins on stone shelves, where dead women lay without being dead among white lilies. A woman sat up in her stone coffin; the lilies tumbled off her. She was Sundanese, like those he had seen in London: he could tell from her fine white cotton dress, her pallid brown skin and the healed slashes on her cheeks. She had the wanton face, the leer, the degraded mouth of a French prostitute he had seen in a pornographic photograph at school, sitting clothed but with her skirt pulled up, her legs open, her great hairiness exposed. She sat up in her roughly chiseled coffin, leering, the lilies falling off her, and she said, holding out her hand, "Nigger, give me a dollar."
>
> So that even here, though he had been lost since the beginning of time, though he was lost in time itself, and didn't know who or what he was, he was betrayed, his secret know. (G, pp. 280-281)

With the death of Jane, Jimmy is truly lost and can only call upon "massa" to assist him. His ties to the dominant culture is so complete that in this moment of loss and desolation, he can only plead to Roche: "You must come, massa. There's no one else I can ask. They've left me alone, massa." (G, p. 292) Alone, therefore in his state of loss and dispossession, the last word we hear in the novel from Jimmy, is a weakened, weak-kneed cry for "Massa." (G, p. 292)

Thus for V. S. Naipaul all the talk about "revolutionary struggle," "Independence," "equality," "dispossession" are only other ways of blacks (i.e. colonial peoples) to call upon "massa" for his approval. All these words are only cries and abstractions of a society, black and poor, capable of nothing, bereft of all human possibilities and dangerous only to themselves. For him, colonial societes are only a gigantic negation.

Thus, A. N. Jones was essentially correct when he suggested that:

> This is not the sort of novel that one reads "for the story," in the usual sense of wanting to know what happens next. In this respect, it differs from Graham Greene's novels which, in other ways, it resembles. The chief merit of *Guerrillas* lies in the questions it raises about people's beliefs about other people's beliefs about race, and the insights and conjectures it offers to assist in understanding these subtleties of feeling. The characters might be said to be more "real" than in some of Mr. Naipaul's other novels, but this raises the question of his ideas of "reality" since he is inclined to suggest that nothing "real" happens in the suburbs of the world—and the character of Jimmy Ahmed, so lifelike but so obviously not a "real" symbol or spokesman of anything, illustrates and develops the author's engagement with this idea.[24]

It is precisely because V. S. Naipaul belives that nothing real can happen in the suburbs of the world that we are presented with the obvious futility of any kind of violent struggle to achieve the goals of equality and liberation. Indeed V. S. Naipaul needed any event or series of events, typical or non-typical, indigenous or non-indigenous, authentic or inauthentic to present his recurrent views of Caribbean failures.

Where Juminer sees the need for revolutionary struggle and the possibilites of collective violence freeing the colonial man from the crippling disease of the colonial psychosis, all that V. S. Naipaul sees is a struggle of misguided and meaningless activity by an equally misguided, meaningless and superfluous people. Therefore Vere W. Knight suggests that:

> Juminer was led by his political convictions to preach a revolutionary doctrine and was intent on showing how a tradition of revolt existed in the history of Caribbean peoples. The maroons also gave him the opportunity to avoid portraying individual heroism and to show the virtue of collective effort.[25]

Naipaul, in his turn, sees an entirely different tradition which he expresses in *Guerrillas* and his other works. For Naipaul the islands in the Caribbean are:

manufactured societies, labour camps, creations of empire; and for long they were dependent on empire for law, language, institutions, culture, even officials. *Nothing was generated locally; dependence became a habit. How, without empire, do such societies govern themselves?* What is now the source of power? The ballot box, the mob, the regiment? When, as in Haiti, the slave-owner leaves, and there are only slaves, what are the sanctions?[26]

It is obvious that each writer brings to bear a different conception of history upon his society and draws entirely different conclusions from the same set of historical facts. Where Juminer sees a tradition of revolt (resistance), Naipaul sees a tradition of negation and dependency. Frantz Fanon sees only dignity in the soul of his people and urges Juminer: "Have confidence in your people and consecrate yourself to their dignity and their fulfilment. For us there is no other way."[27] Naipaul, on the other hand, sees only the absurdity, indignity, and lunacy in these people. For him:

Something of the Carnival lunacy touches all these islands where people, *first as slaves and then as neglected colonials, have seen themselves as futile, on the other side of the real world.*[28]

From this collective insanity there is, nor can there be, any reprieve. Thus as we examine these novels we observe that *Au seuil d'un nouveau cri*'s central thematic movement, which shifts from the countryside in "The Cry" to Paris in "The Echo," has its genesis in Frantz Fanon's *The Wretched of the Earth*. Fanon asserted that when the lumpen-protelariat moves from the countryside to urban centers, then it will begin to constitute the spearhead of the revolutionary forces of the colonized people. Fanon says:

In fact the rebellion, which began in the country districts, will filter into the towns through that fraction of the peasant population which is blocked on the outer fringe of the urban centres, that fraction which has not yet succeeded in finding a bone to gnaw in the colonial system. The men whom the growing population of the country districts and colonial expropriation have brought to desert their family holdings circle tirelessly around the different towns, hoping that one day or another they will be allowed inside. It is within this mass of humanity, this people of the shanty towns, at the core of the *lumpen-proletariat* that the rebellion will find its urban spearhead. For the *lumpen-proletariat*, that horde of starving men, uprooted from their tribe and from their clan, constitutes one of the most spontaneous and the most radically revolutionary forces of a colonised people.[29]

Bozambo's Revenge, through a system of cultural reversals, examines the nature of guerrilla warfare in the urban centers. Thus, Juminer's novels are directed to Caribbean people's dignity and the manner in which revolutionary struggle carries foward that process. Indeed Juminer's novels reflect a tradition of resistance and identifies some of the main obstacles which colonial people must overcome in order to reintegrate into themselves and to achieve their authentic being. More importantly, Juminer seems to suggest that the nature of the struggle in the twentieth century must transcend the narrow question of race (even though this problem is still important) and operate on a higher plane of class-awareness.

In V.S. Naipaul we see the antithesis of our stated position even though the substance of his thematic movement is generated from the base of resistance. V.S. Naipaul does not see any sense of possibilities for these small forgotten islands which have been stranded in time. In order to do so he must recognize their capacity for creativity, not only at the sensuous-aesthetic level but also at the practical-revolutionary level, where people restructure their reality through revolutionary struggle. Having denied the creativity of the people, having denied them even a history of any purposeful activity, he is forced, correspondingly, to deny the possibility of any revolutionary activity at any given level and to treat it as a squalid farce whenever it appears. Indeed, Naipaul can only explain the social activity of the people within the context of "bad-Johnism" and the "robber-talk" of the legendary midnight robbers of Trinidad and Tobago carnival.

The works of Juminer and Naipaul build on the thematic concerns which the previous novelists developed. While Juminer is concerned about the purgatory through revolutionary violence and the need to move from *dependence* to *independence* through structured revolutionary struggle, all that Naipaul sees is chaos, confusion, and negation.

Alejo Carpentier and Wilson Harris are assigned the task of working out that new relationship in more cosmic and universal terms and suggesting some new method of conveying that content. To them the question is the way in which Caribbean men can transcend the legacy of a "conquest-ridden society" and restructure a new dialogue which has validity not only for Caribbean man but for all men.

BACK INTO HISTORY AND MANHOOD:
The Kingdom of this World
The Whole Armour
Explosion in a Cathedral

THE Indianist movement was pervasive in early Caribbean literature and the Indian emerged as the symbol of patriotism and resistance to European slavery. That movement gave way to the national liberation movement in which the negro slaves contested for their freedom, and the slave narrative and the romantic novel of the Spanish Caribbean began to occupy an especial place in our literature. The victory of the slaves in Haiti gave the African and his culture in the Caribbean a new sense of importance and self-pride which allowed the Haitian writers to contest the racist theories which arose in the latter half of the nineteenth century and demonstrated to the Haitians the importance of their cultural achievements to the rehabilitation of the race. Thus arose the first incipient underpinnings of the Negritude movement.

During the first half of the twentieth century, many of the Caribbean islands were faced with the problem of contesting the imperialist conquest of foreign powers. As a result, many reviews and publications arose to contest the foreign ideologies of the colonizers by articulating those features of Caribbean culture that were unique to the area. Turning to the triple gods of Communism, Realism and Surrealism, these writers used these concepts and their attendant methodology to probe their past and to understand their societies and peculiarities of their historical being.

While the writers of the Caribbean were attempting to discover an indigenous form to convey the content of their experiences and to respond to the presence of a foreign power, the writers of Cuba also had to come to grips with the contribution of their indigenous population. In short they had to recognize the African presence in Cuban national life. But in Haiti where, for example, the African population was a majority, in Cuba they were a minority who were not fully integrated into the country's life— in spite of the fact that Antonio Maceo, the famed "Bronze Titan," was one of the triumvirate of "Cuba's struggle for independence."[1]

Thus by the turn of the century, the problem of assimilating the African population fully into the Cuban nation still proved to be intractable. As Professor Roberto González Echevarría has argued:

> Since independence, the racial composition of Cuba has been a controversial issue. Blacks had filled the ranks in the wars of independence and demanded a better place in a society they had helped to forge, first as slaves and later as soldiers. In spite of the best intentions on the part of revolutionary leaders and some of the first legislators of the republic, the white majority was not eager to assimilate blacks into a society whose class divisions were largely (though not entirely) drawn along racial lines.
>
> Cuba's black population had tenaciously maintained its cultural identity, partly because many blacks were of recent arrival from Africa, but mostly because of the alienation to which slavery and later economic oppression had subjected them.
>
> African customs and religious practices thrived in the island. In spite of incipient racial mixing (which dates to the sixteenth and seventeenth centuries), blacks stood apart, not only by the color of their skin and general impoverishment, but because they clung to their ancestral traditions. Drums beat in the countryside and the outskirts of towns punctuating the social schism, and often calling to rebellion. The answer to that call took various forms as the political waters of the republic became more turbulent.[2]

Because of the tenacity of the African presence and their corresponding exclusion from the society (which resulted in the Negro Revolt of 1912), the early ethnographic studies of Fernando Ortiz (his first volume of *Hampa Afro-Cubana, Los Negros Brujos* appeared in 1906[3]), their centrality in the social and cultural life of the country (the backbone of the sugar industry and the musical life), and a certain amount of fashionableness of the Negroes at that moment of history (that is, the Negro became a pure, primitive, simplified reality in the eyes of his [white beholders]) the twenties ushered in the era of Afro-Cubanism.[4]

But while Afro-Cubanism arose primarily in response to the social conditions of the Blacks in Cuba, it served (its secondary manifestations, if you will) as a break to the cultural predominance of European cultural forms in Cuba and provided a rich alternative to the past. As Echevarría has suggested

> Afro-Cubanism called for a radical break and a new beginning. There was in it the sportive, frivolous élan of the avant-garde, directly opposed to the

246

mentality of the good bourgeois for whom life was the performance of appointed tasks. In the black, the new artists found, readily at hand, a being that fulfilled all the requirements of the new spirit: the pure primitive way of expressing a simplified reality; his angular art; his jerky, percussive music and dance; the unintelligibility of his religious expression, which permeated all aspects of his culture.[5]

One of the major literary movements which began to exalt Afro-Cubanism was *Vanguardismo*. One of its chief proponents was Nicolás Guillén who readily embraced most of the elements of the movement. In 1929, Guillén's poem, "Motivos de Son," appeared in the newspaper: another of his poems, "Ideales de una Raza," was dedicated to exposing the problems of racism in Cuba. The impact of these poems was immense. Not only did Guillén use the folk elements of his culture to structure his verse, but he was able to turn the eyes of the populace to the important role of the Blacks in the culture. As Guillén testified:

CBR: What valid contributions did those poems make to the black movement? And which were not so valid?

NG: I believe that they made the eyes of public criticism turn to a phenomenon up to then considered not important or even non-existent — the rôle of the Negro in our national culture, and the proof was in those poems whose rhythms indicated the possibility of injecting a mulatto element into the Spanish romance, that is, to Cubanise it, returning it to its pristine state as in the times of the Ma Teodora. Look . . . one thing is certain, and it is that when concern for things Negro (la moda de lo negro) came to Cuba, not directly from Africa, but by way of Montparnasse and the Latin Quarter, it was converted into a way of seeing (modo) determined by the historical formation of our people, product of the African cultures coming to our country for more than three centuries, mixed with the Spanish culture. For we all are acquainted with the examples of Góngora and Lope; but in the Cuban environment, with Afro-Hispanic roots, it was not a matter of an adventure, or of an endeavour, as in those men of talent, but of establishing the serious contribution of one culture to another, in an incessant and vital interchange.[6]

In the 1930s Guillén wrote two books of poems (*Sóngoro Cosongo* [1931] and *West Indies Ltd.* [1934]), which were instrumental in launching the Afro-Cuban movement and which ushered in a new direction in Cuban literary history. Within that period, President Machado, the brutal Cuban president, had fallen from power, and the poetry of Guillén, like the literature of Afro-Cubanism itself, moved from being purely "black poetry. . . to Cuban poetry (*color cubano*), from poetry with social outlines it ha[d] gone on to full social poetry."[7] Indeed, it seemed as though Afro-Cubanism had challenged the entire country and asked it to face up to itself and the fecundity of originality that lay within its breast.

Thus where the poetry of *Sóngoro Cosongo* pleads:

This is the song of the bongo:

—Here the most refined
will respond, if I call.
Some say: right away,
others say: in a while.
But my hoarse sound,
but my deep voice,
summons both black and white,
dancing to the same "son",
brown skinned or black souled
more from blood than from sun,
for who is not night on the outside
has already turned black from within . . . .

Someone will manage to insult me,
but not from any deep feeling;
someone may even spit on me in public,
although he embraced me when we were alone.

To that man, I say:
                —Brother,
    Soon you'll ask my forgiveness,
    soon you'll share my stew,
    soon you'll say I'm right
    soon you'll feel my rhythm,
    soon you'll dance to my music,
    soon we'll walk arm in arm,
    soon you'll be where I am:
    soon you'll rise from below,
    for here I am the greatest![8]

On the other hand, the poetry of *West Indies Ltd.* is anti-imperialist in its sentiments and came a long way from the almost exclusive concern that Guillén showed for the Black Cuban in his earlier poetry. More importantly, the dramatic decline of the sugar industry in the early part of the 1930s only demonstrated how vulnerable the Cuban blacks were to the fortunes of the sugar industry and how much a part of the national framework they were. As the long poem "West Indies Ltd.," affirms:

West Indies! West Indies! West Indies!. . .
This is the grotesque head office of companies and
    trusts.
Here are the pitch lake, the iron mines,

the coffee plantations,
the port docks, the ferry boats, the ten cents. . .
This is the region of all right
where everything is very bad;
this is the region of very well
where no one really is.

Here are the servants of Mr. Babbit,
Those who educate their children at West Point.
Here are those who shriek: hello baby,
and smoke Chesterfield and Lucky Strike.
Here are the foxtrot dancers,
and the boys of the jazz band
and the summer holiday makers from Miami and
    Palm Beach.
Here are those who ask for bread and butter
and coffee and milk.

Here are the absurd syphilitic youths,
smokers of opium and marijuana,
flagrantly displaying their chancres,
and cutting a new suit every week.
Here is the best of Port-au-Prince,
the purest of Kingston, the high life of Havana. . .
But here also are those who row among tears,
dramatic galley slaves, dramatic galley slaves. . . [9]

With these two books of poems, Guillén was able to bridge the gap between his blackness and his Cubanness, to bring an important new dimension to Cuban poetry and to broaden the scope of Caribbean literature. As one critic suggested:

"Nicolás Guillén is the revelation . . . he is Cuban in body and soul. He is our first poet to discover a rhythm, extract an observation, create a form. He is equidistant from France and Spain. He is not Darío or Chocano, nor Juan Ramon Jiménez. He is Guillén. And when the attempt is made to sketch a history of our poetic evolution and many names fall away into silence, drowned in the mediocrity of their work and in the poverty of their creation, the name of Nicolás Guillén will remain. And with Nicolás Guillén his book of revelation, Sóngoro Cosongo. . . . Among us only Nicolás Guillén has

249

created and discovered anything. He is, then, something more than a great poet. He is the poet of Cuba whose muse is mulatto."[10]

What Guillén was doing for poetry, Alejo Carpentier was doing for the novel. Like Guillén, Carpentier participated in Vanguardismo and Afro-Cubanism. In 1929, while he was imprisoned in Cuba, Carpentier wrote a novel called ¡Ecue-Yamba-O!, which he rewrote in Europe and published in 1933. The title itself is written in ñáñigo dialect, one of the African languages still spoken in Cuba.[11] The story itself tells of a black man who is born on the San Lucio sugar plantation and who is finally initiated in the Ñáñigo society through an elaborate ceremony. As Captentier commented about his work some thirty years later:

> In a time characterized by its great interest in Afro-Cuban folklore, recently discovered then by the intellectuals of my generation, I wrote a novel—!Ecue-Yamba-O!—whose characters are blacks of the rural classes of the period. I must explain that I was brought up in the Cuban countryside, in contact with rural blacks and their sons, that later, very interested in santeria and naniguismo, I attended innumerable ceremonial rituals. With this, "documentation" I wrote a novel published in Madrid in 1932 [sic], during the apotheosis of European nativism. Well, twenty years of research about the syncretic realities of Cuba made me realize that everything profound and real, everything universal about the world that I had pretended to portray in my novel had remained outside my field of observation.[12]

But the twenties and thirties were a period in which the novel itself was going through a period of crisis and a time when Caribbean writers were seeking new ways in which to express themselves. As Echevarría observed, "from the very start, Carpentier is experimenting within an aesthetic movement that rejected the tenants and practices of Realism and the classical nineteenth century novel."[13] Indeed, the very uniqueness of the Ñáñigos allowed Carpentier to experiment within a new form of expression that was unique to the Caribbean.

Reading extensively about America, Carpentier renounced his first novel, ¡Ecu-Yamba-O! (1933) in the belief that it rendered anthropological fact without penetrating the "essencias" of the Caribbean experience or capturing its "intra-historical" meaning. As Luis Harss and Barbara Dohmann point out:

> A studious smattering of folk mythology, he [Carpentier] discovered, was no substitute for intuition. A more thorough grounding was needed in the ways of a place to reveal its spirit. Documents were not enough. They could be not only misleading but an actual stumbling block. After all, native cosmogonies were

not so much a system of thought as a way of feeling. "Rationals," the Indians used to call their white brothers, who were always trying to reason out the things they could not understand.[14]

The teluric background of Latin America's vastness (Carpentier perceived the Caribbean as one region of Latin America) is always overshadowing man. With prolific vegetation, and the modern and the ancient always palpably present, man is at once young and old in the Caribbean, a phenomenon which quickly merges into legend. The cyclical process of death and regeneration is constantly at work, and the "age-old struggle for survival and renewal"[15] becomes the *sine qua non* of existence. In 1949 Capentier was able to structure these concerns into a more consistent premise which he called "magical" or "marvelous realism." From the Ñáñigos of Cuba, Carpentier turned to the rich mysteries of Haitian history to express the uniqueness of the Caribbean literary contribution to the world. It was in his prologue to *el reino de este mundo* (1949) [*In the Kingdom of This World*] that Carpentier finally rejected the surrealist and realist method of probing into reality as being an inadequate manner of examining the reality of the Caribbean at that moment in time. It was his feeling that the reality of the Caribbean possessed a magical or a marvelous quality of experience that was unique to the area. As he stated:

At the end of 1943, I had the luck to visit the kingdom of Henri Cristophe—the poetic ruins of Sans-Souci; the hulk, imposingly intact in spite of lightning and earthquakes, of the Citadel La Ferrière—and to get to know the yet Normand City of the Cape, the Cap Français of the late colony, where a street of longest balconies leads to the quarried palace inhabited long ago by Pauline Bonaparte. After feeling the magic of the Haitian land (none too exaggerated), after finding magical warnings in the red roads of the Central Plateau, after hearing the drums of Petro and Rada, I was led to compare this recently experienced marvelous reality to the tired pretension of invoking the marvelous, which characterized certain European literatures of these last thirty years. The marvelous, searched for among the old clichés of the jungle of Brocelandia, the knights of the Round Table, Merlin the enchanter and the Arthurian cycle; the marvelous, poorly suggested by the activities and deformities of circus characters—won't the young French poets ever get tired of the phenomenal types and the clowns of the "fête foraine", from whom Rimbaud had already departed in his *Alchemy of the Verb?*—; the marvelous, obtained with sleight-of-hand tricks, bringing together objects that never usually meet (that is, the old and deceiving story of the fortuitous encounter between the umbrella and the sewing machine over a dissection table) generating the ermine spoons, the snails in the raining taxi cab, the head of a lion in a widow's pelvis, the surrealist exhibits. Or, even yet, the marvelous literary: the king of Sade's *Juliette*, Jarry's *supermacho*, Lewis's monk, the frightening props of the Black comedy in England, such as ghosts, walled priests, lycanthropies, hands nailed onto castle doors.[16]

Rejecting all of these old "tricks" of European literature which presented themselves as "the supreme invention of reality,"[17] Carpentier argued that in fact these "tricks" resulted from a "poverty of imagination"[18] and a tiredness of the society itself.

Contrasted with Europe, Carpentier argued that the "marvelous truth" of Caribbean reality is so powerful and overwhelming that it not only "devours" the artist, but that it renders the artist's *subject-matter* a more significant reality than the individual artist himself. As he confessed:

This was made particularly evident during my stay in Haiti, when I found myself in daily contact with something that we might call "marvelous reality." I was standing on a land where thousands of men yearning for liberty had believed in the lycanthropic powers of Mackandal, to the point that the collective faith produced a miracle the day of his execution. I knew already the prodigious story of Bouckman, the Jamaican initiate. I had been in the Citadel La Ferrière, a work without architectural precedents, solely announced in the *Imaginary Prisons* of Piranese. I had breathed the atmosphere created by Henri Christophe, a ruler with incredible longings, much more astounding than any of the cruel kings invented by the surrealists, who fancied imaginary tyrannies, though never suffered them. At every step I found "marvelous reality." But I also thought that the presence and relevance of marvelous reality was not a privilege unique to Haiti, but instead patrimony of America as a whole where a compilation of cosmogonies has not yet been established. Marvelous reality found at every step in the lives of men who inscribed dates in the history of the Continent and left surnames that are carried even now: from the searchers for the Fountain of Eternal Youth and the golden city of Manoa to some of the most recent rebels and even some modern heroes of the wars of independence of as mythological a figure as Colonel Juana de Azurduy.[19]

It was to this historical source of marvelous realism that Caribbean writers ought to turn if they wished to produce a literature that was authentic. It was to this untapped reservoir of the marvelous and mythological that all literary production of the Caribbean should draw upon if it wished to make any contribution to the world of literature. One need not turn to the realism or surrealism of the European writers for in the Caribbean there existed a number of historical characters whose historical reality could surpass the wildest imagination of any literary artist of Europe. For example, there was Makandal, of whom "a whole mythology remains, accompanied by magic hymns preserved by a whole people, which are still sung in the Vaudou ceremonies."[20]

For Carpentier, the Caribbean writer needed to turn his glance inward in order to discover that which was special and original to his culture. For it is, "the virginity of the landscape, the formation of its own ontology, the faustic presence of the Indian and the Negro, the Revelation which constituted its recent discovery, the fecund cross-breeding which it promoted [which makes] America very far from having exhausted the wealth of its mythologies."[21] It is this wealth of mythology that inheres in the very life, history and landscape of the Caribbean that constitutes its unique contribution to a universal literature.

Carpentier saw the entire history of the Caribbean as one of magical realism and the fit and major base on which all Caribbean literature should rest. As J.A. George Irish correctly points out:

> The magic quality he discerns in the geography, history and cultural patterns of the region. The virgin forests with their amazing freshness, rich vegetation, vastness and stupendous architectural formations are seen on the continent as well as in Dominica or Nevis. The fascinating lives of Cortez and the dashing conquistadors and maroons, Victor Hughes of Guadeloupe and other heroes of American history demonstrate the same mysterious enchantment. The folk songs, dances, rhythms, myths, superstitions, miraculous cures of Negroes are no less bewitching among the indigenous peoples of the continent. These are the inexhaustible constants of the fascinating reality of the area. Carpentier envisages a long future for magical realism in West Indian art. There is a wealth of potential for an extensive mythology to be created around the various stages and the history of the region—the discovery and conquest, colonization and exploitation, slavery and the slave uprisings, wars of independence, revolutions up to the Castro regime, and the prevailing conditions of millions of Negroes and Indians in this very generation. Carpentier is not interested in merely recording historical facts for their own sake, nor even in building up a story around these facts just for the sake of telling a story. His main order is to capture "the intra-historical meaning of American history.[22]"

It is this attempt to penetrate to the "essencias" of the Caribbean experience that offers the most fruitful exploration for the Caribbean novelist. This recognition was made not only by Carpentier, it was made also by J.S. Alexis of Haiti and Wilson Harris of Guyana.

In 1965, J.S. Alexis presented his concept of what "marvelous realism" meant to him, from a French Caribbean point of view. In a paper entitled "Of the Marvelous Realism of the Haitians" that was presented to the First International Conference of Negro Writers and Artists, J.S. Alexis, in discussing the development of marvelous realism in Haiti, first spoke about its principal contributions to the Haitian culture. Among them were those of the Taine-Chemes Indian, the African contribution which, he claimed, predominated, and the Western (particulary the French). Drawing on what he called the "cultural confluence" of the area, he felt that Haitian culture presented very much the same elements of fecundity as that which made up "marvelous realism" in the whole Caribbean area. Arriving at almost the same conclusions as Carpentier, Alexis explained:

> Haitian art, in effect, presents the real with its accompaniment of the strange and fantastic, of dreams and halflight, of the mysterious and the marvelous; beauty of form is not in any of its fields an accepted premise, a primary purpose, but Haitian art achieves it from all angles of approach, even that of said ugliness. . . . It seems to us that Haitian art, like that of its African cousins, is profoundly realistic, notwithstanding that it is indissolubly linked to the myth, the symbol; the stylized, the heraldic, even the hieratic. Stripping down, the search for the characteristic sonorous, plastic or verbal feature, goes very well with accumulation and richness. Each element is stripped down to its very essence, but these elements together may constitute a formidable accumulation. This art demonstrates the falseness of the theories of those who would reject the marvelous on the pretext of realistic purposes, claiming that the marvelous in these drily and pretendedly realistic works miss their mark and do not touch certain peoples. Down with this analytic and reasoning realism, which does not touch the masses. Up with a living realism, linked to the magic of the Universe, a realism which stirs not only the mind, but also the heart and the whole network of the nerves.[23]

It is this same world of the real and the fantastic that Carpentier draws upon to reach the essence of Caribbean experience. In taking up surrealism, Césaire attacked Western rationalization. So, too, had Claude McKay in *Banjo*. In his article, Alexis renounced the art of "the West of Greco-Latin descent, which tends too often to intellectualization, to idealisation, to the creation of perfect canons, to the logical unity of the elements of feeling, to a pre-established harmony."[24] In presenting the Haitian art's marvelous realism, Alexis reemphasizes the new direction Caribbean art should take. As he points out, its sole criterion should be: "Does it throw light upon man and his destiny, his day to day problems, his optimistic combats and his enfranchisements?"[25] With these words Alexis anticipates Fidel Castro's famous pronouncements in *Words to the Intellectuals*. Alexis continues:

> the miracle is that, in contrast with the intellectualist constructions of a certain decadent West, its cold blooded surrealistic researches, its analytic games, Haitian art, like that of peoples of Negro origin, *leads always to men, to the fight for hope and to free art and the ivory tower*. It was in this sense that most of us perfectly understood what our beloved Aimé Césaire meant when he said "Blood is a powerful voodoo! . . . " Blood, yes, but all the blood; in other

words, we would never be the disciples of a narrow particularism which would divide the world into water tight compartments of antagonistic races and categories.[26] [Italics mine.]

This movement is universal, outward rather than inward, for magical realism was conceived as the Caribbean's peculiar contribution to universal advancement of man, to the "revindication of man" through art, as Castro puts it.[27] The staid imitation of the West, which *Légitime Défense* criticized, had to be replaced by a more indigenous and wholesomely distinctive creation. It is this "mystic conception of the world"[28] by which the Caribbean people seek to "express their whole consciousness of reality"[29] and into which they fuse unconsciously, placing it in the "service of realizing specific and actualized struggles."[30]

While Carpentier and Alexis present magical and marvelous realism from their specific Spanish and French angles of vision, Wilson Harris has an English perception. His essays and works point toward the same course and reiterate the same perceptions as inspiration for the Caribbean writer although he has not called his conception specifically marvelous realism.

In May 1964, Wilson Harris delivered an address, "Tradition and the West Indian Novel," to West Indian students in London and stated his view on marvelous realism in the West Indian novel. He enlarged upon this theme in another article, "The Writer and Society." C. L. R. James, that grand old man of West Indian culture, who was among the first to recognize the importance of the piece, comments: "The point that shocked me was that Harris, grappling with a West Indian problem, had arrived at conclusions which dealt with the problem of language as a whole in the world at large. . . . Harris obviously thinks that creative originality in literature is a sign, a portent, evidence of creative originality in politics, and in social life."[31] How then did Harris perceive magical realism in the Caribbean novel? Harris feels that the most remarkable thing about the West Indian (Harris includes Central and Latin America in the West Indies) is the depth of the "series of subtle and nebulous links which are latent within him, the latent ground of old and new personalities."[32]

These are links and a depth of experience on which both Carpentier and Alexis draw. Arguing against the novel of persuasion in which the writer selects and leads up to a situation "which yields self-conscious and fashionable judgments, and self-conscious and fashionable moralities"[33] (characteristic of many West Indian novels), Harris argues for a literature that grows out of the Caribbean environment, which he says

. . . is steeped . . . in such broken conceptions as well as misconceptions of the residue and meaning of conquest. No wonder in the jungles of Guiana and

Brazil, for example, material structural witnesses may be obliterated or seem to exist in a terrible void of unreality. Let us look once again at the main distinction which for convenience one may describe as the divide pre-Columbian/post Columbian. The question is—how can one begin to reconcile the broken parts of such an enormous heritage, especially when those broken parts appear very often like a grotesque series of adventures, volcanic in its precipitate effects as well as human in its vulnerable settlement? This distinction is a large, a very large one which obviously has to be broken down into numerous modern tributaries and other immigrant movements and distinctions so that the smallest area one envisages, island or village, prominent ridge or buried valley, flatland or heartland, is charged immediately with the openness of imagination, and the longest chain of sovereign territories one sees is ultimately no stronger than its weakest and most obscure connecting link.[34]

When Harris criticizes the Jamaican novelist, John Hearne, for not using *At the Stelling* to inculcate the problem of "relevant conceptions and misconceptions,"[35] he argues that Hearne did not allow the story to reflect "the transforming imperative to endure (which is the highest moral principle)."[36] Harris argues here for the same realization and affirmation—that the greatness of man lies in his capacity to struggle and endure—that Ti-Noel makes in *The Kingdom of This World*.

In "The Writer and Society" (1967), Harris emphasizes the importance of memory and in "The Unsolved Constitution" (1968), he emphasizes this more clearly when he rather categorically states that "the direction in which I would like the West Indian novel to move . . . would be towards an *act of memory*."[37] [Italics mine.] He sees the writer involved in a "drama of consciousness . . . in which . . . in his work, he sets out again and again across a certain territory of primordial but broken recollections in search of a community or species of fiction whose existence he discerns."[38] Restating what one critic calls the "grim stoicism"[39] of Carpentier's vision, Harris contends:

> The creative writer at whom we have been looking—both transcends and undermines (or deepens if you will) the mode of society since the truth of community which he pursues is not a self-evident fact: it is neither purely circumscribed by nor purely produced by economic circumstance. To put it in another way—the so-called economic unity of man (the story-line of progress) is an illusion, in particular when it is maintained as a blanket moral proposition over the actual and obscure moral crises in the heart of those it professes to change.[40]

Harris' marvelous realism has in common with Carpentier and Alexis' ideas the archetypal notion of the writer plummeting to the "primordial but broken recollections" and the cyclical concept of history. E.K. Skinner interprets these archetypal patterns in the works of Carpentier by utilizing the concepts of "monomyths" and "cosmogogic round"[41] as presented in Joseph Campbell's *The Hero With a Thousand Faces.*

Magical realism, which supplanted the Indian and Negro as the focal point in Caribbean literature, argued for looking at the "context," as Carpentier calls it, for trying to capture the "intra-historical meaning," for seeking the "essence," and attempting to posit that experience in archetypal and universal terms with a mythology and cosmology particularly Caribbean.

Because Alejo Carpentier sees the role of Latin America as "ecumenical" and thinks that writing should be epic and about grand movements, no one was better suited to write the Caribbean epic than he. Harss says of Carpentier: "In word and deed, Carpentier is something of a prototype of the Latin-American intellectual: home-grown but culturally crossbred, an appropriate formula in a society that, as he says, is the product of racial symbiosis and spiritual miscegenation."[42] Having spent seven months in prison for signing a manifesto against the dictator Machado, which he felt was "premonitory of the principles of the Cuban revolution," Carpentier sees himself as a man engaged in struggle from the beginning; in fact, he became one of the first writers to support the Cuban Revolution.[43]

Carpentier accepted surrealism as a means of liberation initially and contributed to *Révolution Surréaliste*, the magazine of surrealists whom he felt had a decisive influence "in discovering the Latin American continent for Western culture."[44] Even though he later rejected surrealism, it did open him to the marvelous realism of the New World, which he first used in *The Kingdom of This World.*

Divided into four parts, the story (realto) spans Haitian history from the rise of Macandal (1758) to the end of Boyer's reign (1820-1843). The first part revolves around the factual/legendary Macandal, who dies in 1758 after his reign of poisonous terror; the second part centers on Jamaican Bouckman, who went to Haiti and led the 1791 Haitian Revolution until Toussaint took over; the third part focuses on the equally legendary Henri Cristophe, whose reign ended when he was killed in 1820 with, some say, a silver bullet; and the fourth part centers on the ascendency of the mulatto aristocracy under the leadership of Jean-Pierre Boyer (1820-1843).

Although the novel has a progression of heroes (Macandal, Bouckman, Cristophe and Ti Noël in the fourth part) who sacrifice themselves for the liberation of their people, the cyclic nature of the cosmogonic round—a cyclical progression that E. K. Skinner describes as "an evolution from the purely temporal and particular toward that which is increasingly more timeless and universal"[45]—gives the work its tremendous epic impact.

All action in the novel is seen through the eyes of the slave, Ti Noël. The story begins with the half legendary/half factual Macandal, *houngman* of the Rada rites, who,

> invested with superhuman powers as the result of his possession by the major gods on several occasions, was the Lord of Poison. Endowed with supreme authority by the Rulers of the Other Shore he had proclaimed the crusade of extermination, chosen as he was to wipe out the whites and create a great empire of free Negroes in Santo Domingo. Thousands of slaves obeyed him blindly. Nobody could halt the march of the poison. (KW, p. 36)

With this almost frightening incantation, poison, a dreaded weapon of extermination, becomes the symbol of the black masses' resistance with Macandal, *houngman* or "Lord of poison," the chief instigator. When the French capture Macandal and burn him to death, the blacks rejoice, knowing in their esoteric awareness the whites will still be "chrismed by the great Loas." (KW, p. 51) The author puts it this way:

> That afternoon the slaves returned to their plantations laughing all the way. Macandal had kept his word, remaining in the Kingdom of This World. Once more the whites had been outwitted by the Mighty Powers of the Other Shore. And while M. Lenormand de Mezy in his nightcap commented with his devout wife on the Negroes' lack of feelings at the torture of one of their own— drawing therefrom a number of philosophical considerations on the inequality of the human races which he planned to develop in a speech larded with Latin quotations—Ti Noël got one of the kitchen wenches with twins, taking her three times in a manger of the stables. (KW, pp. 52-53)

After death, the life of Macandal takes on legendary proportions in stories told and retold by Ti Noël and other slaves.

Twenty-five years later Bouckman picks up where Macandal left off. Ti Noël, a faithful follower of Macandal, transfers his allegiance to Bouckman without forgetting Macandal. Bouckman is convinced that a pact sealed between "the initiated on this side of the water and the great Loas of Africa" (KW, p. 66) necessitates a war of liberation against the whites when the time is favorable. The Haitian revolution begins and Ti Noël is the first to lead the onslaught against his master just as he was the first to poison his master's two best cows when Macandal gave the word.

During the revolution Ti Noël travels to Cuba, then returns to Haiti, "a land where slavery had been abolished forever," only to find that the murderous cycle of slavery continued under the auspices of Henri Cristophe, a black (KW, p. 108) Ti Noël's first act on arrival is to give thanks for having returned safely. At first the splendors of the soldiers and the beauty of Sans Souci, the favorite residence of King Cristophe, assail him. While admiring the palace splendor, he is felled by a heavy blow across his back and finds himself in prison when he returns to consciousness. To his dismay, Ti Noël is enslaved again. He is given a brick and forced to join "children, pregnant girls, women, and old men, each of whom carried a brick," (KW, p. 116) to the Citadel La Ferrière where there is a bust of Pauline Napoleon, wife of Leclerc, who led the expedition against the black people of Haiti. On his departure from France, Leclerc disdainfully announced: "All the niggers, when they see an army, will lay down their arms. They will be only too happy that we pardon them."[46] The bust of this man's wife, famed for her licentiousness, graces the mighty and impregnable fortress of Citadel La Ferrière.

Paradoxically, the slave, who joined Macandal's campaign, poisoned his master's two best milk cows, and sacked his master's house at Bouckman's signal, returns to his land where he thought slavery was abolished forever only to be enslaved by his own kind. As presented by Carpentier, Cristophe's excesses and inhumanity are dismaying. The paradox causes Ti Noël to ponder:

Walking, walking, up and down, down and up, the Negro began to think that the chamber-music orchestras of Sans Souci, the splendor of the uniforms, and the statues of naked white women soaking up the sun on their scrolled pedestals among the sculptured boxwood hedging the flower-beds were all the product of a slavery as abominable as that he had known on the plantation of M. Lenormand de Mézy. Even worse, for there was a limitless affront in being beaten by a Negro as black as oneself, as thick-lipped and wooly-headed, as flat-nosed, as low-born, perhaps branded, too. It was as though, in the same family, the children were to beat the parents, the grandson the grandmother, the daughters-in-law the mother who cooked for them. Besides, in other days, the colonists—except when they had lost their heads—had been careful not to kill their slaves, for dead slaves were money out of their pockets. Whereas here the death of a slave was no drain on the public funds. As long as there were black women to bear their children—and there always had been and always would be—there would never be a dearth of workers to carry bricks to the summit of Le Bonnet de l'Évêque." (KW, pp. 122-123)

We are presented with the cyclical progression of events against this "series of repetitions and circularities."[47] as González Echevarría puts it. Ti Noël is bewildered. In another ironic and paradoxical act, Ti Noël runs to his former slave master's home, seeking refuge from the cruelty of Cristophe and his men.

Happy at the end of Cristophe's rule, Ti Noël faces a new aristocracy: the mulattoes under Boyer's leadership. Once more a new regime comes into power upon the backs of "hundreds of Negro prisoners" (KW, pp. 184-185) plowing and clearing the land for the mulattoes. Once more the peasant masses, caught in the same cycle of repression, are forced to flee to the hills like the Maroons of old. Ti Noël is last seen as he hurls "his declaration of war against the insolent works of the mulattoes in power." (KW, p. 185) It is as if Ti Noël, in his last "sacrificial act similar to that of his mentor Macandal, again unleashes the energy from the primordial source which could restore the kingdom to the Negroes and thus reactivate the cycle of cosmologic round."[48]

If, as Harris contends, "the story-line progress of man is an illusion," and man must constantly set out "across certain territory of primordial but broken recollections" (see footnote 38), it seems fairly evident that to regenerate himself and start anew, man must constantly tap the primordial source ("the Lords of Back There [Africa], headed by Damballah, the Master of the Roads, and Ogoun, Master of the Swords,") found in Haitian mythology. (KW, p. 42) Within this context Ti Noël discovers

> that a man never knows for whom he suffers and hopes. He suffers and hopes and toils for people he will never know, and who, in turn, will suffer and hope and toil for others who will not be happy either, for man always seeks a happiness far beyond that which is meted out to him. But man's greatness consists in the very fact of wanting to be better than he is. In laying duties upon himself. In the Kingdom of Heaven there is no grandeur to be won, inasmuch as there is an established hierarchy, the unknown is revealed, existence is infinite, there is no possibility of sacrifice, all is rest and joy. For this reason, bowed down by suffering and duties, beautiful in the midst of his misery, capable of loving in the fact of afflictions and trials, man finds his greatness, his fullest measure, only in the kingdom of this world. (KW, pp. 184-185)

In *The Kingdom of This World*, the saga of an age is telescoped through the principal figures and legends of an island. One small detail is enought to illuminate the entire age of a resistance which is metamorphosed into a larger human struggle against elements that seek to diminish, stifle, and enslave man. Man's nobility lies in his capacity to struggle, even if the degree of success is seen only in relative terms and even if history repeats the same repressive forces (the French, the blacks, and mulattoes under Cristophe) under different guises. Only through struggle, which Carpentier affirms as a human imperative, can man find the capacity to endure.

The same theme and archetypal patterns of death and regeneration resonate in Wilson Harris' *The Whole Armour*. In the 1973 edition of *The Whole Armour*, Harris appraises his work:

> *The Whole Armour*. . . is set in a landscape saturated by traumas of

conquest. A bitter thread or scale runs through Carib and Arawak pre-Columbian vestiges capable of now relating themselves afresh to the value-turned-bias structure of twentieth century man. Thus it would seem, we are involved in a peculiar juxtaposition at the heart of our age—renascent savagery and conquest-ridden civilization. (WA, p. 8)

Harris perceives vision as a capacity "to resense or rediscover a scale of community" (WA, p. 8) by accepting and relating ourselves once more to the "monsters" that have created the polarization and alienation of the races in our conquest-ridden civilization. He believes these monsters are "native to psyche; native to a quest for unity through contrasting elements, through the ceaseless tasks of the creative imagination to digest and liberate contrasting spaces rather than to succumb to implacable polarization." (WA, p. 8) Thus, the Caribbean writer's task is to take up "the whole armour of God, that ye may be able to withstand in the evil day, and having done all, to stand."[49] Thus the writer must take up the "whole armour" of magical realism to withstand the pressures and conflicts of civilization and to endure and regenerate.

Harris draws on a large scale of community consisting of ancestral Indians, Caribs, Arawaks, African slaves and European immigrants. His geographical area involves overwhelming proportions located in timeless dimension at the source of the Pomeroon River, a region of no "true geographical location"; (WA, p. 22) "a region of absurd displacement and primitive boredom, the ground of dreams, long-dead ghosts and still-living sailors, ancient masters and mariners, and new slaves, approaching the poor uncharted Guiana coast and beckoning the aboriginal mummy for whom all trespass beyond the sculpture of death was an act of brutal unimaginable faith." (WA, pp. 22-23)

Cristo, the major protagonist of the novel, returns to this source of his multifaceted origin in order to retrieve his sense of self and his feeling of community. But, he is accused of killing the rival of his sweetheart, Sharon. Abram, the father of all men and lover of his mother, Magna, the whore, protects him. When Cristo is also accused of killing Abram, he retreats further into the community of his forebearers who have lived for several hundred years in the region. A wake is held for Cristo to hoodwink the authorities into believing he is dead. But dead spiritually, Cristo assumes a new persona, born of his immersion in the primordial source. With this new sense of self, he and his lover, Sharon, the virgin, are reunited. The authorities eventually capture and kill Cristo, but by this time he and Sharon have produced a son to whom Cristo gives "the legacy of every ancestral ghost—the appraisal as well as the execution of the last fictions in time." (WA, p. 130)

Before his death, Cristo, with his new consciousness, discovers his generation's ties to its ancestors and acknowledges that his generation constitutes the real beginning of a new order. He exclaims joyfully:

> "I wish with all my life, one could show them that they're *our* problem child after all, that we're *hundreds of years* older than they dreamed to be. And why? Because we have begun to see ourselves in the earliest grassroots, in the first tiny seed of spring"—he paused a fraction of an instant and then proceeded fiercely—"the ancestral tide and spring of Jugsaw Bay, I swear, and that's why we're so different. We're reborn into the oldest native and into our oldest nature, while they're still Guiana's first aliens and arrivals." . . . . He glanced across the river and knew, whatever he suffered, *he would remain at all cost*. He had returned and he would not fly again. (WA, p. 114)

Having returned from the dead and been born into a new consciousness, Cristo cries out for expression and understanding; having penetrated his primordial existence, he is reborn into the recognition that the new generation of Caribbean people is "the first potential parents who can contain the ancient house." (WA, p. 116) They must not look backward as their parents did but forward to a new order and a new unity.

Like Carpentier, Harris struggles with a new form (baroque, in a way) to deal with this new content of the Caribbean experience. Characters begin by being untouched by, and not responsible for, each other's lives; after a series of almost irrational and unbelievable murders, they all draw from the same primordial source and realize the need for a new collective identity. As the author says, "Time had come for everybody to discard their foul vest of hypocrisy! Let us see ourselves for what we are." (WA, p. 93) Like Carpentier, Harris also moves from the particular Caribbean experience to the universal, for in the Caribbean are seeds for a new appraisal of man in the twentieth century.

Harris genuinely believes that twentieth-century man is "capable of relating himself afresh" to these ancestral vestiges by retrieving his ancestors' "monsters" into his psyche and relating to them in spatial rather than in physical terms. Although technologically oriented twentieth-century man cannot return to nature physically, the Caribbean's ancestral legacy offers man a new hope only if he can discard the rational and delve again into the primordial:

> We've got to pick up the seeds again where they, our ancestors, left off. It is no use worshipping the rottenest tacouba and tree-trunk in the historical topsoil. There's a whole world of branches and sensation they've missed, and we've got to start again from the roots up even if they look like nothing. Blood, sap, flesh, veins, arteries, lungs, heart, the heartland, Sharon. (WA, pp. 115-116)

Here is new hope. All the men in *The Whole Armour* die in their pursuit of community. By taking up the "whole armour" of the past, Cristo gives his son the "legacy of every ancestral ghost that ye may be able to withstand in the evil day" and the chance to start afresh. Man will gird himself for the future when "having done all, will stand." Ti Noël affirms the same impulse in *The Kingdom of This World*: "A man never knows for whom he suffers and hopes . . . man's greatness consists in the very fact of wanting to be better than he is. . . . " It is this capacity to endure and struggle that typifies both novels.

In *Explosion in a Cathedral* Carpentier uses a design of epic proportions. As he says, "I like big themes. . . . They are the ones that confer the greatest richness to the characters and plot of the novel."[50] This novel is important for several reasons. First, it was written during the Cuban Revolution (Carpentier began the novel in 1956 and finished it in 1962) and was influenced by many of the revolution's ideas. Second, as Emil Volek affirms, it is one of the "chief achievements of the new Hispanic-American era [and] also opens up a rich perspective to this Cuban writer's whole works of his mature period."[51] Third, the work inculcates in the largest dimension possible the uses of resistance as a theme in the Caribbean novel. It presents not only the local phenomenon of resistance but its inseparable relationship to international resistance. As in his previous works, Carpentier is still working out the question of man's struggles, the circularities of those struggles and their unceasing nature. The novel traces the immediate reaction of the French Revolution upon the New World and its influence on the concept of social equality that was to have devastating effects upon the hegemony of the New World.

The novel opens the night Victor Hughes' store burns down in the Haitian Revolution. Hughes enters the world of Sophia and Esteban, to whom life is a game devoid of any responsibility. They live in a world of trivia, "discovering the world by books" (EC, p. 29) in the domesticity of their home. Arriving at their house on Easter morning, Victor Hughes penetrates their cloistered world. When we are introduced to Hughes, he is a socialist who believes in the progressive ideas of equality and the abolition of private property. During the novel he degenerates until he rejects his former ideas. Early in the book he returns to the New World, approving of the guillotine and urging the Emancipation Proclamation but, after eight years in the Caribbean, he restores slavery with as much alacrity and resoluteness as he used in his first affirmation, "All men were born equal." (EC, p. 43) This leads Sophia to observe, "Eight years before he had shown a persistence, and almost superhuman energy in abolishing slavery, and now he was showing the same energy in restoring it. She was amazed at the lack of integrity of a man who could do both good and evil with the same cold courage." (EC, p. 322)

The circularities of history that we observed in *The Kingdom of This World* are also present in *Explosion in a Cathedral.* While Hughes degenerates with the revolution, Sophia, who has no idea of revolutionary struggle, rejects the decadence of Hughes' world and chooses the regeneration of humanitarian ideas inspired by the French Revolution: "I want to return to the world of the living, where people believe in something." (EC, p. 335) She summons her courage and returns to Esteban, who is imprisoned in Spain. We last see her as she joins the Spanish revolutionary struggle in 1808. Like Ti Noël in *The Kingdom of This World*, Sophia willingly hurls herself into the struggle, starting again the cycle of regeneration and liberation.

The novel's sweep is enormous, its vision panoramic, and its literary achievement astounding. Like Harris, Carpentier retraces the Caribs' great migration across the archipelago and their confrontation with the "unsuspecting unsuspectable invaders": Carpentier outlines this in epochal and archetypal dimensions:

> Two irreconcilable historical periods confronted one another in this struggle where no trace was possible. Totemic Man was opposed to Theological Man. For the disputed Archipelago had suddenly become a Theological Archipelago. The islands were changing their identity, and were being integrated into the great, all-embracing sacramental drama. The first island discovered by these invaders from a continent inconceivable to the islanders themselves had received the name of Christ, and the first cross, made of branches, was planted on its shore. For the second they had gone back to the Mother, and had called it Santa María de la Concepción. The Antilles were being transformed into an immense stained-glass window, flooded by sunlight. . . . (EC, pp. 244-245)

This archetypal impulse to search for a better world inevitably leads to a clash between two primal forces. The Caribbean offers the possibility of utopia; indeed Sir Thomas More selected Cuba as the site for his Utopia. But the impulse that drives the Caribs on their migration is the same one that drives the Europeans on their quest for new land. This movement from the particular to the universal in a continuing drama interests Carpentier most:

> The Caribs had conceived of this Better World in their own terms just as in his turn Ferdinand and Isabella's High Admiral had imagined it, here by the seething Dragon's mount, where he had been enlightened and illuminated by the taste of water from afar. . . . The Encyclopaedists had discovered a Better World, in the society of the Ancient Incas, just as the United States had seemed to be a Better World, when they sent ambassadors to Europe without wigs, who

wore buckled shoes, spoke clearly and simply, and bestowed blessings in the name of Freedom. (EC, p. 247)

By using the Caribbean particularity, Carpentier moves toward universal vision in *Explosion in a Cathedral*. Caribbean magical realism culminates in this novel for Carpentier creates the present-in-the-past by telescoping the past centuries of Caribbean experience and simultaneously creating the sensation that what takes place in the twentieth century is the cyclic repetition of what took place in the nineteenth. Galvan's *Enriquillo* similarly recreates the sixteenth century while working in the nineteenth. Harris works in the same timeless dimension.

Explosion in a Cathedral's message, like that in *The Kingdom of This World*, is the same, and certainly much more explicit, warning when Esteban exclaims:

We must beware of too much fine talk, of Better Worlds created by words. Our age is succumbing to a surfeit of words.

The only Promised Land is that which man can find within himself.

As he said this Esteban thought of Ogé, who had been so fond of quoting a sentence from his master Martínez de Pasqually: "A human being can only become enlightened if we awaken the divine faculties within him, kept dormant by the predominance of matter. (EC, p. 261)

Ti Noël was also led astray by the promise of a better world. Esteban suffers the same fate and, like Ti Noël, returns to the struggle at the price of constant vigilance which, translated into the Caribbean context, means continual resistance.

*   *   *

These novelists saw their vision as magical/marvelous realism within a cyclical view of history. However, most writing of this period of Caribbean literature should rightly be called "critical realism," for we should understand the development of history as being spiral rather than cyclical. In an attempt to discover the "essence" of Caribbean experience, these novels contain social analyses of that reality; they reflect the belief that this struggle confers some noble meaning to man's existence and the perception that experience proceeds forward in an opening or spiral development which is neither magical nor cyclical.

As stated earlier C. L. R. James maintains that the hallmark of Harris' discovery lies in his recognition that "creative originality is a sign, a portent, evidence of creative originality in politics, in social life," (see note 31) yet how can this be equated with the marvelous or the magical? Harris' question as he views the Caribbean's long history is "how can one begin to reconcile the broken parts of such an enormous heritage, especially when those broken parts appear very often like grotesque series of adventures, volcanic in its precipitate effects as well as human in its vulnerable settlements?" (see note 34) Certainly, movement is through history and the suggestion of historic continuity is implicit. While it is true, in the negative sense, that "the truth of community . . . is neither purely circumscribed nor purely produced by the economic unity of man . . . " (see note 40) in a positive sense, the truth of community, like the truth of man, lies in the synthesis of the economic and the social dimensions of man. Because comminity is created by the constant collision of social forces driving man foward and evolving into a higher synthesis, social development should be perceived as spiral rather than cyclical. The correctness of this observation can be seen from the tremendous strides man has made in science and technology. It is therefore with the use of history as process that we see the consistent forward development of the Caribbean experience and, as a consequence, its literature.

For Harris, "the highest principle is in the capacity of man to endure." (see note 36) For Carpentier, man finds his greatest measure in his capacity to struggle and endure, and for Alexis, all Caribbean literature leads to man and the fight for hope. The movement is therefore towards man and his great capacity to endure in the "kingdom of this world."

In critical realism, social analysis and typification of character exist and depict one social order giving way to another in the struggle for human dignity. The conflict between individuals and society is usually the subject of penetrating analyses, with most of the attention concentrated on society's fate. These are Harris's and Carpentier's major concerns. But the final central concern of the writers of magical realism (i.e., critical realism) is their crying need to understand the "inter-historical" meaning of the Caribbean experience; to reconcile the alienation separating man's condition in his society and the objective reality of his existence. But on what is this inter-historical meaning founded?

The fascinating lives of Cortez and the dashing conquistadores and explorers, the Haitian revolutionaries, the Jamaican maroons, Victor Hughes of Guadeloupe and other heroes of American history demonstrate the same mysterious enchantment. The folk songs, dances, rhythms, myths, superstitions, miraculous cures of Negroes are no less bewitching among the indigenous peoples of the continent. These are the inexhaustible constants of the fascinating reality of the area. Carpentier envisages a long future for magical realism in West Indian art. There is a wealth of potential for an extensive mythology to be created around the various stages and the history of the region—the Discovery and Conquest, colonization and exploitation, slavery and the slave uprisings, Wars of Independence, Revolutions up to the Castro regime, and the prevailing conditions of millions of Negroes and Indians in this very generation.[52]

These are the realities, and there is nothing magical about them. Only in understanding what Cortez and his civilization meant to our civilization can we bridge the chasm of our alienation: reconciliation becomes the result of the critical rather than the magical exploration of reality. Magical realism embodies elements of the metaphysical inclination of the surrealists who totally reject the grounding of their work in material reality. The adjective "magical" (defined as the "pretended art of producing effects beyond the natural human power by means of supernatural agencies or through command of occult forces in nature") ought to be discarded because it does not accurately or truthfully reflect the cause of phenomena, for the events which Carpentier and Alexis describe as magical were in fact real, having as their origin   the conditions of the exploitation and oppression out of which contemporary realism in the Caribbean grew.

The literature is critical for several reasons. First, it examines Caribbean experience in a methodolgical and systematic way. Second, its method represents an historical epistemology, drawing artistic forms, images and symbols from the Caribbean experience. Third, it reflects a particular Caribbean ontology that grows out of the material basis of the Caribbean. Critical realism is not to be regarded as a separate principle, but as two facets (critical and real) of a single experience. Therefore, because it examines the Caribbean literary experience in a systematic way, it reflects the essence of the Caribbean experience.

Carpentier's search for evidence to authenticate reality proves categorically that he did not only rely on intuition but also drew on the region's history, which is filled with inexhaustible examples of the concept of forward development. Documents do sharpen intuition, but intuition is not a substitute for documentation. With documentation we hope to learn from the past and avoid making the same mistakes. With greater documentation, with greater social analysis, more incisive perception and intuition into the facts, history will proceed forward spirally rather than circularly and aimlessly repetitious. Castro is not a repetition of Toussaint, for there has been a movement toward a more egalitarian society as Ti Noël, burdened as he was with suffering, would testify could he appear in contemporary Cuba. Thus, critical realism and the forward development of history become the terms of reference and definition for major Caribbean writers.

CONCLUSION:
CRITICAL REALISM AND THE
DEMOCRATIC SENTIMENT

He only earns his freedom and existence,
Who daily conquers them anew.[1]

IN reviewing the major characteristics of Caribbean literature and arguing for the acceptance of resistance as the aesthetic-political theme that fashions and structures it, it is important to observe that the literature itself is determined by democratic postulates. For if resistance acts as the determining factor in the "how" of the literature, then the "what" of it is fashioned by the persistent struggle for democracy—this can be perceived as the "democratic sentiment" that is inherent in our literature.

In using the term "democratic," however, one must be careful not to include its bourgeois connotations that imply revolution from above, but to stress the surging activity of the masses from below who are the catalytic agents in the shaping of Caribbean history. Or, to put it more precisely, to show how little people struggle constantly for the democracy that ultimately shapes the literary history of the area. For after any quick observation, it becomes readily apparent that most of the major characters whom we have studied are these little people, or, in the vulgarized sense, the "ordinary people" (even though people are never ordinary) making history—Juan, Montejo, Cecilia, Banjo, Manuel, Pa Campbell, Shephard, Modestine/Sonson, Ti Noël, Cristo, Esteban—that is, a slave, a Maroon, a mulatto, a ragamuffin, a peasant, a Maroon descendant, a half-crazed liberator, a slave Maroon, a semi-proletariat. Little, ordinary people,— they are the fulcrum around which the history of the development of Caribbean society revolves. When we study the idealized characters (Enriquillo and Mencia) and the broken aristocrats (Sophia and Esteban), their sentiments are seen to be progressive and are in harmony with those of the oppressed people, who are struggling for their dignity.

The term democratic is justified for several reasons. First, the characters, as they are depicted novelistically, are shown resisting and rebelling against

269

an unjust social order. Second, the novels are set, for the most part, within a context of the oppressors versus the oppressed—that is, the Spanish oppressing and consequently liquidating the indigenous Indian civilization; the slave masters oppressing the slaves, which subsequently culminated in the liberation struggle; the rigors of white "rational" civilization oppressing the "instinctual" one of black civilization; the cruelty of Europeans as they exploit their colonial societies; the occupation of the United States forces as they oppress and dispossess the peasant societies of the Caribbean (which is juxtaposed to the struggle for independence). The growing acknowledgment that the struggle must be seen within the context of class rather than race, with the ever increasing need to understand history as process which develops spirally rather than cyclically, also testifies to the democratic sentiments that are to be found within the literature.

This democratic sentiment is not to be perceived as being something novel within the literature. For, in speaking of the historical romances of Sir Walter Scott, Boris Suchkov makes the point that "the idea that the practical activity of perfectly ordinary people is at the same time historical activity gave Scott's novels an epic dimension and a democratic flavour."[2] This "democratic flavour," or what I prefer to call the democratic sentiment, became for the Caribbean writer the point of departure for his analysis of the literature. The classicism of Galván was a manifestation of the pre-romantic movement which at first perceived the struggle (that is, in characterization) in a certain "idealized" way, even though there were elements of "historicism" or "historical activity" inherent in the work. The spirit of resistance, however, and the elements of "romanticism" were able to carry the literature forward and, in a way, anticipate (strictly in a thematic sense) the spirit of revolutionary romanticism that was to follow in the works of *Cecilia Valdés, The Early Life of Juan Manzano* and *The Autobiography of a Runaway Slave*. It is in these works that we begin to see elements of realism which would have tremendously important ramifications for our literature.

These revolutionary romantics were important, not only because they recognized "the antagonistic character of social relations and gradually realized that the masses, carrying the burdens of progress on their shoulders, were the force which was moving history forward", but also because they recognized that the very content of those burdens were "leading them to understand the true nature of the historical processes and preparing their transition to realism."[3] That transition to realism is very important because it is possible to study thrugh the literature the oppressed colonial individual in his complex inter-relationship with the oppressing colonial order.

The study of the colonial order and its inherent man-killing racism became the social task of Maran and McKay and even Roumain (in whom we see elements of critical realism), who set out to portray in graphic details the essence of the socio-political order. The socio-psychological aspect of realism supplements that of the socio-political method of realist inquiry in that it uses the psychological condition of the colonial man as a point of departure to examine his social conditions. As we know, George Lamming was the chief proponent of this form.

But the questions which must be asked are in what way was realism of such great importance and why was it so interlinked with the democratic sentiment? The answer is that realism as an artistic method and a concrete historical phenomenon by its use of "selection, evaluation and portrayal by the artist of reality in his desire to reveal natural laws inherent in contradictory real phenomena"[4]. was able to elucidate the causal relationship between the opposing tendencies in Caribbean society, which are the particular essence of the Caribbean experience. However, because the essence of that experience is the constant and persistent struggle for liberation and justice, it automatically imposes upon the writer the task of achieving democracy within the society, either explicitly or implicitly.

In a novel where the democratic sentiment is present, the hero usually acts in a particular manner; his actions are not the result of accident but reveal causality, the results of injustice, or oppression, the aim of which is usually to rectify the cause of this injustice, and to create a condition where such actions are no longer possible. The culmination of this process results in the creation of an entirely new and democratic society .

Inherent in this contention is the recognition that there are those writers who will reject (explicitly) this democratic aim as a determining function of the literature. This position, is only the other side of the same reality, in that those who reject this position implicitly accept or recognize it as the starting point or framework for any analysis of Caribbean literature. By way of example, the position of V. S. Naipaul readily comes to mind. Here is a Caribbean writer who takes the position that in the "West Indian islands slavery and latifundia created only grossness, men who ate 'like cormorants' and drank 'like porpoises'; a society without standards, without noble aspirations, nourished by greed and cruelty,"[5] and, of course, his now famous position that "history is built around achievement and creation; and nothing was created in the West Indies." Even though one can argue very convincingly that Naipaul is wrong, these positions, by their very nature, reveal not only an elitist way of looking at the world, but judge history as only and exclusively the acts of the colonizers (i.e., the oppressors). It negates the humanistic element of the democratic struggle of the masses for liberation, and it reveals Naipaul's antidemocratic sensibilities. It is precisely because history is the dynamic and creative activity of the masses that we in the Caribbean not only created history by our very acts of resistance, but literally created our "revolutionary selves." To blame the oppressed masses for the inhumanity of the oppressor is not only the vulgarization and dangerous rewriting of history but is also the manifestation of a class position, fashioned by a myopic and misguided misanthropy.

This anti-democratic and nihilistic Naipaulian tendency has been embraced by other Caribbean writers such as John Hearne, Orlando Patterson, and Derek Walcott. Yet, one would be equally metaphysical if, like Edward Brathwaite, one simply demanded that "words" should be used as the starting point to refashion the nature of Caribbean reality ("I must be given words to refashion futures like a healer's hand," says Brathwaite.) One can only reiterate that the *practical activity* of Caribbean man comes first; then comes his *literary activity* which is used as a vehicle to reveal, record, and shape the nature of his practical activity (albeit at the emotional and spiritual level) in a meaningful and non-chaotic manner; thereby expanding the dialogue on Caribbean reality in the pursuance of our search for national identity and autonomy. In this process, the quest for meaning and understanding of Caribbean reality is elevated to a higher and higher plane. Thus, even in their denial of the Caribbean past and possibilities (i.e. in their implicit rejection of their "democratic task" and their advocacy of clearly anti-democratic positions), these writers merely reveal the other side of the democratic sentiment in our literature and so affirm rather than deny its presence.[6]

It is not to be argued that the creativity which most of our post-1960 novelists have shown, their expanded capacity for detailed social analysis and typification of characters, and their increased attention to the fate of society, all became crystallized at a time when swift historical changes were taking place before their very eyes. Indeed, it was a time in Caribbean literature when we saw the full coming-into-being of "critical realism"; a realism that fully understood, and was able to analyze through the novel, the fundamentally important fact that one social order was giving way to another. Theirs was the task to analyze the cause of our oppression and to show the way towards liberation, using critical realism, as T. Motyleva puts it, "to convey the stormy dynamism of the times and to reveal the greatly increasing complications of relations between the individual and society."[7] Indeed, it was a time when all the "progressive, democratically inclined critical realist writers took up their stand on the side of the peoples fighting against fascism during the years of bitter historical tribulation. . . ."[8] and when we in the Caribbean, particularly, were struggling against colonialism and neocolonialism, demanding the right to create new societies free from capitalist exploitation.

It is in this sense that Caribbean writers, sharing common concerns, merge with their Third World counterparts and force their consciousness upon not only the national but upon the world's literary process as well. T. Motyleva puts it this way:

In our day, the literary map of the world is being augmented by regions heretofore little known from this viewpoint such as Asia, Africa and Latin America. Today it is hard to imagine world literature without Muktar Auezov, Chinghiz Aitmatov, Kobo Abe, Miguel Angel Asturias, Jacques Stephen Alexis, Nicolás Guillén, Pablo Neruda, Leopold S. Senghor, Semben Usman, Nazim Hikmet and many others. A literature posing the fundamental problems of the life of nations is developing on all continents and in all forms, engendering unexpectedly complex blends of the basically national and borrowed, primeval and ultra-modern.[9]

In Chapter IV we argued that each work of art should "propose a concrete liberation from all alien forms of oppression" and that the literature should produce a "symbiotic and synthetic unity between man's essence and his existence, thereby allowing for the less intense and gradual elimination of alienation and the development of the human personality." As Suchkov has pointed out in another context, because "this conflict between the individual and society was the subject of penetrating examination in critical realist writing,"[10] we found that critical realism, more than any other method to date, has provided us with the artistic tools to examine these conditions and has been able to suggest, at some levels, tangible ways in which some of these conflicts can be resolved. Given the possibilities of resolution, critical realism creates the conditions in which there can be a basis for the reconciliation of essence and existence (i.e., the individual and society), resulting in the gradual elimination of alienation.

This is precisely why I argue that the term, "magical realism" as a descriptive literary category becomes the incorrect way in which to define this literary phenomenon. In the end, because critical realism is a manifestation of the democratic consciousness of the masses, in the full realization that only through total and consistent democracy can their societies be transformed, it became the rallying cry of our contemporary writers.

Another indication of the "democratic sentiment" in our literature, is the continuous struggle to create a society which is based on a "humanism" in the sense that Friere speaks about it. For in the quest for liberation, in the very nature of resistance, there is a burning away of "egotism," "individualism," and "selfishness," which is replaced by a more acute collective consciousness, creating a greater awareness of societal needs. This, in its turn, allows for the collective focusing on the goal of liberty and ushers in many elements of an egalitarian society and a democratic humanism. Indeed, it may be argued that the "democratic sentiment" in Caribbean literature lays the basis for a particular Caribbean humanism (another manifestation of general humanism) that glorifies the moral integrity of the little man, his firm determination and faith in human dignity.

Alas, one must point out the central weaknesses of critical realism: even though it has been our best vehicle for the analysis of our struggle, and a basis for our humanism, it still exists at a particular level of contemplation and noninvolvement. It is from this point of view that Suchkov argues: "Realizing the need to struggle against reaction the critical realist challenged it with the power of the word, continuing to believe in contemplative humanism and beginning to regard history as a tragic balance of reason and barbarity."[11] This, we must remember, seems to be the identical sentiment that Carpentier reflects upon when he exclaimed, "We must beware of too much fine talk, of Better Worlds created by words. Our age is succumbing to a surfeit of words. The only promised land is that which man can find within himself." But the "power of the word," the "surfeit of words" can and does lead to "contemplative humanism," i.e., metaphysical humanism which finds its "promised land . . . within (him)self." This humanism is largely speculative and, even though at particular historical moments within the context of struggle it is important, it tends to exaggerate the "metaphysical" at the expense of the materialist basis of life; as a consequence it begins to create some level of false consciousness. Such are the limits of critical realism. But it is with "socialist realism," which has as its centrality "conscious historicism," that we begin to perceive the resolution of these limitations. It was Mikhail Sholokhov who, in his 1965 Nobel Prize speech, proclaimed the virtues of socialist realism:

> I am speaking of the realism that expresses the idea of life's rejuvenation, its refashioning for the good of mankind. I am speaking, of course, of the realism we now call socialist. Its specific feature is a view of the world that rejects mere contemplation of or retreat from reality, and calls to battle for the progress of mankind, makes it possible to achieve aims dear to the heart of millions and illuminates the paths of the struggle.[12]

Indeed, it is this vision of the world that calls for the active and full collective participation of the masses.

To claim the democratic sentiment for our literature and to argue that it is of the masses is not to suggest that the literature in fact reached the people en masse. As such it did not serve to alter mass consciousness in the vital process of transforming the society from one socio-political and socioeconomic order to the next, for it remained the luxury of the elites of our society and a way of measuring the "cultured" individuals. It is not necessary even to consider the argument that the very nature of our colonial society, which has newly attained independence, means that of necessity many of our elites cling to things foreign and insists that a knowledge of Shakespeare is the measure of the truly cultured individual. If Caribbean literature is to play more than a decorative function in our society there is a need for its mass dissemination among the population, with a greater thrust of our writers towards "socialist realism"—the position in which the political masses take up the struggle. It is to this new consciousness from which, and to which, the writer must now speak.

When, in his panoramic sweep, Galván surveyed the struggle of Enriquillo for independence, he wondered aloud, "We do not know whether or not the Spanish statesmen of those times, who gave Enriquillo's rebellion the importance it deserved, had a sense that history must eventually take this course [the course of resistance] but were discreet enough to keep it to themselves." When Carpentier polished his prose through the revolutionary reconstruction of the Cuban society, he understood that the struggle of man is both archetypal and eternal—the imperative of man if he is to retain his liberty and his sense of person. The story of Caribbean literature, as one tries to impose some order upon it, is the struggle of man for freedom and dignity, with resistance to any form of oppression that would deny him his right to be a person. In this transitional epoch, our literature must now concern itself with the rejuvenation of life and the onward march for consistent democracy.

Truly, throughout its long march of "classicism," "romanticism," "realism," "socio-psychological realism" "magical realism" and "critical realism," the Caribbean novel must be perceived in the largest sense as being "democratic in conception," and as revealing a "democratic sentiment" fashioned by the recurrent thematic motif of resistance that makes itself manifest in the works.

NOTES

INTRODUCTION

1. Karl Marx and Frederick Engels, *Selected Works*, Vol. I (Moscow: Progress Publishers, 1969), p. 186.
2. Vladimir Shcherbina, *Lenin and Problems of Literature* (Moscow: Progress Publishers, 1974), p. 22.
3. *Ibid.*, p. 22.

CHAPTER I

1. C. L. R. James, *The Black Jacobins* (New York: Alfred A. Knopf, Inc. and Random House, 1963) 2nd ed., p. 334.
2. Sylvia Wynter, "We Must Learn to Sit Down Together and Talk a Little Culture, Reflections on West Indian Writing and Criticism, Part I," *Jamaica Journal, Quarterly of the Institute of Jamaica*, vol. II. no. 4 (December, 1968), p. 31.
3. Julio Le Riverend, *Economic History of Cuba* (Havana: Ensayo Book Institute (1967), pp. 15-16.
4. Karl Marx and Frederick Engels, *Selected Works*, Vol. II, p. 102.
5. A. Z. Manfred, ed., *A Short History of the World* (Moscow: Progress Publishers, 1974), I, p. 251.
6. Marx and Engels, *Selected Works*, p. 133.
7. Manfred, *A Short History of the World*, p. 350.
8. Felipe Pichardo Moya quoted in Manuel Maldonado-Denis, *Puerto Rico: A Socio-Historical Interpretation* (New York: Random House, 1942), p. 14.
9. Riverend, *Economic History of Cuba*, p. 55.
10. *Ibid.*, p. 83.
11. *Ibid.*, p. 81
12. Eric Williams, *Capitalism and Slavery* (New York: Capricorn Books, 1966), p. 7.
13. Eric Williams, *From Columbus to Castro: The History of the Caribbean, 1492-1969* (New York: Harper and Row, 1970), p. 30.
14. *Ibid.*, pp. 31-32.

15. Juan Angel Silén, *We, the Puerto Rican People* (New York: Monthly Review Press, 1971), p. 23.

16. Riverend, *Economic History of Cuba*, p. 82.

17. Williams, *From Columbus to Castro*, p. 37.

18. *Ibid.*, pp. 66-67.

19. Sidney King, "A Birth to Freedom," *New World*, vol. II, no. 4, 1966, p. 22.

20. The word "maroon" is derived from the Spanish cimarron, which in the New World "originally referred to domestic cattle that had taken to the hills in Hispaniola, and soon after to Indian slaves who had escaped from the Spaniards as well. By the end of the 1530s, it was already beginning to refer primarily to Afro-American runaways and had strong connotations of fierceness, of being wild and unbroken." The phenomenon of maroonage, characteristic of the slave experience in the New World, is not only confined to Jamaica, as might be suggested from the enormous attention paid to the Jamaican Maroons in this chapter. For a further reading of maroonage in the New World see Richard Price, ed., *Maroon Societies: Rebel Slave Communities in the Americas* (Garden City, N.Y.: Doubleday, 1973).

21. Carey Robinson, *The Fighting Maroons of Jamaica* (Jamaica: William Collins and Sangster Ltd., 1971), p. 19.

22. *Ibid.*, p. 38.

23. *Ibid.*, p. 51.

24. *Ibid.*, p. 51.

25. *Ibid.*, p. 31.

26. Monica Schuler, "Akan Slave Rebellions in the British Caribbean," *Savacou*, vol. I, no. 1 (June, 1970), p. 9.

27. *Ibid.*, p. 10.

28. *Ibid.*, p. 18.

29. Cheddi Jagan, *The West on Trial* (New York: International Publishers, 1966), p. 33.

30. Schuler, "Akan Slave Rebellions," p. 20.

31. King, "A Birth to Freedom," p. 27.

32. *Ibid.*, p. 22. Sidney King's article, "A Birth to Freedom" is a very good analysis of the Berbice Rebellion (King prefers to call it the Berbice Revolution) of 1763. His claims, however, are somewhat extravagant, i.e., when he says, "But in so far as he [the slave] constituted the labor force of a capitalist enterprise sustained by shareholders of private capital, or the capital of some Company-State, and in which money was invested for profits, insofar as he was a toiler without property of his own, the West Indian slave was a proletarian." King is very wrong here. In the first place, to impose categories of "capitalist social relations of production" on a "slave mode of production" is incorrect; and secondly to claim that the "West Indian slave was a proletarian" is particularly false. Capitalist relations had not crystallized within the slave world since there was not a wage-earning proletariat necessary to enact commodity relations which are the chief prerequisites for the formation of a proletarian class. Further, even though there might have been "private capital" there was not a wage-earning class to establish capitalist production relations. Put very

simply, the slaves could not buy what they produced simply because they had no money; neither could they sell their "labour power" because they were owned totally by the slaveowner. (S. R. C.)

33. Robinson, *The Fighting Maroons*, p. 154.

34. James, *The Black Jacobins*, p. 221.

35. *Ibid.*, pp. 12-13.

36. T. Lothrop Stoddard, *The French Revolution in San Domingo* (Boston: Houghton Mifflin Co., 1914), pp. 14-16.

37. *Ibid.*, p. 51.

38. James, *The Black Jacobins*, p. 18.

39. Edward Kamau Brathwaite in his introduction to Melville J. Herskovits' *Life in a Haitian Valley* (New York: Doubleday, 1971) says that the first independent black settlement in the New World was actually established in 1631 at Palmares in Pernambuco, Brazil, and lasted for 65 years. "Unlike Haiti, however, Palmares was not able to move from autonomy to recognized independent statehood." *See* p. xiii.

40. Ramiro Guerra y Sánchez, *Sugar and Society in the Caribbean* (New Haven: Yale University Press, 1964), p. 33.

41. There were, of course, slave rebellions in Cuba in 1538, 1731, and 1795; the last was led by a free slave, Morales, who demanded equality for blacks and whites and the distribution of lands to blacks. That Cuba supplied to Jamaica bloodhounds that were trained to hunt down slaves gives us a fair picture of what the treatment of slaves in Cuba was at the time. For a further description of the treatment of slaves in Cuba, see Hugh Thomas, *Cuba: The Pursuit of Freedom*, Chapter XIII.

42. Guerra y Sánchez, *Sugar and Society*, p. 22.

43. *Ibid.*, p. 76.

44. *Ibid.*, p. 45.

45. *Ibid.*, p. 46.

46. *Ibid.*, p. 74.

47. *Ibid.*, p. 86.

48. *Ibid.*, p. 97.

CHAPTER II

1. Roger Bastide, *African Civilizations in the New World* (New York: Harper and Row, 1971), p. 47.

2. *Ibid.*, p. 9.

3. James, *The Black Jacobins*, p. 391.

4. Bill Riviere, "Ideology in Caribbean Education," *Shango, The Magazine of the Caribbean*, vol. 1, 3, (Summer, 1973), p. 12.

5. Walter Rodney, *How Europe Underdeveloped Africa* (Dar es Salaam: Bogle-L'Ouverture Publications, 1972), p. 264.

6. Julius K. Nyerere, *Ugamaa: Essays on Socialism* (New York: Oxford University Press, 1971), p. 46.

7. Silén, *We, the Puerto Rican People*, p. 100. Also see pp. 93-102 for a discussion of education in Puerto Rico.

8. Paulo Freire, *Pedagogy of the Oppressed* (New York: The Seabury Press, 1970), p. 39.

9. *Ibid.*, p. 39.

10. Bill Riviere, *Oppression and Resistance: The Black Condition in the Caribbean* (Ithaca: Cornell University, African Studies and Research Center), Monograph Series no. 1, p. 39.

11. Peter D. Curtin, *Two Jamaicas: The Role of Ideas in a Tropical Colony, 1830-1865* (New York: Greenwood Press, 1968), p. 26.

12. Riviere, *Oppression and Resistance*, p. 39.

13. See Edward Kamau Brathwaite, "The African Presence in Caribbean Literature." *Daedalus*, vol. 103, no. 2 (Spring, 1974).

14. Mary Reckord, "The Jamaican Slave Rebellion of 1831," in Richard Frucht, *Black Societies in the New World* (New York: Random House, 1971), p. 54

15. *Ibid.*, p. 57.

16. *Ibid.*, p. 63.

17. The distinction is made in Jamaican society among three distinct groups: the whites, who form the planter class; the Negro slaves and their descendants, who form a lower class; and in the middle is found the colored group, formed by the union of black and white. During the 50s and 60s this group would divide into two blocks: those supporting the aspiration of the blacks, e.g., William Gordon, and those aligning with the whites, e.g., Robert Osborn. (S. R. C.)

18. Curtin, *Two Jamaicas*, p. 7.

19. Thomas Carlyle, "Occasional Discourse on the Negro Question," *Fraser's Magazine* (December, 1849), pp. 7-8.

20. Lord Olivier, *The Myth of Governor Eyre* (London: The Hogarth Press, 1933), p. 29.

21. See Sidney Mintz, "The Caribbean Region," *Daedalus* vol. 103, no. 2 (Spring, 1974).

22. Lord Olivier, *The Myth of Governor Eyre*, pp. 87-88.

23. *Ibid.*, p. 113.

24. Mavis Christine Campbell, *The Dynamics of Change in a Slave Society* (Rutherford: Fairleigh Dickinson University Press, 1976), p. 335.

25. Lord Olivier, *The Myth of Governor Eyre*, p. 167.

26. *Ibid.*, p. 207.

27. John Henrik Clarke, ed., *Marcus Garvey and the Vision of Africa* (New York: Random House, 1974), p. 80.

28. Lord Olivier, *The Myth of Governor Eyre*, p. 314.

CHAPTER III

1. Manuel Maldonado-Denis, *Puerto Rico: A Socio-Historic Interpretation*, p. 21.

2. *Ibid.*, p. 39.

3. *Ibid.*, p. 38.

4. *Ibid.*, p. 40.

5. Silén, *We the Puerto Rican People*, p. 31.

6. Maldonado-Denis, speculating on the success of the War of Yara and the failure of the War of Lares, contends that the War of Lares failed for the following four reasons: (a) the overwhelming predominance of African slaves in Cuba—5.7 times as many as were in Puerto Rico; (b) the inability of the Puerto Ricans to develop a revolutionary consciousness because of the short duration of the revolt; (c) the absence of a great leader experienced in war, (d) the geography of Cuba made it more appropriate for guerrilla warfare. (S. R. C.) *See Puerto Rico; A Socio-Historical Interpretation, loc. cit.*, pp. 43-47 for further discussion.

7. Franklin W. Knight, *Slave Society in Cuba during the Nineteenth Century* (Madison: University of Wisconsin Press, 1970), p. 6.

8. *Ibid.*, p. 10.

9. Henry Clay, from Hugh Thomas, *Cuba; The Pursuit of Freedom*, p. 104.

10. Ralph Korngold, *Citizen Toussaint* (New York: Hill and Wang, 1947), p. 161.

11. Walter Rodney, *West Africa and The Atlantic Slave Trade* (East Africa Publishing House, Nairobi, 1967), p. 5

12. Hugh Thomas, *Cuba*, p. 161.

13. It must be remembered that the most active participant in the slave trade in the nineteenth century was the southern United States. As Dr. Rodney has pointed out, "it was the new nation of the United States which played the biggest part in the last fifty years of the Atlantic Slave-Trade taking away slaves at a greater rate than ever before." *See* Walter Rodney, *West Africa and the Atlantic Slave-Trade, loc. cit.* p. 5.

14. José L. Franco, "Maroons and Slave Rebellions in the Spanish Territories," in Richard Price, *Maroon Societies;* p, 48.

15. Knight, *Slave Society in Cuba*, p. 154.

16. A. N. Yakovlev, ed., *Fundamentals of Political Science* (Moscow: Progress Publishers, 1975), pp. 64-65.

17. Knight, *Slave Society in Cuba*, p. 159.

18. *Ibid.*, p. 162.

19. Thomas, *Cuba*, p. 265.

20. Walter Millis, *The Martial Spirit* (Cambridge, Mass.: Riverside Press, 1931), p. 13.

21. *Ibid.*, pp. 17-18.

22. Roberto Fernández Retamar, "Caliban: Notes Towards a Discussion of Culture in Our America," *The Massachusetts Review*, vol. XV, nos. 1-2 (Winter-Spring, 1974), p. 42.

23. Fidel Castro, *History Will Absolve Me* (Havana: Cooperative Obrera, 1961), p. 31.

24. *Ibid.*, p. 33.

25. Millis, *The Martial Spirit*, p. 41.

26. Williams, *From Columbus to Castro*, p. 420.

27. Suzy Castor, "The American Occupation of Haiti (1915) and the Dominican Republic (1916-1924)", *The Massachusetts Review* vol. XV, nos. 1-2 (Winter-Spring, 1974), p. 253.

28. Smedley D. Butler, "America Armed Forces, 2. 'In Time of Peace'; the Army," *Common Sense*, vol. IV, no. 2 (1935), p. 8.

29. Rayford W. Logan, *Haiti and the Dominican Republic* (New York: Oxford University Press, 1968), p. 100.

30. Castor, "American Occupation of Haiti," p. 262.

31. *Ibid.*, p. 254.

32. *Ibid.*, p. 256.

33. Logan, *Haiti and the Dominican Republic*, p. 97.

34. *Ibid.*, p. 97.

35. Castor, "American Occupation of Haiti," pp. 256-257.

36. *Ibid.*, p. 259.

37. *Ibid.*, p. 262.

38. Logan, *Haiti and the Dominican Republic*, p. 121.

39. Castor, "American Occupation of Haiti," p. 266.

40. *Ibid.*, p. 267.

41. Naomi M Garret, *The Renaissance of Haitian Poetry* (Paris: Presence Africaine, 1963), p. 59.

42. *See* Edward Brathwaite, Introduction to Melville Herskovits' *Life in a Haitian Valley*, *loc. cit.*, p. xvi.

43. Gordon Lewis, *The Growth of the Modern West Indies* (New York: Monthly Review Press, 1969), p. 88,

44. *Ibid.*, p. 175.

45. Reckford, "Jamaican Slave Rebellion of 1831" in Frucht's *Black Societies*, *loc. cit., p. 58.*

46. *Ibid.*, p. 58.

47. Riviere, *Oppression and Resistance*, pp. 56-57. (Also *see* Appendix I for a description of the activity of the black militia prior to the 1860s.)

48. *Ibid.*, p. 60.

49. Silén, *We, the Puerto Rican People*, p. 51.

50. Walter Rodney, *The Groundings with My Brothers* (London: Bogle-L'Ouverture Publications, Ltd., 1969), p. 12.

51. Maldonado-Denis, *Puerto Rico*, p. 117.

52. *Ibid.*, p. 118.

53. *Ibid.*, p. 128.

54. K. S. Karol, *Guerrillas in Power* (New York: Hill and Wang, 1970), p. 63.

55. *Ibid.*, p. 72.

56. *Ibid.*, p. 81.

57. See Appendix II for a further discussion on this point.

58. C. L. R. James, *A History of Pan-African Revolts* (Washington, D.C.: Drum and Spear Press, 1969), p. 92.

59. *Ibid.*, p. 92.

60. Jagan, *The West on Trial*, p. 178.

61. Castro, *History Will Absolve Me*, p. 75.

62. Jagan, *The West on Trial*, p. 37.

63. Lewis, *Growth of Modern West Indies*, p. 264.

64. Jagan, *The West on Trial*, pp. 18-19.

65. Lewis, *Growth of Modern West Indies*, p. 264.

66. *Ibid.*, p. 272.

67. Jagan, *The West on Trial*, p. 264.

68. *See* Castro, *History Will Absolve Me*, particularly pp. 72-79.

69. Leo Huberman and Paul M. Sweezy, *Cuba; An Anatomy of a Revolution* (New York: Monthly Reveiw Press, 1961), p. 17.

70. *Ibid.*, p. 22.

71. *Ibid.*, p. 29

72. *Ibid.*, p. 57.

73. *Ibid.*, p. 63.

74. *Ibid.*, pp. 78-83.

75. *Ibid.*, p. 93.

76. Walter Rodney, "The Black Scholar Interviews: Walter Rodney," *Journal of Black Studies and Research*, vol. 6, no. 3 (November, 1974), pp. 44-45.

77. George L. Beckford, "Toward Independent Economic Development for the Betterment of the Caribbean," *The Massachusetts Review*, vol. XV, nos. 1-2 (Winter-Spring, 1974), p. 119.

78. See Appendix III for the lyrics of the calypso. I was introduced to this calypso by my brother, a nonacademic without even a high school diploma, with the following words, "Dis is a calypso I want yo' to hear." I don't think that he has ever read Marx or, for that matter, Beckford or Rodney. However, when the condition is articulated in song he readily knows what's happening. (S. R. C.)

79. Huberman and Sweezy, *Cuba*, p. 93.

80. Allan Williams, "Report on Castle Bruce" (unpublished), p. 13.

81. *Ibid.*, pp. 45-46.

CHAPTER IV

1. Fidel Castro quoted in Retamar, "Caliban: Notes Towards a Discussion of Culture in Our America," p. 68.

2. Boris Suchkov, *A History of Realism* (Moscow: Progress Publishers, 1973), p. 10.

3. *Ibid.*, p. 10.

4. Grigory Oganov, *Freedom of Art Under Socialism* (Moscow: Novosti Press Agency Publishing House, 1975), p. 48.

5. *Ibid.*, p. 17.

6. Marx and Engels, *Selected Works*, Vol. I, p. 503.

7. Margaret Dickinson, *When Bullets Begin to Flower* (Nairobi, Kenya: East African Publishing House, 1972), p. 24.

8. *Ibid.*, p. 29.

9. Oganov, *Freedom of Art*, p. 66.

10. Dickinson, *When Bullets Begin to Flower*, pp. 80-82.

11. *Ibid.*, pp. 116-127.

12. Roberto Fernández Retamar, *Retamar's Revolutionary Poems, Cuba 1959-1974* (Mona, Jamaica: Savacou Publishers, Ltd., 1974), p. 11.

13. A. Mushmin, "Analytic Approach to a Work of Art," *Social Science* (October, November, December, 1971), p. 138.

14. *Ibid.*, p. 145.

15. *Ibid.*, p. 149.

16. Amílcar Cabral, *Return to the Source* (New York: African Information Service, 1973), p. 40.

17. *Ibid.*, p. 69.

18. Price, *Maroon Societies*, p. 10.

19. Cabral, *Return to the Source*, p. 69.

20. Jacques Ehrmann, "On Articulation: The Language of History and the Terror of Language," *Yale French Studies*, 39, p. 23.

21. *Ibid.*, pp. 23-24.

22. Jean Paul Sartre, *What is Literature?* (New York: Harper and Row, 1965), p. 59.

23. Cirilo Villaverde, *Cecilia Valdés* Sydney G. Gest, trans. (New York: Vantage Press, 1962), pp. 15-16.

24. Ehrmann, "On Articulation," p. 25.

25. Franz Fanon, *The Wretched of the Earth* (New York: Grove Press, Inc., 1966), p. 187.

26. Leon Trotsky, *Literature and Revolution* (An Arbor: The University of Michigan Press, 1960), p. 70.

27. M. Petrosyan, *Humanism Its Philosophical, Ethical and Sociological Aspects* (Moscow: Progress Publishers, 1972), p. 71.

28. There are those critics who argue from the Marxian perspective that the complete elimination of alienation can only occur with the complete liquidation of private property (i.e., capitalist social relations) and the achievement of communism. This, however, need not concern us here since Cuba is the only Caribbean country that has opted for the "socialist road," and secondly, because any exhaustive study of alienation is somewhat outside our purview. S. R. C.)

29. R. M. Lacovia, "English Caribbean Literature, A Brave New World," *Black Images*, vol. 1, no. 1, p. 22.

30. *Ibid.*, p. 22.

31. Kenneth Ramchand, *The West Indian Novel and Its Background* (London: Faber and Faber, 1970), p. 7. I am not particularly convinced that Ramchand gives the correct reason for the "partial" success of *A House for Mr. Biswas*. Indeed, one is convinced that both Lacovia and Ramchand suffer from being

"uncritical" in their analysis of *A House for Mr. Biswas*. The novel, one can argue, must be seen against the especial nature of the historical, political, social and cultural experience of the Caribbean (one is calling here, not so much for the recital of the historical facts but more for the identification of the essence of the given experience that the facts manifest; that is, for the use of dialectical as opposed to formal logic) and more precisely against the quality of Naipaul's particularly alienated ontological vision of Caribbean society, which is spelt out rather categorically in his book *The Middle Passage*.

32. V. S. Naipaul, *The Middle Passage Impressions of Five Societies—British, French, and Dutch in the West Indies and South America* (London: Andre Deutsch, 1963), p. 29.

33. Gordon Rohlehr, "The Ironic Approach," in *The Islands in Between*, Louis James, ed. (London: Oxford University Press, 1968), p. 123.

34. Diana T. Laurenson and Alan Swingerwood, *The Sociology of Literature* (New York: Schocken Books, 1972), p. 250.

35. *See* G. Orwell, "Politics vs. Literature: An examination of Gulliver's Travel," in *The Orwell Reader: Fiction, Essay and Reports* (New York: Harcourt Brace Javanovich, 1956), particularly the last page, and Sartre, *What is Literature?, loc. cit.*, p. 57-58

36. Lacovia, "English Carribbean Literature," p. 15.

37. Richard Greeman, "Victor Serve: Is Proletarian Literature Possible?" *Yale French Studies*, 39, p. 158.

38. Retamar, *Retamar's Revolutionary Poems*, pp. 60-61.

39. Sylvia Wynter, "We Must Learn to Sit Down Together," p. 31.

CHAPTER V

1. Jacques Roumain, *Ebony Wood* (New York: Interworld Press, 1972), pp. 29-30.

2. *See* M. A. Korestovovtsev, "On the Concept, 'The Ancient East,' " *Soviet Studies in History*, vol. 1, no. 2 (Fall, 1970) for a good discussion of the Ancient East. The parallels with the Indian civilization are obvious. (S. R. C.)

3. *Ibid.*, p. 129.

4. I say "initially" since we know that at least in the early part of the expansion of the Indian civilizations in both central and South America, a certain amount of prosperity was brought to the states that were overtaken. These constant wars among the Indians, however, began eventually to lead to a condition of uneven development, where instead of bringing some measure of prosperity to the captured states, they began to lead to their impoverishment. The prisoners taken in battle were subsequently enslaved and made to till the soil. The warriors who distinguished themselves in battle received more of the booty and the choice lands in the conquered territory. This led to great inequalities in the society and the subsequent resistance of the tribes who refused to be subdued by the conquering group. The ultimate unevenness of development that resulted as this system matured ultimately led to the underdevelopment of

the "conquered territory," and a lack of prosperity for the conquered territory. Hence we find that the Mayas for example, "at the end of the fifteenth century and the beginning of the sixteenth century were in the midst of a gradual transition to a class society with the appropriate forms of state power." Manfred, *A Short History of the World, loc. cit.*, p. 249.

5. Lewis Hanke, *The Spanish Struggle for Justice in the Conquest of America* (Boston: Little, Brown and Co., 1965), p. 124.

6. *Ibid.*, p. 172. Lewis Hanke, for example, in discussing las Casas' work *Apologetic History* in which las Casas claims that "the American Indians compared very favorably with the peoples of ancient times, were eminently rational beings, and in fact fulfilled every one of Aristotle's requisites for the good life," adduces from this that "the history of human exaggeration shows few more interesting exhibits than the *Apologetic History*" (Hanke, *The Spanish Struggle*, p. 123). The fact is that most evidence shows the Indians as having surpassed the "ancients" in many ways, a fact that neither Mr. Hanke of the present day nor the Spaniards of those inglorious days were willing to accept. (S. R. C.)

7. Sylvia Wynter, "Creole-Criticism: A Critique," *New World Quarterly*, 2, no. 5 (1972), p. 27.

8. G. R. Coulthard, "the Emergence of Afro-Cuban Poetry," *Caribbean Quarterly*, vol. 2, no. 3 (1952), p. 14.

9. Hanke, *The Spanish Struggle*.

10. Roumain, *Ebony Wood*, pp. 2-30, 45.

11. Kenneth Schwartz, *A New History of Spanish American Fiction*, Vol. 1, (Coral Gables, Florida: University of Miami Press, 1972), p. 68.

12. Coulthard, "Emergence of Afro-Cuban Poetry, p. 14.

13. Boris Suchkov, "Realism and Its Historical Roots," in S. Mozhnyagun, *Problems of Modern Aesthetics* (Moscow: Progress Publishers, 1969), p. 323.

14. Suchkov, *A History of Realism*, p. 103.

CHAPTER VI

1. Suchkov, *A History of Realism*, p. 57.

2. Jean Franco, *An Introduction to Spanish-American Literature* (Cambridge, London: University Press, 1969), p. 47.

3. *Ibid.*, p. 59.

4. *Ibid.*, p. 181.

5. Suchkov, *A History of Realism*, pp. 102-103.

6. The term "anti-slavery movement" is not used here in the classical sense of the formal and organized movement against slavery, e.g., the Anti-Slavery Movement which we witnessed in the U.S. (Frederick Douglass and others) or in England (i.e., Wilberforce and others). It is used here to describe the mass–popular democratic movement of the African slaves for freedom, which perforce had to be anti-slavery. Needless to say, this anti-slavery movement was a pro-resistance and a pro-freedom movement.

7. The systems approach to literature is an important means of literary analysis in that it seeks not only to discuss the content, "artistic concepts," structure of the work," etc., but it also seeks to explore the interrelations of the component parts of a literary work; that which gives to a work its "tonality, the highly developed system of emotional projections inherent to them, their emotional-expressive accents and nuances, in short that system which alone provides the framework for aesthetic assimilation of the world." Mikhail Khrapchenko, "Systems Analysis in Literature," *Social Sciences*, vol. VII, no. 1 (1976), p. 167.

8. *Ibid*, p. 167.

9. See *Cecilia Valdés, A Romance of Old Havana*, translated from the Spanish by Mariano Lorente, Boston. Issued for the St. Botolph Society by L. C. Page and Co., 1935.

10. Suchkov, *A History of Realism*, p. 81.

11. Richard Wright, *Native Son* (New York: Grosset and Dunlap, 1940), p. 358.

12. Fanon, *The Wretched of the Earth*, p. 187.

13. Sarah Grimke quoted in Theodore Weld's *American Slavery As It Is* (New York: Arno Press and *The New York Times*, 1968), p. 23.

14. *See Time and the Cross, Vol. 1, The Economics of American Negro Slavery* (Boston: Little Brown & Co., 1974) in which the authors advance the argument that slavery in the U. S. was not so bad as it has been presented, and with the use of economics the authors set out to prove that slavery was indeed beneficial to slaves.

15. Suchkov, *A History of Realism*, p. 27.

16. *Ibid.*, p. 24.

17. This relentless pursuance of freedom by Juan is manifested even in the poetry. One of the most revealing aspects occurs in the ode, "Religion":

> Oh, that its light were shed on those whose deeds
> Belie the doctrines of the church they claim;
> Whose impious tongues profane their father's creeds,
> And sanction wrong, e'en in religion's name.

> Oh, God of mercy, thronged in glory high,
> O'er earth and all its miseries, look down!
> Behold the wretched, hear the captives' cry,
> And call thy exiled children round thy throne!
> There would I fain in contemplation gaze,
> On thy eternal beauty, and would make
> Of love one lasting canticle of praise,
> And ev'ry theme but that, henceforth forsake.

(Juan Manzano, *Poems*, R. R. Madden, trans. [London: Thomas Ward and Co., 1840].)

18. A national-democrat is defined as one who advances a "revolutionary concept of democracy which transcends the limits of traditional bourgeois ideas. Briefly it can be defined as a combination of far-reaching social change in the interest of the working people designed to further the introduction of economic democracy and social justice, on the one hand, and the granting of

political rights, freedoms and scope for civic activities to the popular masses, on the other." (R. Ulyanovsky, *Socialism and the Newly Independent Nations*, p. 102.) More particularly for those who may want to classify Fidel at that historic period as a revolutionary-democrat, one can see the revolutionary-democrat being in the "progressive strata within the national-democracy which are moving nearer and nearer to scientific socialism" (137). In other words, the revolutionary-democrat is the precursor to Marxist-Leninist if he is successful: hence national-democrat, revolutionary-democrat, and Marxist-Leninist. One can see this transition in the career of Fidel Castro. Suffice it to say when the speech *History Will Absolve Me* was given, Fidel Castro was indeed a national-democrat. (S. R. C.)

19. Petrosyan, *Humanism*, p. 33.
20. Ferdinand Oyono, *Boy!* (New York: Collier Books, 1970), pp. 22-24.
21. *Ibid.*, pp. 89-90.
22. William Wells Brown, *Clotel, or The President's Daughter* (New York: Arno Press, 1969), p. 69.
23. *Ibid.*, pp. 70-72.
24. *Ibid.*, p. 67.

CHAPTER VII

1. René Despestre quoted in Aimé Césaire, *Discourse on Colonialism* (New York: Monthly Review Press, 1972) p. 75.
2. Antenor Firmin quoted in G. R. Coulthard, *Race and Colour in Caribbean Literature* (New York: Oxford University Press, 1962) p. 41.
3. Hannibal Price quoted in Coulthard, *Race and Colour*, p. 63.
4. *Ibid.*, p. 63.
5. Garret, *Renaissance of Haitian Poetry*, p. 234.
6. Normil G. Sylvain, "Chronique-Programme," *La Revue Indigène*, vol. 1, no. 1 (July, 1972), p. 2.
7. Garret, *Renaissance of Haitian Poetry*, p. 234.
8. Edmund Wilson, "The Marcelins—Novelists of Haiti," *The Nation*, (October 14, 1950), p. 341.
9. Garret, *Renaissance of Haitian Poetry*, p. 64.
10. Phillipe Thoby-Marcelin, "Haiti's Writers Find the People," *Americás*, vol. no. 4 (June, 1949), p. 39.
11. *Ibid.*, p. 39.
12. *Ibid.*, p. 39.
13. Garret, *Renaissance of Haitian Poetry*, p. 202.
14. *Ibid.*, p. 203.
15. F. A. Irele, *Literature and Ideology in Martinique: René Maran, Aimé Césaire, Frantz Fanon* (Buffalo: State University of New York, 1972), p. 8.
16. Lilyan Kesteloot, *Black Writers in French* (Philadelphia: Temple University Press, 1974), p. 76.
17. *Ibid.*, p. 78.

18. Irele, *Literature and Ideology*, p. 6.

19. Kesteloot, *Black Writers in French*, p. 76.

20. *Ibid.*, p. 72.

21. Césaire, *Discourse on Colonialism*, p. 72.

22. Michael Dash, "The Marxist Counterpoint—Jacques Roumain: 1930s to 1940s," *Black Images*, vol. 2, no. 1 (1973), p. 25.

23. Édouard Glissant, "Le romancier noir et son peuple: notes pour une conference" (The Black Novelist and His People), *Presence Africaine*, no. 16 (October-November, 1957), p. 25.

24. Edmund Wilson, *Red, Black, Blond and Olive; Studies in Four Civilizations: Zuni, Haiti, Soviet Russia, Israel* (New York: Oxford University Press, 1957), p. 25.

25. Bastide, *African Civilizations in the New World, p. 28.*

26. F. Ojo-Ade, "René Maran and the Racial Question: The Literature Of Alienation and Frustration," *Black Images*, vol. 2, nos. 3-4 (1974).

27. Wilson, *Red, Black, Blond and Olive*, pp. 116-119.

28. Silén, *We, the Puerto Rican People*, p. 39.

29. Maldonado-Denis, *Puerto Rico*, p. 4.

30. María Teresa Babín and Stan Steiner, *Borinquen: An Anthology of Puerto Rican Poetry* (New York: Vintage Books, 1974), p. 129.

31. Maldonado-Denis, *Puerto Rico*, p. 5.

32. Kesteloot, *Black Writers in French*, p. 26.

33. *Ibid.*, p. 40.

34. Suchkov, *A History of Realism*, p. 51.

35. In trying to understand the philosophical underpinnings of this period, particularly in reference to Césaire who openly accepted Marxism, then and still is a Marxist, it is necessary to understand the law of the Unity of and Struggle of Opposites and the law of the Negation of Negation: Very briefly put, the essence of the former posits that "all things, phenomena and processes possess internal contradictions, opposing aspects and tendencies that are in a state of interconnection and mutual negation; The struggle of opposites gives an internal impulse to development, leads to the building up of contradictions, which are resolved at a certain stage in the disappearance of the old and the appearance of the new." (p. 152). In looking at the Law of the Negation of Negation we must first understand that "negation" in the Marxist sense doesn't simply mean "no" but is the necessary condition for any further development. Development, however, is not confined to one simple act of negation. There is a "first negation" since what is preserved in the first negation is opposite to what existed in the initial form. The relationship between *initial form* and *first negation* is a relationship of two opposite forms. When, however, the first negation has achieved its full development by exhausting itself, it gives way to a higher and newer form. This is the *Second Negation*, the negation of the first negation, and hence its name the Negation of Negation. Development in this sense is seen as "spiral" rather than "straight," the first point culminating with the latter but at a higher moment of development. It is against this background that we can better understand Cesaire's negations and particularly that great work, *Return to My Native*

Land. (S. R. C.) Also please see F. V. Konstantinov et. al., *The Fundamentals of Marxist-Leninist Philosophy* (Moscow: Progress Publishers, 1974), pp. 152-159, for a fuller discussion of these two laws.

36. Senghor quoted in Kesteloot, *Black Writers in French*, p. 84.

37. Léon Damas quoted in Kesteloot, *Black Writers in French*, p. 232.

38. It must be pointed out categorically that the early writings of Negritude are nothing more or less than Caribbean literature. Antenor Firmin, Hannibal Price, Price-Mars, Claude McKay, Léon Damas, Aimé Césaire, René Maran, Entienne Léro and all the other principal writers of Negritude were from the Caribbean, and used the Caribbean condition as the source of their material. With the exception of Senghor, all of the early members of the Negritude movement were in fact from the Caribbean. Although the movement has been termed Negritude because of its return to African roots and the emphasis of the African personality, it cannot be emphasized too strongly that most of the important contributions from the early Negritude Movement came from Caribbean writers. The literature is, therefore, an integral part of Caribbean literature.

39. Ellen Conroy Kennedy, "Léon Damas: Pigments and the Colonized Personality," *Black World*, vol. XXI, no. 3 (1972), p. 4.

40. Léon Damas, "Poems from Pigments," *Black World*, vol. XXI, no. 3 (192), pp. 19-20.

41. Damas quoted in Kesteloot, *Black Writers in French*, pp. 140-141.

42. Bertène Juminer, "Hommage à Frantz Fanon," *Présence Africaine*, First Quarter, (1962), p. 126.

43. Kesteloot, *Black Writers in French*, p. 143.

44. Irele, *Literature and Ideology*, pp. 15-16.

45. Kesteloot, *Black Writers in French*, p. 159.

46. Gerald Moore and Ulli Beire, *Modern Poetry from Africa* (Middlesex: Penguin Books, 1963), p. 51.

47. Albert Gomes, *Through a Maze of Colour* (Port of Spain, Trinidad: Key Caribbean Publications, Ltd., 1974), pp. 16-17.

48. *Ibid.*, p. 20.

49. *Ibid.*, p. 20.

50. *Ibid.*, p. 21.

51. Kenneth Ramchand quoted in C. L. R. James, *Minty Alley* (London: New Beacon Books, Ltd., 1971), p. 7.

52. Alfred H. Mendes, *Black Fauns* (London: Duckworth, 1934), pp. 89-90.

53. C. L. R. James, "Discovering Literature in Trinidad: The Nineteen Thirties," *Savacou*, no. 2 (September, 1970), p. 56.

54. *Ibid.*, p. 55.

55. Daniel L. Racine, "A Profile of Leon-Gontran Damas," *Negro History Bulletin*, vol. 42, no. 3 (1979), p. 61.

56. *Ibid.*, p. 62.

57. Ian Munro and Reinhard Sander, eds., *Kas-Kas: Interviews With Three Caribbean Writers* (Austin, Texas: The Unviersity of Texas, 1972), p. 36.

58. James quoted in Munro and Sander, *Kas-Kas*, pp. 36-37.

59. Suchkov, *History of Realism*, p. 80.
60. Suchkov, "Realism and its Historical Roots," p. 325.
61. Nikolai Leizerov, "The Scope and Limits of Realism," *Problems of Modern Aesthetics*, p. 318.
62. G. R. Coulthard, *Caribbean Literature* (London: University of London Press, 1966), p. 69.

CHAPTER VIII

1. C. L. R. James, *The Case for West-Indian Self Government* (London: Leonard and Virginia Woolf at the Hogarth Press, 1933), pp. 8-9.
2. *Ibid.*, p. 12.
3. *Ibid.*, p. 32.
4. Mercer Cook, "The Haitian Novel," *The French Review*, vol. XIX, no. 6 (May, 1946), p. 410. This article contains a good introduction to the Haitian peasant novels of the period.
5. George Lamming, *The Pleasures of Exile* (London: Michael Joseph, 1960), p. 45.
6. There is a peculiar relation that goes on between the "heroes" of these novels and their women as it relates to their vocation, which in turn is dictated by their ideological commitment. In speaking about the "man/woman relationship" as it exists in his novel, *The Natives of My Person*, Lamming comments that "if the man/woman relationship is aborted, is perverted, there will be a corresponding perversion in the relationship between man and what he calls his work or his conception of his fulfillment." It is precisely this "abortion" in the relation between Davie and Lucille that led to the failure or the perversion, if you will, of the original notion of independence that Davie had envisaged for his colony.

   This peculiar relationship seems to run through most of the novels discussed. Initially, Enriquillo complained that if he wasn't married to Mencia he would not have endured the indignities which he had suffered so long. He, however, is able to break away from those inhibitions and finally frees himself. A process that Mencia herself aids in. In Lamming's *Of Age and Innocence*, Shephard's whole drive for independence is propelled and distorted by an English woman (unnamed), and an aborted relationship (unexplained) that he had with her pushed him on like a "madman" to come to grips with the problem of the independence of San Cristobal. This relationship also perverts his dream for independence, which Ma Shephard, his mother, sees very clearly. In *Au seuil d'un nouveau cri*, we are faced with the same issue of Modestine/Pierre caught up in a relationship that inevitably causes him to modify his demands for independence and make claims for a larger kind of freedom. For it is in the recognition that this white woman was going through precisely the same oppression that he was going through and he, faced with running away, leaving her to face her oppressors, would have meant partially abandoning the fight for liberty. Modestine masters the relationship and eventually triumphs.

   In *Explosion in a Cathedral* the problem is a little different. Sophia is particularly naive in her cloistered world, whereas Victor is a man of the world and possesses the correct political instincts. Through the course of the novel their positions change 360 degrees. Whereas Sophia is the one who carries on the struggle, Victor has completely degenerated into a man of a completely amoral character.

The man/woman relationship therefore emerges in a very important context in these novels and by careful analysis readily illuminates the struggle for liberation; its success or failure is subtly predicated upon by the man/woman relationship that exists in the novels.

7. James, *Case for West-Indian Self Government*, pp. 30-31.

8. Roger Mais, *The Three Novels of Roger Mais*, Introduction by Norman Washington Manley (London: Jonathan Cape, 1970), pp. vi-vii.

9. Barrie Davies, "The Novels of Roger Mais," *The International Fiction Review*, vol. 1, no. 1 (July, 1974), p. 141.

10. Jean Creary, "The Novels of Roger Mais" in Louis James, ed., *The Islands in Between* (London: Oxford University Press, 1968), p. 53.

11. Campbell, *The Dynamics of Change in a Slave Society*, p. 273. Mavis Campbell's account of this incident is highly instructive. She reports:

In this badly punctuated document, with its quaint language, Gordon described a place of temporary confinement called the "lockup" at Morant Bay, which he thought the "most disgusting and revolting to human nature." Many were jammed in this small confinement and for days or weeks, locked up together "and perform the calls of nature in the same place on the ground, and imbibe its miserable stench—Eno' to breed pestilence." Gordon said it would hardly be believed that "such a state of matters would be witnessed in a British colony in connection with prison discipline." He pointed out that the Rector of the Parish, the Reverend Cooke had actually sent "a poor sick man" to this place who had applied to him for alms. The wretched man spent days in the "Privy" of this unventilated place, "there he ate and drank and slept," undergoing the "slow process of poisoning." Gordon submitted that it was a case for the attorney general, and that it warranted an inquiry by the governor, because the "instincts of humanity plead in this case." He pointed out other abuses in the district prison of Morant Bay and drew the governor's attention to the fact that the extensive parish of St. Thomas-in-the-Vale was without a hospital, a poor or alms house, or a debtor's jail and often debtors were thrown into the district criminal prison. He called upon the governor to institute inquiries in such cases.

12. Rex Nettleford, in his introduction to *Dread: The Rastafarians of Jamaica*, has defined Rastafarianism in the following manner:

In the wake of a generation and a half of preachments, prophecies and protest about Africa, the Rastafarians have given to Jamaica, the Caribbean and Plantation America, *Rastafarianism*—a still developing system of religious thought and a style of practical living that summon a groping and equivocating society to honesty and moral certitude. It even suggests itself as a viable alternative to that dominant body of beliefs which inheres in the operation of a political, social and economic system that renders the mass of people not only unemployed but unemployable, without a sense of place or a sense of purpose. (Joseph Owens, *Dread: The Rastafarians of Jamaica* [Kingston, Jamaica: Sangsters, 1976], p. vii.)

13. James, *The Case for West-Indian Self Government*, p. 8.

14. Rex M. Nettleford, *Mirror Mirror: Identity, Race and Protest in Jamaica* (Jamaica: Williams Collins and Sangster Ltd., 1970), pp. 47-48.

15. Rodney, *The Groundings with my Brothers*, p. 61.

16. Wilbert J. Roget, "Image of Africa in Writings of Glissant," *CLA Journal*, vol. XXI, no. 3 (March, 1978), p. 391.

17. In terms of its unique contribution to the social and cultural development of the world, the importance of the Caribbean seems to best be stated by another Caribbean writer, Alejo Carpentier:

> This development is of such significance that it must be considered the most important event in history. Because in the history of the world there is an enormous difference between the person who preceded the discovery of the Americas and the person who came after.
>
> For a variety of reasons that you well know, after their discovery the Americas, and in particular the Caribbean, suddenly became the setting of the first meeting and first symbiosis in recorded history between three races which had never before met as such: the white race of Europe; the Indian race of the Americas, which had been completely unknown until then; and the African race, which, although it was known by Europe, was totally unknown on this side of the Atlantic. The monumental symbiosis of these three races was of extraordinary importance because of the richness of the cultures that were brought together and the entirely original civilization that was created.
>
> There is something more which confers a special and primordial importance on the Caribbean: the Caribbean has played a privileged, unique role in the history of the continent and the world.
>
> Firstly, as I said a moment ago, the discovery of this new continent, of the existence of different lands and different vegetations, was recorded in Columbus' diary. Through this diary and the letters he sent to their Catholic majesties describing his voyages, the Americas became established in people's minds and for the first time humankind acquired a real idea of the world in which it lived. People now knew that the world was round and when they explored it they now knew where they were going. For the first time in history people knew the world they lived in.

"The Culture of Caribbean Peoples," *Gramma* (August 26, 1979), p. 7.

18. Roget, *The Image of African*, pp. 398-399.

19. Gerard Pierre-Charles, "A Human Microcosm," Third World, vol. 2 (July, 1979), p. 10.

20. Nyunai, "La Lézarde: opinion d'un juene," *Presence Africaine*, no. 22 (October-November, 1958), p. 119.

21. Glissant, "The Black Novelist and His People," p. 30.

22. Ramchand, *The West Indian Novel and its Background*, p. 183.

CHAPTER IX

1. Mozhnyagun, *Problems of Modern Aesthetics*, p. 332.

2. George Lamming, *The Pleasures of Exile*, p. 9.

3. *Ibid.*, p. 13.

4. Michael Montaigne, *The Essayes of Michael Lord of Montaigne*, John Florio, trans. (London: George Routledge and Sons, Ltd., 1891), p. 94.

5. *Ibid,.* p. 96.

6. *Ibid.*, p. vii.

7. William Shakespeare, *The Tempest*, G. B. Harrison, ed. (London: Penguin Books, 1937), p. 14.

8. *Ibid.*, p. 34.

9. Montaigne, *Essayes*, p. v.

10. Suchkov, "Realism and its Historical Development," in Mozhnyagun, *Problems of Modern Aesthetics*, loc. cit., p. 320.

11. R. F. Retamar begins with the arrival of Columbus who, in his *Diario de Navegacion* (Navigation Log Books) records the first impression of the Caribs, who referred to as 'Canniba'. "They were men with one eye and others with dog's muzzles and who ate human beings" on the island of Haiti, whom the people called "cannibals," which he contends indicated "the deformation which the name Carib had undergone."

   Lamming in his turn draws on the adventures reported by Richard Hakluyt who in 1562 refers to Dominica "as an Island of Canybals" and from these elaborates on the connection between 'the Canybals' and Caliban." Retamar provides us with much more tangible evidence of this connection. He reports that by 1580, Montaigne's essay "De los canibales" (On Cannibals) appeared, and by 1603 it was translated into English by Giovanni Flora, who was a very close friend of Shakespeare. Shakespeare received a copy of this work which is still preserved today, and drew heavily upon this translation when he did *The Tempest* (1612). To Shakespeare *Caliban/cannibal* emerges as a "savage and deformed slave who cannot be degraded enough."

   It is this myth or symbol: the symbol of the Caribs depicted as Cannibals that many writers have been trying to analyze for a long time. However, it is only with O. Manoni's *Prospero and Caliban* (1950) that Caliban is identified for the first time with the colonial. It is this relationship that Lamming picked up in 1960 in *The Pleasures of Exile* and which, by 1969, would be taken up "with pride as our symbol by three Antillean writers (Aimé Césaire (Martinique), Edward Brathwaite (Barbados); and Robert Fernández Retamar (Cuba)—each of whom expressed himself in one of the three great colonial languages of the Caribbean." By 1971, however, the symbol of Caliban, once a despicable symbol and myth is now taken up and proposed as the new symbol of Caribbean peoples in that Caliban now represents "the rude and unconquerable master of the island."

12. Retamar, *Caliban*, p. 13.

13. Lamming, *Pleasures of Exile*, p. 15.

14. Retamar, *Caliban*, p. 24.

15. Césaire, *Discourse on Colonialism*, p. 68.

16. Anonymous, "George Lamming: The Search for Freedom," *Manjak* (April, 1974), p. 8.

17. Lamming, *Pleasures of Exile,* p. 9.

18. George Lamming, *Season of Adventure* (London: Allison Busby, 1979) p. 17.

19. *Ibid.*, p. 18

20. Wilson Harris, "The Unsolved Constitution," *Caribbean Quarterly*, 14, nos. 1-2 (1968), p. 46.

21. Lamming, *Pleasures of Exile*, p. 34.

22. Wynter, "Creole Criticism," p. 20.

23. Shakespeare, *The Tempest*, pp. 33-34.

24. George Kent, "A Conversation with George Lamming," *Black World*, vol. XXII, no. 5, pp. 90-91

25. *Ibid.*, p. 92.

26. Marxist scholars differentiate between *revolutionary violence*, a legitimate weapon in the struggle for achieving the liberation of the colonial masses, and *counter-revolutionary violence* which is used by the colonizer to suppress the legitimate aspirations of the majority of the colonized people and to ensure its position of dominance. The "Declaration of the Meeting of the Communist Parties of Latin America and the Caribbean" articulated this distinction between the two types of violence in the following manner:

    The utilization of all legal possibilities is an indispensible obligation of all the anti-imperialist forces, and the defense of the right of the peoples to decide, through democratic means, the transformation they demand, is a constant principle of our struggle.

    Revolutionaries are not the first to resort to violence. But it is the right and duty of all peoples and revolutionary forces to be ready to answer *counterrevolutionary violence* with *revolutionary violence* and open the way, through various means, to the peoples' action, including armed struggle to the sovereign decision of majorities. (Havana: *Granma*, June 22, 1975), p. 3.

27. Wilson Harris, *Tradition, the Writer and Society* (London: New Beacon Publications, 1979), 37.

CHAPTER X

1. Irene L. Gendzier, *Frantz Fanon: A Critical Study* (New York: Vantage Books, 1974), p. 81.

2. Suchkov, *History of Realism*, p. 51.

3. Vere W. Knight, "Negritude and the Isms," *Black Images*, vol. 3, no. 1 (1974), p. 16.

4. Randolph Hezekiah, "Bertene Juminer and the Colonial Problem", *Black Images*, vol. 3, no. 1 (1974), p. 35.

5. *Ibid.*, p. 33.

6. Bertène Juminer, "Hommage à Frantz Fanon," *Presence Africaine*, First Quarter (1962), p. 125.

7. *Ibid.*, pp. 126-127.

8. Because imperialism is seen as the last stage of capitalist development, *colonial exploitation* can be viewed as yet another form of *imperialist oppression*. Hence the same economic system which required African slaves at

its commencement now requires low wage-earning Africans to continue its existence and continued growth.

9. One can differentiate between *revolutionary violence*, a spontaneous and unplanned activity, and *revolutionary struggle*, which is a planned activity and is directed towards the achievement of statehood.

10. Pierre-Charles, "A Human Microcosm," p. 10.

11. Benedetti, p. 107.

12. V. S. Naipaul, *The Middle Passage* (London: Andre Deutsch, 1962), p. 29.

13. V. S. Naipaul, *The Overcrowded Barracoon and Other Articles* (Middlesex: Penguin Books, 1976), p. 275.

14. *See* Michael Abdul Malik, *From Michael de Freitas to Michael X* (London: Andre Deutsch, 1968).

15. D. A. N. Jones, "Little Warriors in Search of a War," *Times Literary Supplement* (September 12, 1975), p. 1013.

16. V. S. Naipaul, "The Life and Trials of Michael X," *The Sunday Times Magazine* (May 19, 1974), p. 27. This article, with a few additions, reappeared in V. S. Naipaul. *The Return of Eva Peron with The Killings in Trinidad* (New York: Alfred A. Knopf, 1980) as "Michael X and the Black Power Killings in Trinidad."

17. *Ibid.*, p. 29.

18. *Ibid.*, p. 37.

19. *Ibid.*, p. 41.

20. *Ibid.*, (May 12, 1974) p. 33.

21. *Ibid.*, p. 33-34.

22. *Ibid.*, p. 21.

23. It is to be noted that in "The Life and Trials of Michael X," Naipaul argued that, "An autobiography can distort; facts can be realigned. But fiction never lies: it reveals the writer totally. And Malik's [Jimmy's] primitive novel is like a pattern-book, a guide to later works." p. 138.

24. Jones, "Little Warriors," p. 1013.

25. Vere W. Knight, "Edouard Glissant: The Novel as History Rewritten," *Black Images*, vol. 3, no. 1 (1974), p. 67.

26. Naipaul, *Overcrowded Barracoon*, p. 254.

27. Juminer, "Hommage à Frantz Fanon," p. 125.

28. Naipaul, *Overcrowded Barracoon*, p. 247.

29. Fanon, *Wretched of the Earth*, p. 103.

CHAPTER XI

1. Phillip S. Foner, *Antonio Maceo* (New York: Monthly Review Press, 1977), p. 2. The two other members of this triumvirate are José Martí and Maximo Gomez. This work provides a remarkable account of this great man.

2. Roberto González Echevarría, *Alejo Carpentier: The Pilgrim at Home* (Ithaca: Cornell University Press, 1977), pp. 43-44.

3. While Professor Echevarría recognizes the important role that Fernando Ortiz played in the birth of Afro-Cubanism, he argues that "Ortiz became interested in African culture for what it could reveal about crime in Cuba . . . just as Indians represented for Argentino an obstacle in his program of civilization, so did the blacks appear to Ortiz as a regressive force." (*Alejo Carpentier*, pp. 46-48.)

4. It is incorrect to argue, as G. R. Coulthard has, that Afro-Cubanism was primarily or "largely a literary phenomenon." As he says:

> The Negro with his social and cultural background, not only figures prominently on the Cuban literary scene, but indeed tends to dominate it. For the Negro to have become the main subject of literature and painting in Haiti, Jamaica or Martinique would have been natural and logical, as the majority of the people in these countries are of predominantly African descent. But in Cuba the Negroes are a minority, so the explanation of Afro-Cubanism clearly cannot be sought in the ethnic or social conditions of Cuba. Interest in the Negro in Cuban literature of this period in fact is largely a literary phenomenon, at least within the bounds of the Afro-Cuban movement, although, particularly in the later phase of its development, the Negro appears in a social context, and a strong note of protest against racial discrimination is heard above the sound of the drums and the *maracas*.
>
> (Race and Colour in Caribbean Literature, p. 27)

The facts would seem to suggest that it was the social and economic conditions which gave rise to Afro-Cubanism. First, even though the Negro Revolt of 1912 was put down in a violent military manner in which 7,000 blacks were killed, the tremendous outrage at being excluded from national life lay smouldering in their breasts and on the nation's conscience. Secondly, as Hugh Thomas suggested:

> The capture by North Americans of vast tracts of Bucan territory, as well as of such important industrial concerns, had two effects, both of which were felt politically. First, the old Cuban masters of society were overwhelmed, tempted by the great profits available to them if they sold their mills. Thus old creole society, already deeply injured by the wars of independence, disappeared, and those members of the old master class who survived did so increasingly by assuming North American habits. . . .
>
> The second development was the increasing indentification of the nation of Cuba, such as it was, with the people, the workers, the mill-workers, the Negroes, *los humilde*. Foreigners might control the means of production but Cubans on the whole worked for it (on the whole, other West Indian labour). (*Cuba, The Pursuit of Freedom*, p. 601)

Third, the decline of the sugar industry in the 1920s affected blacks the most and led to labor unrest, while many persons saw in this decade "the decay of the Cuban society." (Thomas, *Cuba*, p. 567) Fourth, so active was racial discrimination that the newspaper, *Ideales de una Raza* devoted part of its Sunday newspaper to voicing such complaints.

It would seem therefore, that the roots of this "literary phenomenon" are to found precisely in the ethnic and social conditions of Cuba.

5. Echevvaría, *Alejo Carpentier*, p. 49.

6. Dennis Sardinha, *The Poetry of Nicolás Guillén* (London and Port of Spain: New Beacon Books, 1976), p. 64.

7. *Ibid.*, p. 66.

8. *Ibid.*, pp. 15-16.

9. *Ibid.*, pp. 23-24.

10. *Ibid.*, p. 18.

11. One of the most distinct and religious African groups that is found only in Cuba is the Abakua group. Its adherents are known by the name Ñáñigo.

    According to Hugh Thomas, the Abakuá was a secret society of the Efors and Efiks, small but independent people settled along the estuary of the Cross River on the Niger Delta, who presumed themselves a specially chosen race in Africa. Their role in slave-trading and commerce had been pre-eminent. They enacted as a part of their religious rite a long saga whose most interesting aspect was that it enabled souls to rest permanently in limbo rather than pursue for ever the path of reincarnation. The cult was carried to Cuba by the Efiks, where it became a secret society, whose adepts became known in the nineteenth century as Ñáñigos. (*Cuba*, p. 521)

12. Carpentier quoted in Echevarría, *Alejo Carpentier*, p. 63.

13. *Ibid.*, p. 56.

14. Luis Harss and Barbara Dohmann, *Into the Mainstream: Conversations with Latin American Writers* (New York: Harper and Row, 196), p. 42.

15. *Ibid.*, p. 43.

16. Alejo Carpentier, *El reino de este mundo* (Santiago, Chile: Editorial Universitaria, 1972), pp. 9-10.

17. *Ibid.*, p. 11.

18. *Ibid.*, p. 10.

19. *Ibid.*, pp. 13-14.

20. *Ibid.*, p. 14.

21. *Ibid.*, p. 14.

22. J. A. George Irish, "Magical Realism: A Search for Caribbean and Latin American Roots," *Revista/Review Interamerican*, vol. IV, no. 3 (1974), p. 419.

23. Jacques Stéphen Alexis, "Of the Marvelous Realism of the Haitians," *Presence Africaine*, no. 8, 9, and 10 (1956), p. 267.

24. *Ibid.*, p. 267.

25. *Ibid.*, p. 268.

26. *Ibid.*, p. 268.

27. Castro quoted in Retamar, "Caliban," p. 68.

28. Alexis, "Of the Marvelous Realism" p. 68.

29. *Ibid.*, p. 269.

30. *Ibid.*, p. 270.

31. C. L. R. James in Harris, *Tradition, the Writer and Society*, pp. 71-73.

32. *Ibid.*, p. 28.

33. *Ibid.*, p. 73.

34. *Ibid.*, p. 28.

35. *Ibid.*, p. 29.

36. *Ibid.*, p. 31.
37. Harris, "The Unsolved Constitution," p. 42.
38. *Ibid.*, p. 45.
39. *Ibid.*, p. 48.
40. *Ibid.*, p. 60.
41. The monomyth is described as "the three part transformative voyage of the hero: separation, initiation and return." The cosmogonic round is described as "cyclic process of emanation and dissolution that serves as the hero's context." (*See* E. K. Skinner, "Archetypal Patterns in Four Novels of Alejo Carpentier," *Graduate Studies on Latin America*, University of Kansas, no. 2 1973, p. 76.
42. Harss, "Into the Mainstream Tradition, The Writer and Society," p. 38.
43. *Ibid.*, p. 39.
44. *Ibid.*, p. 39.
45. Skinner, "Archetypal Patterns," p. 81.
46. James, *Black Jacobins*, p. 274.
47. Roberto González Echevarría, "The Parting of the Waters," *Diacritics*, vol. IV, no. 4 (1974), p. 10.
48. Skinner, "Archetypal Patterns," p. 78.
49. Ephesians, 7:13.
50. Carpentier quoted in Harss, *Into the Mainstream*, p. 42.
51. Emil Volek, "Algunas reflexiones sobre El Siglode Las Lucas ye el arte narrative de Alejo Carpentier," *Casas Las Americas*, vol. XIII, no. 74 (1972), p. 42. (My own translation.)
52. Irish, "Magical Realism," p. 419.

CONCLUSION

1. Johann Wolfgang von Goethe, *Faust* (New York: Washington Square Press, 1971), p. xi.
2. Boris Suchkov, *History of Realism*, p. 86.
3. Suchkov, "Realism and Its Historical Development" in Mozhnyagun Problems of Modern Aesthetics, p. 325.
4. Mozhnyagun, *Problems of Modern Aesthetics*, p. 306.
5. *See* Naipaul, The Middle Passage.
6. The error of presenting history as mostly and exclusively the activity of the oppressor is to be found even in Eric Williams' work, *From Columbus to Castro*. It is no wonder then that he endorses the Naipaul position in the following manner:

    V. S. Naipaul's description of West Indians as "mimic men" is harsh, but true. Finally, psychological dependence strongly reinforces the other forms of dependence. For, in the last analysis, dependence is a state of mind. A too-long history of colonialism seems to have crippled Caribbean self-confidence and Caribbean self-reliance, and vicious circle has been set up: psychological dependence leads to an ever-growing economic and cultural dependence on the outside world. Fragmentation is intensified in the process. And the greater degree of dependence and fragmentation further reduces local self-confidence. (p. 502.)

I wish that this were true, but, alas, it is not. The fragmentation and borrowing of which Williams speaks usually reaches its zenith in those members of society, "the elites," who by education and training have imbibed large doses of "mimicry" from the metropolitan countries, and which might be the case of the Williams' and Naipaul's "psychological dependence. . . and fragmentation" being *imposed* upon the masses and then being *presumed* to be the reality of the masses. It is to be reemphasized that invariably it is the masses who "in keeping their *culture* and *identity*, . . . keep intact the sense of their individual and collective dignity, despite the worries, humiliation, and brutalities to which they are often subject." (Cabral, *op. cit.*, p. 69.) Cultural borrowings are not to be understood always and everywhere as mimicry, nor is it to be forgotten that "ethnic consciousness" is that ingredient which holds any ethnos, ethnikos or nationality (or "national consciousness" at the level of a nation) together and gives it its distinctive features. Moreover, ethnic/national consciousness is to be identified by the qualities which predominate (essence) rather than that which is borrowed (accidents). The need to correct this erroneous approach to history is very apparent. Gordon Rohler's article, "History as Absurdity" in *Is Massa Day Dead?* (Orde Coombs, ed.) also argues the point very cogently. (S. R. C.).

7. T. Motyleva, "The Richness of Modern Realism," *Social Science*, p. 112.

8. Suchkov, "Realism and Its Historical Development," p. 347.

9. Motyleva, Richness of Modern Realism," p. 113.

10. Suchkov, "Realism and Its Historical Development," p. 338.

11. *Ibid.*, p. 344.

12. Mikhail Sholokhov, *Socialist Realism in Literature and Art* (Moscow: Progress Publishers, 1971), p. 87.

BIBLIOGRAPHY

Alexis, Jacques Stephen, "Of the Marvellous Realism of the Haitians," *Presence Africaine*, no. 8-9-10, (1966).

Babín, María Teresa and Stan Steiner, Borinquen, *An Anthology of Puerto Rican Poetry*, Vintage Books, New York, 1974.

Bastide, Roger, *African Civilizations in the New World*, Harper & Row, New York, 1971.

Beckford, George, *Persistent Poverty*, Oxford University Press, New York, 1972.

_____, "Towards Independent Economic Development for the Betterment of the Caribbean," *The Massachusetts Review*, XV, no. 1-2 (1974).

Brathwaite, Edward Kamau, "The African Presence in Caribbean Literature," *Daedalus*, 103, no. 2, (1974).

Brown, Williams Wells, *Clotel or the President's Daughter*, Arno Press, New York, 1969.

Bushmin, A., "Analytic Approach to a Work of Art," *Social Sciences*, no. 4 (6) 1971.

Butler, Smedley D., "America Armed Forces, 2, 'In Time of Peace'; the Army," *Common Sense*, IV, no. II, 1935.

Cabral, Amílcar, *Return to the Source*, African Information Service, New York 1973.

Campbell, Mavis Christine, *The Dynamics of Change in a Slave Society: A Sociopolitical History of the Free Coloreds of Jamaica, 1800-1865*, Farleigh Dickinson University Press, Rutherford, 1976.

Carlyle, Thomas, "Occasional Discourse on the Negro Question," *Fraser's Magazine*, December (1849).

Carpentier, Alejo, *Explosion In a Cathedral*, Victor Gollanez, London, 1973.

_____, *The Kingdom of this World*, Collier Books, New York, 1957.

_____, "The Culture of the Caribbean Peoples," *Gramna*, 26 August (1979).

Casas, Bartolomé de las, *Tears of the Indians*, & Sir Arthur Helps, *The Life of Las Casas*, The John Hilburne Company, Williamstown, Massachusetts, 1970.

Castor, Suzy, "The American Occupation of Haiti (1915-34), *The Massachusetts Review*, XV, no. 1-2, (1974).

Castro, Fidel, *History Will Absolve Me*, Cooperative Obrera, Havana, 1961.

Césaire, Aimé, *Discourse on Colonialism*, Monthly Review Press, New York, 1972.

_____, *Return to My Native Land*, Penguin Books, Middlesex, 1970.

Clarke, John Henrick (ed.), *Marcus Garvey and the Vision of Africa*, Vintage Books, Random House, New York, 1974.

Cook, Mercer, "The Haitian Novel," *The French Review*, XIX, no. 6 (1946).

Coombs, Orde, *Is Massa Day Dead? Black Moods in the Caribbean*, Anchor Press, Garden City, New York, 1974.

Coulthard, G. R., *Race and Colour in Caribbean Literature*, Oxford University Press, New York, 1962.

———, "The Emergency of Afro-Cuban Poetry," *Caribbean Quarterly*, 2, no. 3 (1950).

Curtin, Phillip, D., *Two Jamaicas, The Role of Ideas in a Tropical Country*, Greenwood Press, New York, 1968.

Damas, Leon, "Poems from Pigments," *Black World*, XXI, no. 3 (1972).

Dash, Michael, "The Marxist Counterpoint-Jacques Roumain: 1930's-1940's," *Black Images*, 2, no. 1 (1973).

Davies, Barrie, "The Novels of Roger Mais," *The International Fiction Review*, 1, no. 2 (1974).

Dickinson, Margaret, *When Bullets Begin to Flower*, East African Publishing House, Nairobi, Kenya, 1972.

Ehrmann, Jacques, "On Articulation: The Language of History and the Terror of Language," *Yale French Studies*, Thirty Nine, 1967.

Firmin Antenór, *De l'égalité des races humaines (antropologie positive)*, F. Pichon, Paris, 1885.

Fanon, Frantz, *Black Skin, White Mask*, Grove Press, New York, 1967.

———, *The Wretched of the Earth*, Grove Press, New York, 1966.

Foner, Phillip S., *Antonio Maceo: The "Bronze Titan" of Cuba's Struggle for Independence*, Monthly Review Press, New York and London, 1977.

Franco, Jean, *An Introduction to Spanish-American Literature*, Cambridge at the University Press, London, 1969.

Freire, Paulo, *Pedagogy of the Oppressed*, The Seabury Press, New York, 1973.

Frucht, Richard (ed.), *Black Society in the New World*, Random House, New York, 1971.

Galván, Manuel de Jesus, *The Cross and the Sword*, Indiana Press, Bloomingfield, 1954.

Garret, Naomi M., *The Renaissance of Haitian Poetry*, Presence Africaine, Paris, 1963.

Gendzier, Irene L., *Frantz Fanon, A Critical Study*, Random House, New York, 1973.

Gomes, Albert, *Through a Maze of Colour*, Key Caribbean Publications, Ltd., Port of Spain, Trinidad, 1974.

González Echevarría, Roberto, *Alejo Carpentier: The Pilgrim at Home*, Cornell University Press, Ithaca and London, 1977.

Glissant, Édouard, "Le Romancier Noir et son Peuple, Notes por une conference," *Presence Africaine*, no. 16. (1957).

———, *The Ripening*, George Graziller, Inc., New York 1959.

Gremann, Richard, "Literary and Revolutionary Realism in Victor Serge," *Yale French Studies*, Thirty Nine, 1967.

Hanke, Lewis, *The Spanish Struggle for Justice in the Conquest of America*, University of Pennsylvania Press, Philadelphia, 1949.

Harris, Wilson, "The Unsolved Constitution," *Caribbean Quarterly*, 14, nos. 1 & 2, (1968).

———, *The Whole Armour and the Secret Ladder*, Faber and Faber, London, 1963.

———, *Tradition, the Writer & Society*, New Beacon Publications, London, 1967.

302

Harss, Luis, *Into the Mainstream, Conversation with Latin American Writers*, Harper & Row, New York, 1967.

Henriquez-Urena, Pedro, *Literary Currents in Hispanic America*, Harvard University Press, Cambridge, Massachusetts, 1946.

Herskovits, Melville J., *Life in a Haitian Valley*, Doubleday & Co., Inc., Garden City, New York, 1971.

Hezekiah, Randolph, "Bertène Juminer and the Colonial Problem," *Black Images*, 3, no. 1 (1974).

Hostos, Eugenio María de, *La pergrinacion de Boyoan*, Editorial, Rio Piedras, 1970.

Huberman, Leo & Sweezy, Paul M., *Cuba, An Anatomy of a Revolution*, Monthly Review Press, New York, 1961.

Irele, F A., *Literature and Ideology in Martinique: Rene Maran, Aimé Césaire, Frantz Fanon*, State University at Buffalo, New York, 1972.

Irish, J. A. George, "Magical Realism: A Search for Caribbean and Latin American Roots," *Revista/Review Interamerican*, IV, no. 3, (1974).

Jagan, Cheddi, *The West on Trial*, International Publishers, New York, 1966.

James, C. L. R., *Black Jacobins*, Alfred Knopf, Inc., and Random House, New York, 1963.

———, *The Case for West-Indian Self-Government*, Leonard and Virginia Woolf at the Hogarth Press, London, 1933.

———, "Discovering Literature in Trinidad: The Nineteen Thirties," *Savacou*, no. 2 (1970).

———, *Minty Alley*, New Beacon Books, Ltd., London, 1971.

———, *A History of Pan African Revolt*, Drum and Spear Press, Washington, D. C., 1969.

James, Louis (ed.), *The Island in Between*, Oxford University Press, London, 1968.

Jesus, Carolina María de, *Child of the Dark, The Diary of Carolina María de Jesus*, New American Library, New York, 1962.

Jones, D. A. N., "Little Warriors in Search of a War," *Times Literary Supplement*, September 12 (1975).

Juminer, Bertène, *Au seuil d'un noveau cri*, Presence Africaine, Paris, 1963.

———, *Bozambo's Revenge*, Three Continents Press, Washington, D. C., 1976.

———, "Hommage à Frantz Fanon," *Presence Africaine*, 1st Quarter, 1962.

Karol, K. A., *Guerillas in Power*, Hill and Wang, New York, 1970.

Kennedy, Ellen Conroy, "Leon Damas; Pigments and the Colonized Personality," *Black World*, XXI, No. 3, (1972).

Kent, George, "A Conversation with George Lamming," *Black World*, XXII (1975).

Kesteloot, Lilyan, *Black Writers in French*, Temple University Press, Philadelphia, 1974.

Khrapchenko, Mikhail, "Systems Analysis in Literature," *Social Sciences*, Vol. VII, no. 1 (1976).

———, "The Typological Study of Literature," *Social Sciences*, Vol. 4 (10), 1972.

King, Sidney, "A Birth to Freedom," *New World Magazine*, Guyana, 1966.

Knight, Franklin W., *Slave Society in Cuba in the Nineteenth Century*, Wisconsin Press, Madison, 1970.

Knight, Vere, W., "Édouard Glissant: The Novel as History Rewritten." *Black Images*, 3, no. 1, 1974.

———, "Negritude and the Isms," *Black Images*, 3, no. 1, 1974.

Konstantinov, F. V., *The Fundamentals of Marxist-Leninist Philosophy*, Progress Publishers, Moscow, 1974.

Korestovovtsev, M. A. "On the Concept 'The Ancient East'," *Soviet Studies in History*, 1, no. 2, 1970.

Korngold, Ralph, *Citizen Toussaint*, Hill and Wang, New York, 1947.

Lacovia, R. M., "English Caribbean Literature. A Brave New World," *Black Images*, 1, no. 1, 1972.

Lamming, George, *Of Age and Innocence*, Michael Joseph, London, 1958.

————, *Pleasures of Exile*, Michael Joseph, London, 1960.

————, *Season of Adventure*, Allison & Busby, London, 1979.

Laurenson, Diana T. and Swingerwood, Allen, *The Sociology of Literature*, Schocken Books, New York, 1972.

Le Riverend, Julio, *Economic History of Cuba*, Havana, Ensayo Book Institute, 1967.

Lewis, Gordon, *The Growth of the Modern West Indies*, The Monthly Review Press, New York, 1968.

Logan, Rayford, W., *Haiti & The Dominican Republic*, Oxford University Press, New York, 1968.

M'Callum, Pierre F., *Travels in Trinidad*, W. Jones, Liverpool, 1805.

McFarlane, J. E. Clare, *A Literature in the Making*, The Pioneer Press, Kingston, Jamaica, 1956.

Maldonado-Denis, Manuel, *Puerto-Rico: A Socio-Historical Interpretation*, Random House, New York, 1972.

Mais, Roger, *The 3 Novels of Roger Mais*, Jonathan Cape, London, 1970.

Malik, Michael Abdul, *From Michael de Freitas to Michael X*, Andre Deutsch, London, 1968.

Manfred, A. Z., *A Short History of the World*, Vol. 1, Progress Publishers, Moscow, 1974.

Manzano, Juan Francisco, *The Early Life of the Negro Poet*, (translated) R. Madden, Thomas Ward & Co., London., 1840.

Maran, René, *Batouala: A True Black Novel*, Fawcet Publications, Connecticut, 1972.

Marx, Karl & Engles, Frederick, *Selected Works*, Vol. 1 & 2, Progress Publishers, Moscow, 1969.

Mendes, Alfred, *Black Fauns*, Duckworth, London, 1934.

Millis, Walter, *The Martial Spirit*, Riverside Press, Massachusetts, 1931.

Mintz, Sidney, "The Caribbean Region," *Daedalus*, 103, no. 2, 1974.

Montaigne, Michael, *The Essayes of Michael Lord of Montaigne*, George Routledge and Sons, Ltd., London, 1891.

Montejo, Esteban, *The Autobiography of a Runaway Slave* (ed.), Miquel Barnet, Pantheon Books, New York, 1968.

Moore, Gerald and Beier, Ulli, *Modern Poetry from Africa*, Penguin Books, Middlesex, 1963.

Motylevan, T., "The Richness of Modern Realism," *Social Sciences*, Vol. 3, 1971.

Mozhnyagun, S. (ed.), *Problems of Modern Aesthetic, A Collection of Articles*, Progress Publishers, Moscow, 1969.

Munro, Ian & Sander, Richard, *Kas-Kas, Interviews with Three Caribbean Writers*, African and Afro-America Research Institute, The University of Texas at Austin, Texas, 1972.

Naipaul, V. S., *Guerrillas*, Ballantine Books, New York, 1976.

————, *A House for Mr. Biswas*, McGraw-Hill, New York, 1961.

_____, "The Life and Trials of Michael X," *The Sunday Times Magazine*, May 12 (1974).

_____, *The Middle Passage: Impressions of Five Societies—British, French and Dutch—in the West Indies and South America*, Andre Deutsch, London, 1962.

_____, *The Overcrowded Barracoon and Other Articles*, Penguin Books, Middlesex, 1976.

_____, *The Return of Eva Perón with The Killings in Trinidad*, Alfred A Knopf, 1980.

Nettleford, Rex M., *Mirror Mirror: Identity, Race and Protest in Jamaica*, William Collins and Sangster Ltd., Kingston, Jamaica, 1970.

Nyerere, Julius K., *Ujamma Essays on Socialism*, Oxford Universtiy Press, New York, 1971.

Nyunai, "Le Lézard: opinion d'un juene," *Presence Africaine*, no. 22, October-November (1958).

Oganov, Grigory, *Freedom of Art Under Socialism*, Novosti Press Agency Publishing House, Moscow, 1975.

Ojo-Ade, F., "René Maran and the Racial Question: The Literature of Alienation and Frustration," *Black Images*, 2, nos. 3 & 4, 1973.

Olivier, Lord, *The Myth of Governor Eyre*, The Hogarth Press, London, 1933.

Orwell, George, "Politics vs. Literature: An Examination of 'Guilliver's Travels'," *The Orwell Reader, Fiction, Essays and Reports*, Harcourt, Brace, Javanovich, New York, 1956.

Owens, Joseph, *Dread: The Rastafarians of Jamaica*, Sangsters, Kingston, Jamaica, 1976.

Oyono, Ferdinand, *Boy!*, Collier Books, New York, 1970.

Padmore, George, *Pan Africanism and Communism*, Doubleday & Co., Inc., New York, 1972.

Petrosyan, M., *Humanism, Its Philosophical, Ethical and Sociological Aspects*, Progress Publishers, Moscow, 1972.

Pierre-Charles, Gerard, "A Human Microcosm," *Third World*, no. 2, July (1979).

Price, Hannibal, *De la réhabilitation de la race noire par la republique d'Haiti*, J. Verollot, Port-au-Prince, 1900.

Price, Richard (ed.), *Maroon Societies*, Anchor Press, Doubleday, Garden City, New York, 1973.

Ramchand, Kenneth, *The West Indian Novel and Its Background*, Faber and Faber, London, 1970.

Rancine, Daniel L., "A Profile of Leon-Gotran Damas," *Negro History Bulletin*, 42, no. 3, September (1979).

Reid, Victor, *New Day*, Heinemann Educational Books, London, 1949.

Retamar, Roberto Fernández, "Caliban, Notes Towards a Discussion of Culture in Our America," *The Massachusetts Review*, Winter-Spring, 1974.

_____, *Retamar's Revolutionary Poems: Cuba 1959-1974*, Savacou Publications Inc., Mona, Jamaica, 1974.

Roget, Wilbert, "Édouard Glissant and Antillanité, Ph.D. Dissertation, University of Pittsburgh, 1975.

Riviere, Bill, "Ideology in Caribbean Education," *Shango, The Magazine of the Caribbean*, Vol. 1, no. 3.

_____, *Oppression of Resistance: The Black Condition in the Caribbean*, Cornell University African Studies and Research Center, Series #1, 1974.

Robinson, Carey, *The Fighting Maroons of Jamaica*, William Collins and Sangster (Jamaica) Ltd., 1971.

Rodney, Walter, *The Groundings with My Brothers*, Bogle-L'Ouverture Publications Ltd., London, 1969.

———, *How Europe Underdeveloped Africa*, Bogle-L'Ouverture Publications, Ltd., London, 1972.

———, *West Africa and the Atlantic Slave-trade*, East African Publishing House, Nairobi, 1967.

Roumain, Jacques, *Ebony Wood/Boise D'Ebene*, Interword Press, New York, 1971.

———, *Masters of the Dew*, Collier Books, New York, 1971.

Sardinha, Dennis, *The Poetry of Nicholás Guillén*, New Beacon Books, London and Port of Spain, 1976.

Sánchez-Guerra, Ramiro, *Sugar and Society in the Caribbean*, Yale University Press, New Haven, 1964.

Satre, Jean Paul, *What is Literature?*, Harper and Row, New York, 1964.

Schuler, Monica, "Akan Slave Rebellions in the British Caribbean," *Savacou*, June 1970, Vol. 1, no. 1.

Schwartz, Kessel, *A New History of Spanish-American Fiction*, Vol. 1, University of Miami Press, Florida, 1972.

Shakespeare, William, *The Tempest*, Cambridge at the University Press, London, 1965, (Act 1, Sc. III).

Shcherbina, Vladimir, *Lenin and Problems of Literature*, Progress Publishers, Moscow, 1971.

Sholokov, Mikhail, *Socialist Realism in Literature and Art*, Progress Publishers, Moscow, 1971.

Silén, Juan Angel, *We, the Puerto-Rican People*, Monthly Review Press, New York, 1971.

Stoddard, T. Lothrod, *The French Revolution in San Domingo*, Houghton Mifflin Co., Boston and New York, 1919.

Suchkov, Boris, *A History of Realism*, Progress Publishers, Moscow, 1969.

Thoby-Marcelin, Phillip, "Haiti's Writers Find the People," *Americás*, no. 4, June (1949).

Thomas, Hugh, *Cuba, the Pursuit of Freedom*, Harper and Row, New York, 1971.

Trotsky, Leon, *Literature and Revolution*, The University of Michigan Press, 1960.

Ulyanovsky, R., *Socialism and the Newly Independent States*, Progress Publishers, Moscow, 1974.

Valentino, Lord, "Dis Place Nice," Straker Records, Barbados, 1974.

Vega, Garcilaso de la, *The Incas, The Royal Commentaries of the Inca*, Avon Books, New York, 1964.

Villaverde, Cirilo, *Cecilia Valdés or Angel's Hill*, Vantage Press, New York, 1962.

Volek, Emil, "Algunas reflectiones sobre El Siglode Las Lucas, ye el arte narrative de Alejo Carpentier," *Casa Las Americas*, XIII, no. 74, 1972.

Von Goethe, Johann Wolfgang, *Faust*, Washington Press, New York, 1971.

Weld, Theodore, *American Slavery As It Is*, Arno Press and The New York Times, New York, 1968.

Williams, Allan, "Report on Castle Bruce," 1975 (unpublished).

Williams, Eric, *Capitalism and Slavery*, Capricorn Books, New York, 1970.

———, *From Columbus to Castro*, Harper and Row Publishers, New York, 1970. York, 1970.

Wilson, Edmund, "The Marcelins-Novelists of Haiti," *The Nation*, October 14, (1950).

_____, *Red, Black, Blond and Olive; Studies in Four Civilizations: Zuni, Haiti, Soviet Russia, Israel*, Oxford University Press, New York, 1956.

Wright, Richard, *Native Son*, Grosset & Dunlap, New York, 1940.

Wynter, Sylvia, "Creole Criticism—A Critique," *New World Quarterly*, Vol. 2, no. 5.

_____, "We Must Learn to Sit Down Together and Talk a Little Culture. Reflections on West Indian Writing and Criticism, Part I," *Jamaica Quarterly* of the Institute of Jamaica, Vol. 2, no. 5.

Yakovlev, A. N., *Fundamentals of Political Science*, Progress Publishers, Moscow, 1975.

Index

Abakua group, 298n
Accabreh, 8
Accompongs, 11-12. *See also* Maroons
action, and dialectic, 230, 231
Adams, John, 16
Adoe, 8, 11
Africa, Antillais, image of, 175
African Civilizations in the New World (Bastide), 19
Afro-Cubanism, 246-247, 250, 297n
age, theme of, 187
Agramonte, 32
Agüeybaná, 8
Ainsi parla l'oncle (Price Mars), 118-19, 125
Akan revolts, 9, 12. *See also* slave revolts
Alexis, J. S., 253, 255, 266, 267
Algerian Revolution, 222
alienation, 69, 284n
Almagro, Diego de, 5
American colonialism, 31. *See also* United States
  and Bay of Pigs fiasco, 52
  in Cuba, 49
  and Haitian economy, 37-41
American Slavery As It Is (Weld), 102
Amymara, 5
anti-imperialist struggle, beginning of, 44
Antillian heritage, 174-175
anti-slavery movement, 286n
Aponte, Jose Antonio, 31
Araby, 8
Arawaks, 5, 7, 261
Argentes, Miro, 36
aristocrats, broken, 263-264, 269
arson
  in Cuban resistance, 34
  in San Cristobal, 188
  in San Domingo, 14
Art, Haitian, 254. *See also* Literature, Poetry
At the Stelling (Hearne), 256
Atta, 11
Au seuil d'un nouveau cri (Juminer), 211, 212-223, 243

autobiography, 296n
Autobiography of a Runaway Slave, The (Montejo) xiii, 93, 106, 111, 270. *See also* narrative
Aztecs, 77

Bacon, Francis, 183
Banjo: A Story without a Plot (McKay), 121, 123-125, 135, 142, 254, 269
Baptist Church, 23, 27, 165. *See also* Religion
Baptist War, 23-24, 41
Barbados
  latifundum system in, 17
  literary movement in, 140
  strike action in, 45
Barnet, Miguel, 106
Bastide, Roger, 19
Batista, Fulgencio, 45, 46, 49-50
Batouala: A True Black Novel (Maran), 121, 122-123, 125, 141
Bay of Pigs fiasco, 52
Beacon, The (magazine), 136-137
Beckford, George, 53
Belvis, Ruiz, 29
Benedetti, Mario, 231-232
Benson, Gale, 233
Berbice Rebellion, 278n
Betances, Ramón Emeterio, 29, 30
Bim (magazine), 140, 143
Bishop, Maurice, 47
Bismarck, Otto von, 38
Black Fauns (Mendes), 138
Black Jacobins (James), 139
Black Power, 233
Black Regiment, 23
Blacks
  in Cuba, 246, 248
  first independent settlement in New World of, 279
  free, in Hispanic colonies, 15
Black Skin, White Masks (Fanon), 216
Blanco, Tomas, 128

309